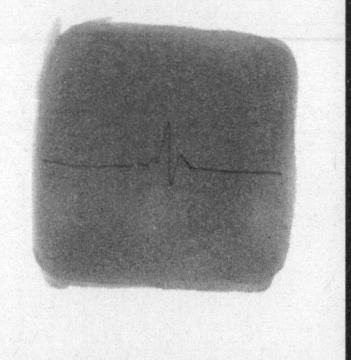

I've started drinking this brand of yogurt every day that a lot of fans have recommended. It's supposedly a magical product that will prevent both colds and allergies.

I hope the magic works!

–Tite Kubo

BLEACH is author Tite Kubo's second title. Kubo made his debut with ZOMBIEPOWDER., a four-volume series for WEEKLY SHONEN JUMP. To date, BLEACH has been translated into numerous languages and has also inspired an animated TV series that began airing in the U.S. in 2006. Beginning its serialization in 2001, BLEACH is still a mainstay in the pages of WEEKLY SHONEN JUMP. In 2005, BLEACH was awarded the prestigious Shogakukan Manga Award in the *shonen* (boys) category.

BLEACH
VOL. 62: HEART OF WOLF
SHONEN JUMP Manga Edition

STORY AND ART BY
TITE KUBO

Translation/Joe Yamazaki
Touch-up Art & Lettering/Mark McMurray
Design/Kam Li
Editor/Alexis Kirsch

Printed in the U.S.A.

Published by VIZ Media, LLC
P.O. Box 77010
San Francisco, CA 94107

10 9 8 7 6 5 4 3 2 1
First printing, November 2014

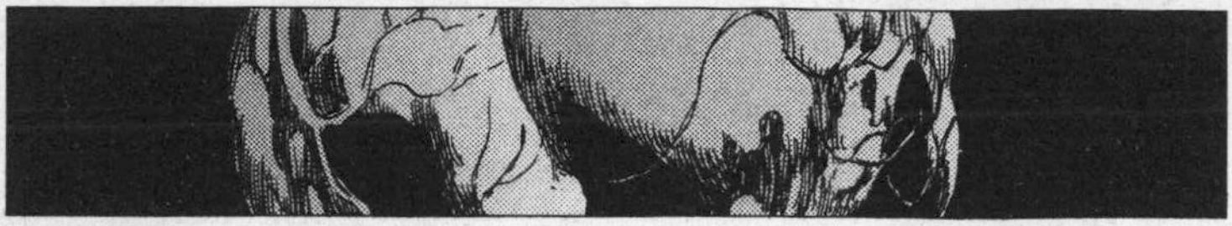

I will continue to fight myself
As long as I have the fangs in my heart

BLEACH 62 | HEART OF WOLF

Shonen Jump Manga

ALL STARS ★ AND

狛村左陣
コマムラサジン

SAJIN KOMAMURA

TOSHIRO HITSUGAYA

日番谷冬獅郎
ヒツガヤトウシロウ

黒崎一護
クロサキイチゴ

ICHIGO KUROSAKI

★ plot

Ichigo Kurosaki meets Soul Reaper Rukia Kuchiki and ends up helping her eradicate Hollows. After developing his powers as a Soul Reaper, Ichigo enters battle against Aizen and his dark ambitions! Ichigo finally defeats Aizen in exchange for his powers as a Soul Reaper.

With the battle over, Ichigo regains his normal life. But his tranquil days end when he meets Ginjo, who offers to help Ichigo get his powers back. But it was all a plot by Ginjo to steal Ichigo's new powers! Ginjo, who was the first ever Deputy Soul Reaper, then reveals to Ichigo the truth behind the deputy badge. However, even after learning the Soul Society's plans for him, Ichigo chooses to continue protecting his friends and defeats Ginjo.

In order to fight the Quincies, Ichigo returns to Oh-Etsu and receives his true Zanpaku-to after facing off against Zangetsu once again. Meanwhile, the invasion of the Seireitei by the Vandenreich commences...

BLEACH

BAMBIETTA BASTERBINE

バンビエッタ・バスターバイン

蒼都 ツァン・トゥ

CANG DU

BAZZ-B

バズビー

STORIES

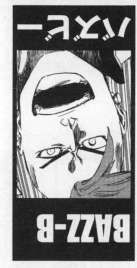

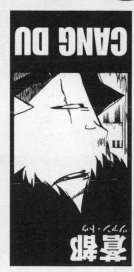

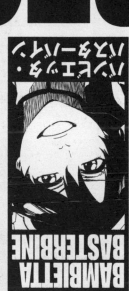

CONTENTS

HEART OF WOLF

BLEACH 628

551. THE BURNT OFFERINGS

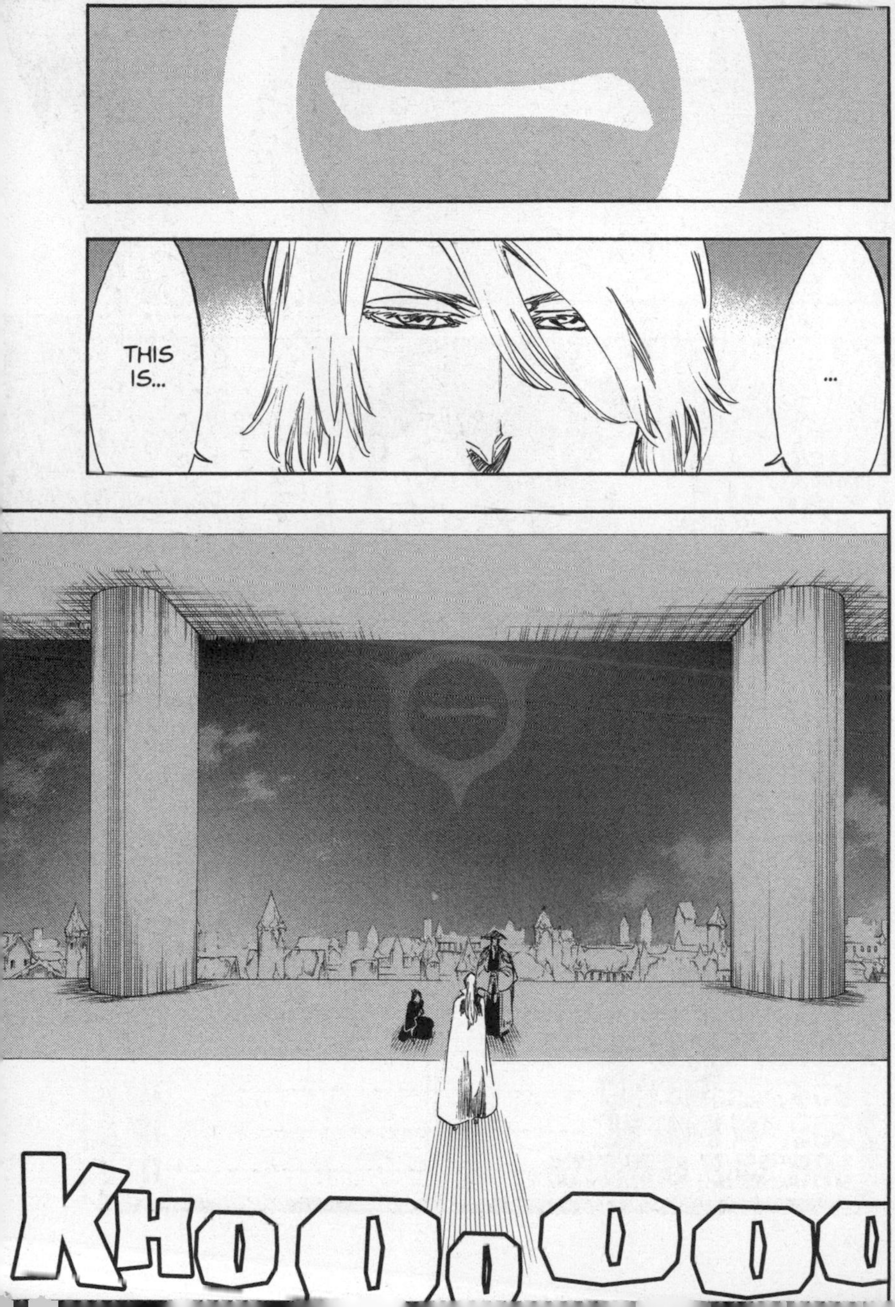
...
THIS IS...
KHOOOOOOO

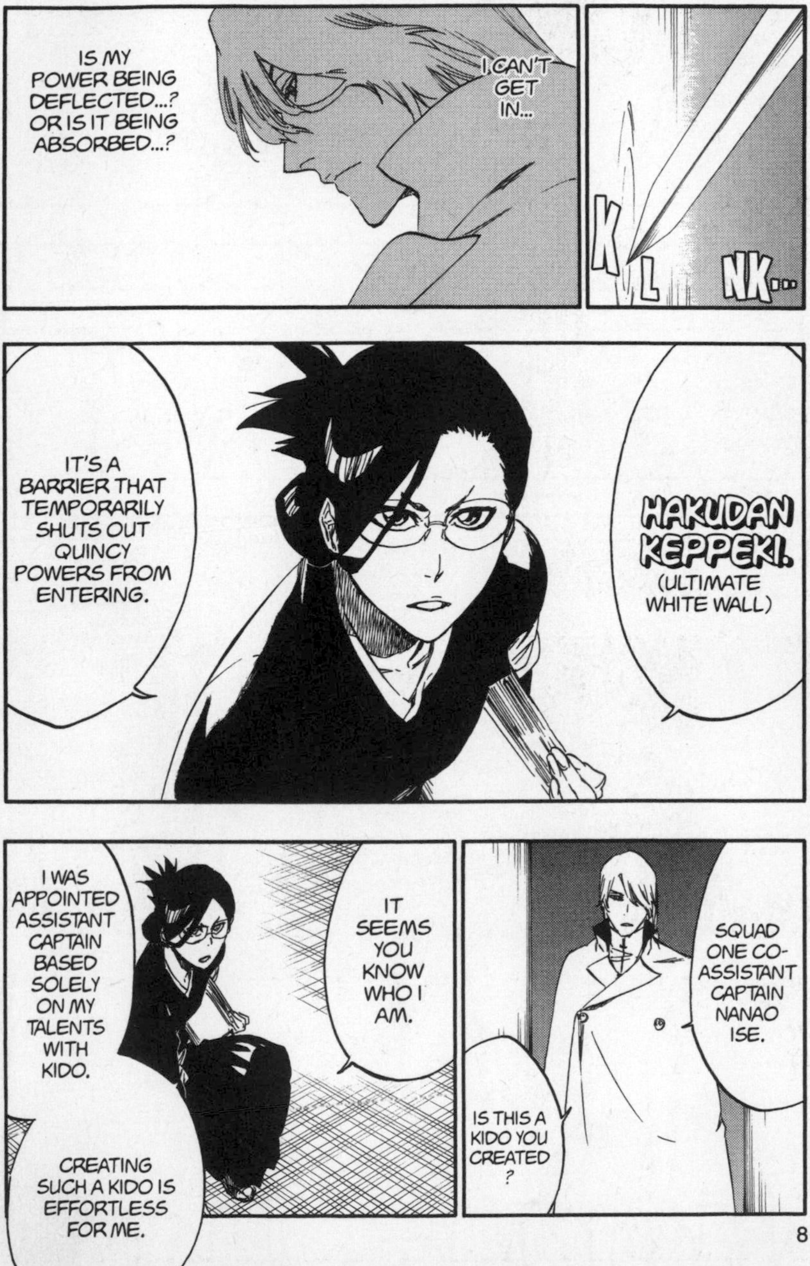
K L NK...
I CAN'T GET IN...
IS MY POWER BEING DEFLECTED...? OR IS IT BEING ABSORBED...?
HAKUDAN KEPPEKI.
(ULTIMATE WHITE WALL)
IT'S A BARRIER THAT TEMPORARILY SHUTS OUT QUINCY POWERS FROM ENTERING.
SQUAD ONE CO-ASSISTANT CAPTAIN NANAO ISE.
IS THIS A KIDO YOU CREATED ?
IT SEEMS YOU KNOW WHO I AM.
I WAS APPOINTED ASSISTANT CAPTAIN BASED SOLELY ON MY TALENTS WITH KIDO.
CREATING SUCH A KIDO IS EFFORTLESS FOR ME.

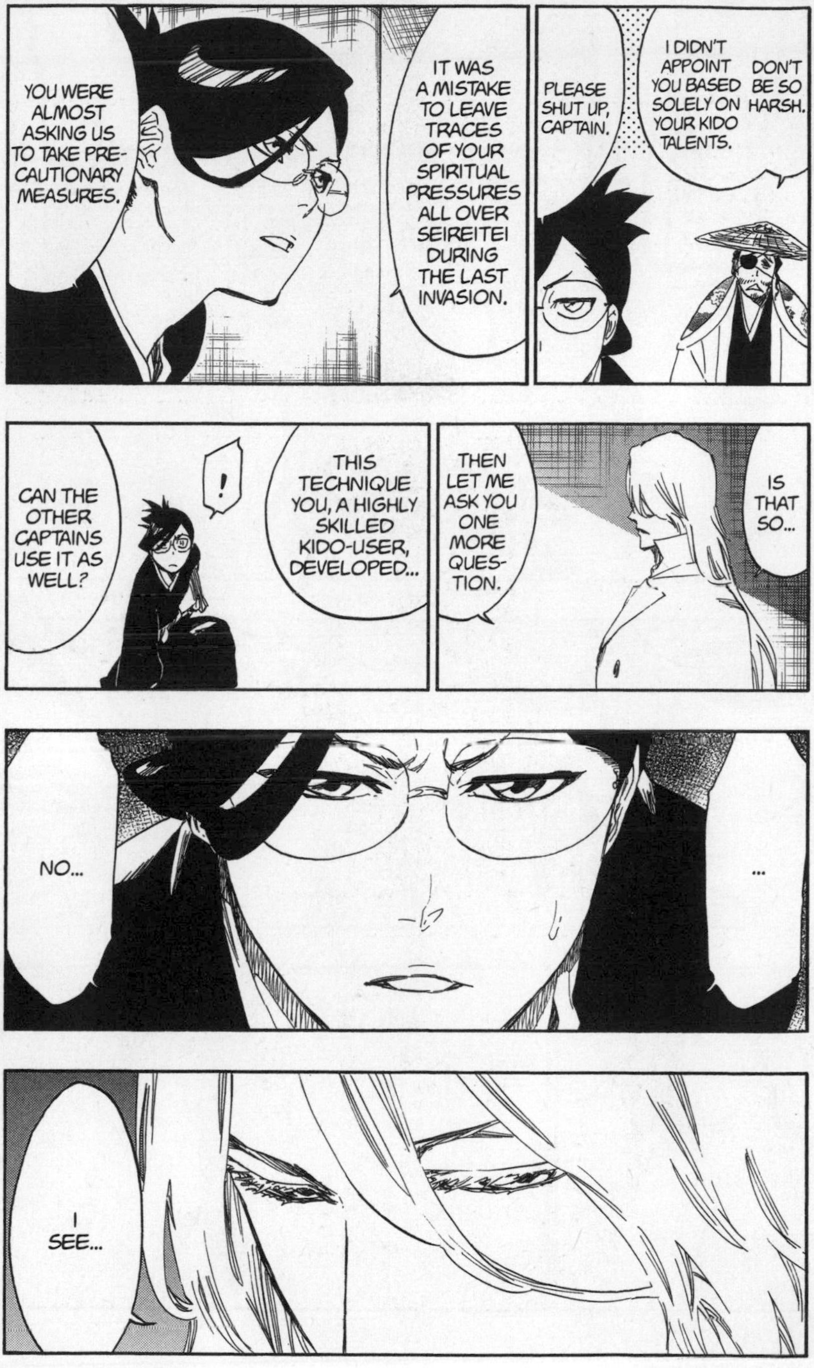
DON'T BE SO HARSH.
I DIDN'T APPOINT YOU BASED SOLELY ON YOUR KIDO TALENTS.
PLEASE SHUT UP, CAPTAIN.
IT WAS A MISTAKE TO LEAVE TRACES OF YOUR SPIRITUAL PRESSURES ALL OVER SEIREITEI DURING THE LAST INVASION.
YOU WERE ALMOST ASKING US TO TAKE PRE-CAUTIONARY MEASURES.
IS THAT SO...
THEN LET ME ASK YOU ONE MORE QUES-TION.
THIS TECHNIQUE YOU, A HIGHLY SKILLED KIDO-USER, DEVELOPED...
!
CAN THE OTHER CAPTAINS USE IT AS WELL?
...
NO...
I SEE...

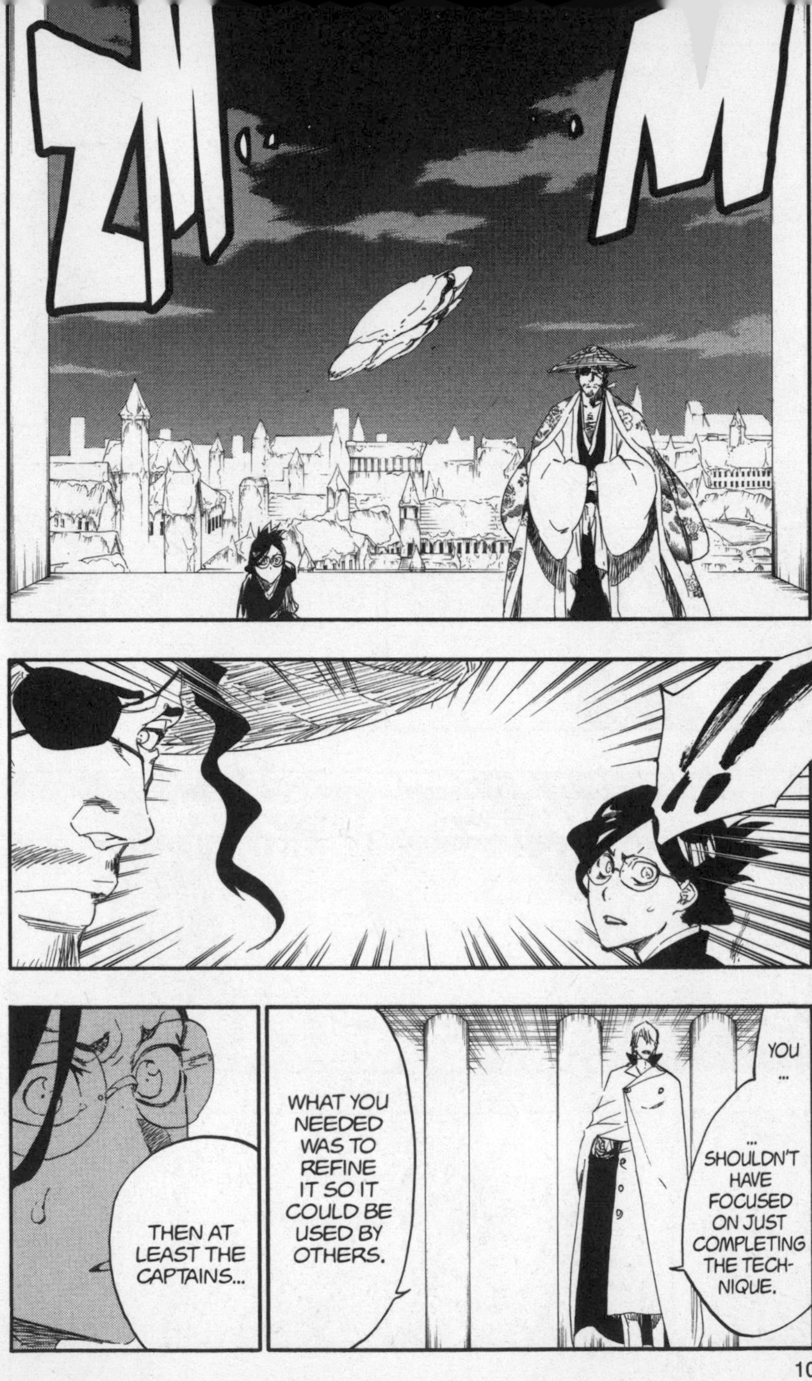

YOU
...
... SHOULDN'T HAVE FOCUSED ON JUST COMPLETING THE TECH-NIQUE.
WHAT YOU NEEDED WAS TO REFINE IT SO IT COULD BE USED BY OTHERS.
THEN AT LEAST THE CAPTAINS...

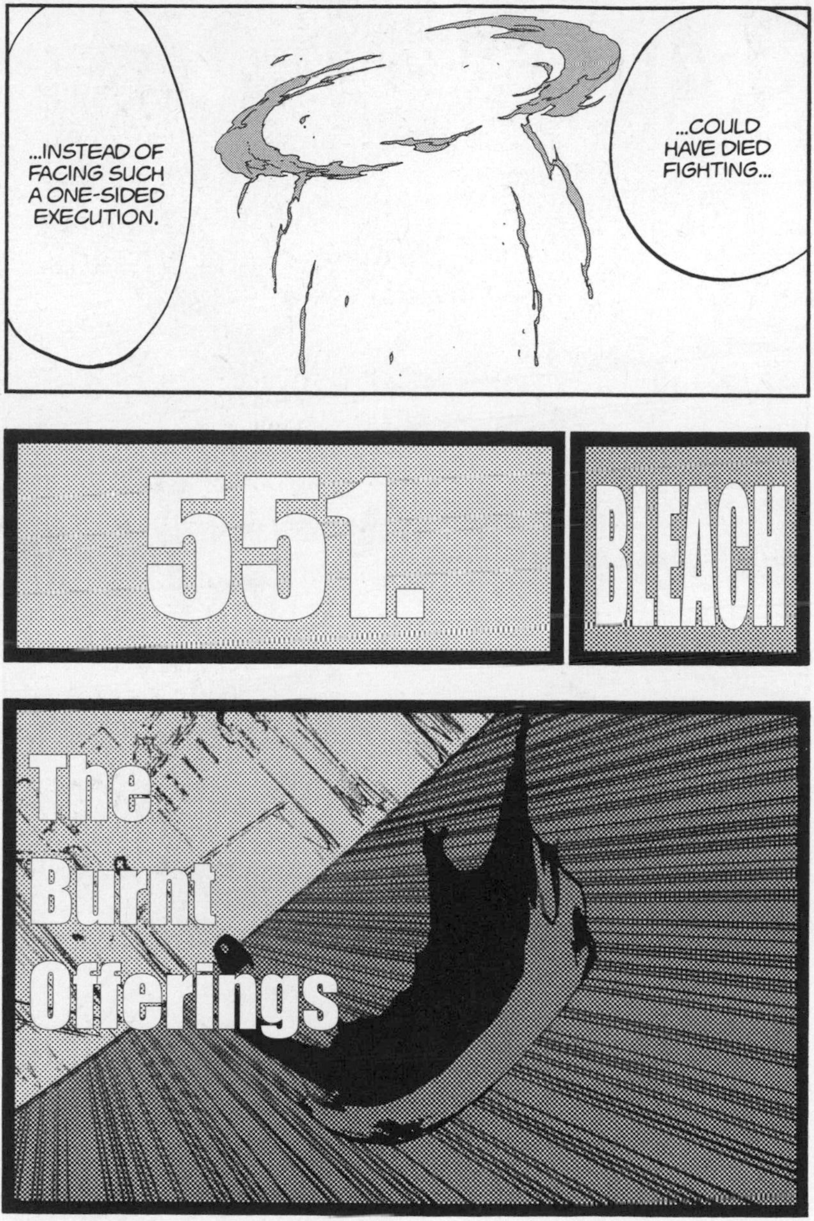
...COULD HAVE DIED FIGHTING...
...INSTEAD OF FACING SUCH A ONE-SIDED EXECUTION.
BLEACH
551.
The Burnt Offerings

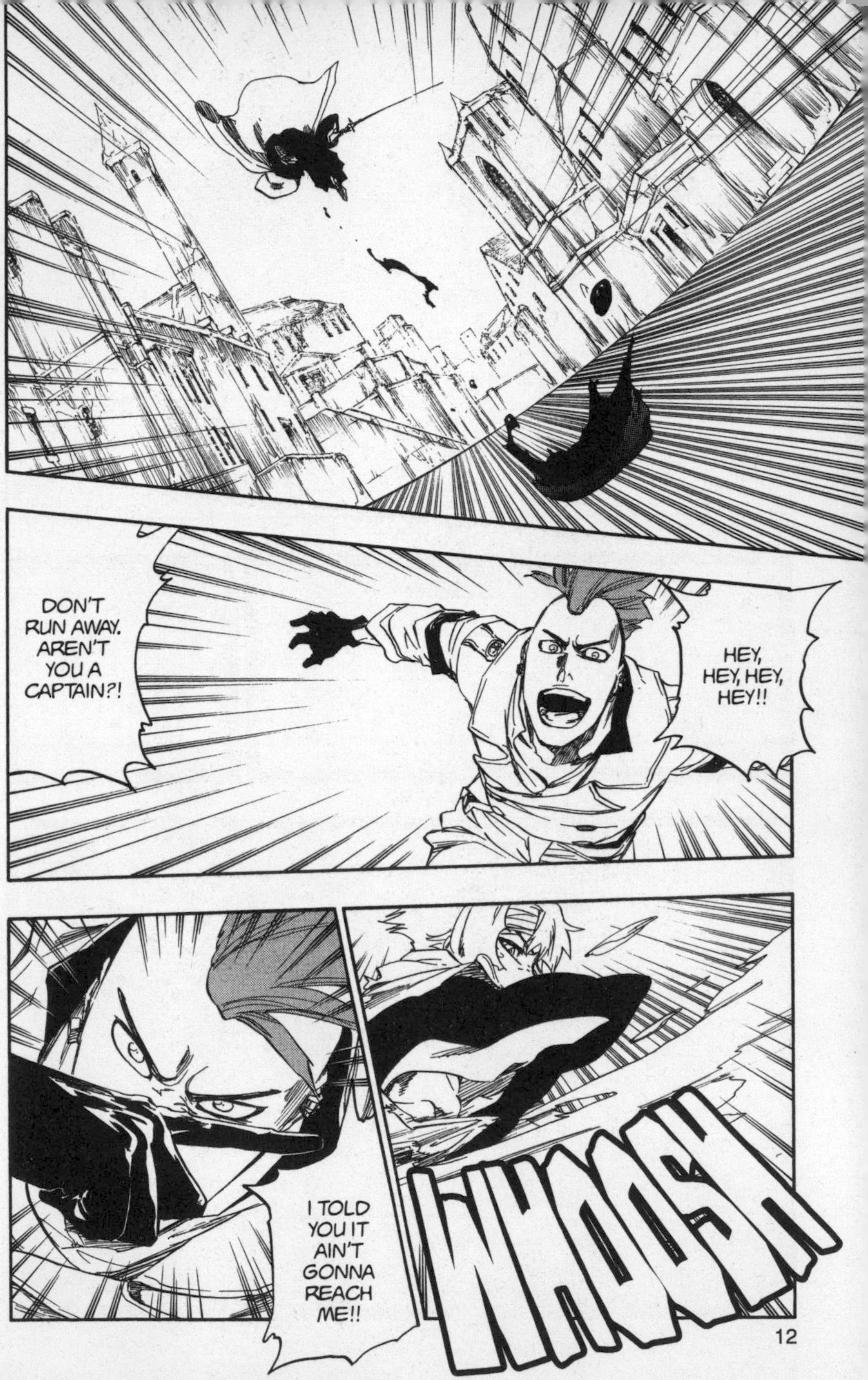
HEY, HEY, HEY, HEY!!
DON'T RUN AWAY. AREN'T YOU A CAPTAIN?!
WHOOSH
I TOLD YOU IT AIN'T GONNA REACH ME!!

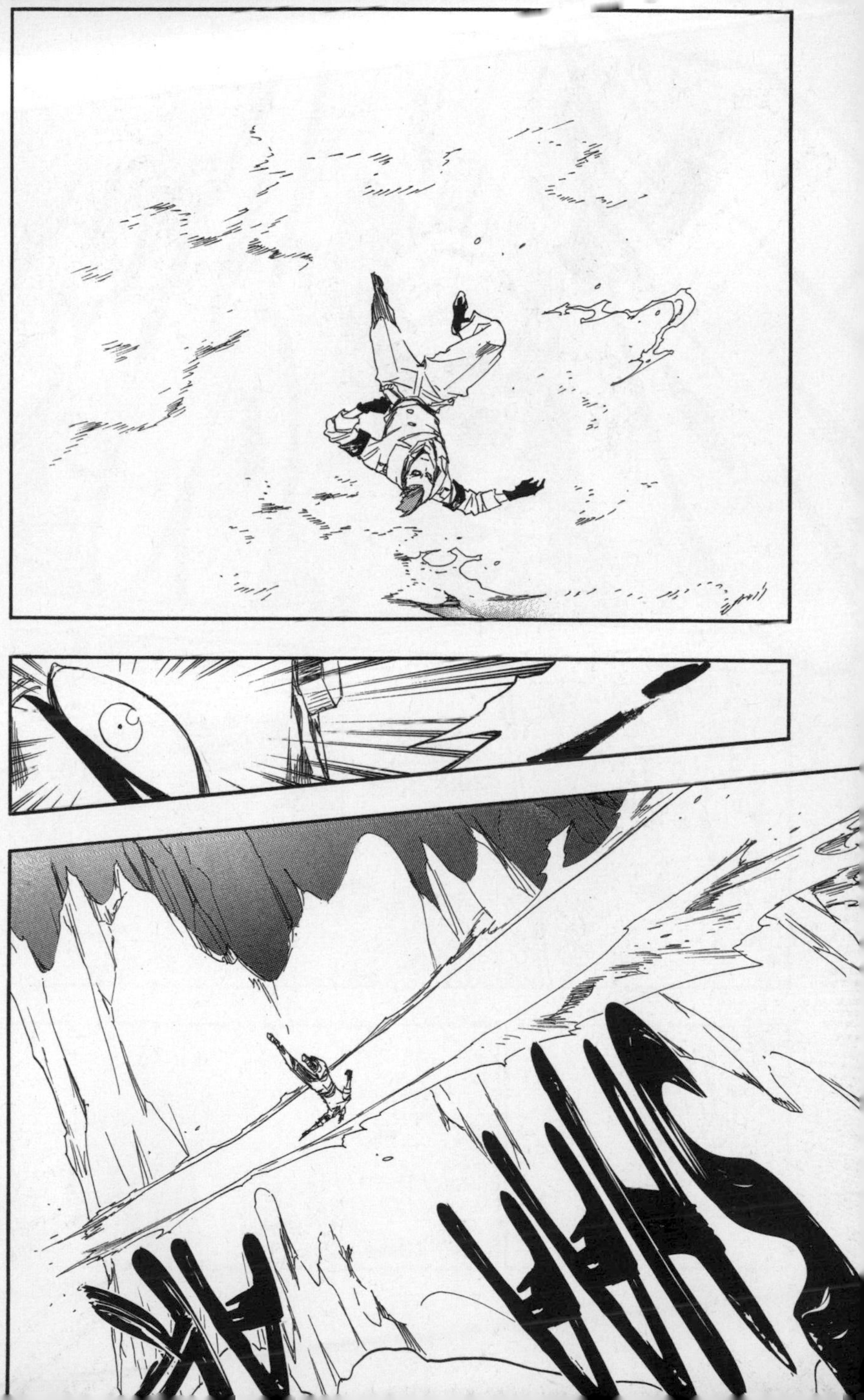

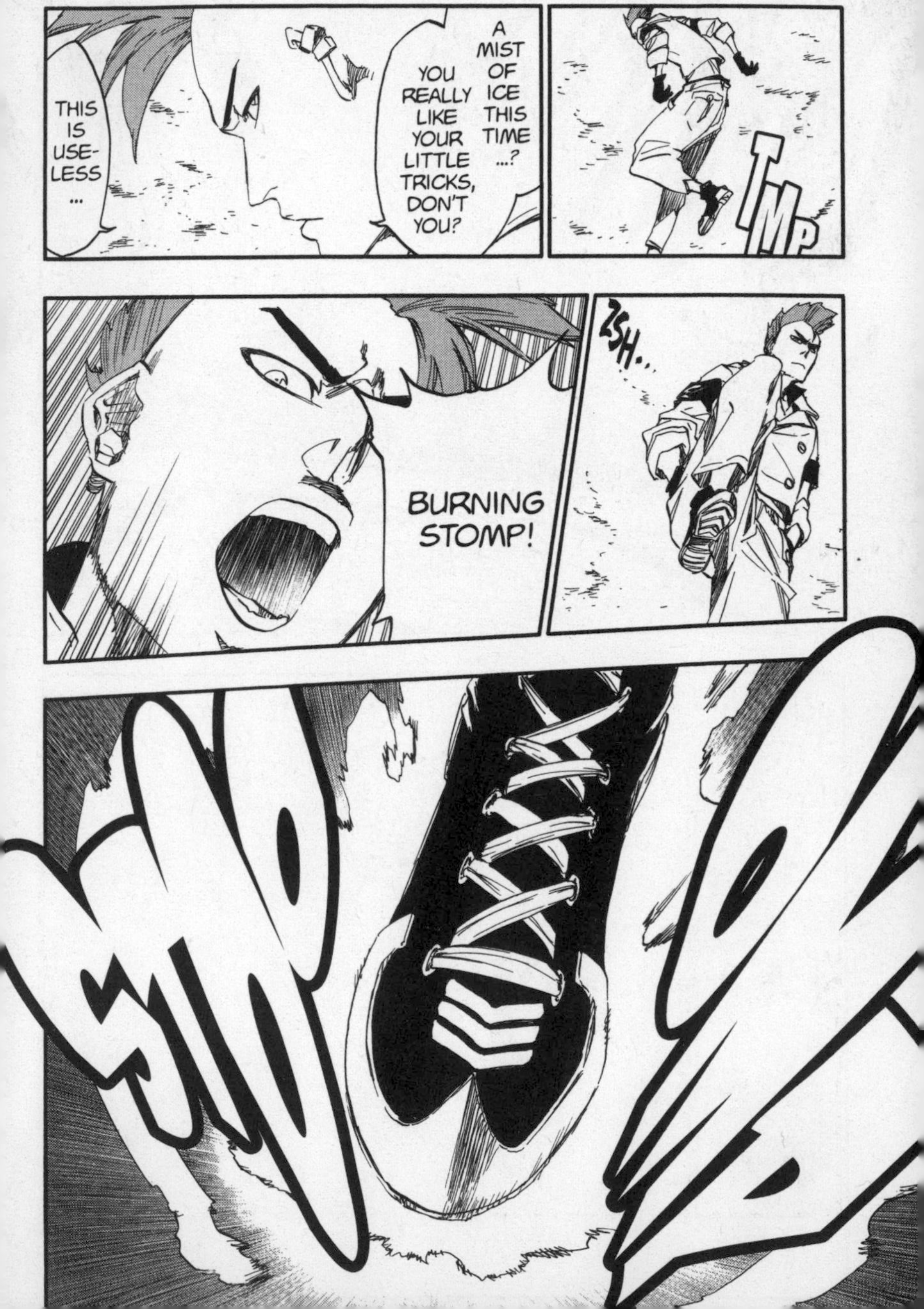
TMP
A MIST OF ICE THIS TIME ...?
YOU REALLY LIKE YOUR LITTLE TRICKS, DON'T YOU?
THIS IS USE-LESS ...
ZSH...
BURNING STOMP!

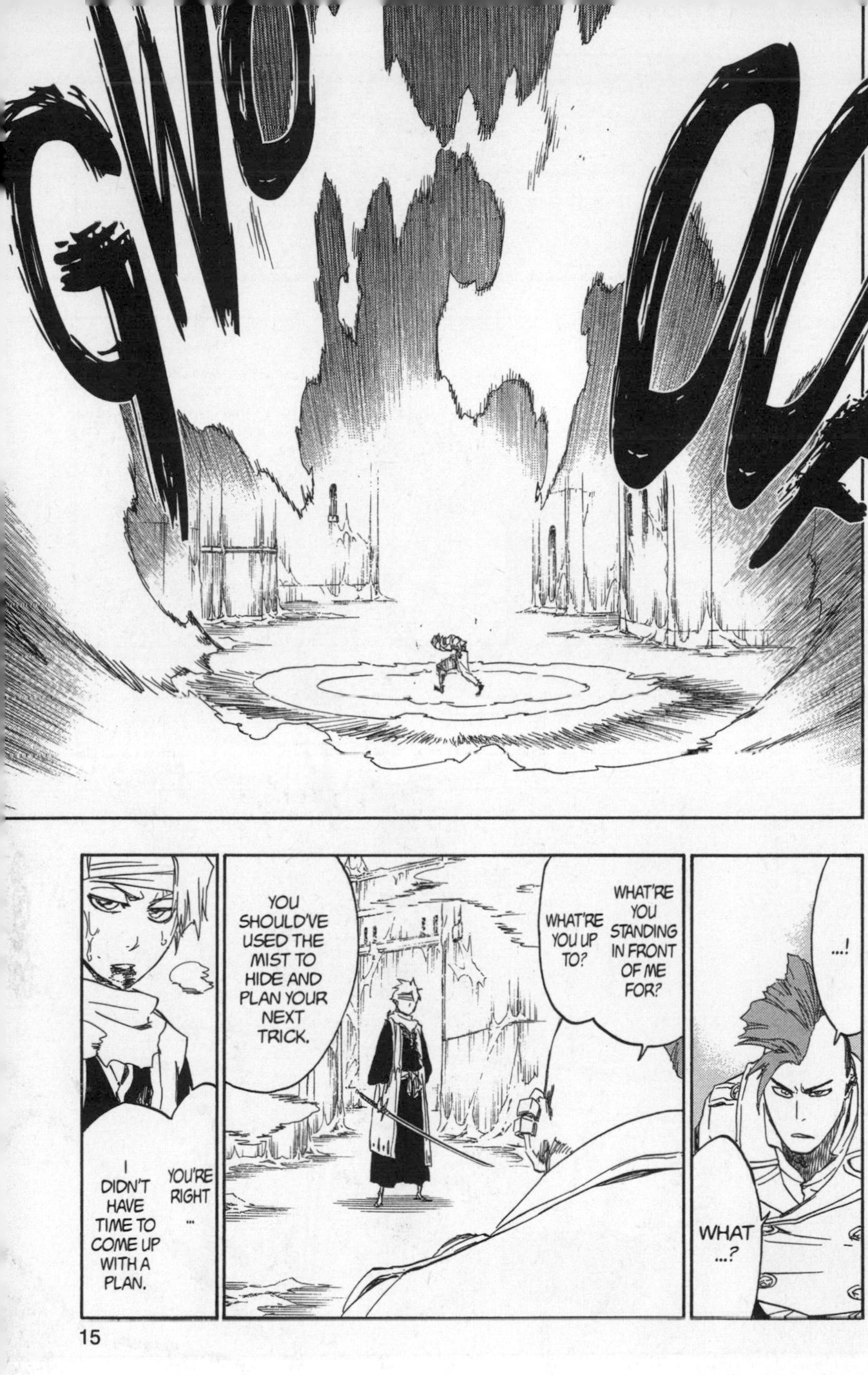
GWOOOOO
...!
WHAT ...?
WHAT'RE YOU STANDING IN FRONT OF ME FOR?
WHAT'RE YOU UP TO?
YOU SHOULD'VE USED THE MIST TO HIDE AND PLAN YOUR NEXT TRICK.
YOU'RE RIGHT ...
I DIDN'T HAVE TIME TO COME UP WITH A PLAN.

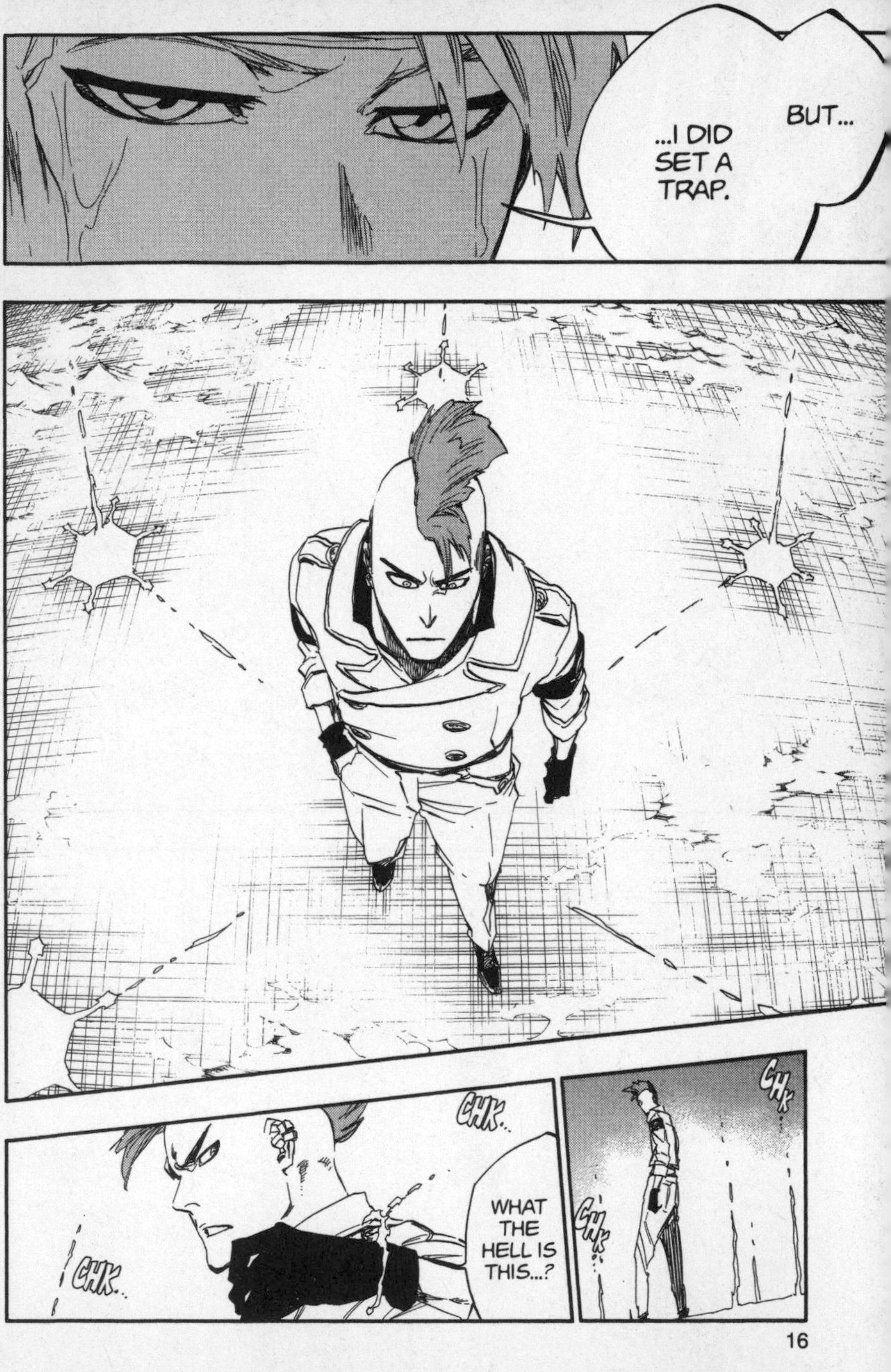
BUT...
...I DID SET A TRAP.
CHK
CHK
CHK...
WHAT THE HELL IS THIS...?
CHK..

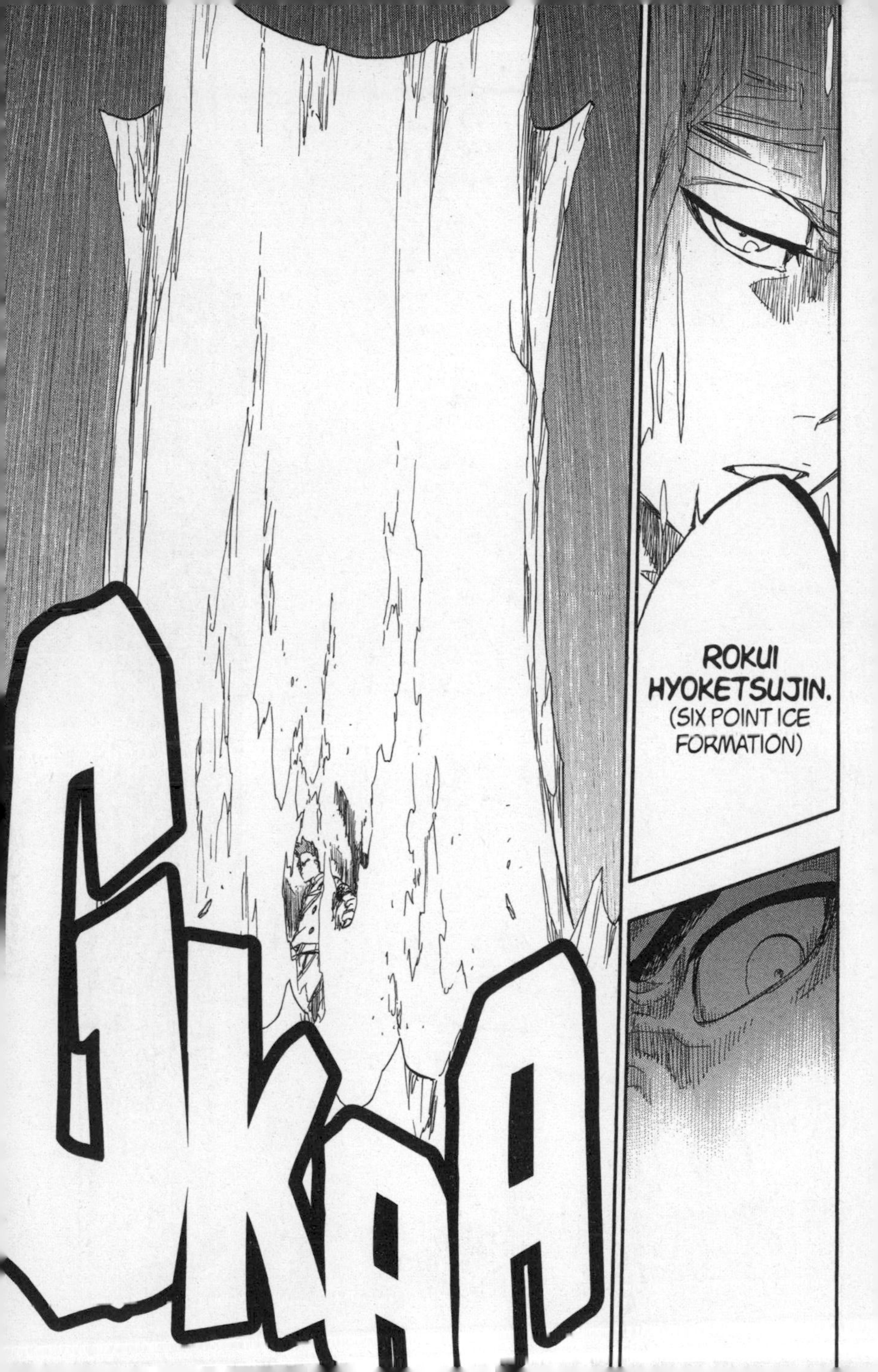
ROKUI HYOKETSUJIN.
(SIX POINT ICE FORMATION)
CKAA

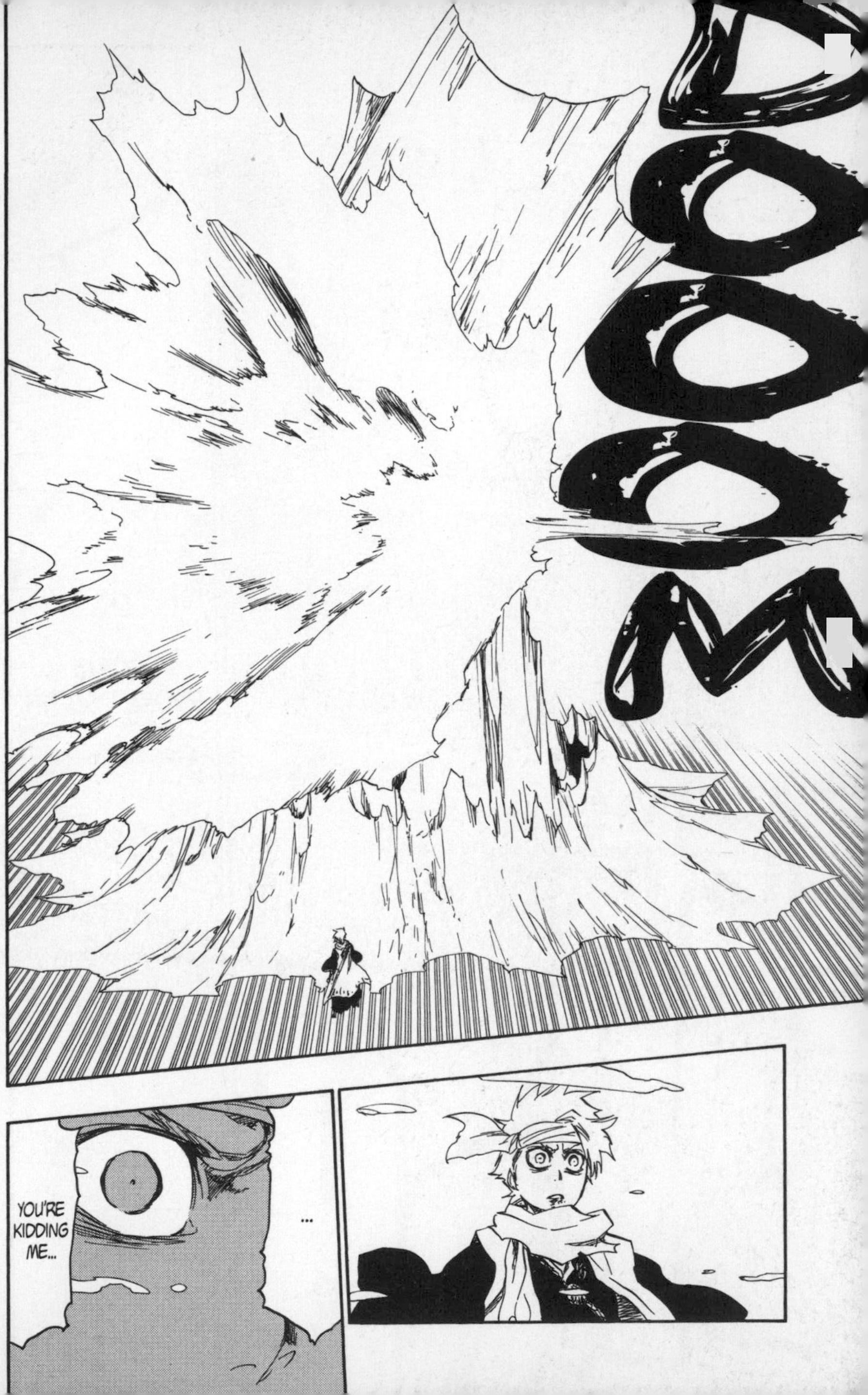
DOOOM
...
YOU'RE KIDDING ME...

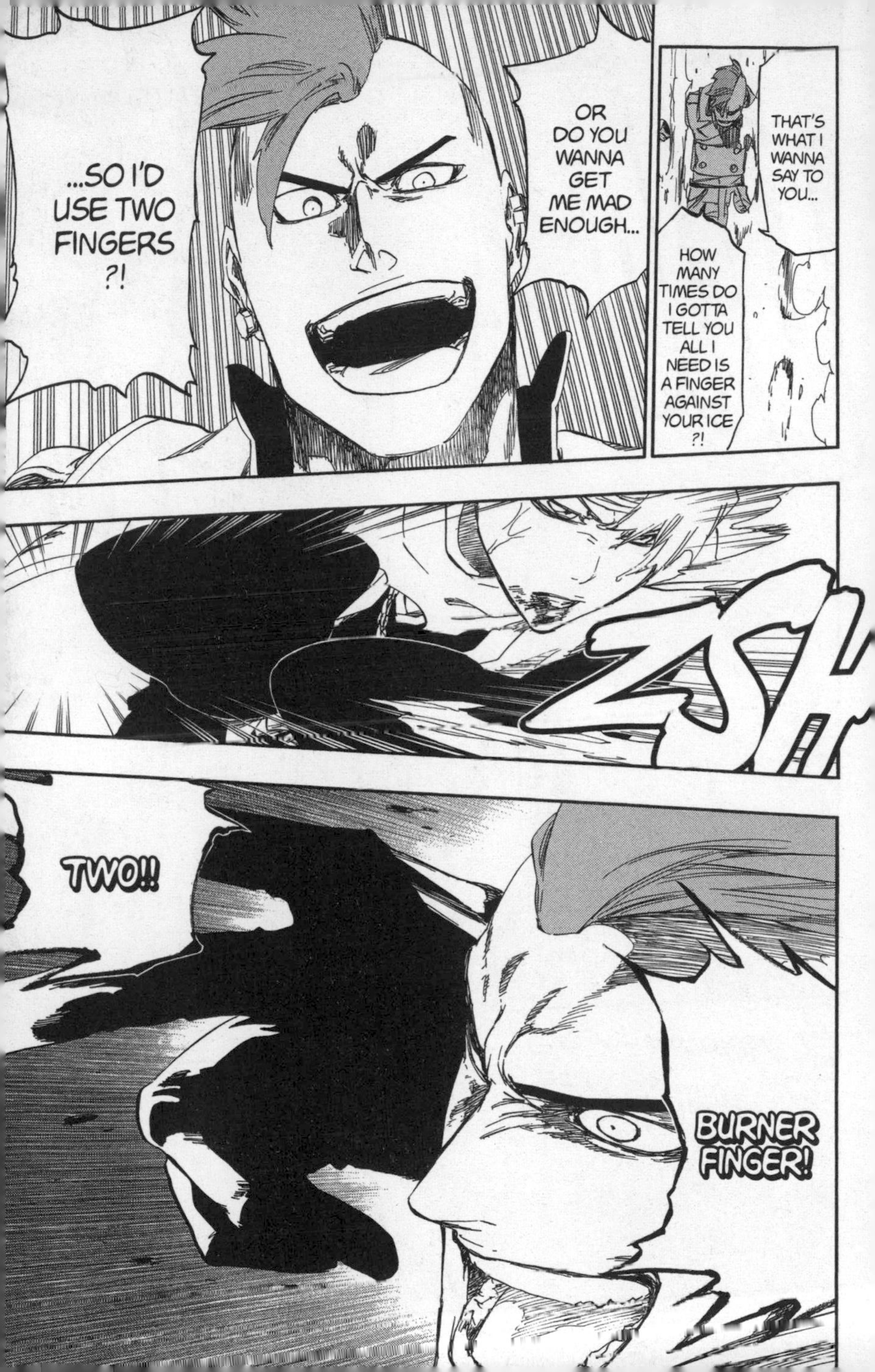
THAT'S WHAT I WANNA SAY TO YOU...
HOW MANY TIMES DO I GOTTA TELL YOU ALL I NEED IS A FINGER AGAINST YOUR ICE ?!
OR DO YOU WANNA GET ME MAD ENOUGH...
...SO I'D USE TWO FINGERS ?!
ZSH
BURNER FINGER!
TWO!!

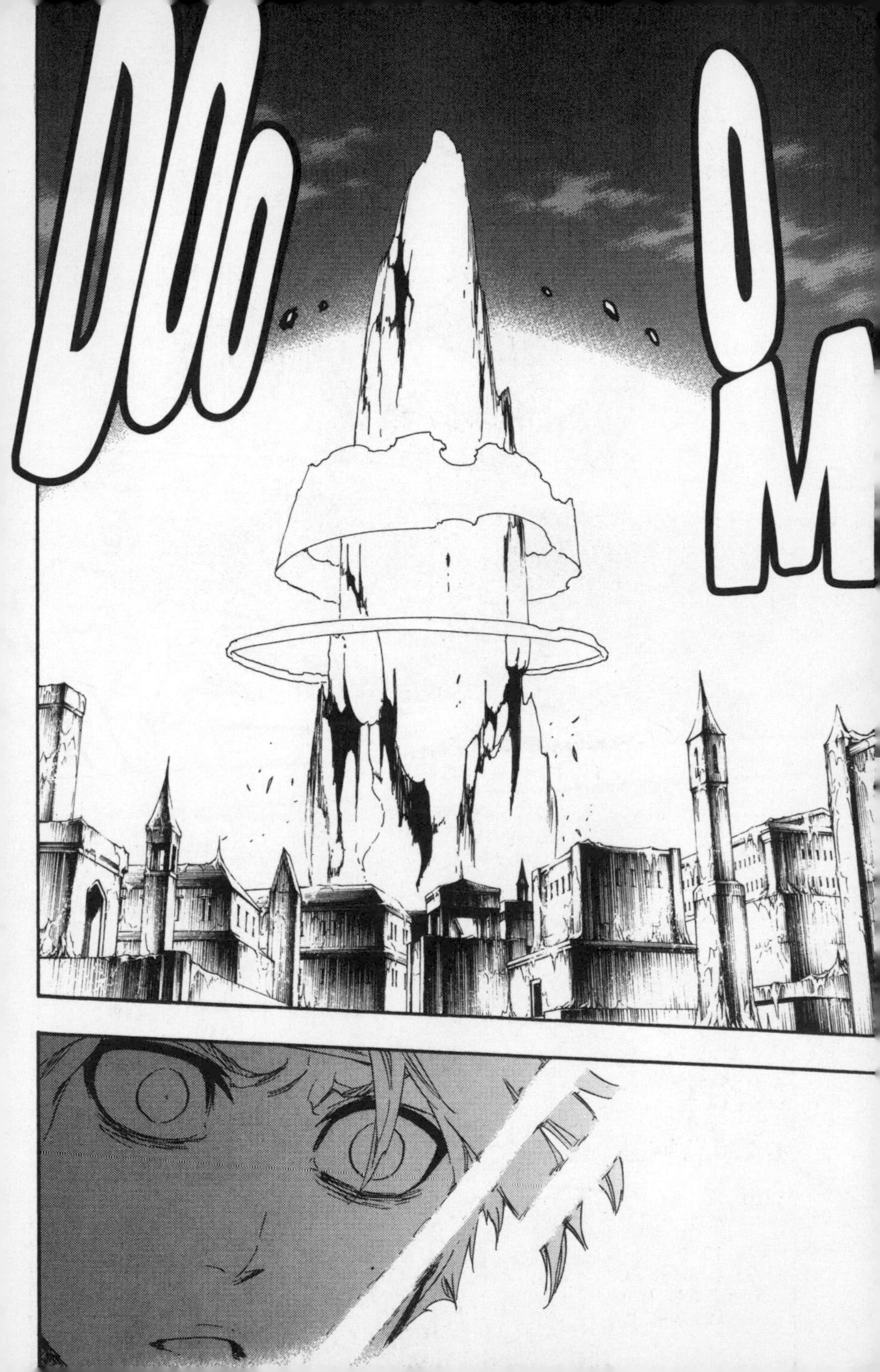
DOO... OM

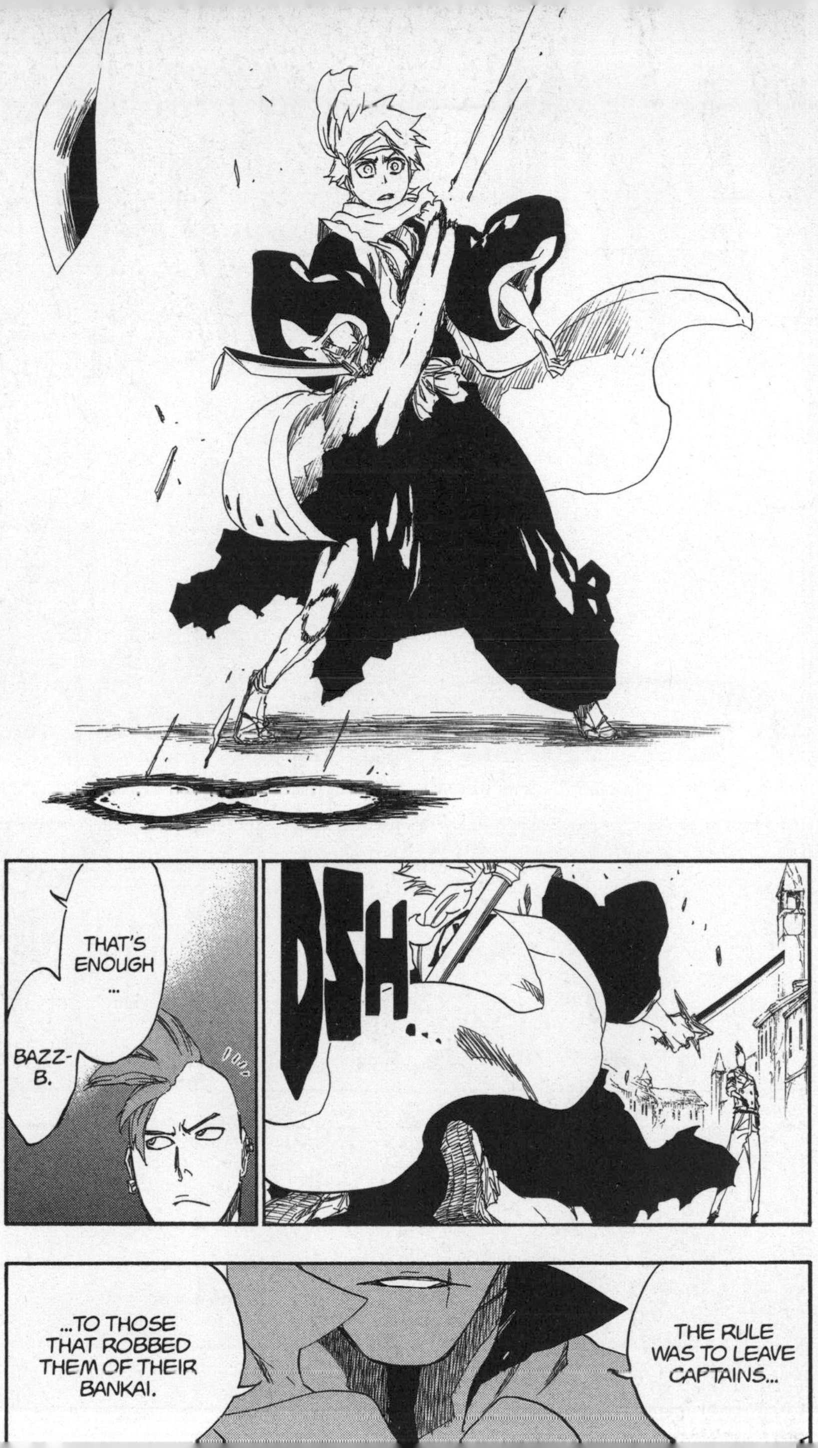
DSH...
THAT'S ENOUGH ...
BAZZ-B.
THE RULE WAS TO LEAVE CAPTAINS...
...TO THOSE THAT ROBBED THEM OF THEIR BANKAI.

TMP
I'LL FINISH HIM.

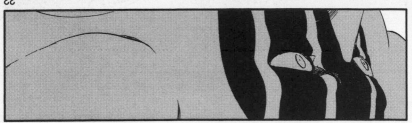

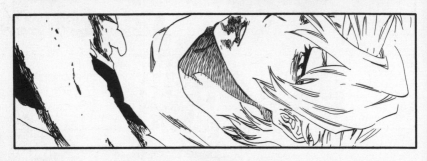

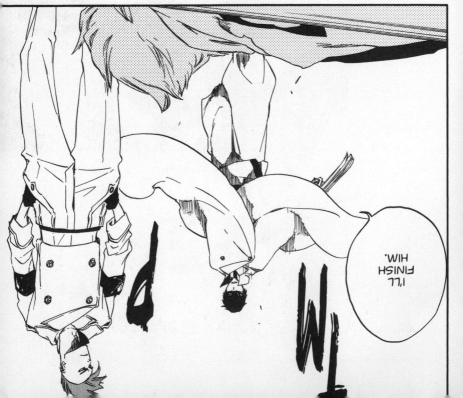

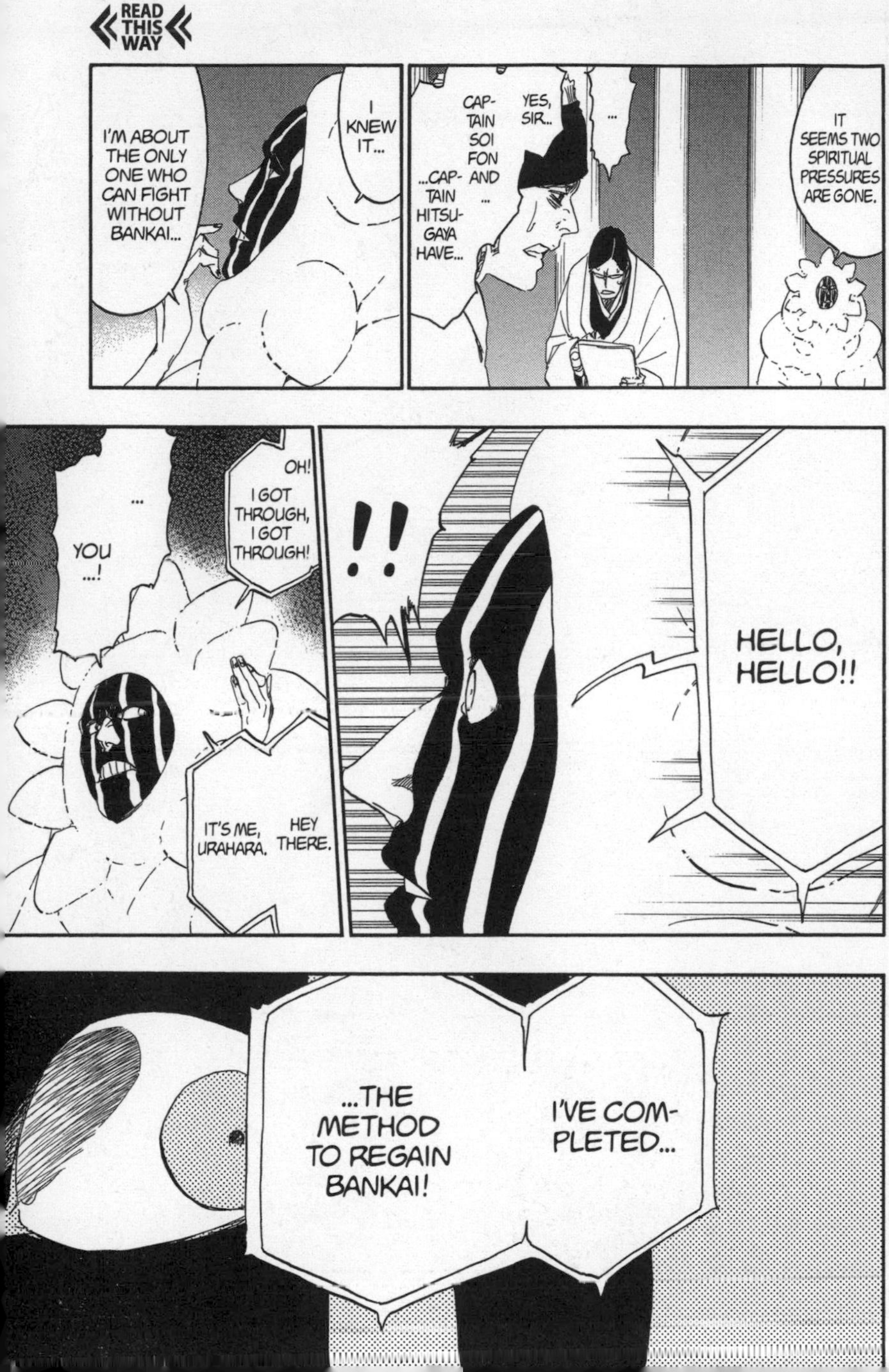
READ THIS WAY
IT SEEMS TWO SPIRITUAL PRESSURES ARE GONE.
...
YES, SIR...
CAPTAIN SOI FON AND ...
...CAPTAIN HITSUGAYA HAVE...
I KNEW IT...
I'M ABOUT THE ONLY ONE WHO CAN FIGHT WITHOUT BANKAI...
HELLO, HELLO!!
!!
HEY THERE.
IT'S ME, URAHARA.
OH!
I GOT THROUGH, I GOT THROUGH!
...
YOU ...!
I'VE COMPLETED...
...THE METHOD TO REGAIN BANKAI!

NUTS
BOLT

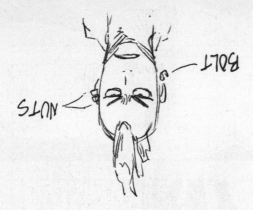

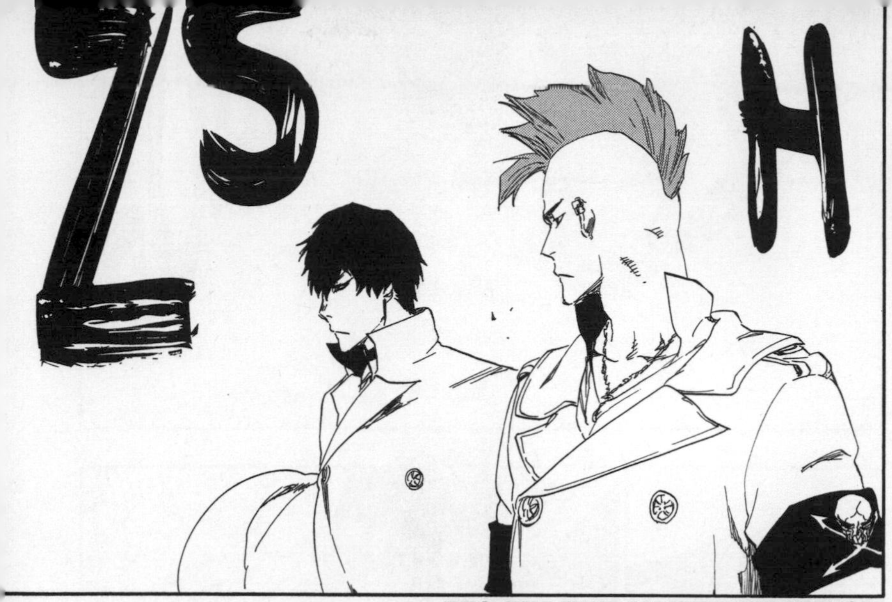

552. THE FUNDAMENTAL VIRULENCE

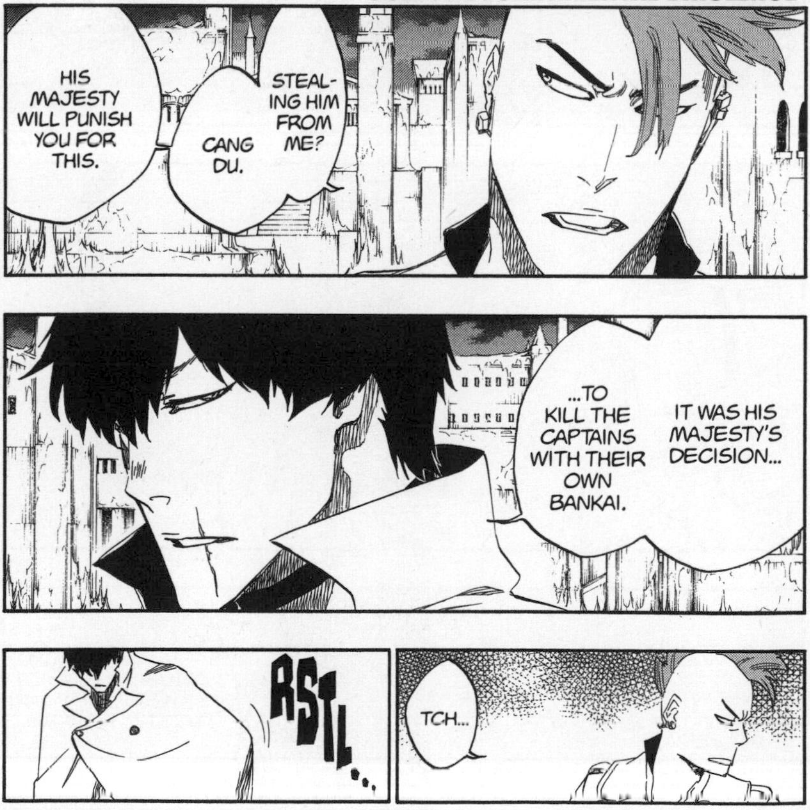
STEAL-ING HIM FROM ME?
CANG DU.
HIS MAJESTY WILL PUNISH YOU FOR THIS.
IT WAS HIS MAJESTY'S DECISION...
...TO KILL THE CAPTAINS WITH THEIR OWN BANKAI.
TCH...
RSTL...

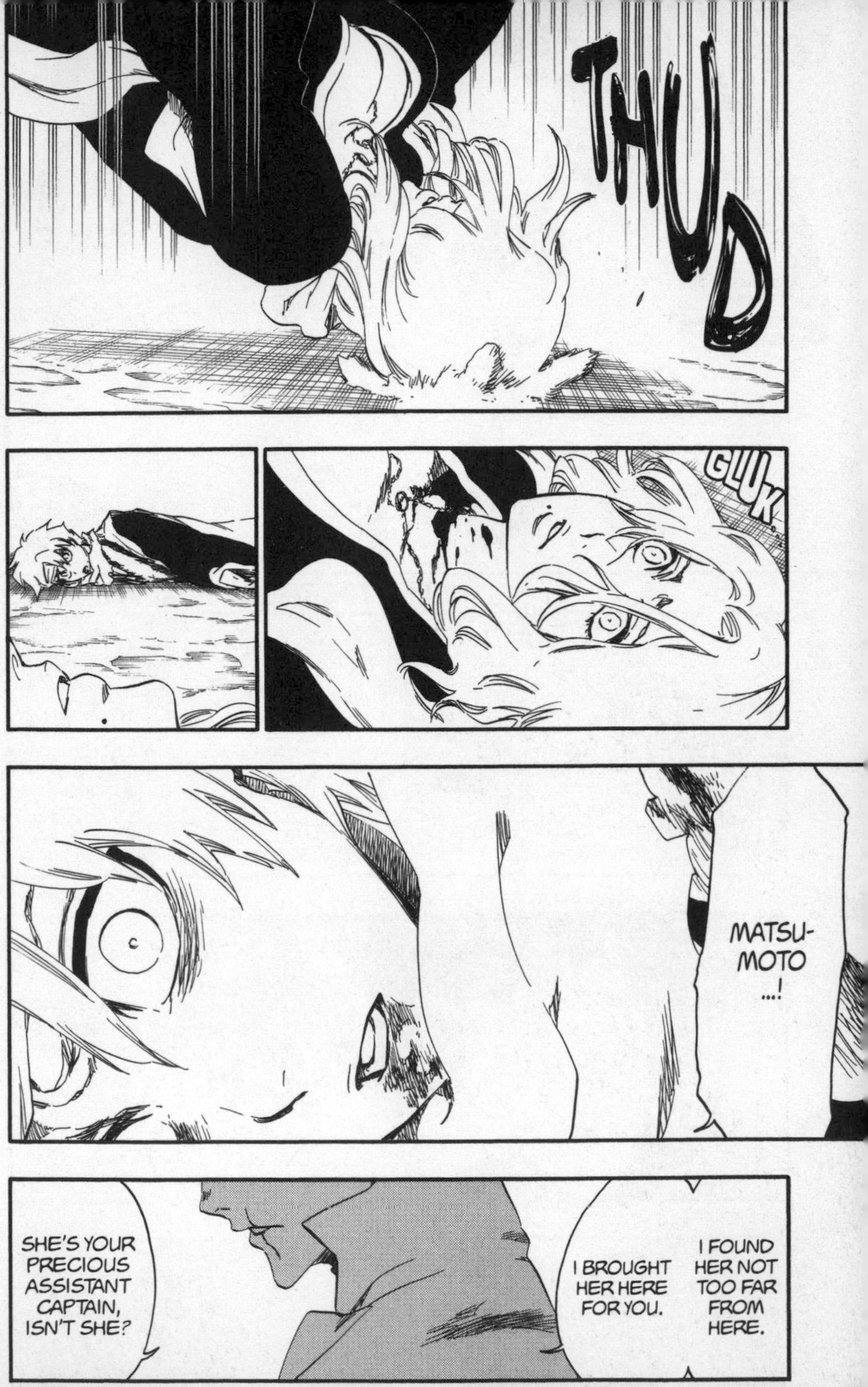
THUD
GLUK
MATSU-MOTO ...!
I FOUND HER NOT TOO FAR FROM HERE.
I BROUGHT HER HERE FOR YOU.
SHE'S YOUR PRECIOUS ASSISTANT CAPTAIN, ISN'T SHE?

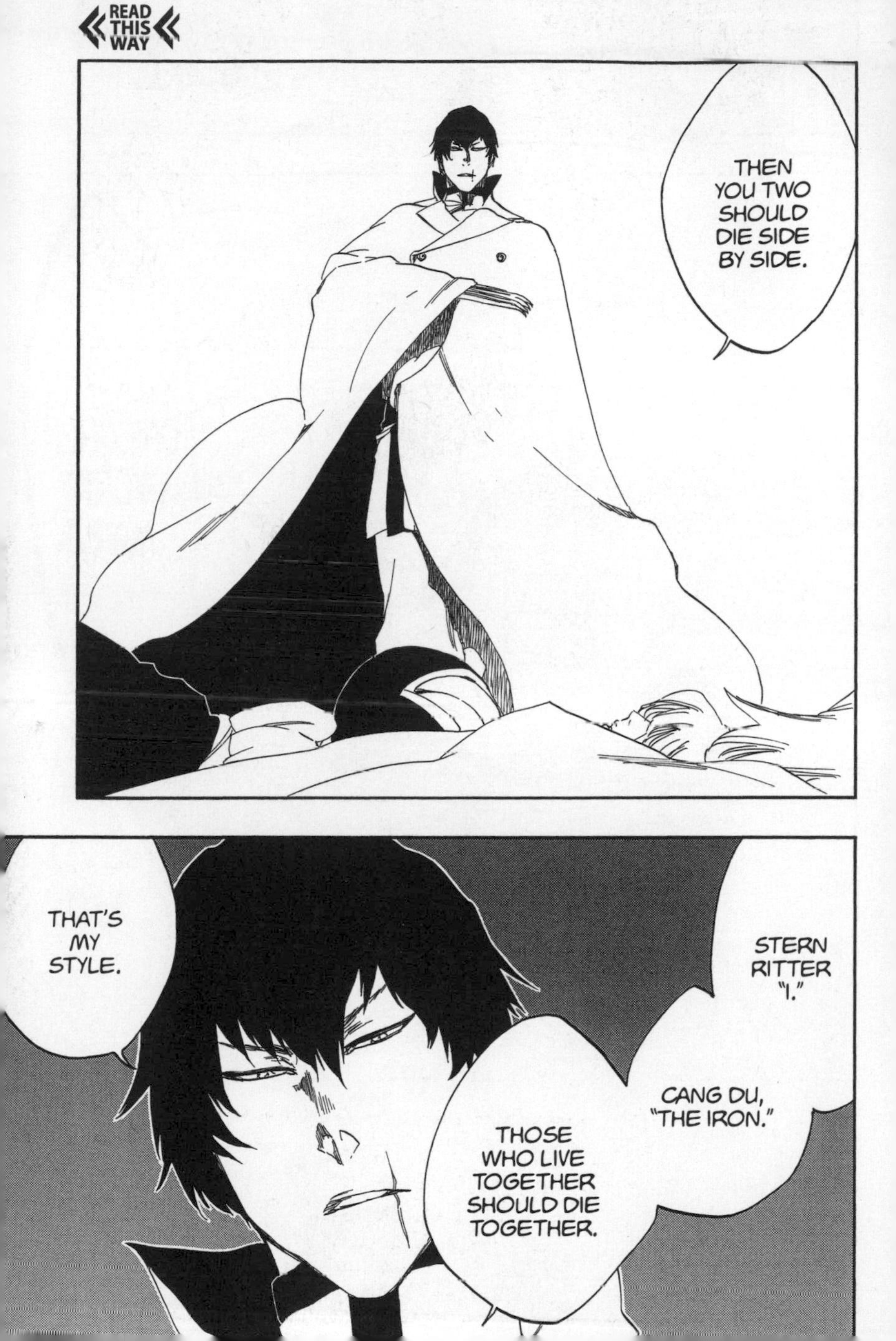
READ THIS WAY
THEN YOU TWO SHOULD DIE SIDE BY SIDE.
STERN RITTER "I."
CANG DU, "THE IRON."
THOSE WHO LIVE TOGETHER SHOULD DIE TOGETHER.
THAT'S MY STYLE.

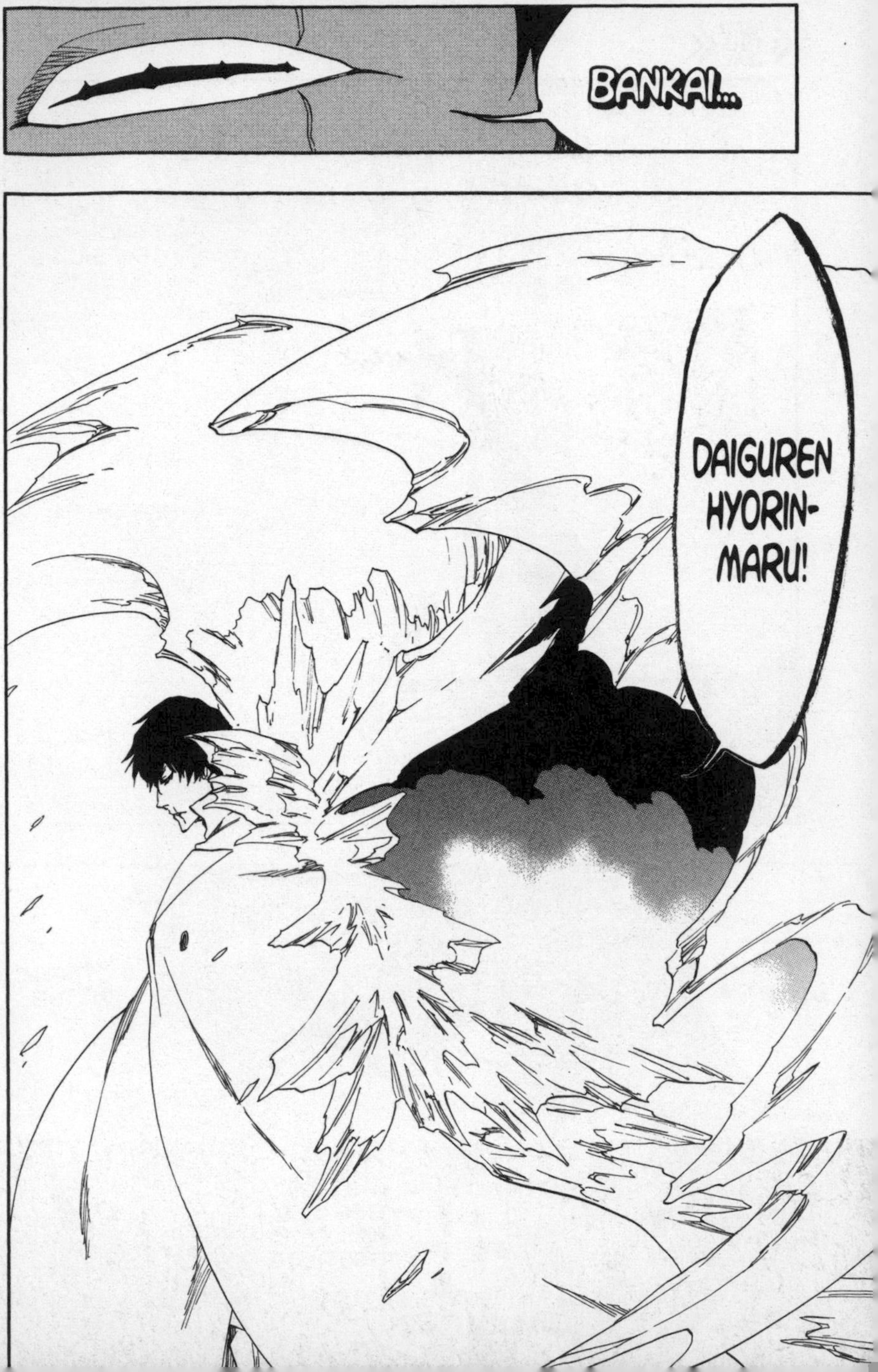
BANKAI...
DAIGUREN HYORIN-MARU!

READ THIS WAY

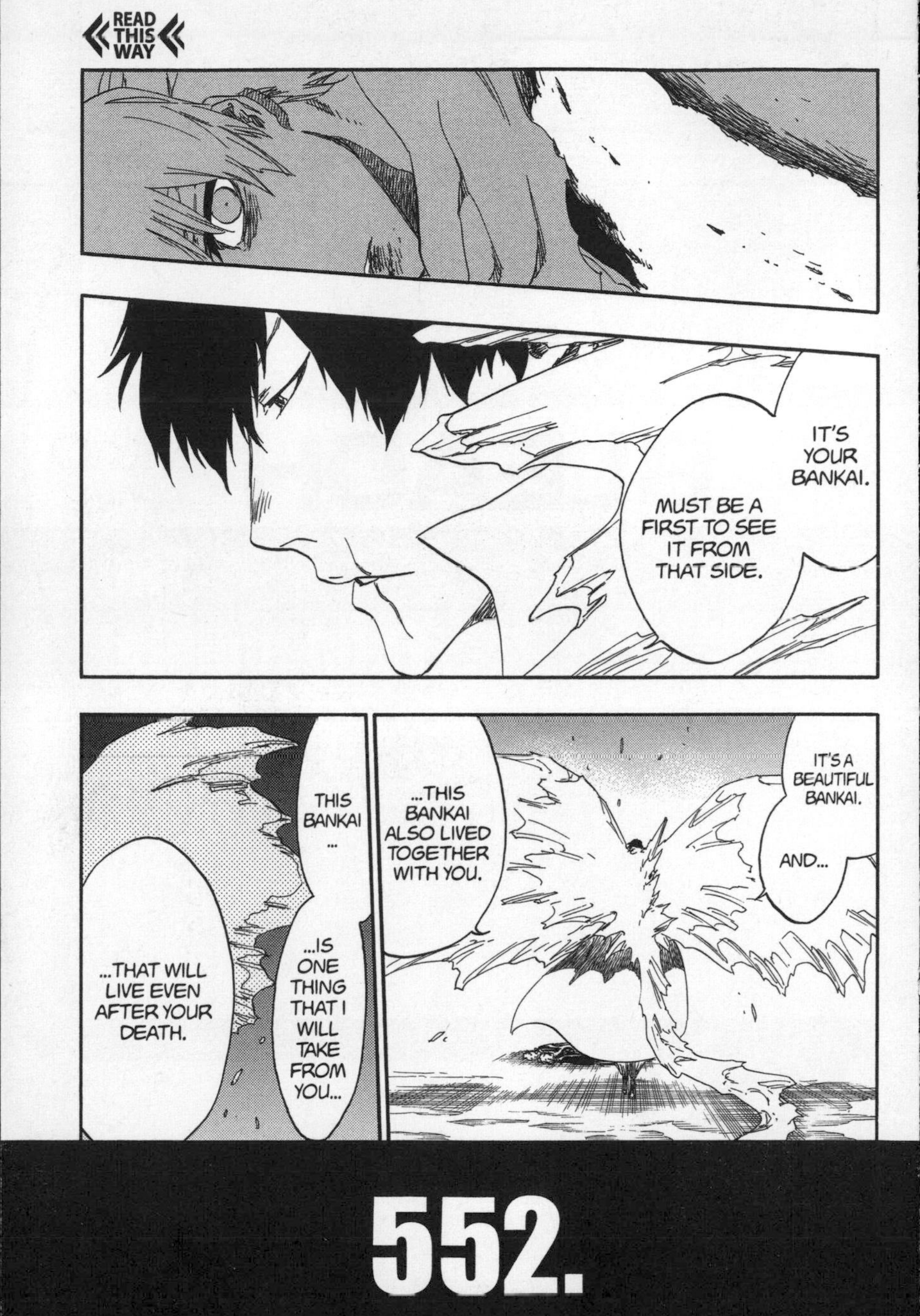
IT'S YOUR BANKAI.
MUST BE A FIRST TO SEE IT FROM THAT SIDE.
IT'S A BEAUTIFUL BANKAI.
AND...
...THIS BANKAI ALSO LIVED TOGETHER WITH YOU.
THIS BANKAI ...
...IS ONE THING THAT I WILL TAKE FROM YOU...
...THAT WILL LIVE EVEN AFTER YOUR DEATH.

552.

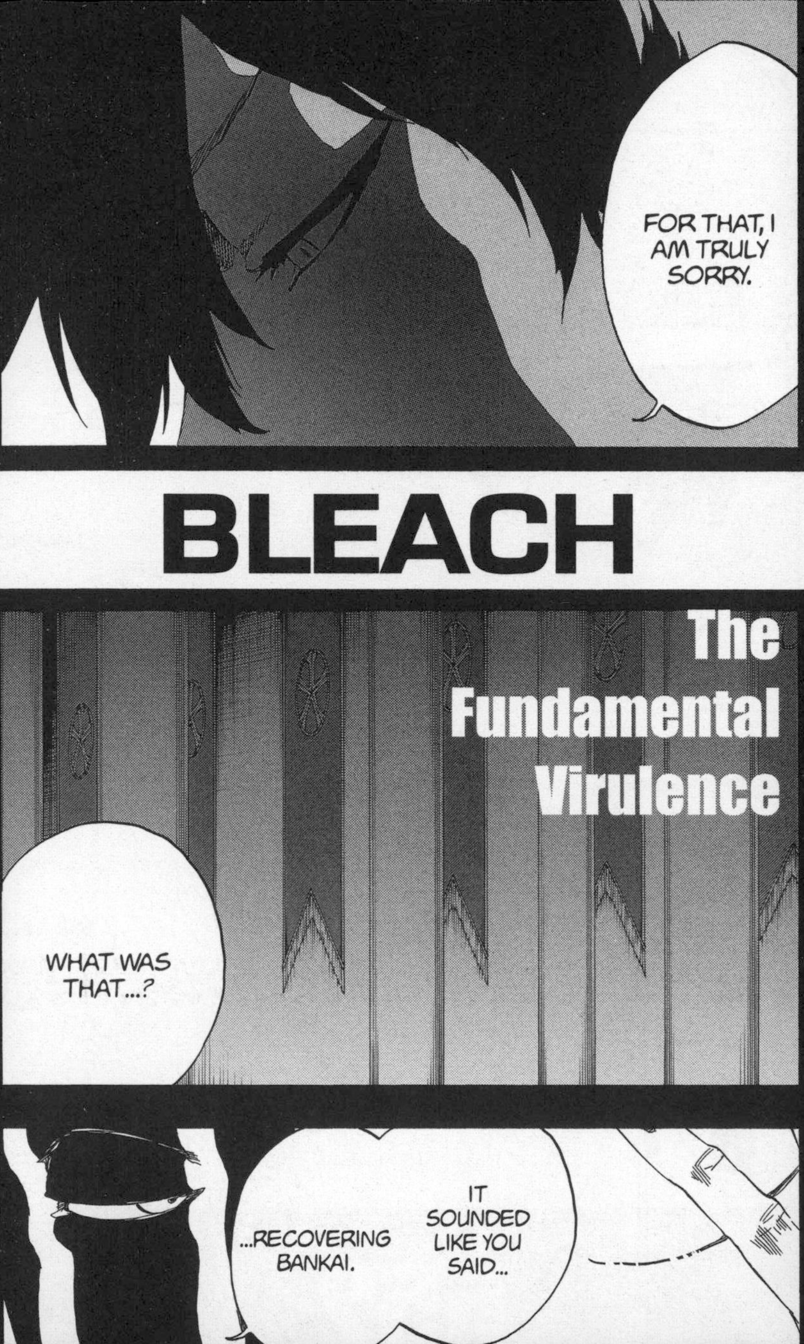
FOR THAT, I AM TRULY SORRY.
BLEACH
The Fundamental Virulence
WHAT WAS THAT...?
IT SOUNDED LIKE YOU SAID...
...RECOVERING BANKAI.

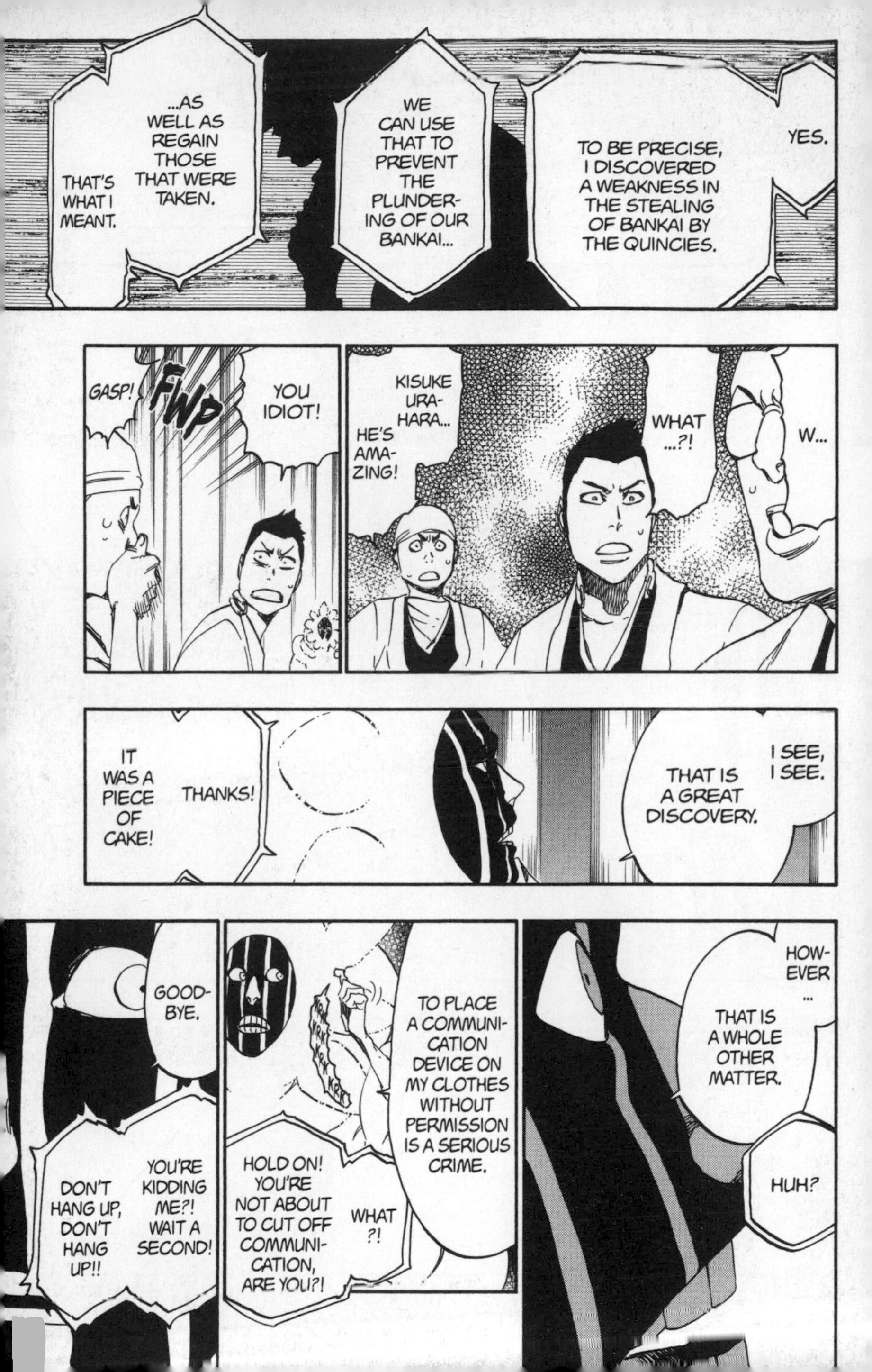
YES.
TO BE PRECISE, I DISCOVERED A WEAKNESS IN THE STEALING OF BANKAI BY THE QUINCIES.
WE CAN USE THAT TO PREVENT THE PLUNDERING OF OUR BANKAI...
...AS WELL AS REGAIN THOSE THAT WERE TAKEN.
THAT'S WHAT I MEANT.
W...
WHAT ...?!
KISUKE URAHARA...
HE'S AMAZING!
YOU IDIOT!
FWP
GASP!
I SEE, I SEE.
THAT IS A GREAT DISCOVERY.
THANKS!
IT WAS A PIECE OF CAKE!
HOWEVER ...
THAT IS A WHOLE OTHER MATTER.
HUH?
TO PLACE A COMMUNICATION DEVICE ON MY CLOTHES WITHOUT PERMISSION IS A SERIOUS CRIME.
WHAT ?!
HOLD ON! YOU'RE NOT ABOUT TO CUT OFF COMMUNICATION, ARE YOU?!
GOOD-BYE.
YOU'RE KIDDING ME?! WAIT A SECOND!
DON'T HANG UP, DON'T HANG UP!!

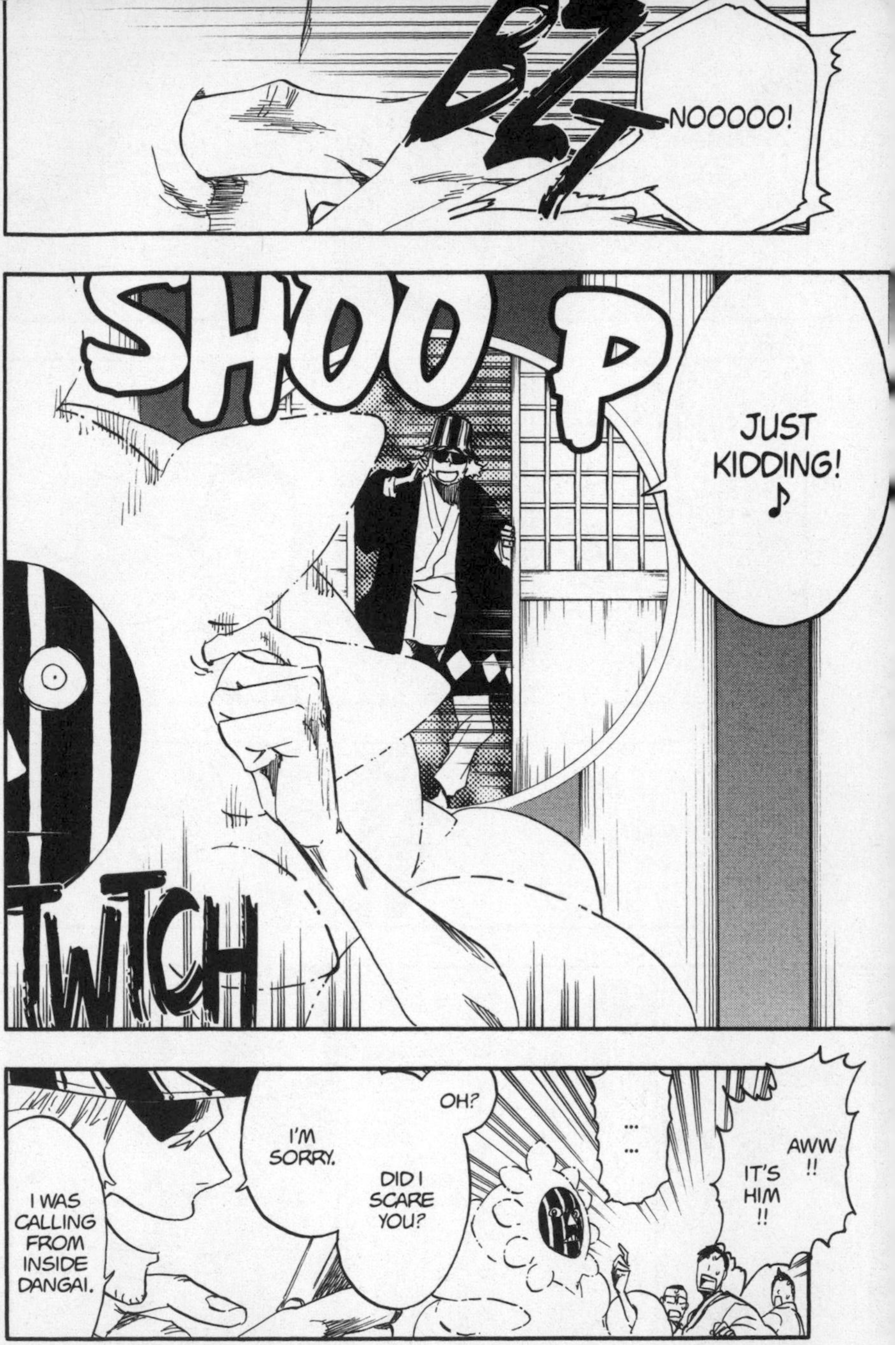
NOOOOO!
BLT
JUST KIDDING! ♪
SHOOP
TWITCH
AWW !!
IT'S HIM !!
... ...
OH?
I'M SORRY.
DID I SCARE YOU?
I WAS CALLING FROM INSIDE DANGAI.

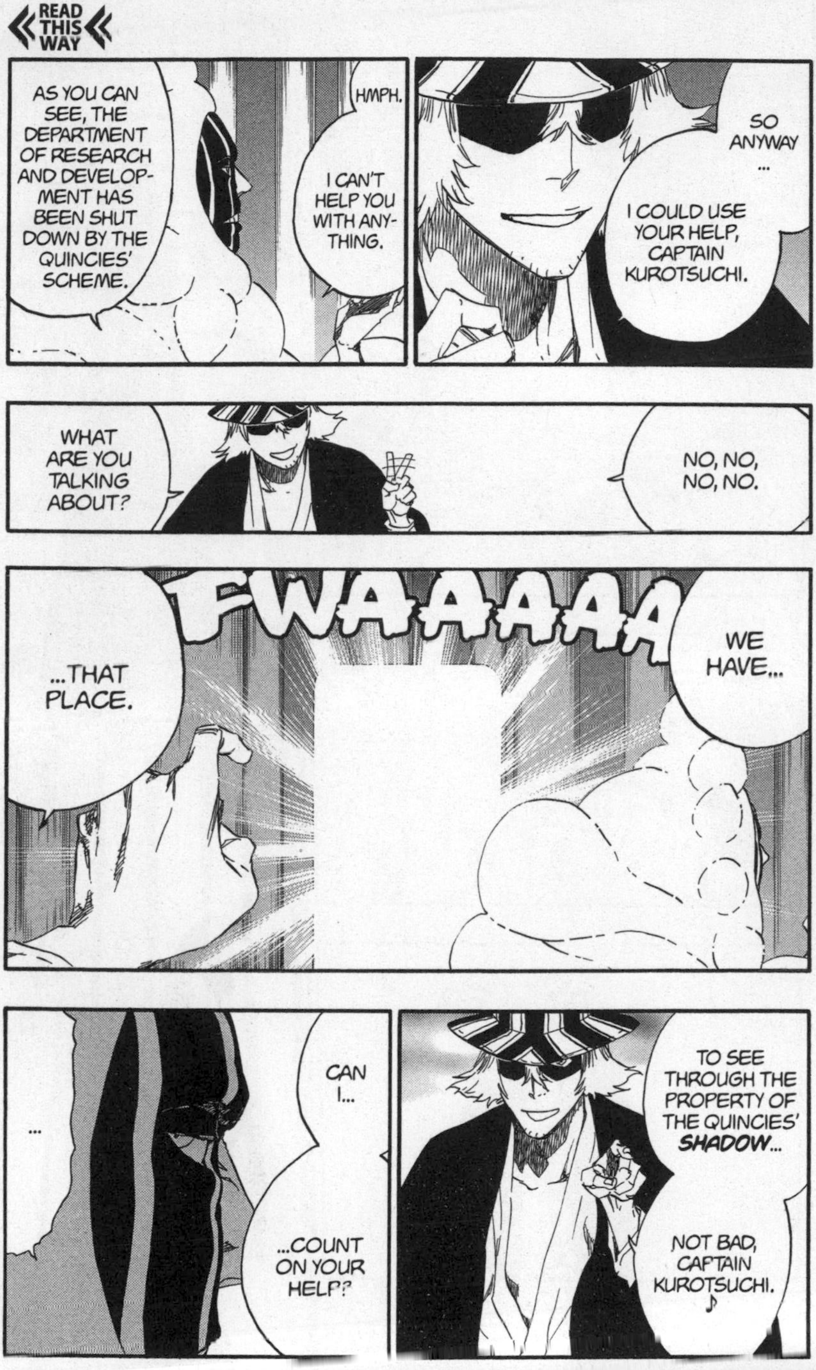
READ THIS WAY
SO ANYWAY...
I COULD USE YOUR HELP, CAPTAIN KUROTSUCHI.
HMPH.
I CAN'T HELP YOU WITH ANYTHING.
AS YOU CAN SEE, THE DEPARTMENT OF RESEARCH AND DEVELOPMENT HAS BEEN SHUT DOWN BY THE QUINCIES' SCHEME.
NO, NO, NO, NO.
WHAT ARE YOU TALKING ABOUT?
WE HAVE...
FWAAAAA
...THAT PLACE.
TO SEE THROUGH THE PROPERTY OF THE QUINCIES' ***SHADOW***...
NOT BAD, CAPTAIN KUROTSUCHI. ♪
CAN I...
...COUNT ON YOUR HELP?
...

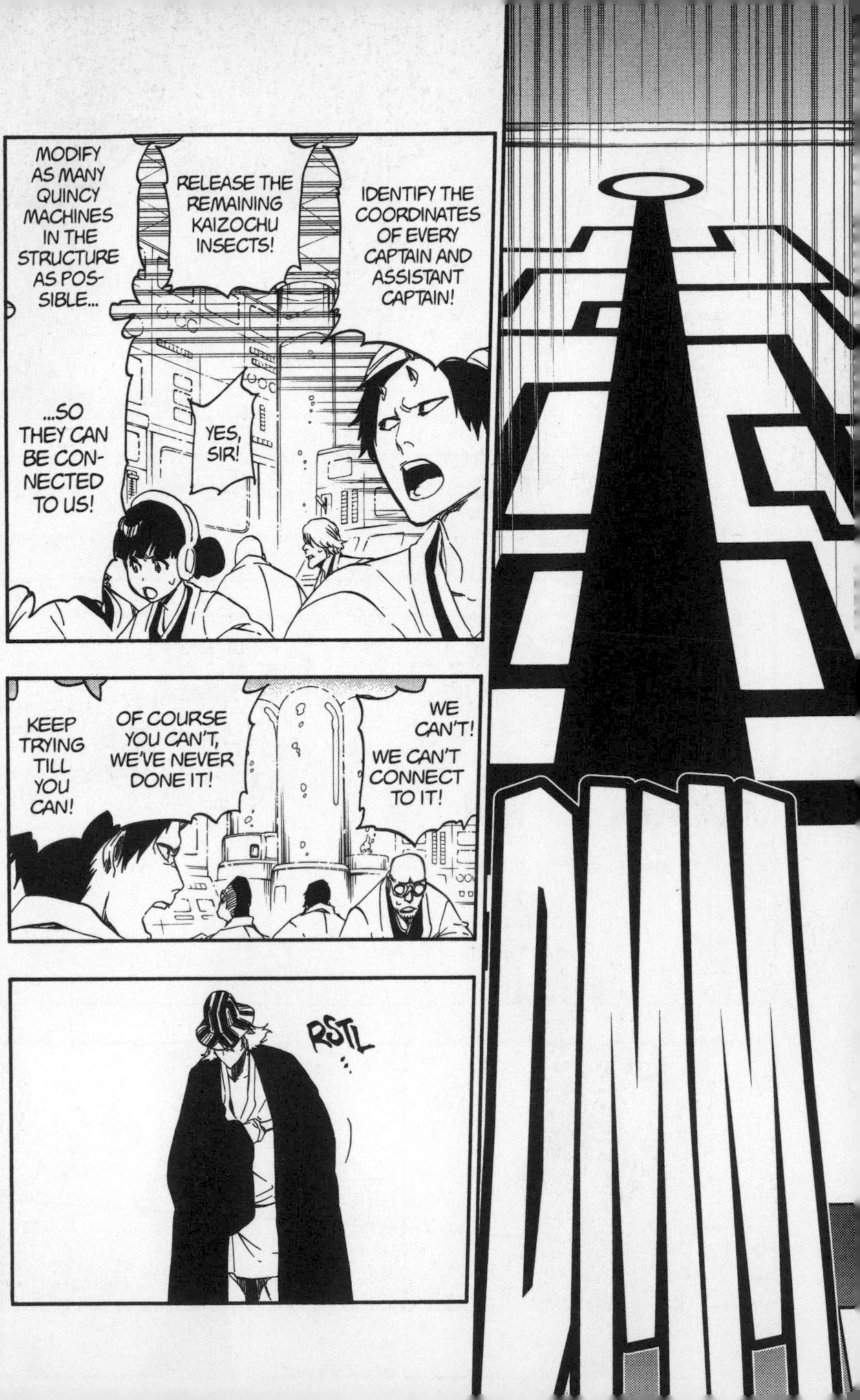
IDENTIFY THE COORDINATES OF EVERY CAPTAIN AND ASSISTANT CAPTAIN!
RELEASE THE REMAINING KAIZOCHU INSECTS!
MODIFY AS MANY QUINCY MACHINES IN THE STRUCTURE AS POS-SIBLE...
YES, SIR!
...SO THEY CAN BE CON-NECTED TO US!
WE CAN'T!
WE CAN'T CONNECT TO IT!
OF COURSE YOU CAN'T, WE'VE NEVER DONE IT!
KEEP TRYING TILL YOU CAN!
RSTL

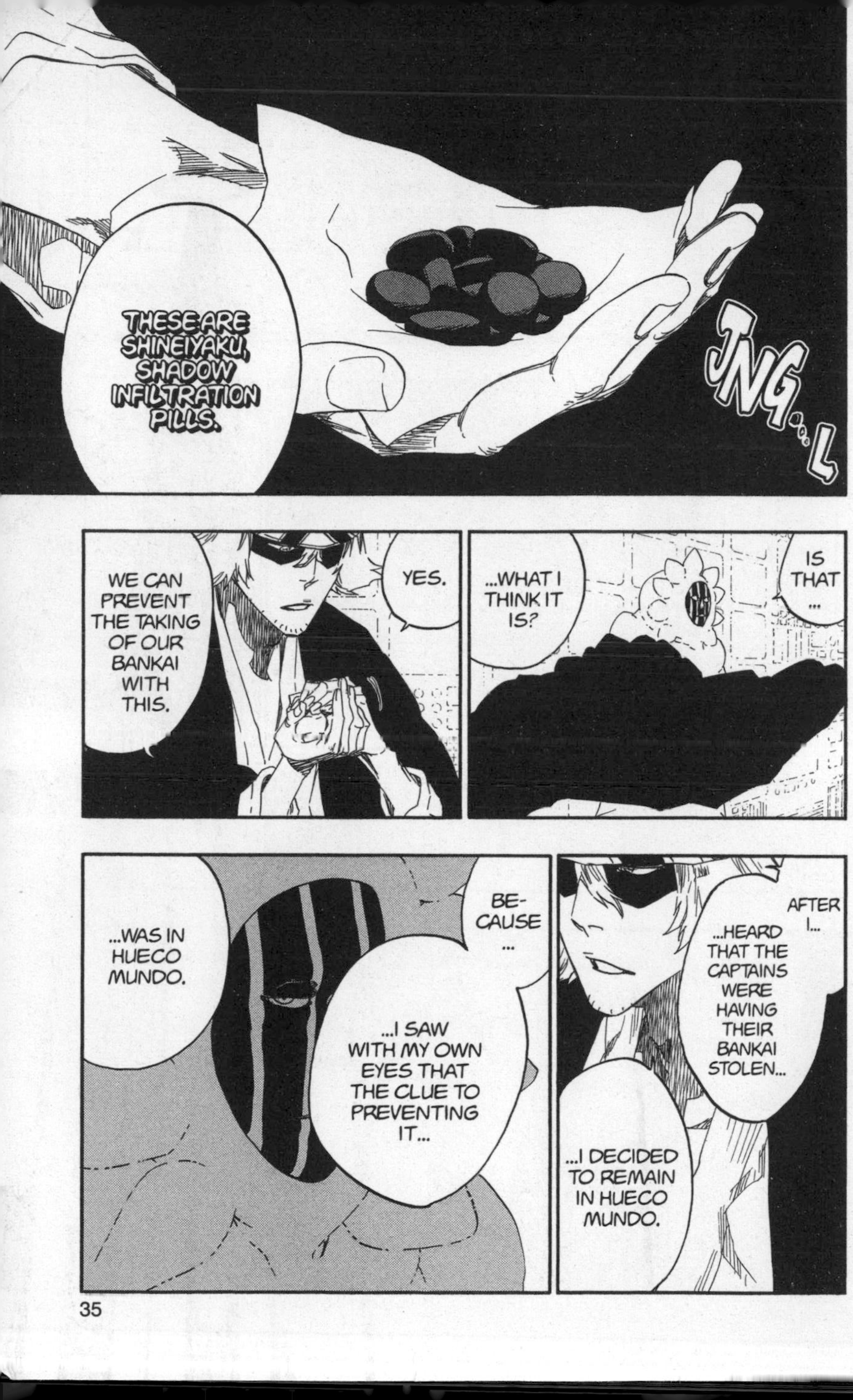
THESE ARE SHINEIYAKU, SHADOW INFILTRATION PILLS.
JNG...L
IS THAT ...
...WHAT I THINK IT IS?
YES.
WE CAN PREVENT THE TAKING OF OUR BANKAI WITH THIS.
AFTER I...
...HEARD THAT THE CAPTAINS WERE HAVING THEIR BANKAI STOLEN...
...I DECIDED TO REMAIN IN HUECO MUNDO.
BE-CAUSE ...
...I SAW WITH MY OWN EYES THAT THE CLUE TO PREVENTING IT...
...WAS IN HUECO MUNDO.

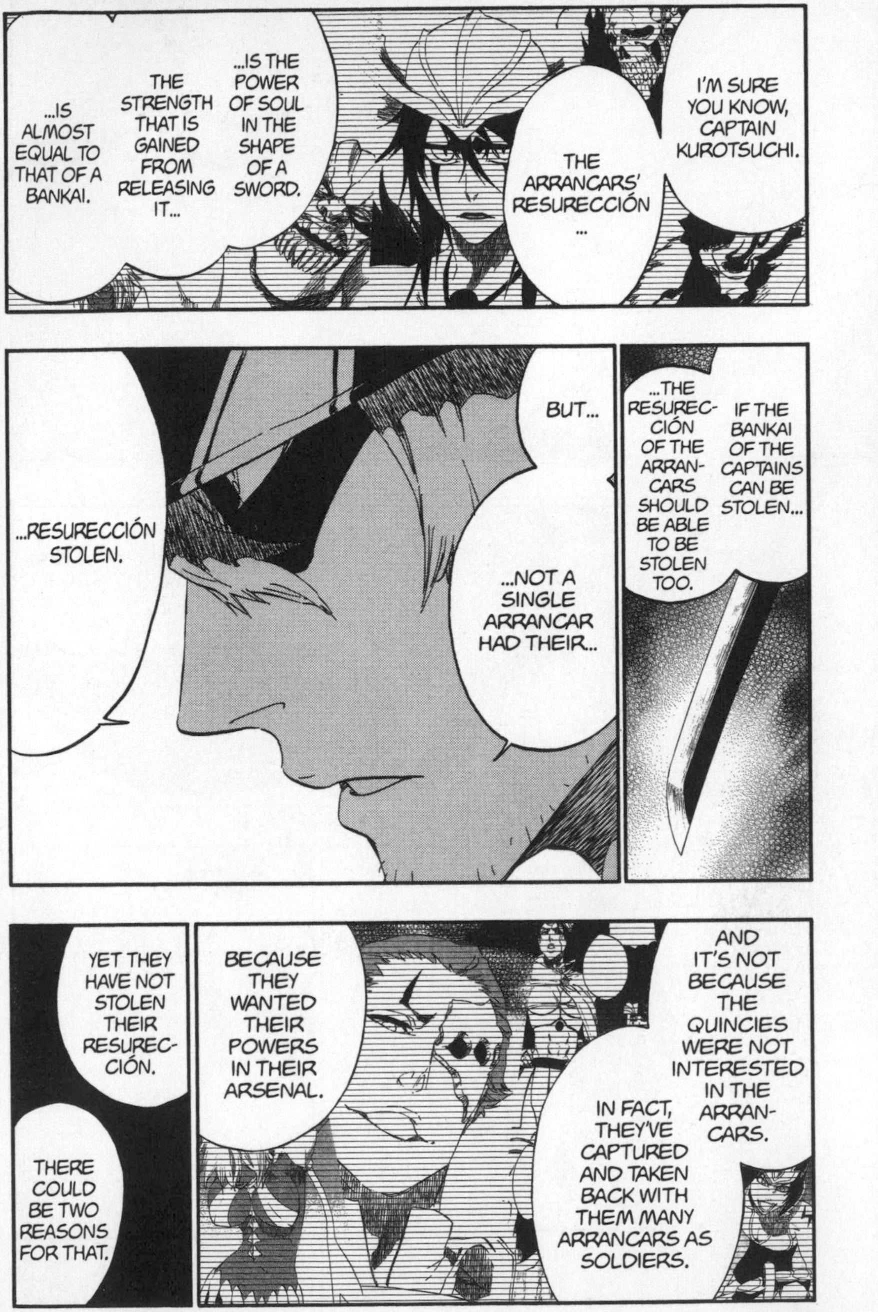
I'M SURE YOU KNOW, CAPTAIN KUROTSUCHI.
THE ARRANCARS' RESURECCIÓN ...
...IS THE POWER OF SOUL IN THE SHAPE OF A SWORD.
THE STRENGTH THAT IS GAINED FROM RELEASING IT...
...IS ALMOST EQUAL TO THAT OF A BANKAI.
IF THE BANKAI OF THE CAPTAINS CAN BE STOLEN...
...THE RESUREC-CIÓN OF THE ARRAN-CARS SHOULD BE ABLE TO BE STOLEN TOO.
BUT...
...NOT A SINGLE ARRANCAR HAD THEIR...
...RESURECCIÓN STOLEN.
AND IT'S NOT BECAUSE THE QUINCIES WERE NOT INTERESTED IN THE ARRAN-CARS.
IN FACT, THEY'VE CAPTURED AND TAKEN BACK WITH THEM MANY ARRANCARS AS SOLDIERS.
BECAUSE THEY WANTED THEIR POWERS IN THEIR ARSENAL.
YET THEY HAVE NOT STOLEN THEIR RESUREC-CIÓN.
THERE COULD BE TWO REASONS FOR THAT.

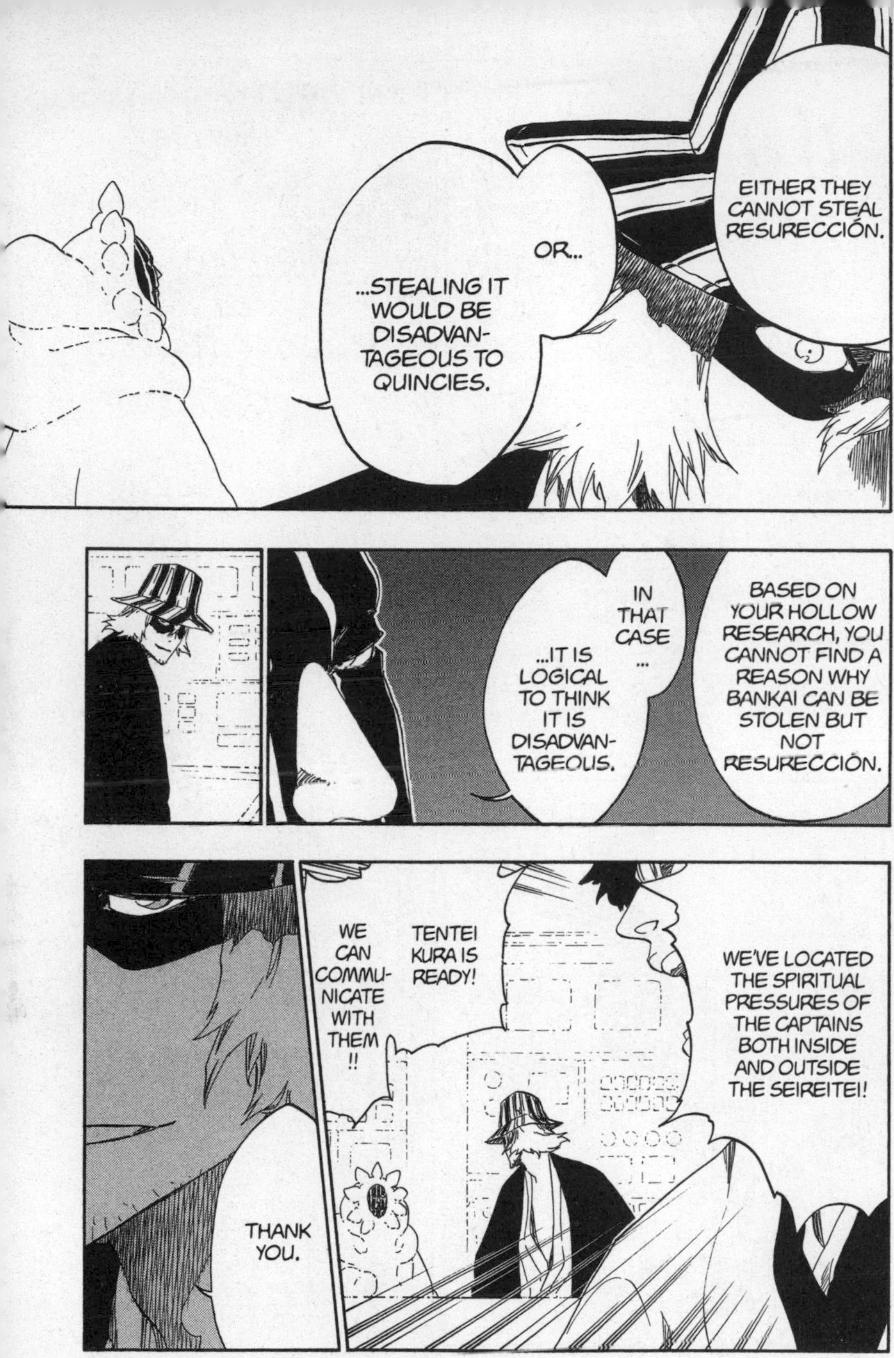
EITHER THEY CANNOT STEAL RESURECCIÓN.
OR...
...STEALING IT WOULD BE DISADVAN-TAGEOUS TO QUINCIES.
BASED ON YOUR HOLLOW RESEARCH, YOU CANNOT FIND A REASON WHY BANKAI CAN BE STOLEN BUT NOT RESURECCIÓN.
IN THAT CASE ...
...IT IS LOGICAL TO THINK IT IS DISADVAN-TAGEOUS.
WE'VE LOCATED THE SPIRITUAL PRESSURES OF THE CAPTAINS BOTH INSIDE AND OUTSIDE THE SEIREITEI!
TENTEI KURA IS READY!
WE CAN COMMU-NICATE WITH THEM !!
THANK YOU.

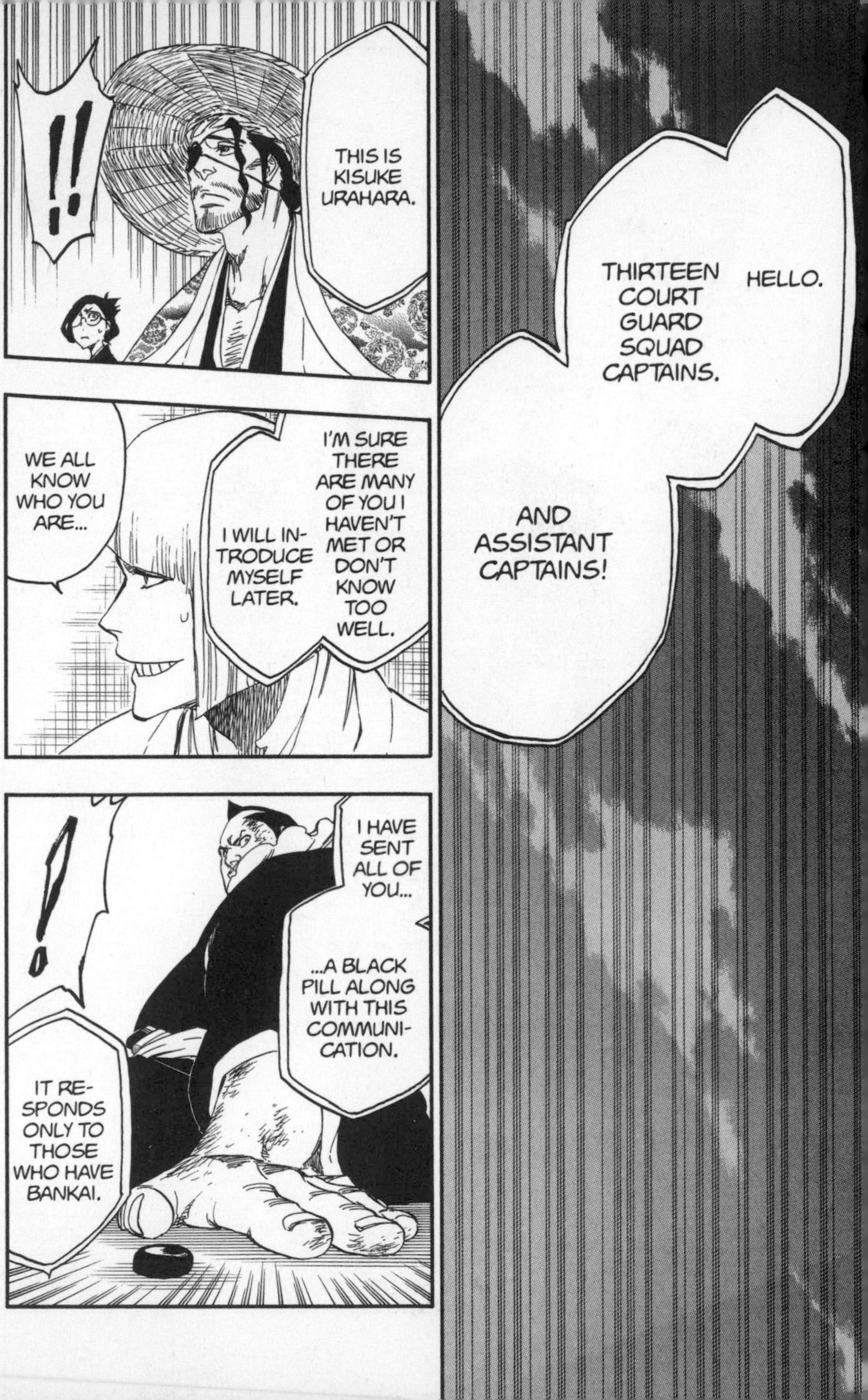
HELLO.
THIRTEEN COURT GUARD SQUAD CAPTAINS.
AND ASSISTANT CAPTAINS!
THIS IS KISUKE URAHARA.
!!
I'M SURE THERE ARE MANY OF YOU I HAVEN'T MET OR DON'T KNOW TOO WELL.
I WILL IN-TRODUCE MYSELF LATER.
WE ALL KNOW WHO YOU ARE...
I HAVE SENT ALL OF YOU...
...A BLACK PILL ALONG WITH THIS COMMUNI-CATION.
!
IT RE-SPONDS ONLY TO THOSE WHO HAVE BANKAI.

PLEASE...
...TOUCH IT WITH YOUR HANDS, LEGS, SWORD OR ANYTHING.
IT WILL BE ABSORBED FROM WHERE YOU TOUCH IT.
THE PILL WILL PERMEATE ALL THE WAY INSIDE YOUR SOUL.
KYW......U
Z..
ZZ...
...
WHAT'S THIS ...?
SOMETHING ...
...HAS BEEN BOTHERING ME ABOUT THE QUINCIES.
THE ABSOLUTE HOSTILITY THEY HAVE AGAINST HOLLOWS...
...MAY NOT STEM FROM RESENTMENT AS IT HAS BEEN SAID.
HOSTILITY IS BORN FROM A DIFFERENCE IN IDEOLOGY.
IT IS IMPOSSIBLE TO CONTINUE HATING THOSE WHO DO NOT HAVE A WILL OR IDEOLOGY.
THERE CAN BE ONLY ONE REASON...
...TO CONTINUE HAVING THAT MUCH HOSTILITY.

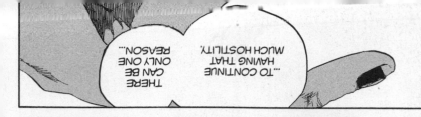

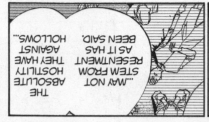

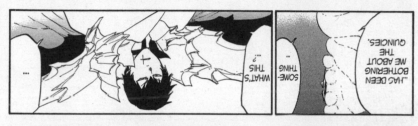

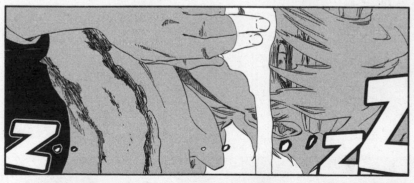

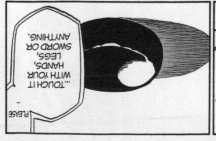

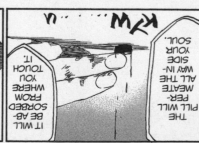

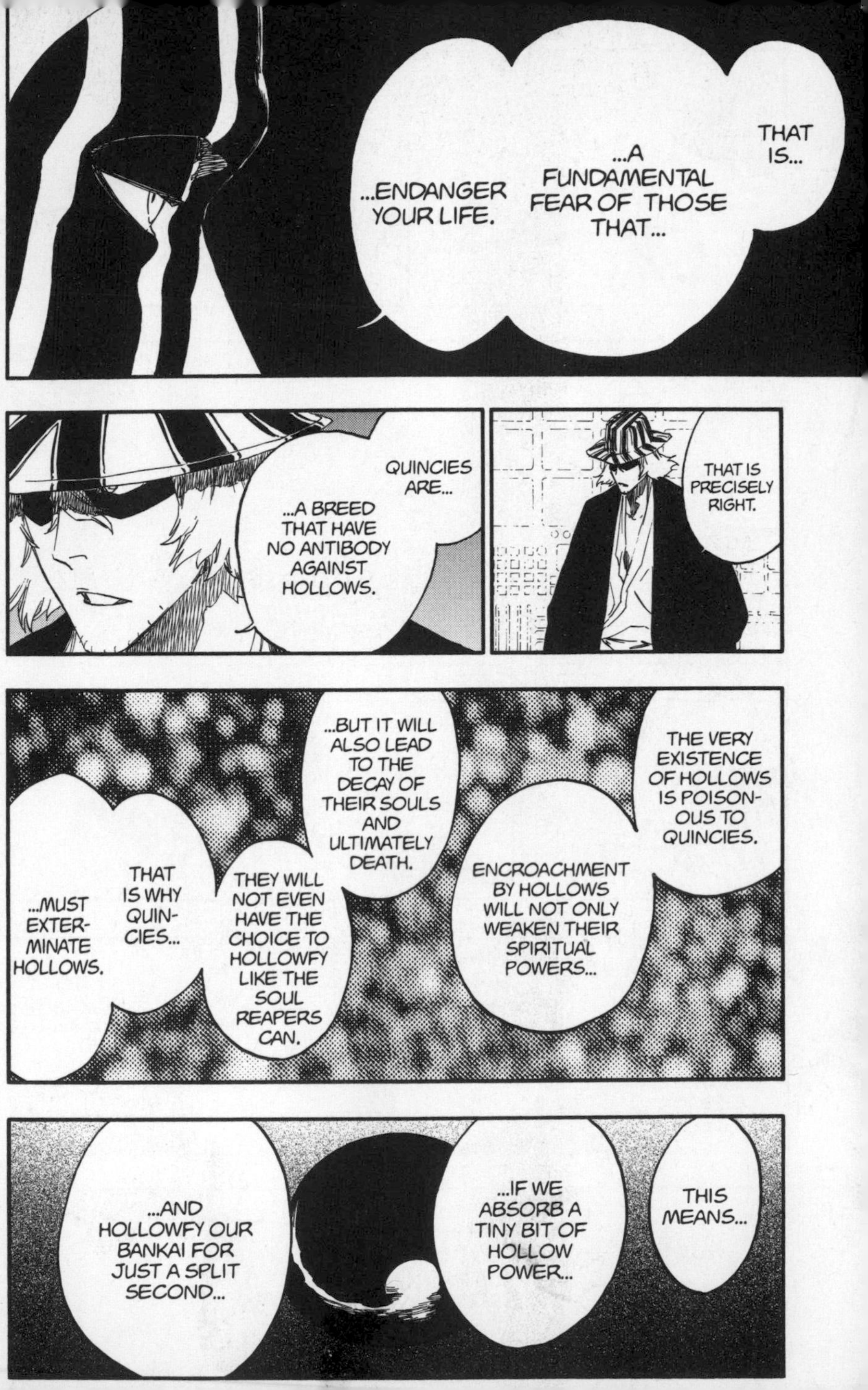
THAT IS...
...A FUNDAMENTAL FEAR OF THOSE THAT...
...ENDANGER YOUR LIFE.
THAT IS PRECISELY RIGHT.
QUINCIES ARE...
...A BREED THAT HAVE NO ANTIBODY AGAINST HOLLOWS.
THE VERY EXISTENCE OF HOLLOWS IS POISON-OUS TO QUINCIES.
ENCROACHMENT BY HOLLOWS WILL NOT ONLY WEAKEN THEIR SPIRITUAL POWERS...
...BUT IT WILL ALSO LEAD TO THE DECAY OF THEIR SOULS AND ULTIMATELY DEATH.
THEY WILL NOT EVEN HAVE THE CHOICE TO HOLLOWFY LIKE THE SOUL REAPERS CAN.
THAT IS WHY QUIN-CIES...
...MUST EXTER-MINATE HOLLOWS.
THIS MEANS...
...IF WE ABSORB A TINY BIT OF HOLLOW POWER...
...AND HOLLOWFY OUR BANKAI FOR JUST A SPLIT SECOND...

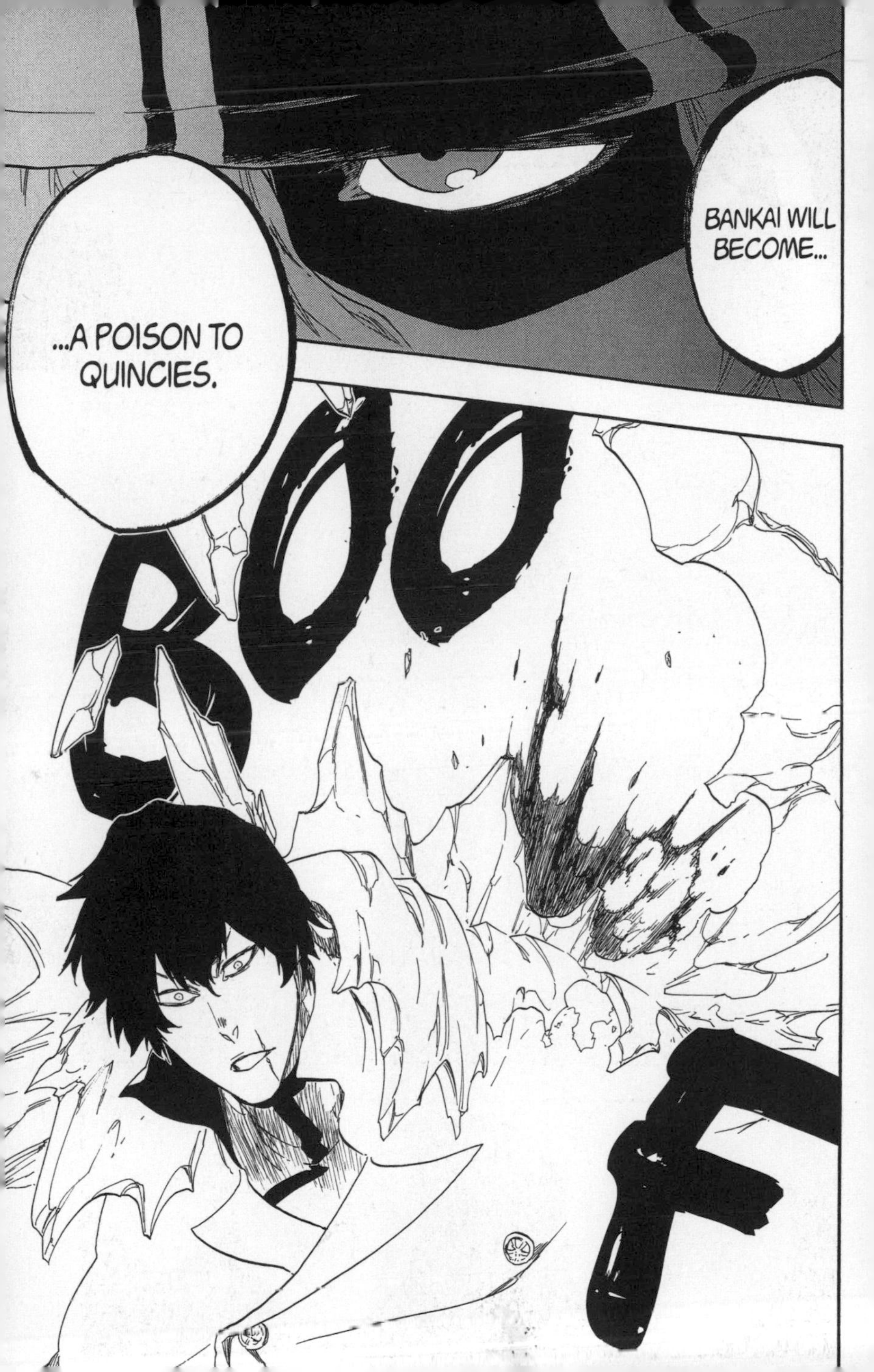
BANKAI WILL BECOME...
...A POISON TO QUINCIES.
BOOF

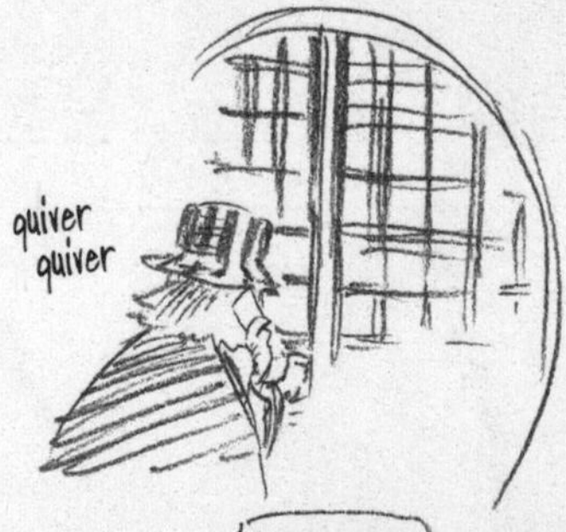
quiver
quiver
ANTICIPATING

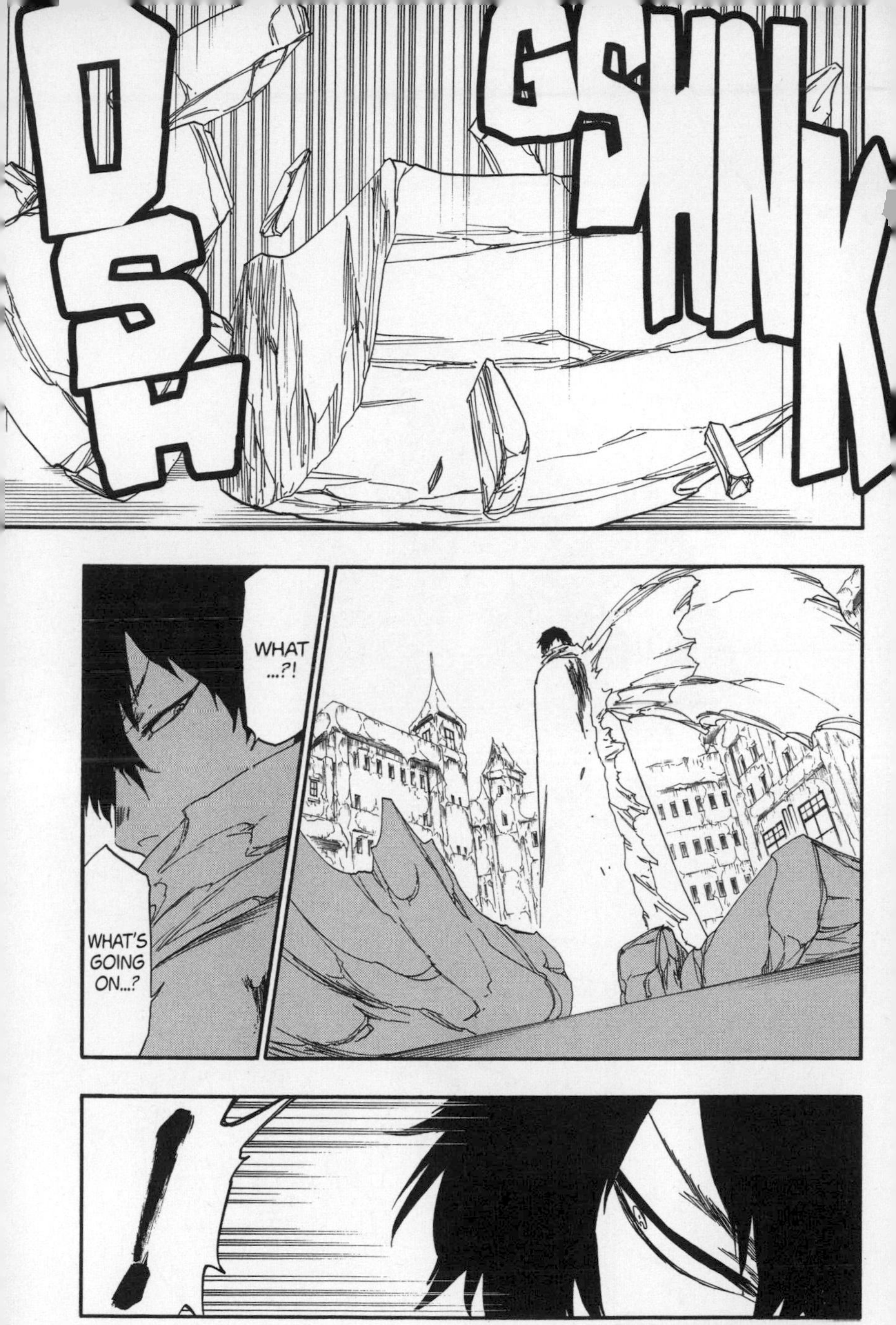
GCHNK
DSH
WHAT
...?!
WHAT'S GOING ON...?
!

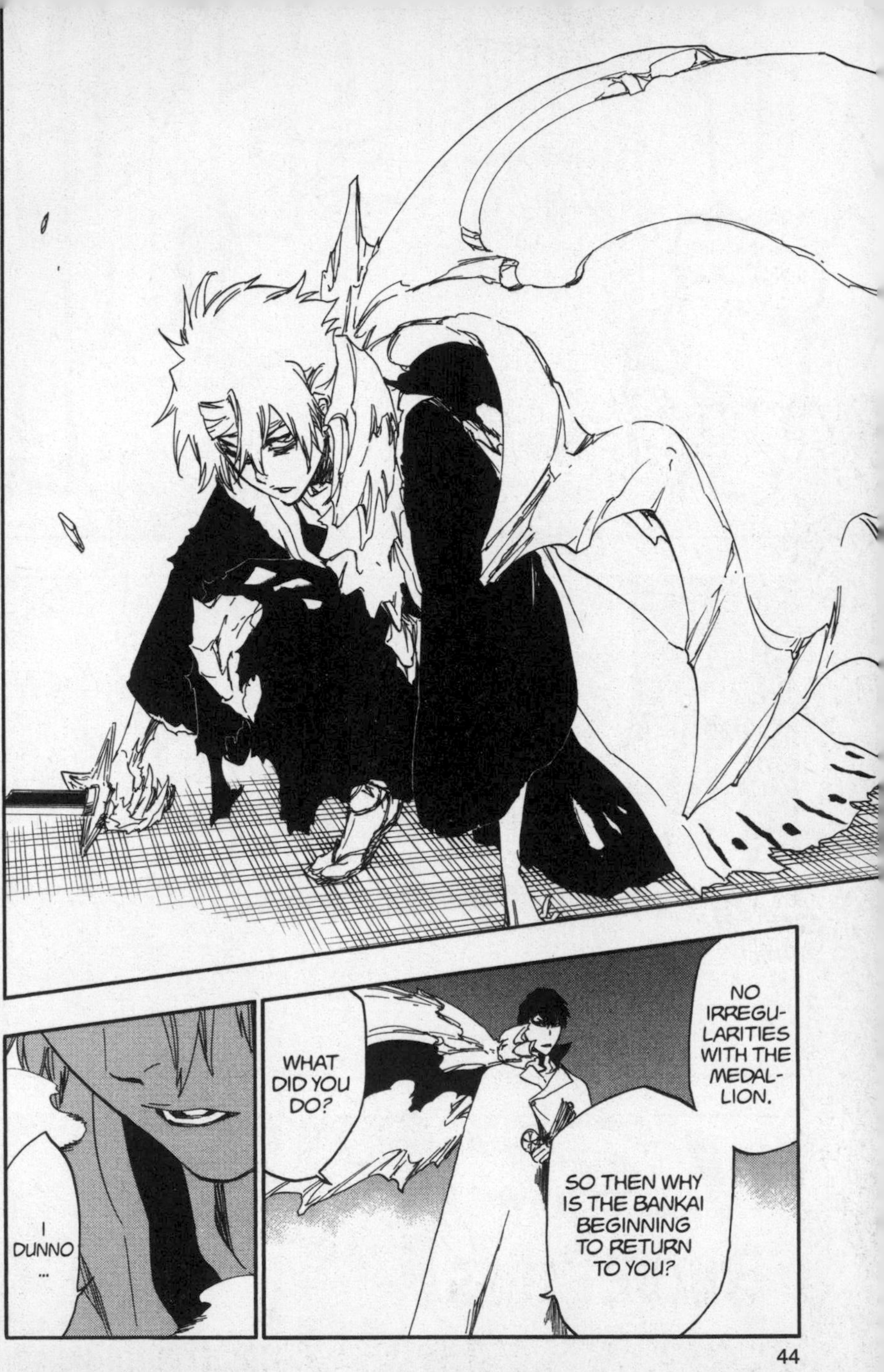
NO IRREGU- LARITIES WITH THE MEDAL- LION.
SO THEN WHY IS THE BANKAI BEGINNING TO RETURN TO YOU?
WHAT DID YOU DO?
I DUNNO ...

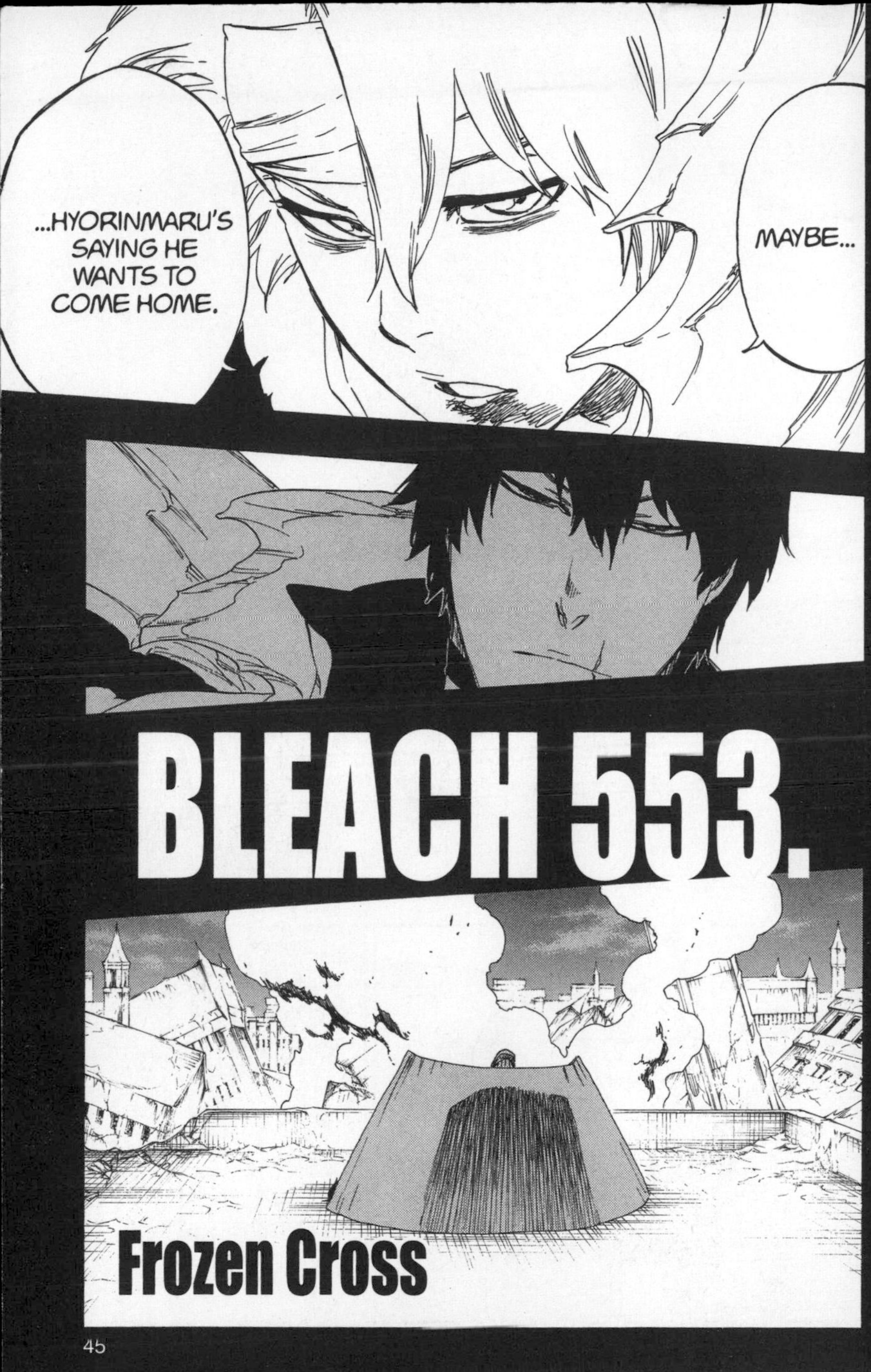
MAYBE...
...HYORINMARU'S SAYING HE WANTS TO COME HOME.
BLEACH 553.
Frozen Cross

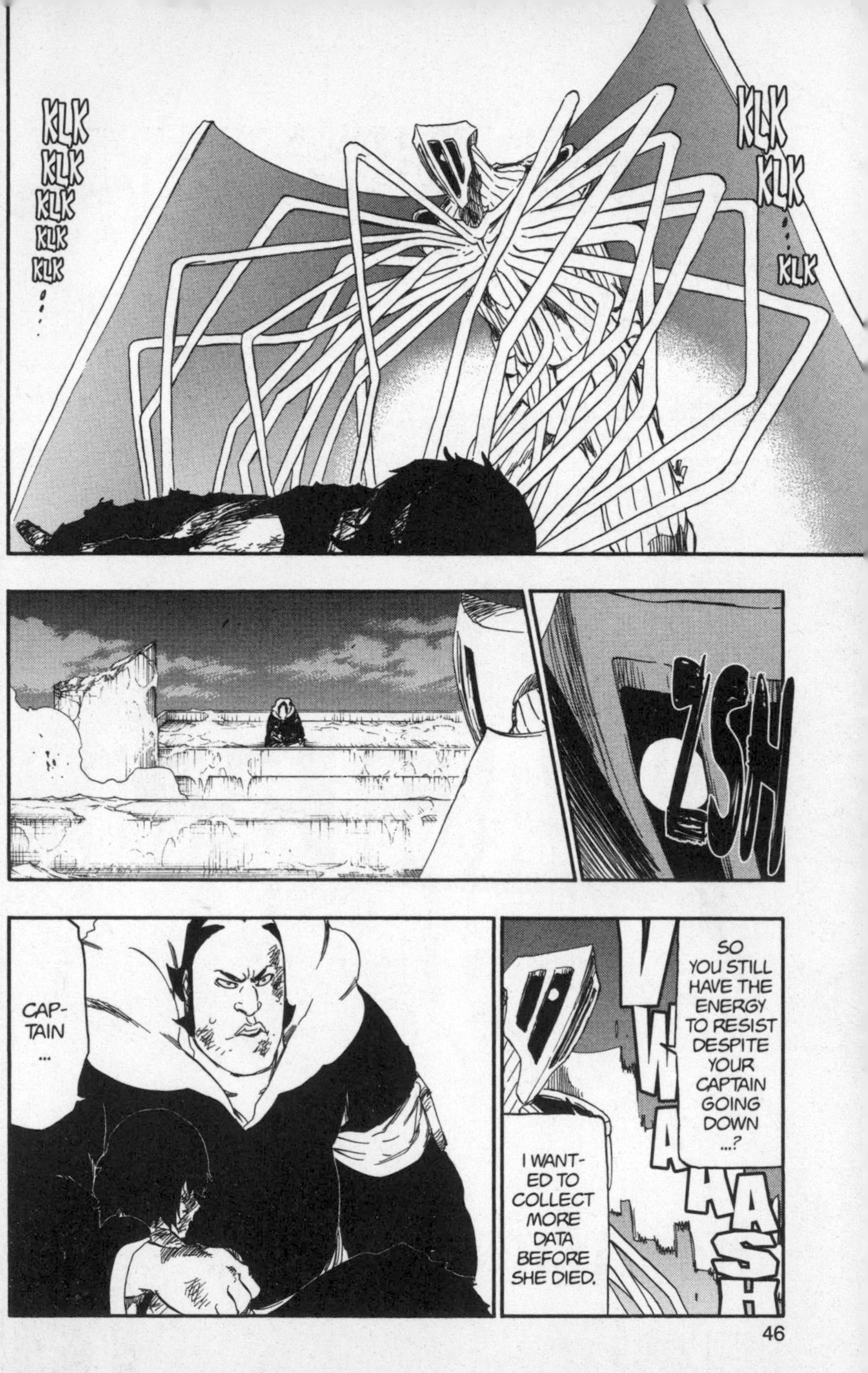
KLK KLK ... KLK
KLK KLK KLK KLK KLK ...
ZSH
SO YOU STILL HAVE THE ENERGY TO RESIST DESPITE YOUR CAPTAIN GOING DOWN ...?
VWAAASH
I WANT-ED TO COLLECT MORE DATA BEFORE SHE DIED.
CAP-TAIN ...

READ THIS WAY

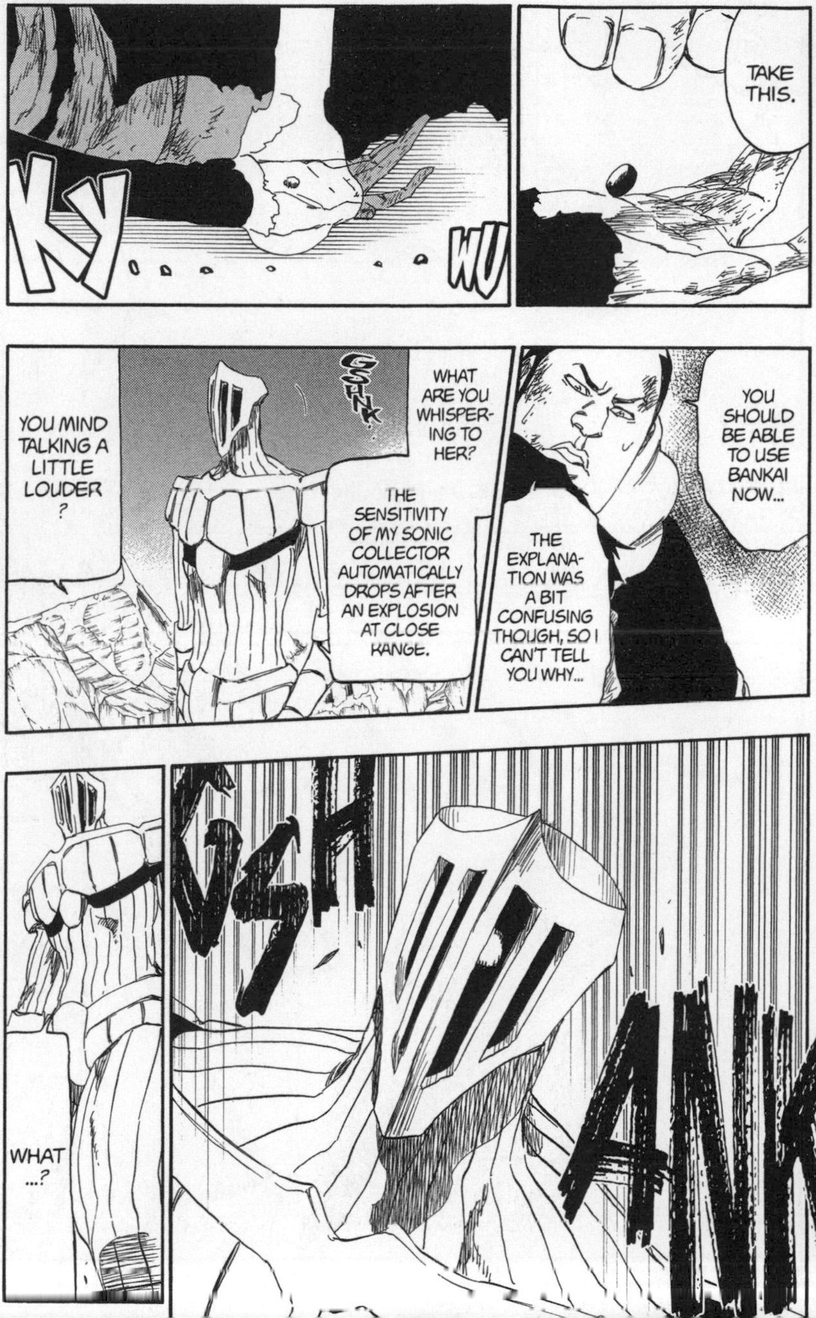
TAKE THIS.
WU
KY
YOU SHOULD BE ABLE TO USE BANKAI NOW...
THE EXPLANATION WAS A BIT CONFUSING THOUGH, SO I CAN'T TELL YOU WHY...
WHAT ARE YOU WHISPERING TO HER?
THE SENSITIVITY OF MY SONIC COLLECTOR AUTOMATICALLY DROPS AFTER AN EXPLOSION AT CLOSE RANGE.
GSHNK.
YOU MIND TALKING A LITTLE LOUDER?
GSH
ANK
WHAT ...?

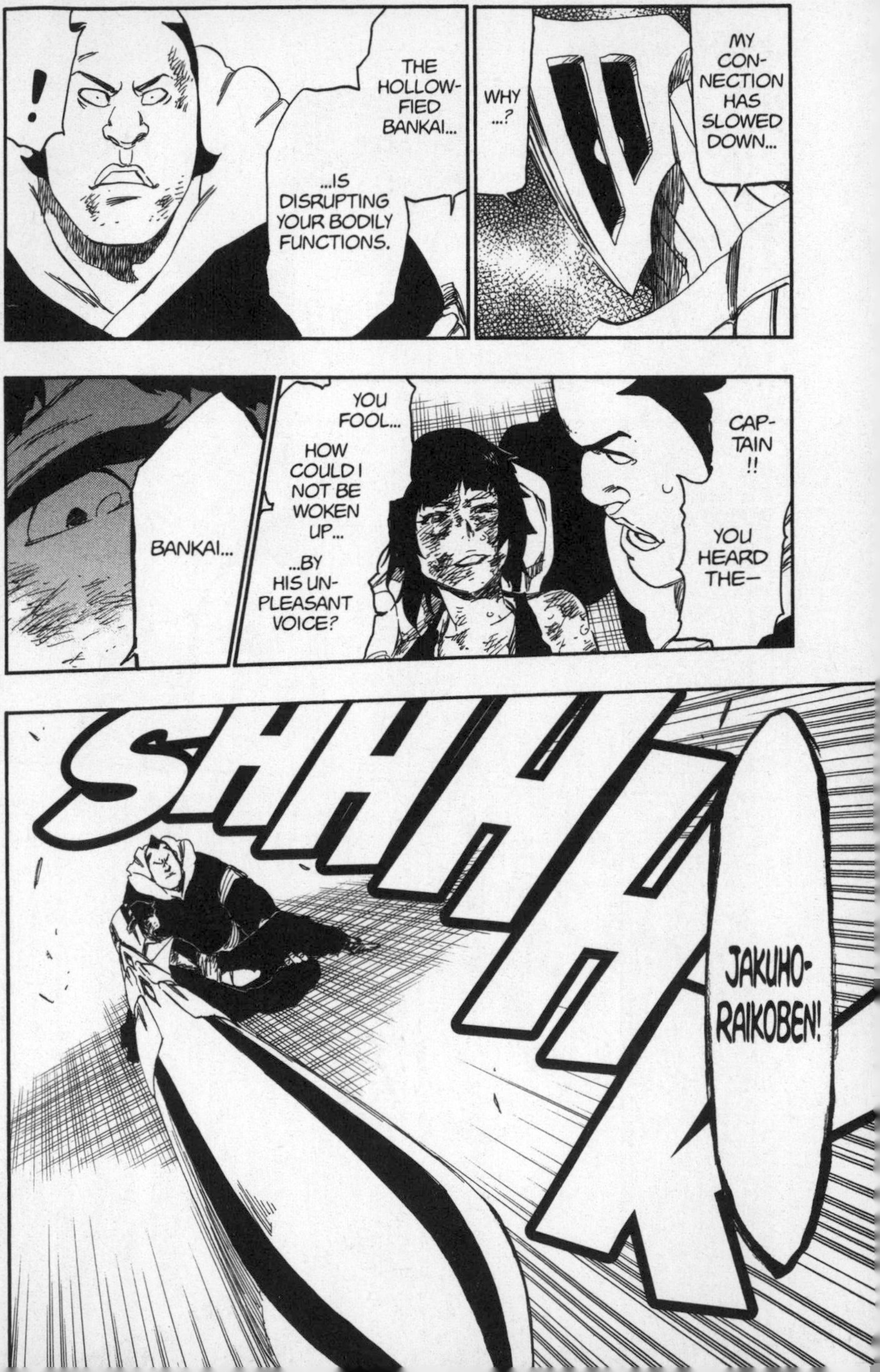
MY CONNECTION HAS SLOWED DOWN...
WHY ...?
THE HOLLOWFIED BANKAI...
...IS DISRUPTING YOUR BODILY FUNCTIONS.
!
CAPTAIN !!
YOU HEARD THE—
YOU FOOL...
HOW COULD I NOT BE WOKEN UP...
...BY HIS UNPLEASANT VOICE?
BANKAI...
JAKUHO-RAIKOBEN!
SHHHA

READ THIS WAY

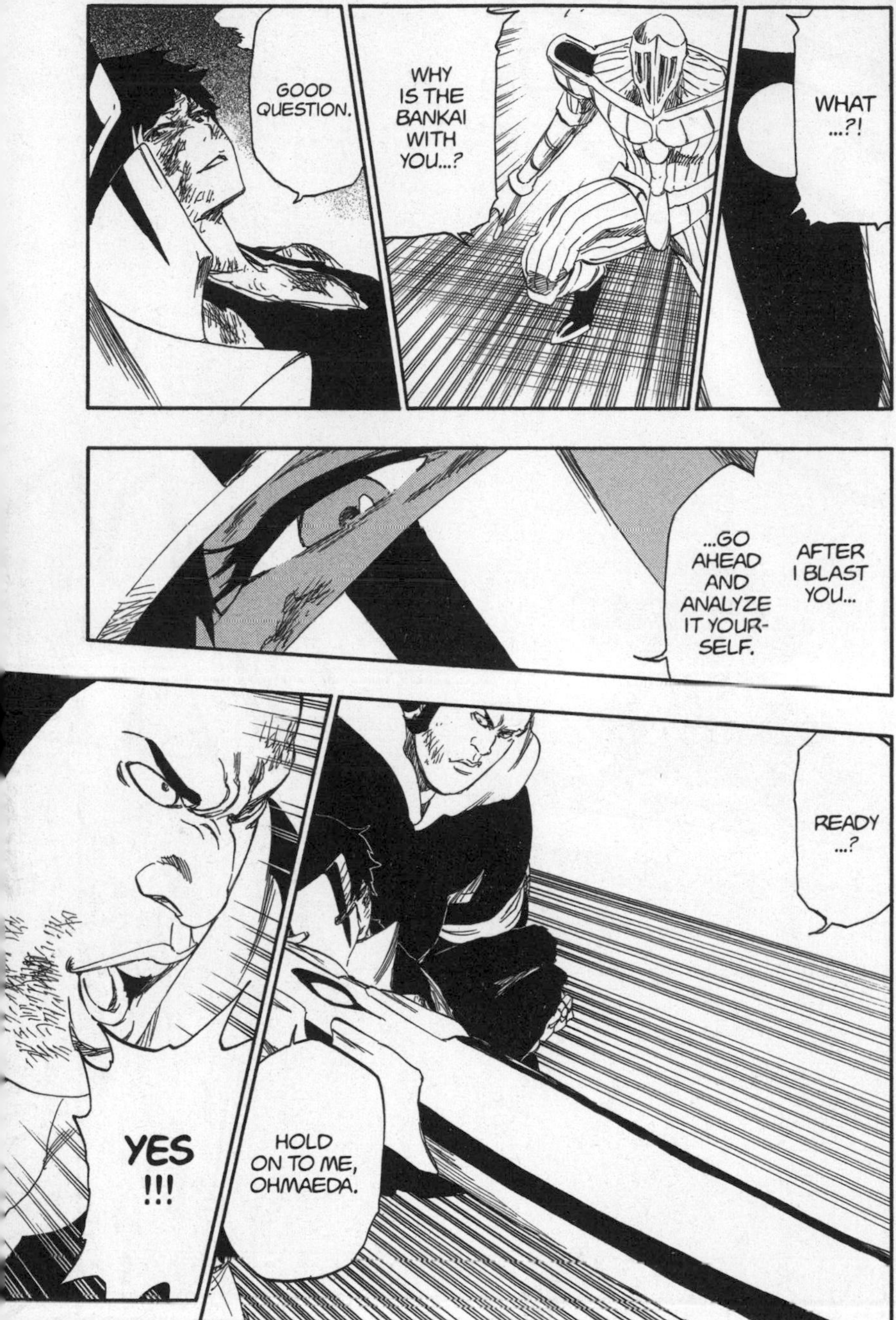
WHAT ...?!
WHY IS THE BANKAI WITH YOU...?
GOOD QUESTION.
AFTER I BLAST YOU...
...GO AHEAD AND ANALYZE IT YOURSELF.
READY ...?
HOLD ON TO ME, OHMAEDA.
YES !!!

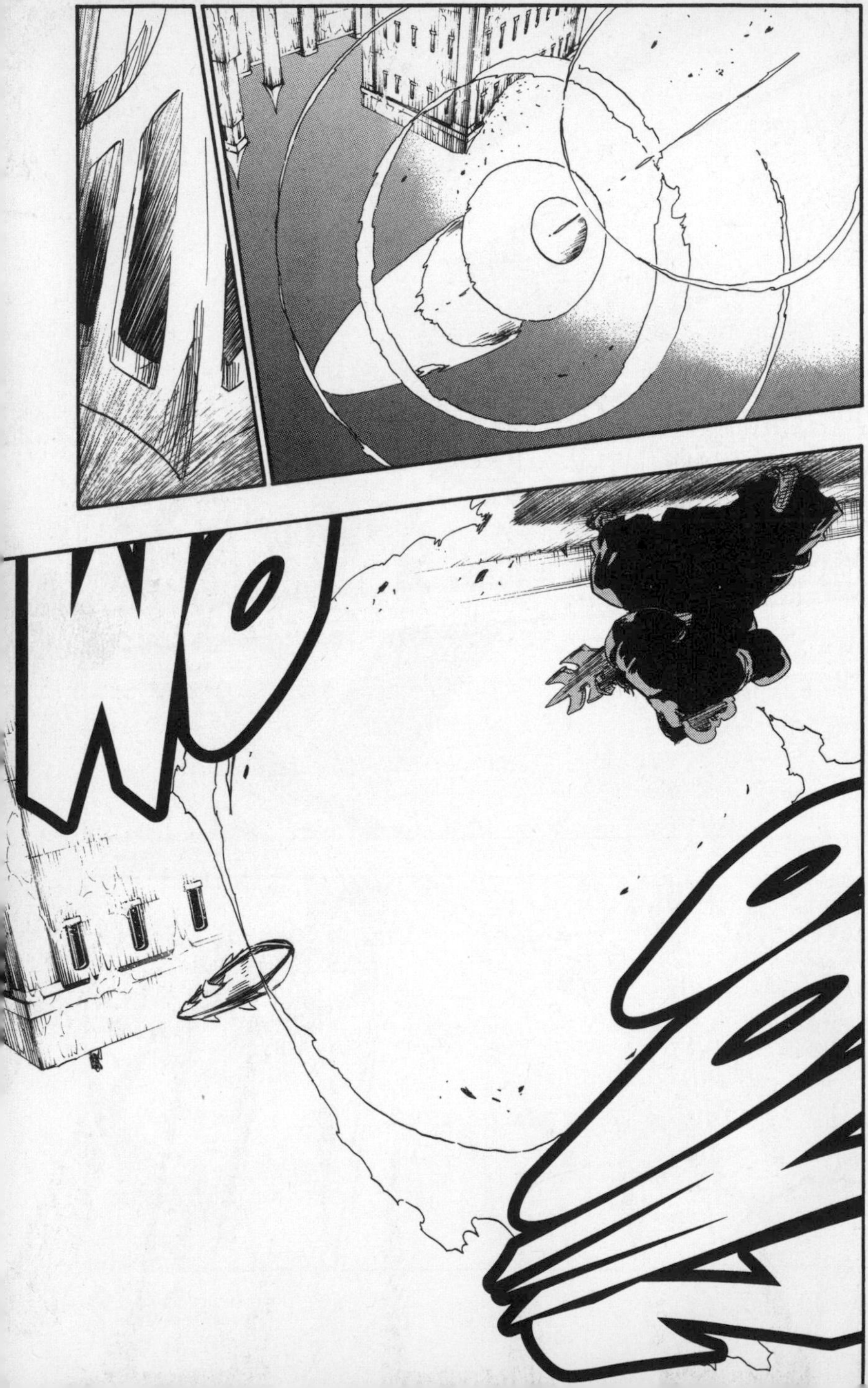

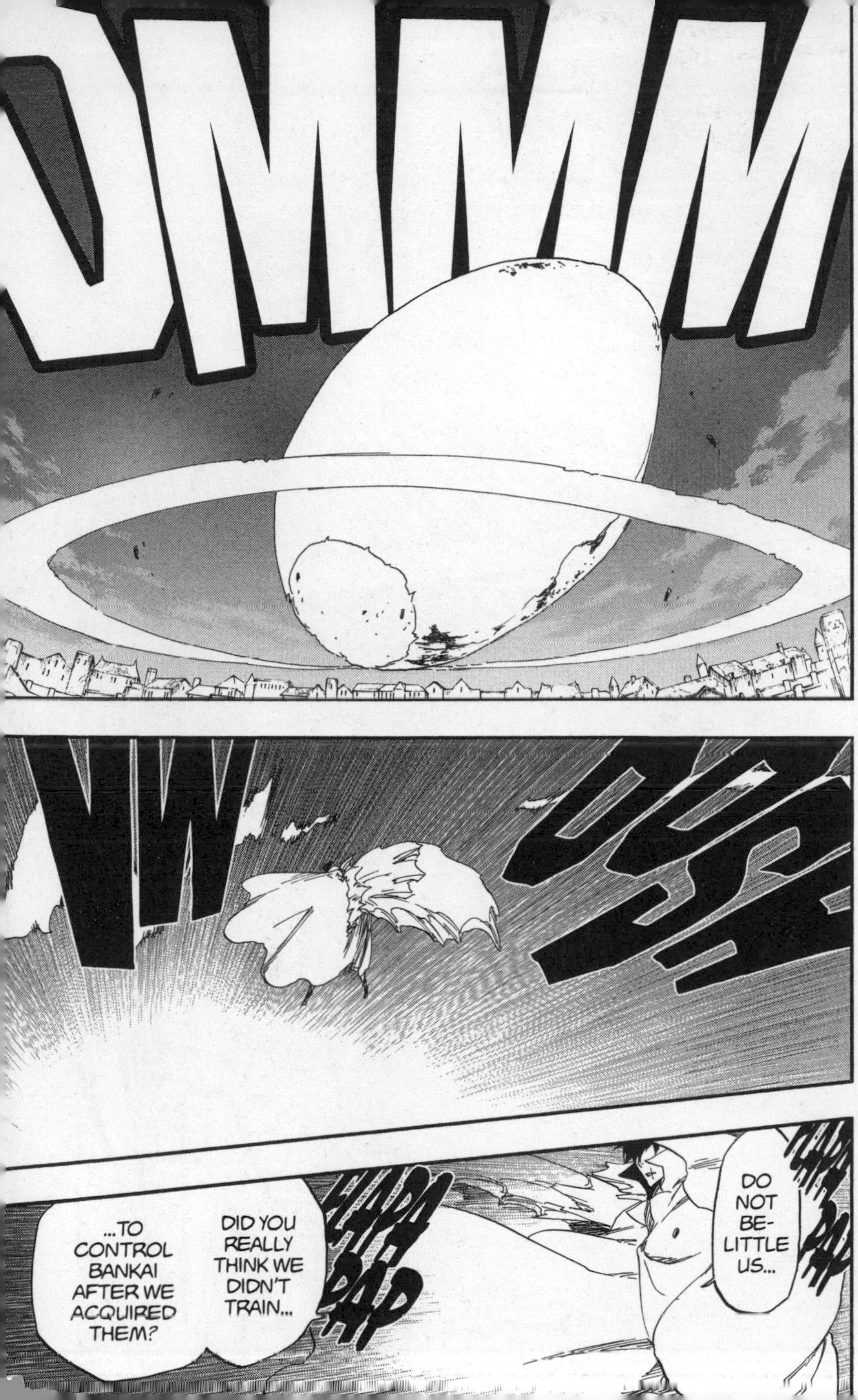
DO NOT BE-LITTLE US...
DID YOU REALLY THINK WE DIDN'T TRAIN...
...TO CONTROL BANKAI AFTER WE ACQUIRED THEM?

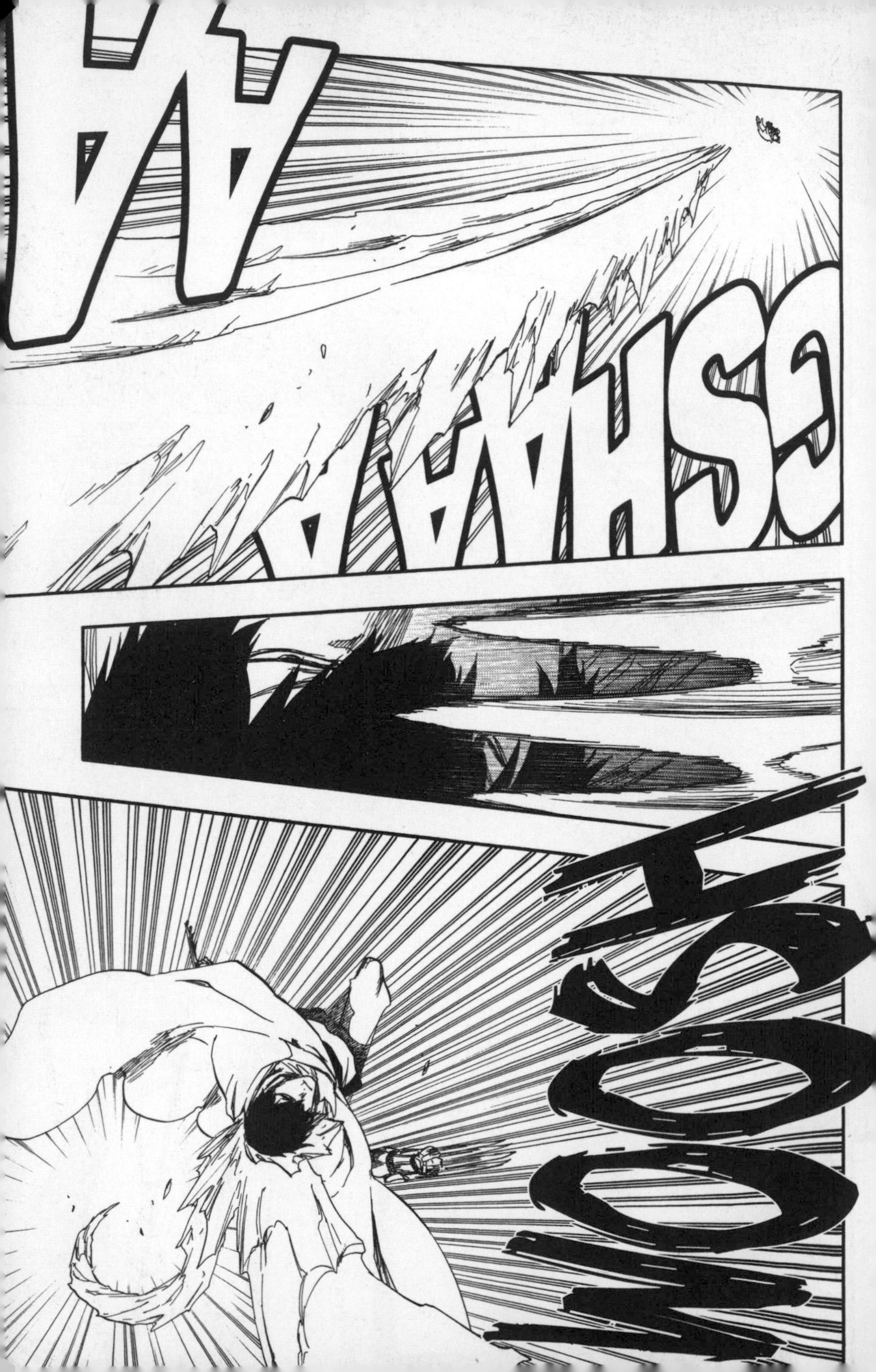
WOOSH

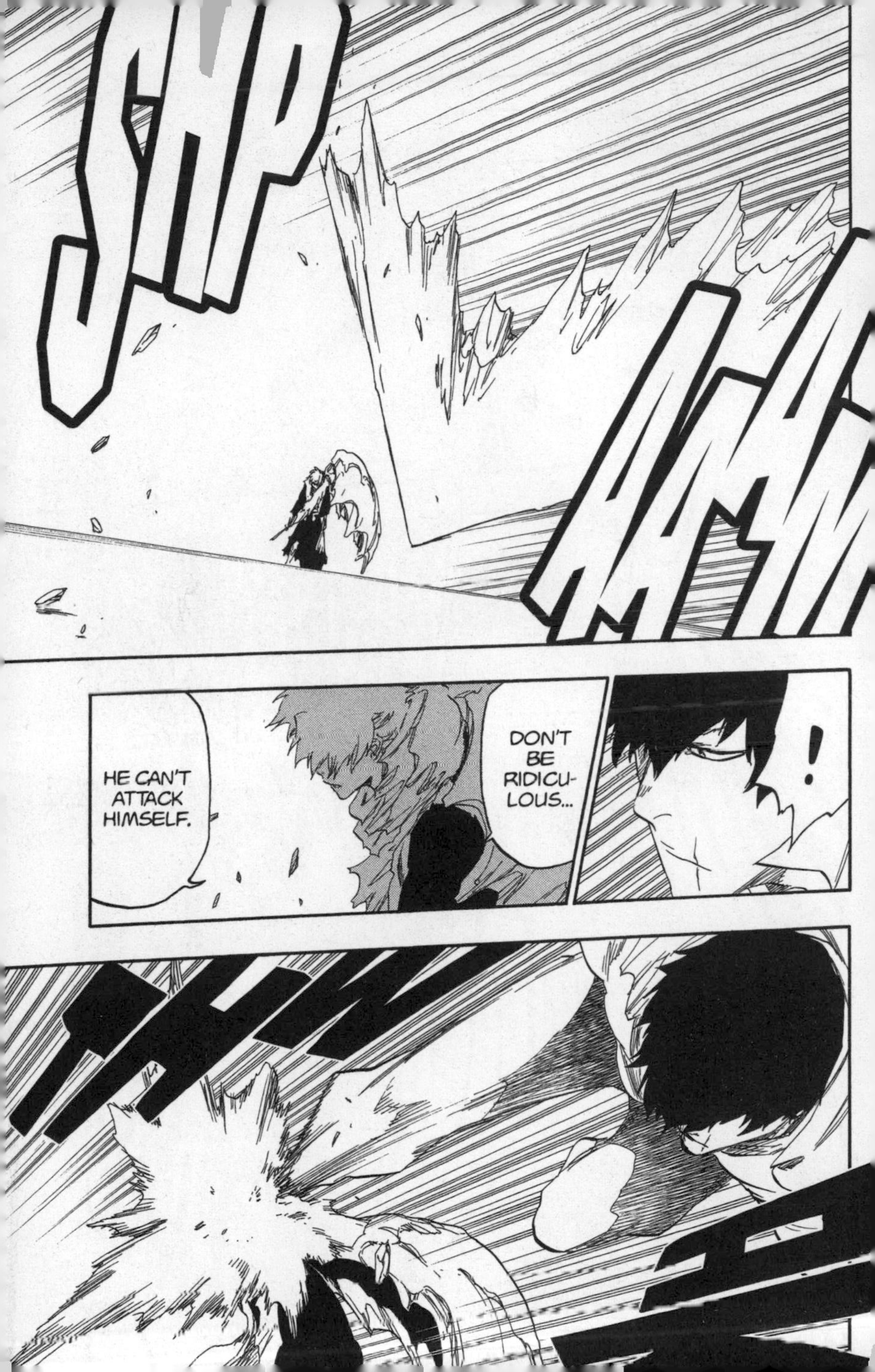
SHP
!
DON'T BE RIDICULOUS...
HE CAN'T ATTACK HIMSELF.

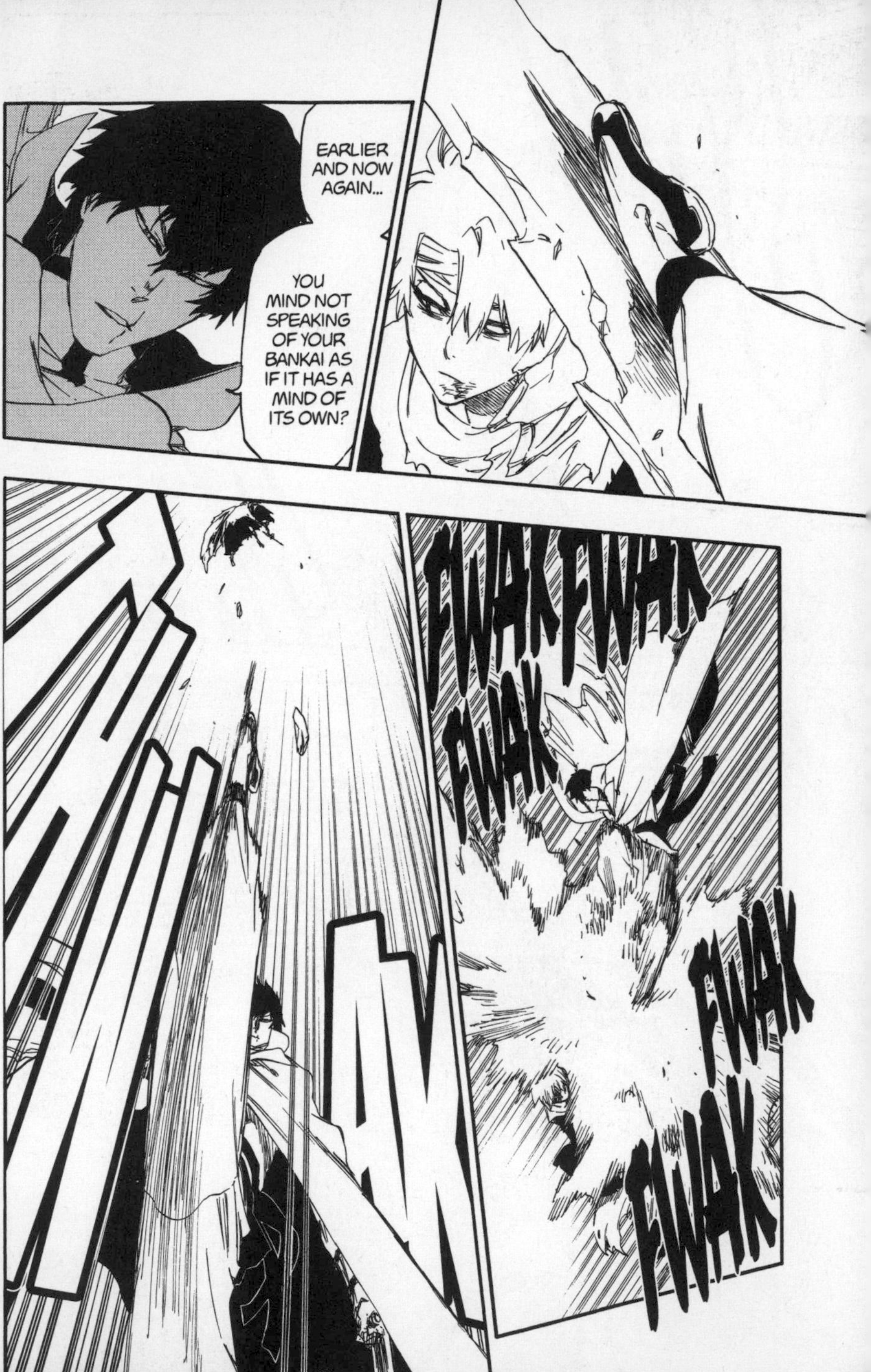
EARLIER AND NOW AGAIN...
YOU MIND NOT SPEAKING OF YOUR BANKAI AS IF IT HAS A MIND OF ITS OWN?
FWAK FWAK
FWAK
FWAK
FWAK

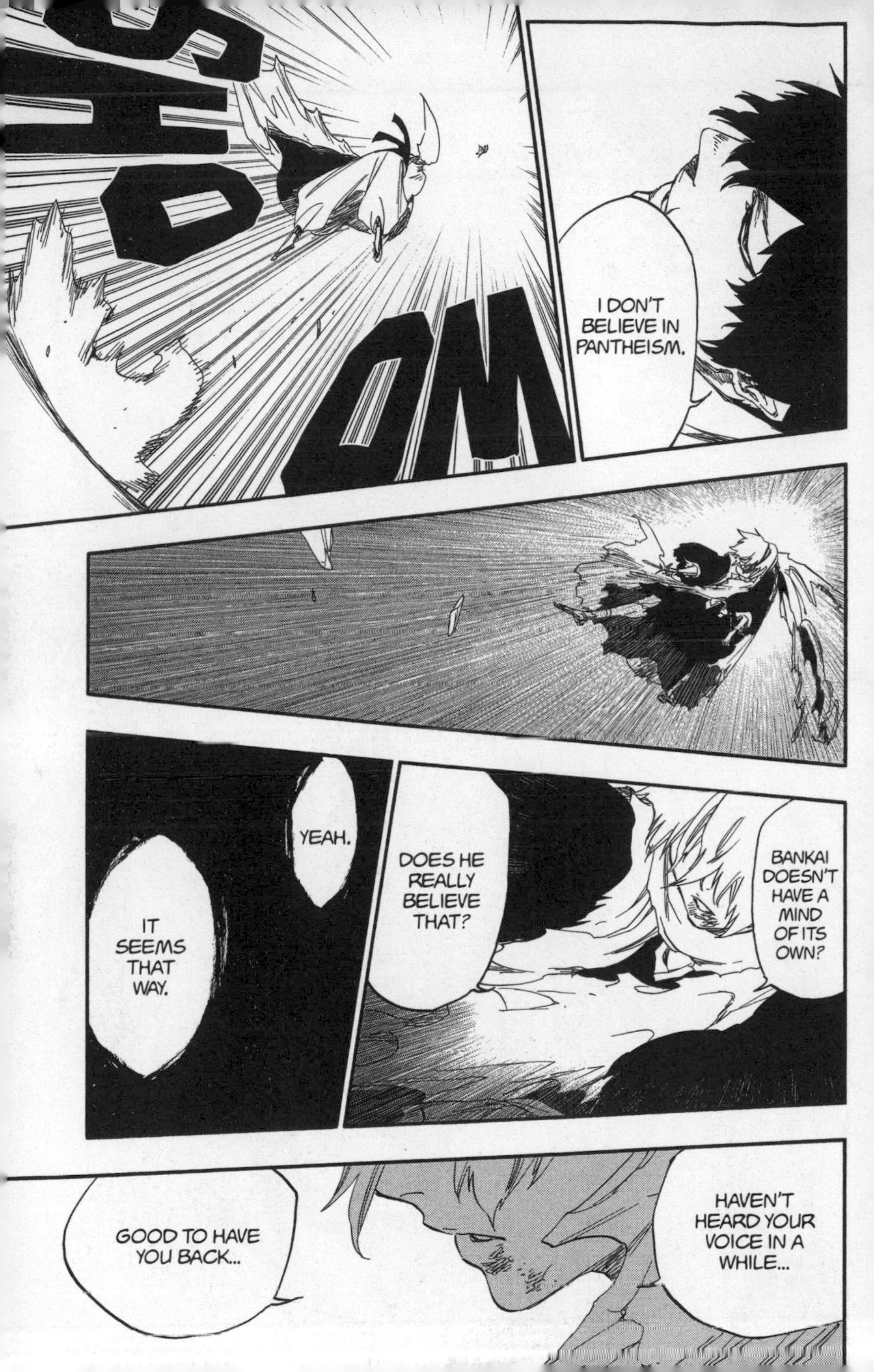
I DON'T BELIEVE IN PANTHEISM.
SHOOM
BANKAI DOESN'T HAVE A MIND OF ITS OWN?
DOES HE REALLY BELIEVE THAT?
YEAH.
IT SEEMS THAT WAY.
HAVEN'T HEARD YOUR VOICE IN A WHILE...
GOOD TO HAVE YOU BACK...

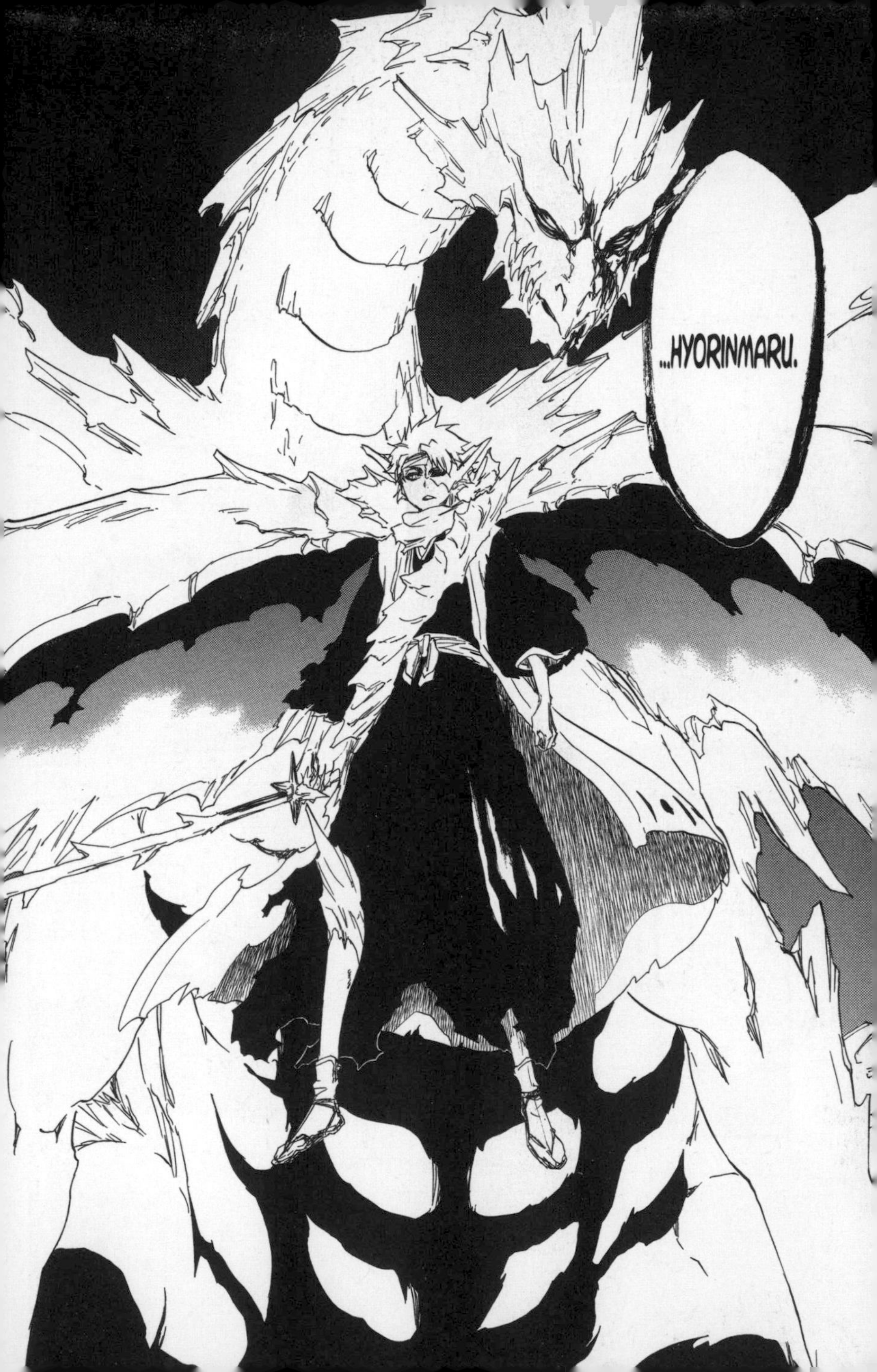
...HYORINMARU.

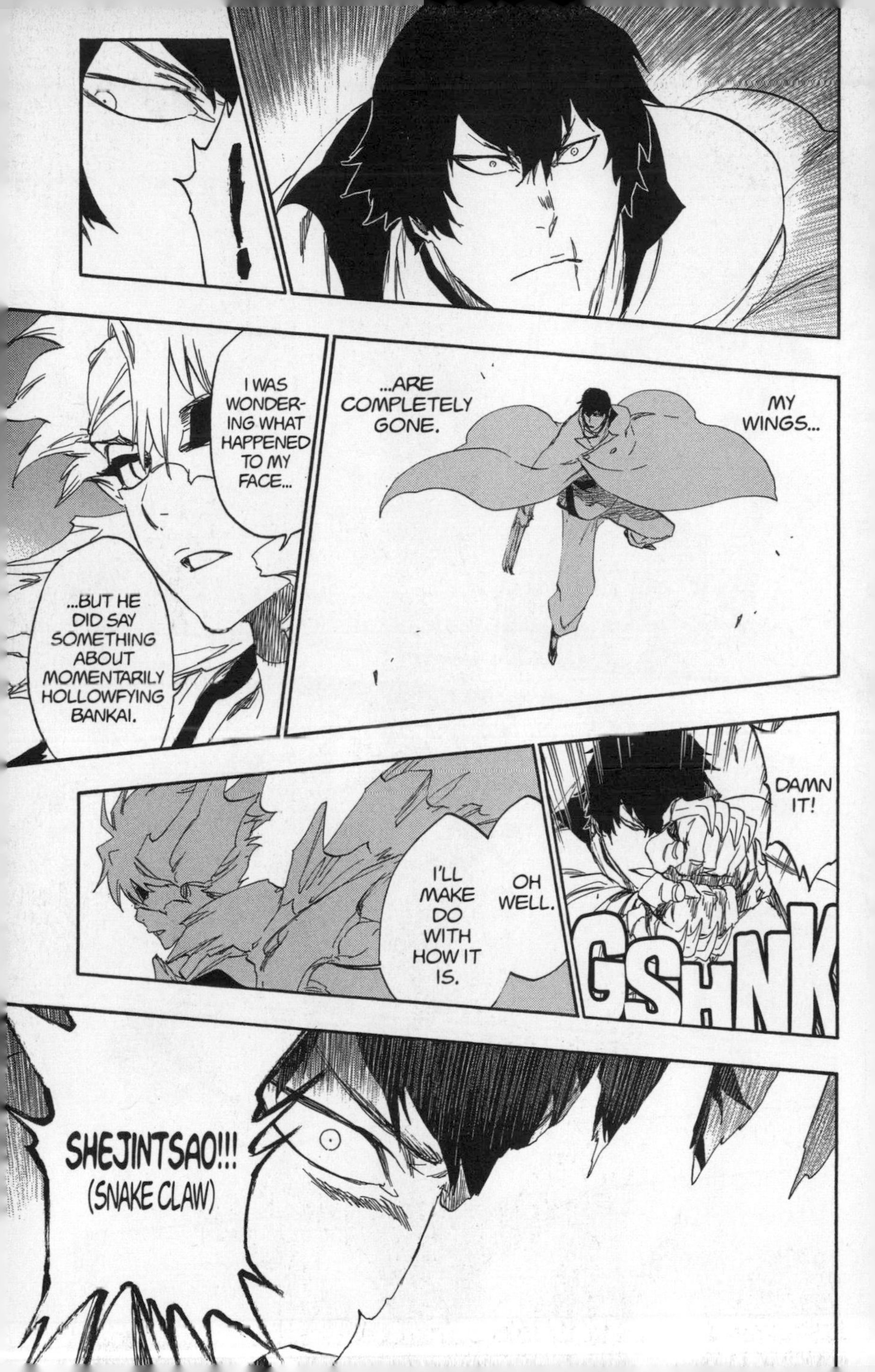
!
MY WINGS...
...ARE COMPLETELY GONE.
I WAS WONDER-ING WHAT HAPPENED TO MY FACE...
...BUT HE DID SAY SOMETHING ABOUT MOMENTARILY HOLLOWFYING BANKAI.
DAMN IT!
GSHNK
OH WELL.
I'LL MAKE DO WITH HOW IT IS.
SHEJINTSAO!!!
(SNAKE CLAW)

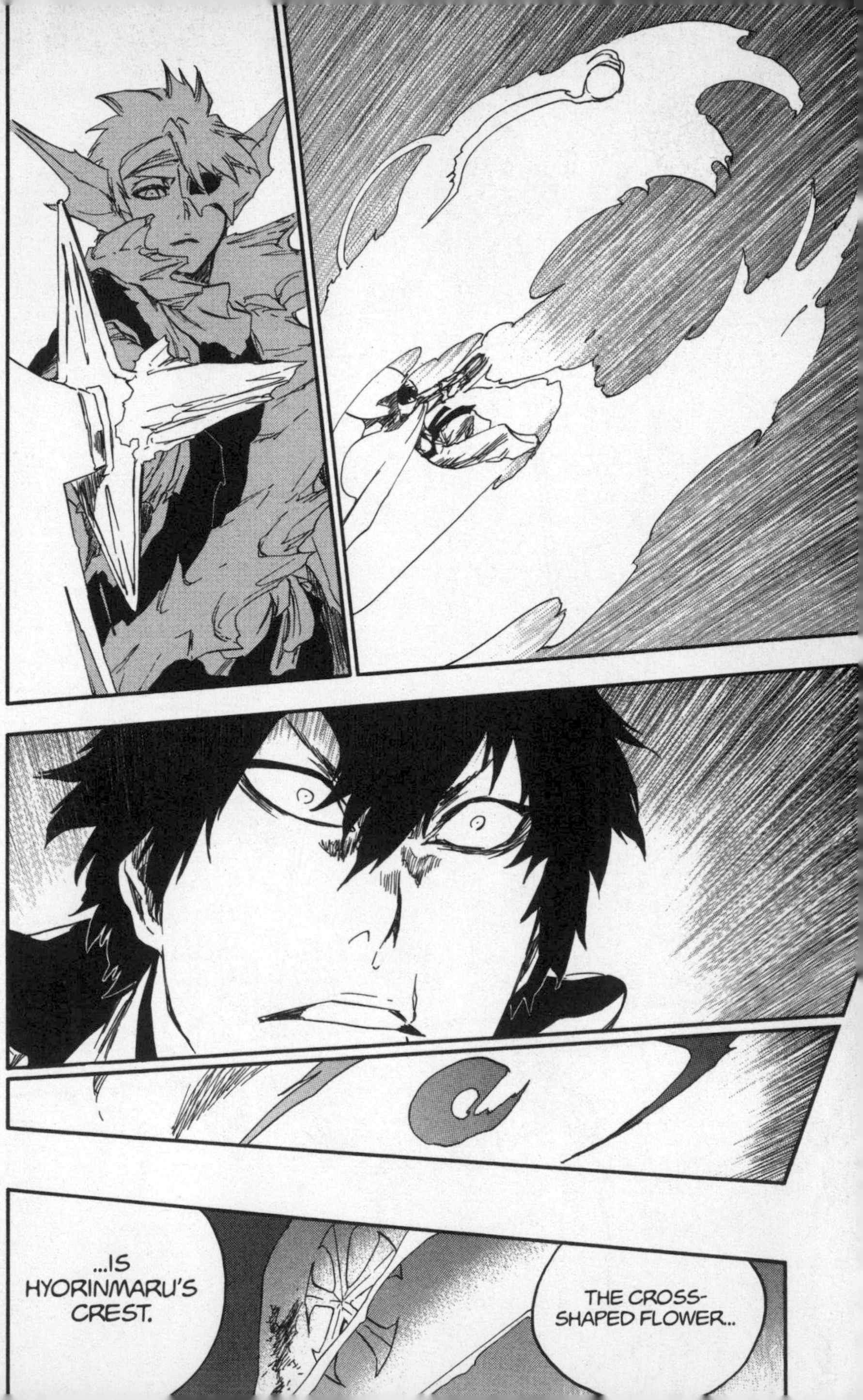
THE CROSS-SHAPED FLOWER...
...IS HYORINMARU'S CREST.

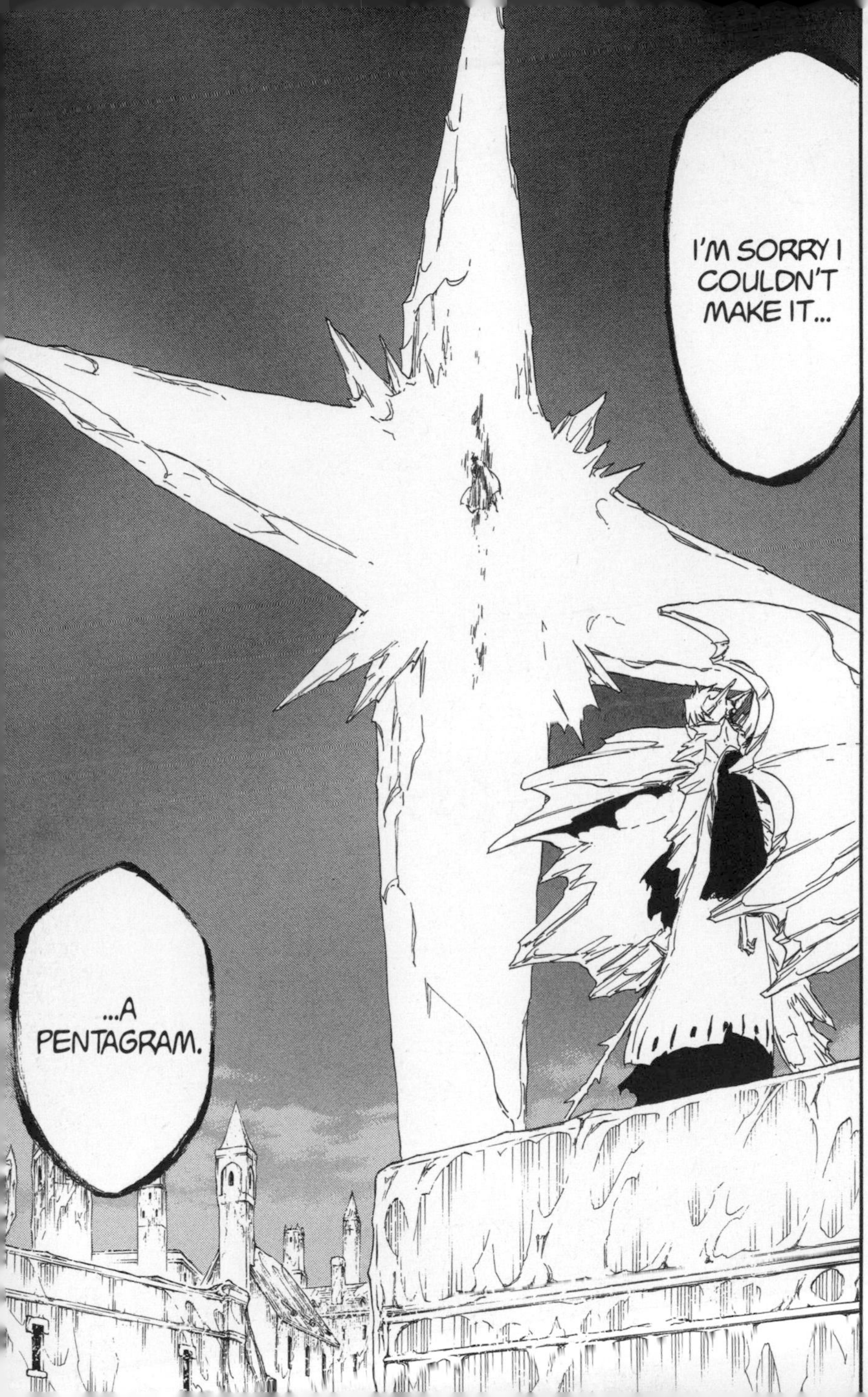
I'M SORRY I COULDN'T MAKE IT...
...A PENTAGRAM.

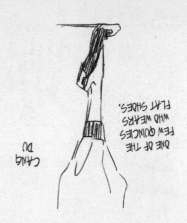

CANG
DU

ONE OF THE
FEW QUINCIES
WHO WEARS
FLAT SHOES.

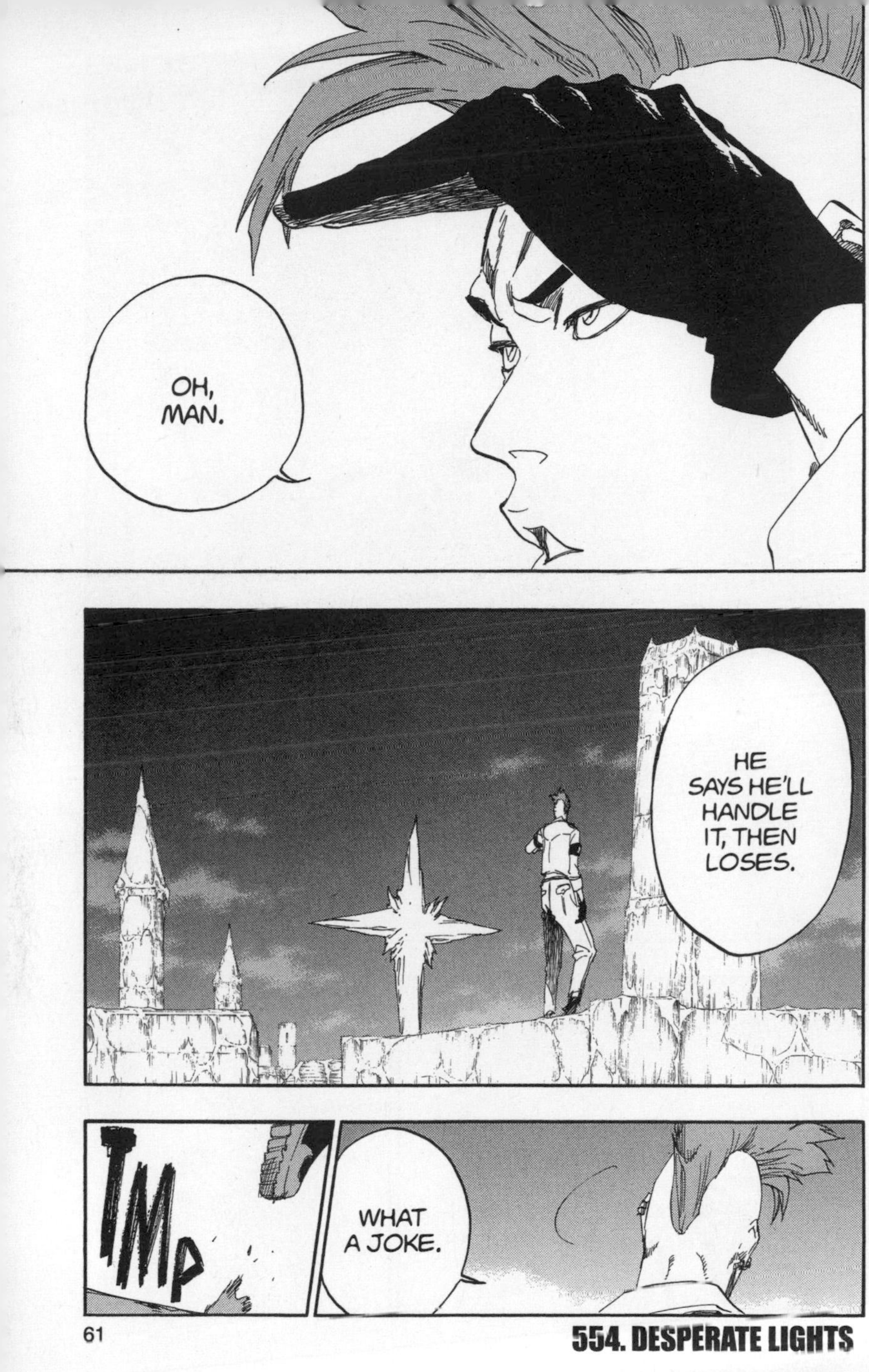
OH, MAN.
HE SAYS HE'LL HANDLE IT, THEN LOSES.
WHAT A JOKE.
TMP

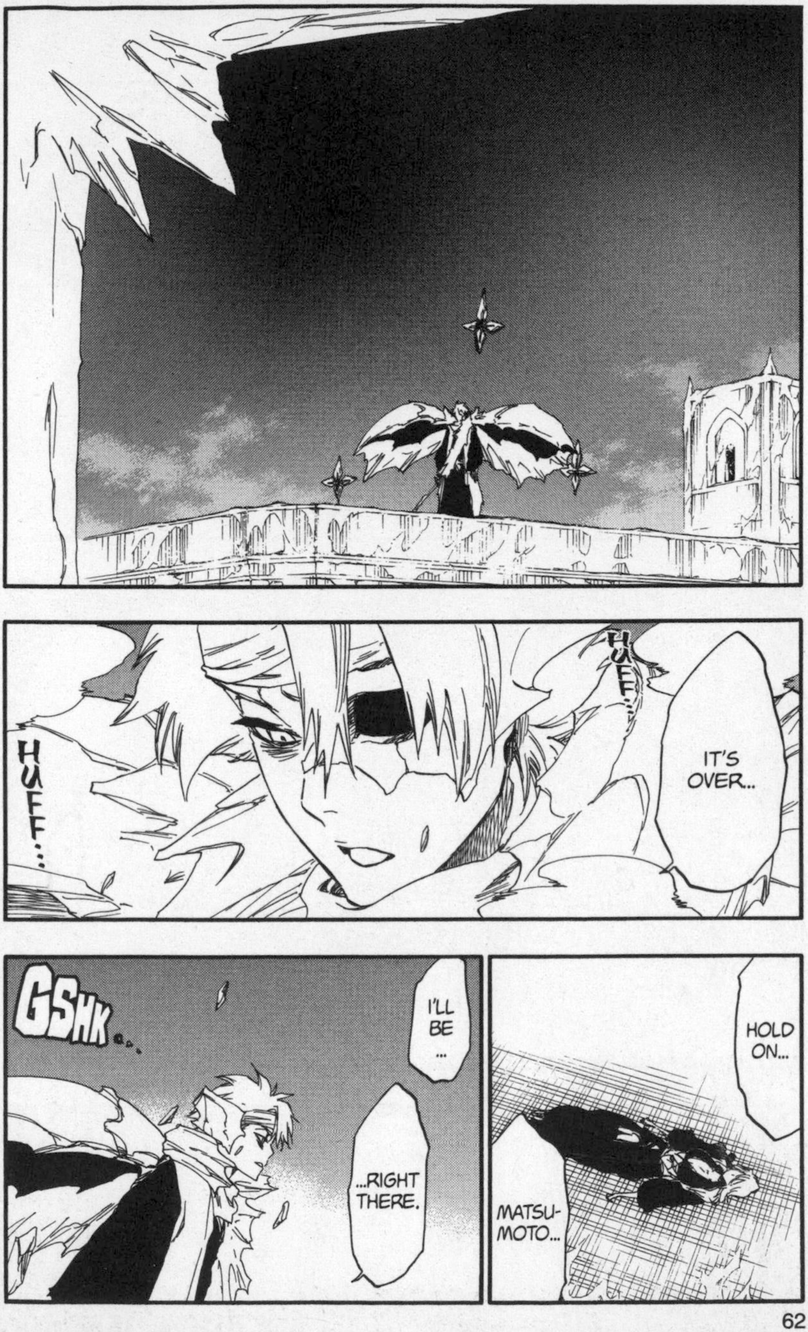
HUFF...
IT'S OVER...
HUFF...
HOLD ON...
MATSU-MOTO...
I'LL BE ...
...RIGHT THERE.
GSHK

READ THIS WAY

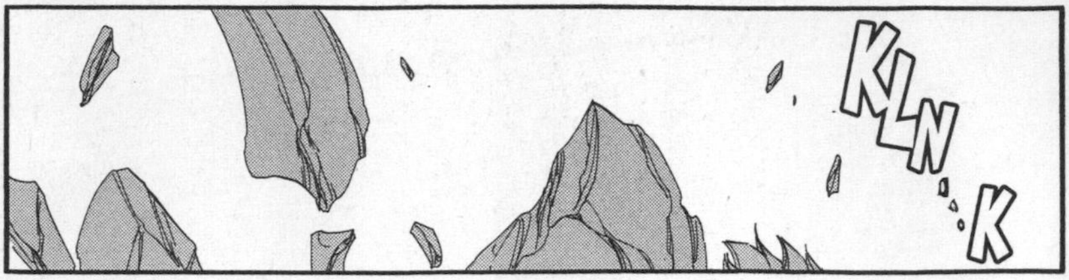
KLN..K

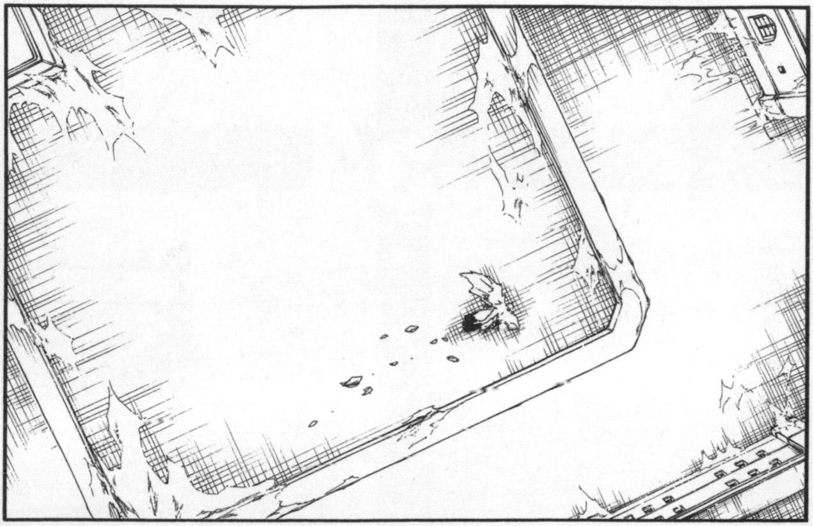

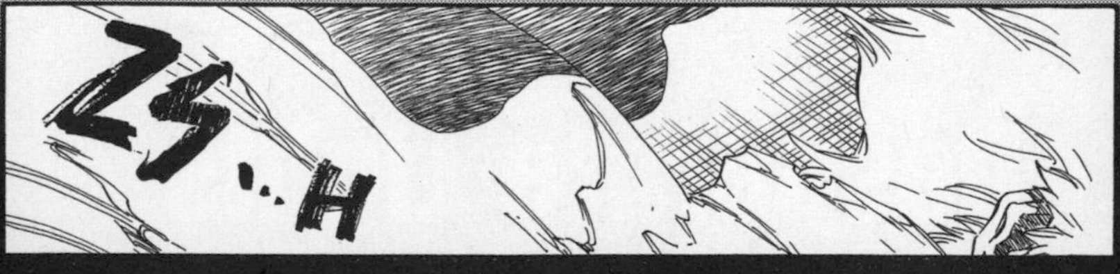
ZS..H

BLEACH

...IS NOW BACK IN THE HANDS OF THE SOUL REAPERS.

SO BANKAI....

Desperate Lights

554.

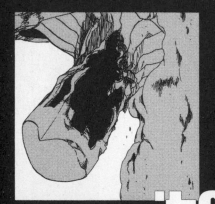
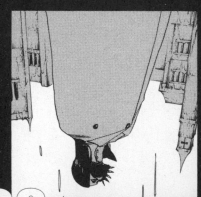

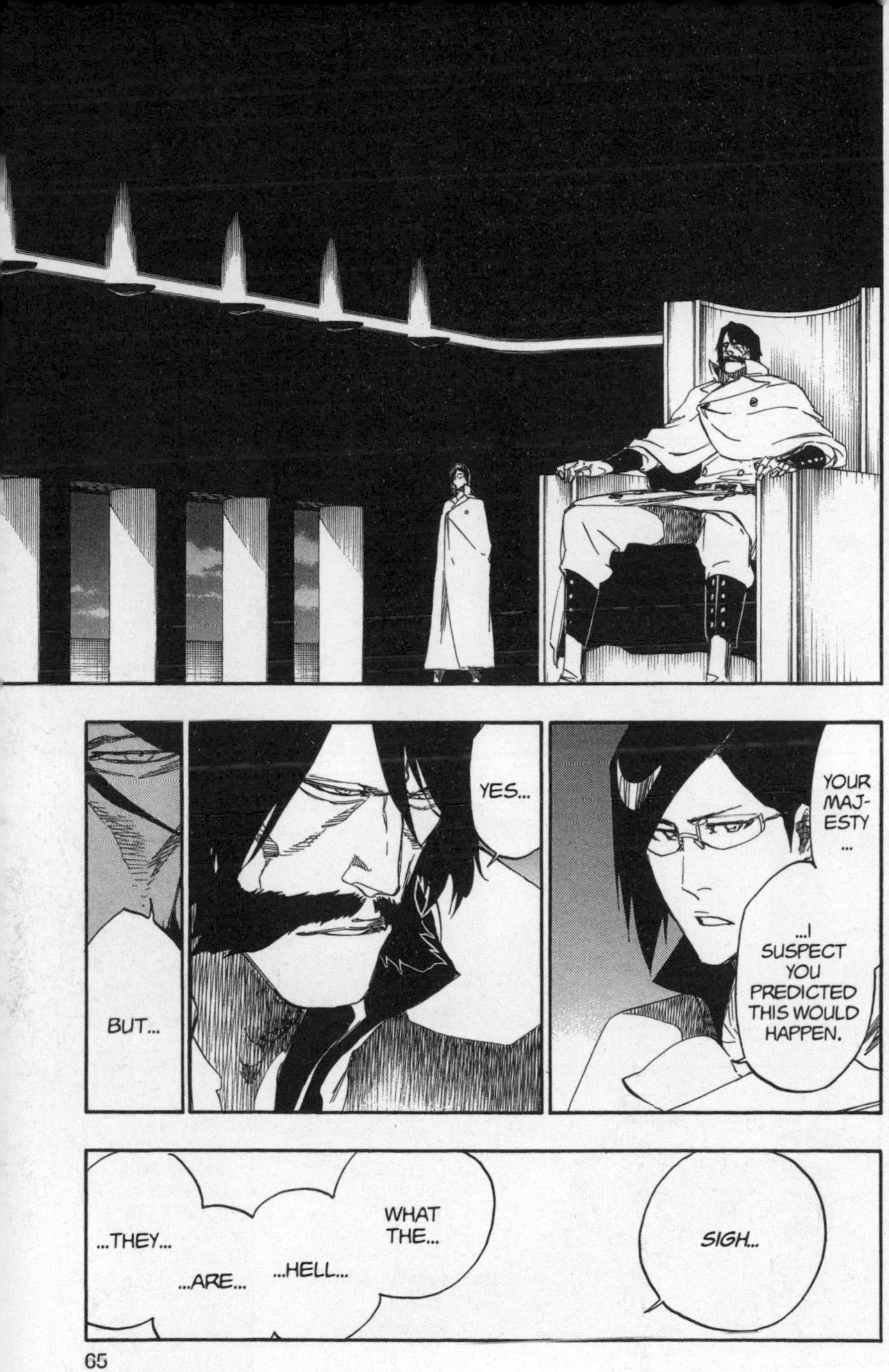
YOUR MAJ-ESTY ...
...I SUSPECT YOU PREDICTED THIS WOULD HAPPEN.
YES...
BUT...
SIGH...
WHAT THE... ...HELL... ...ARE... ...THEY...

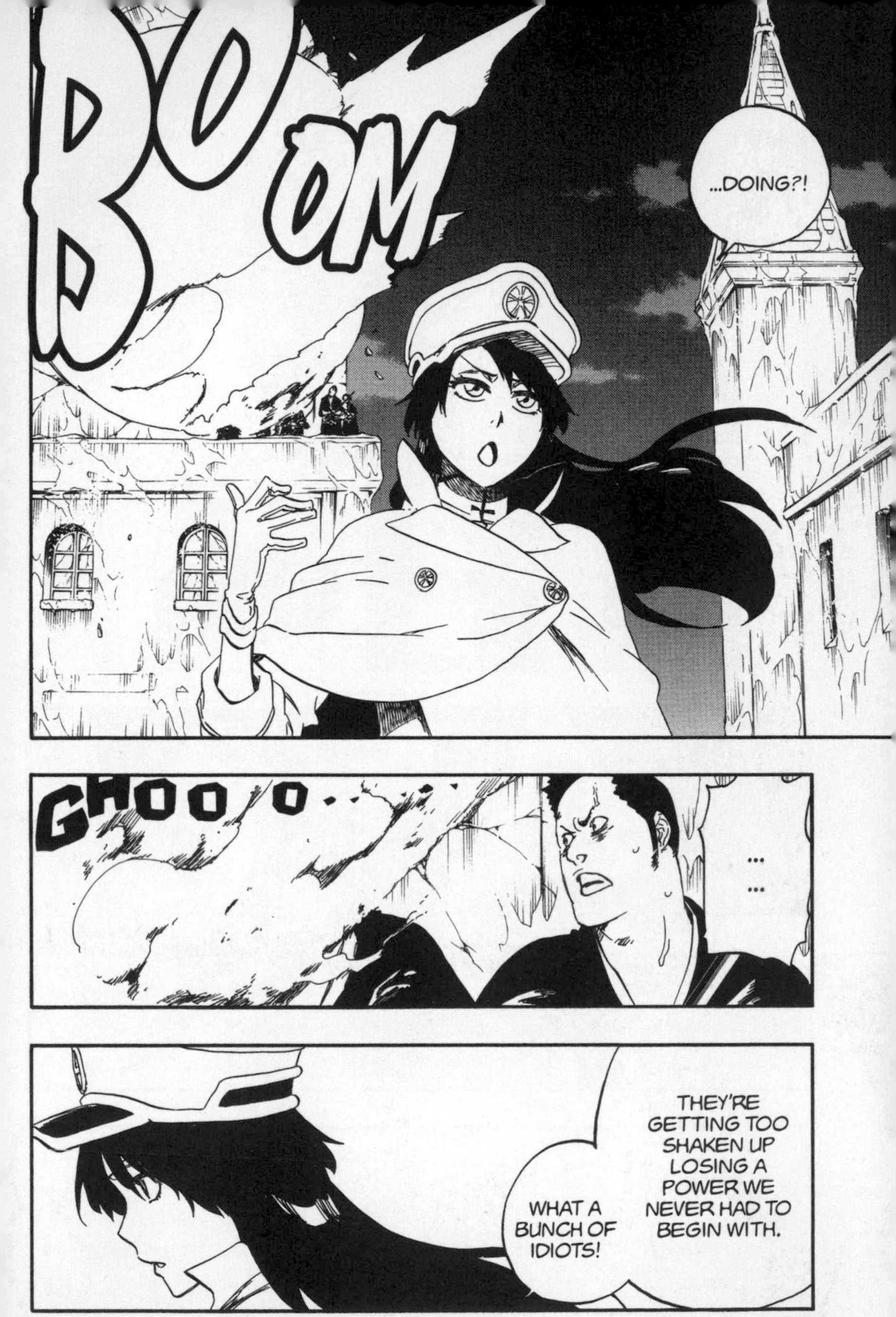
...DOING?!
BOOM
...
...
GHOOO...
THEY'RE GETTING TOO SHAKEN UP LOSING A POWER WE NEVER HAD TO BEGIN WITH.
WHAT A BUNCH OF IDIOTS!

READ THIS WAY

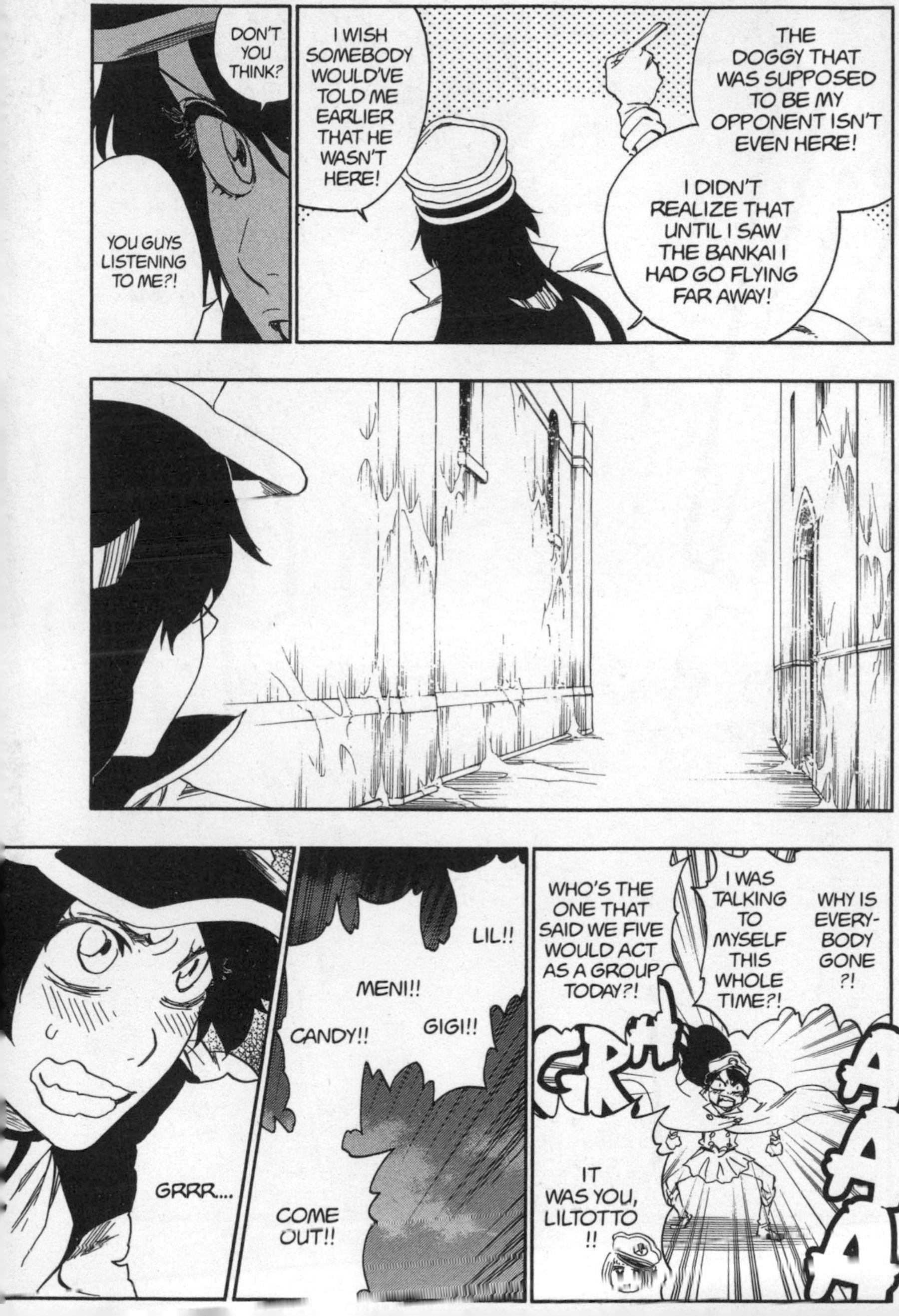
THE DOGGY THAT WAS SUPPOSED TO BE MY OPPONENT ISN'T EVEN HERE!
I DIDN'T REALIZE THAT UNTIL I SAW THE BANKAI I HAD GO FLYING FAR AWAY!
I WISH SOMEBODY WOULD'VE TOLD ME EARLIER THAT HE WASN'T HERE!
DON'T YOU THINK?
YOU GUYS LISTENING TO ME?!
WHY IS EVERY-BODY GONE ?!
I WAS TALKING TO MYSELF THIS WHOLE TIME?!
WHO'S THE ONE THAT SAID WE FIVE WOULD ACT AS A GROUP TODAY?!
AAA
IT WAS YOU, LILTOTTO !!
LIL!!
MENI!!
GIGI!!
CANDY!!
COME OUT!!
GRRR....

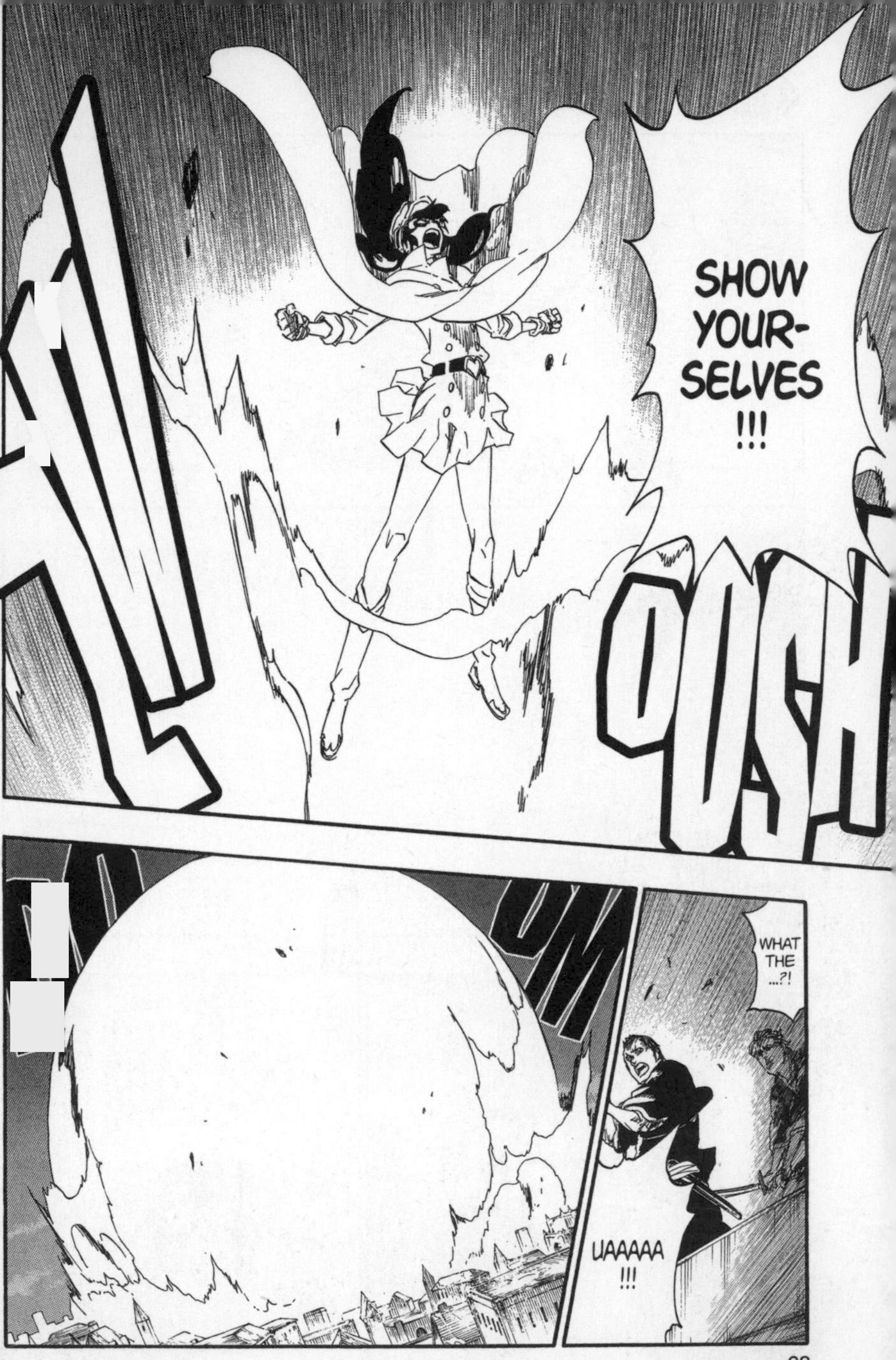
SHOW YOUR-SELVES !!!
WHAT THE ...?!
UAAAAA !!!

READ THIS WAY

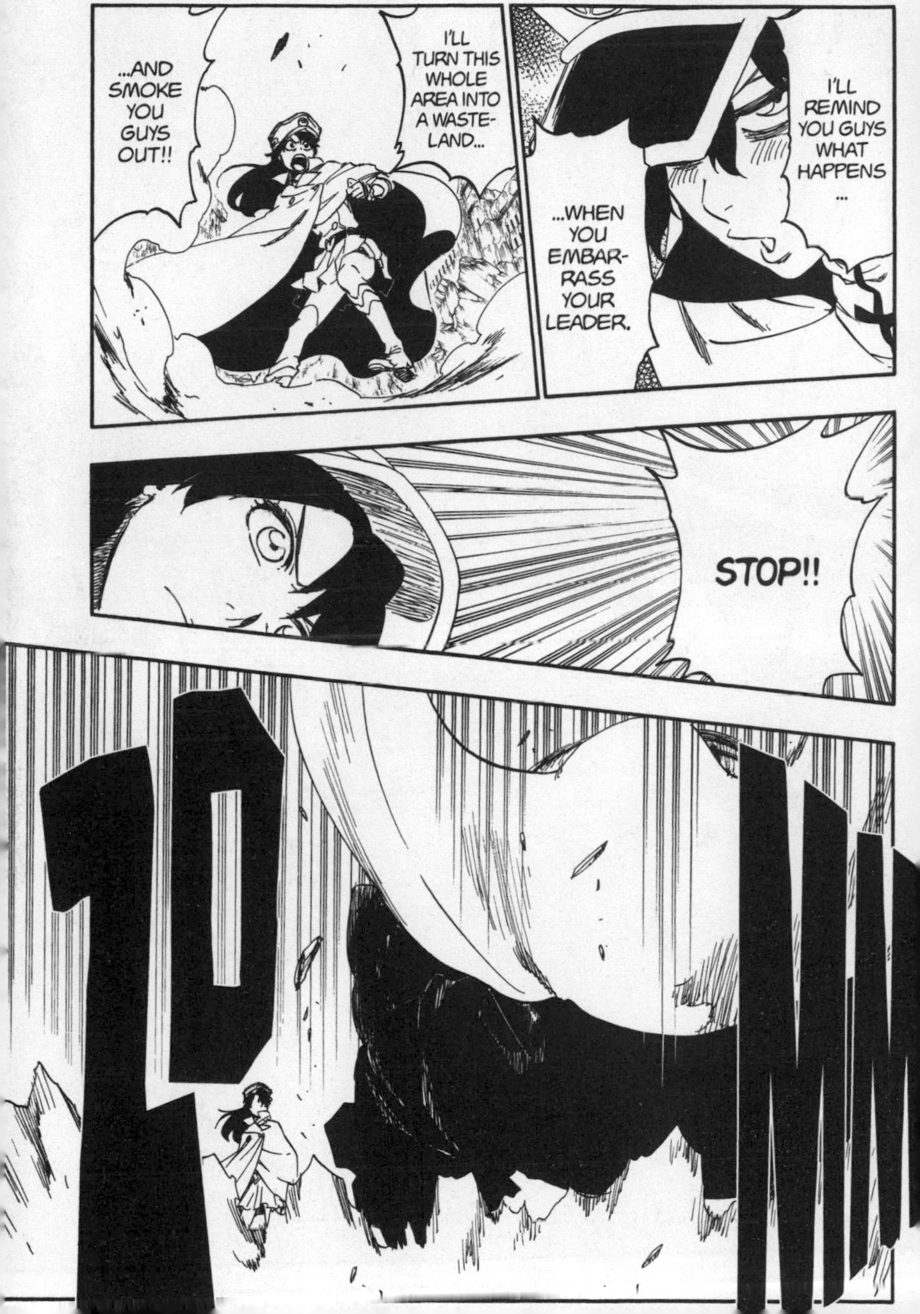
I'LL REMIND YOU GUYS WHAT HAPPENS ...
...WHEN YOU EMBAR-RASS YOUR LEADER.
I'LL TURN THIS WHOLE AREA INTO A WASTE-LAND...
...AND SMOKE YOU GUYS OUT!!
STOP!!

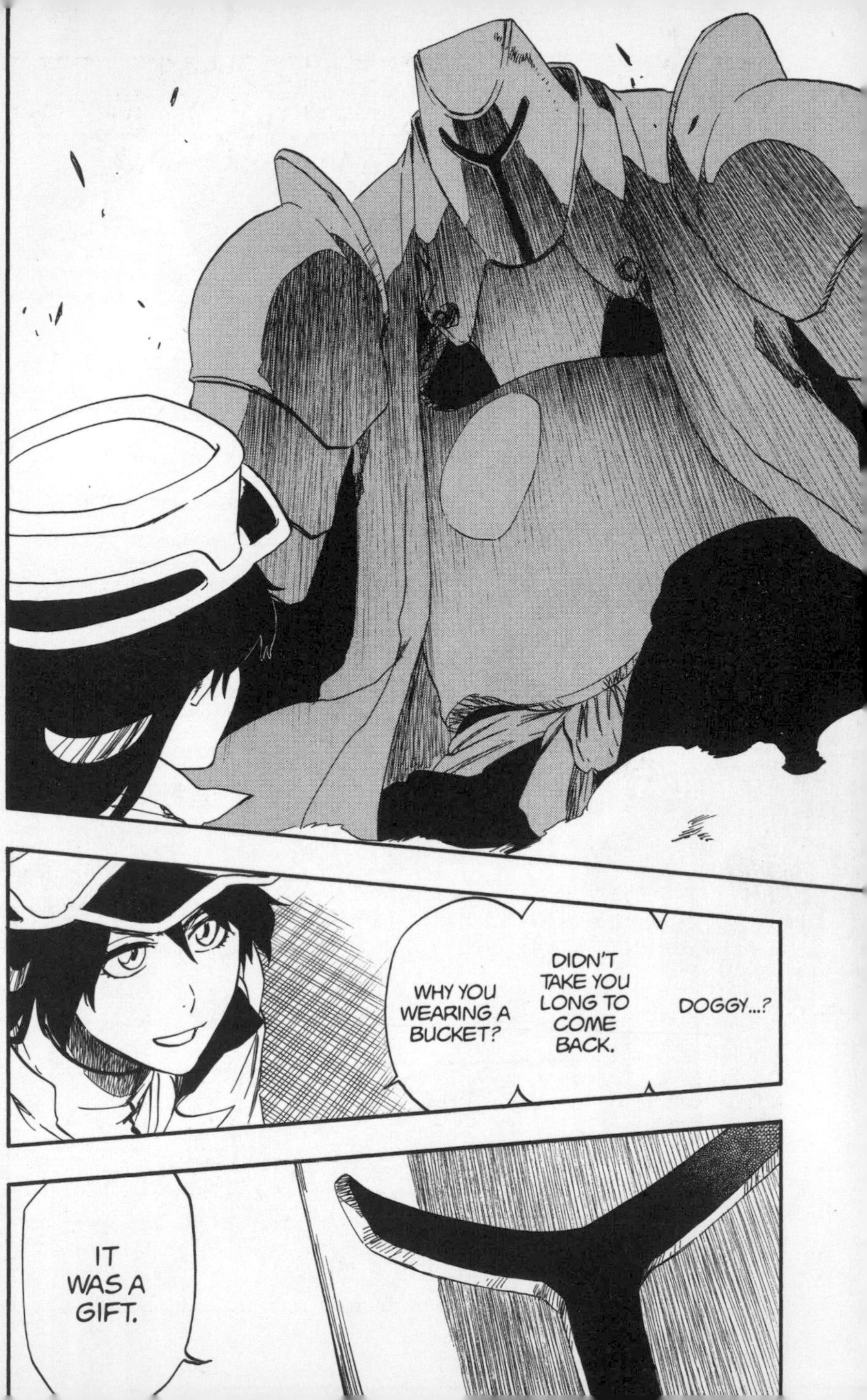
DOGGY...?
DIDN'T TAKE YOU LONG TO COME BACK.
WHY YOU WEARING A BUCKET?
IT WAS A GIFT.

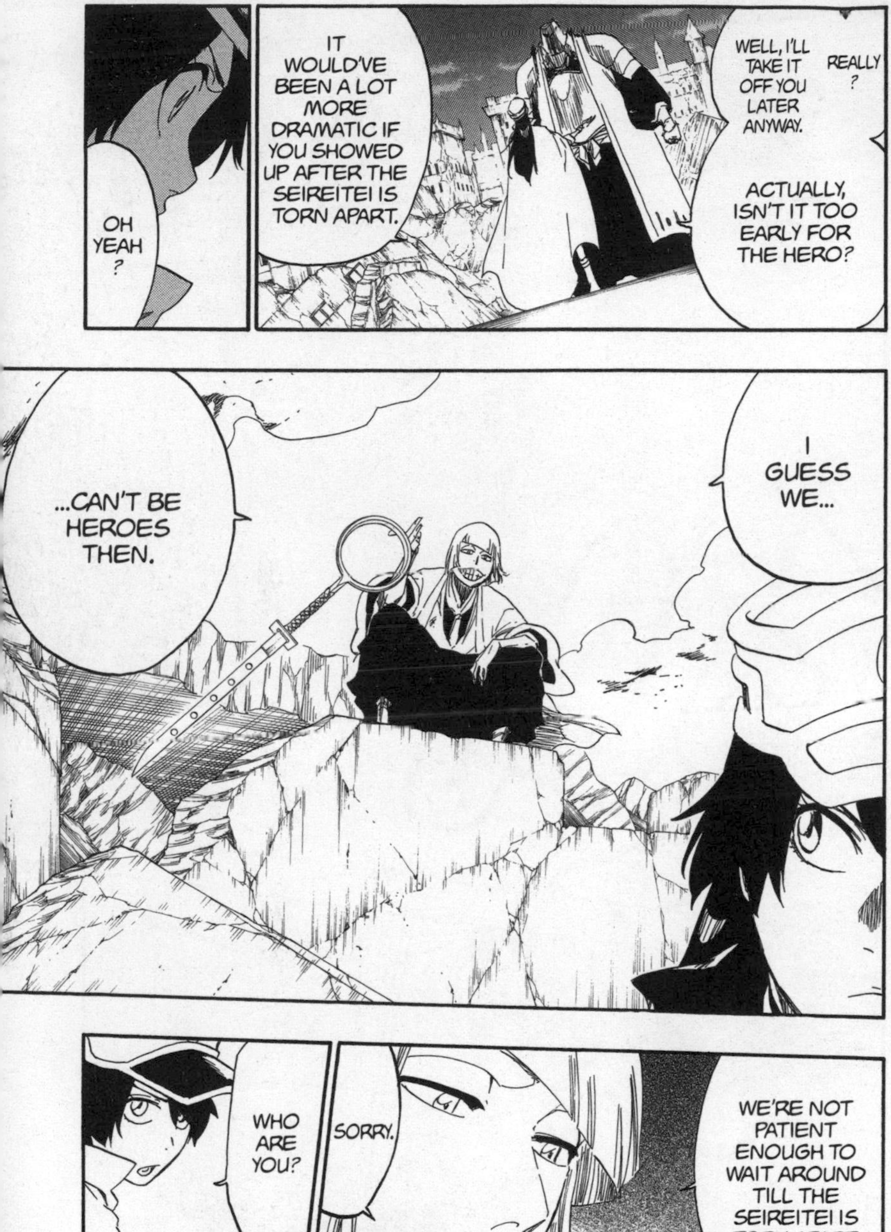
REALLY?
WELL, I'LL TAKE IT OFF YOU LATER ANYWAY.
ACTUALLY, ISN'T IT TOO EARLY FOR THE HERO?
IT WOULD'VE BEEN A LOT MORE DRAMATIC IF YOU SHOWED UP AFTER THE SEIREITEI IS TORN APART.
OH YEAH?
I GUESS WE...
...CAN'T BE HEROES THEN.
WE'RE NOT PATIENT ENOUGH TO WAIT AROUND TILL THE SEIREITEI IS TORN APART.
SORRY.
WHO ARE YOU?

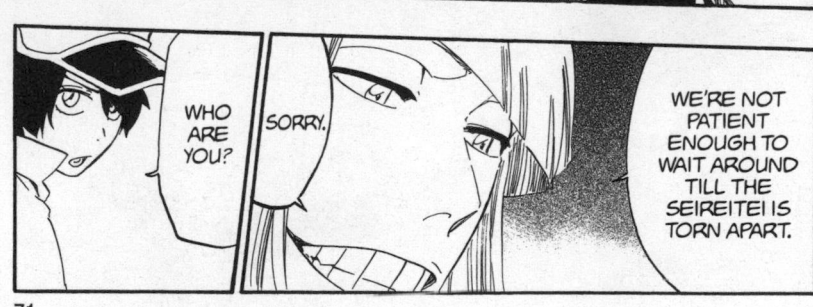

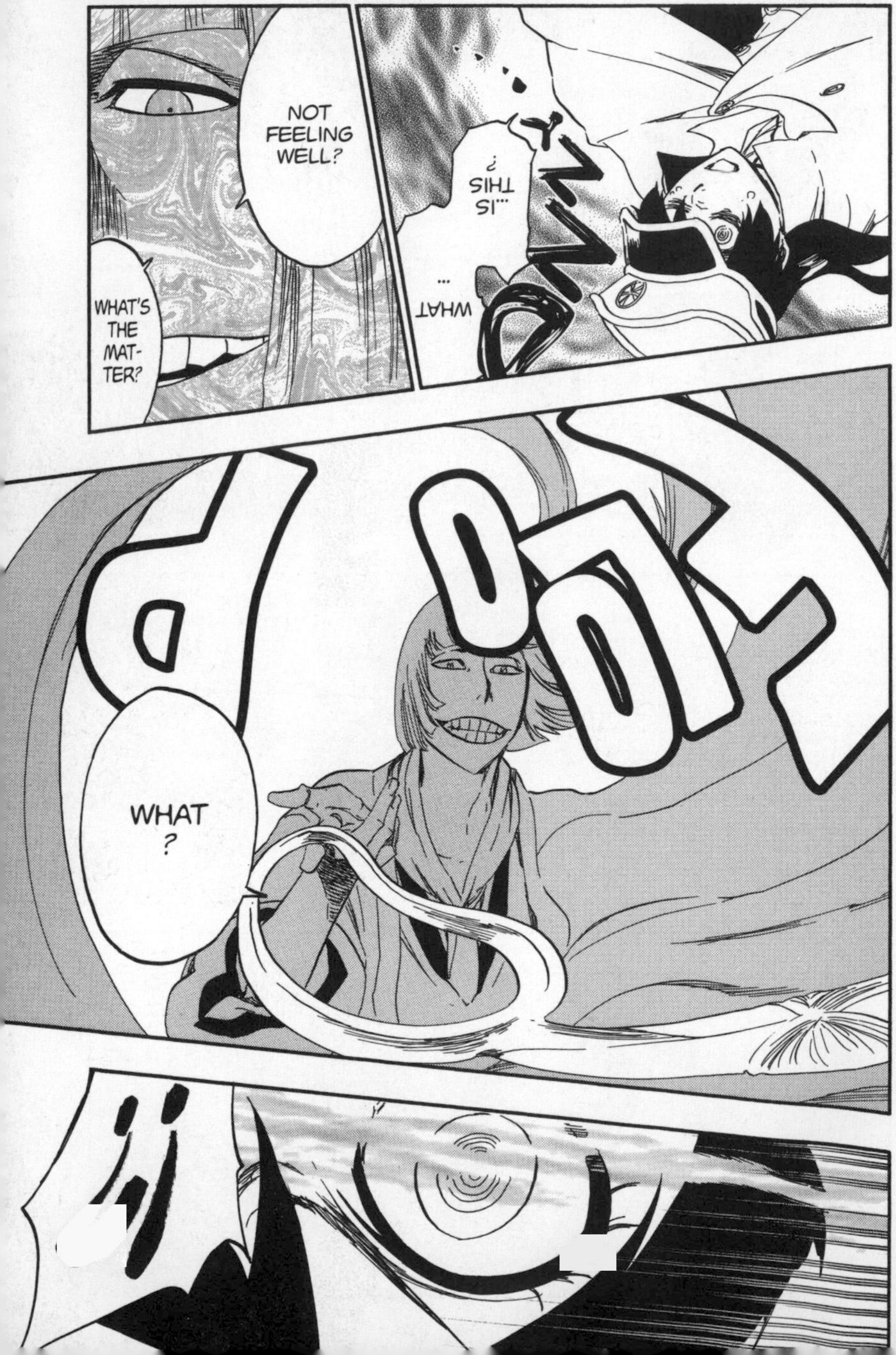
WHAT... ...IS THIS?
NOT FEELING WELL?
WHAT'S THE MAT-TER?
WHAT?

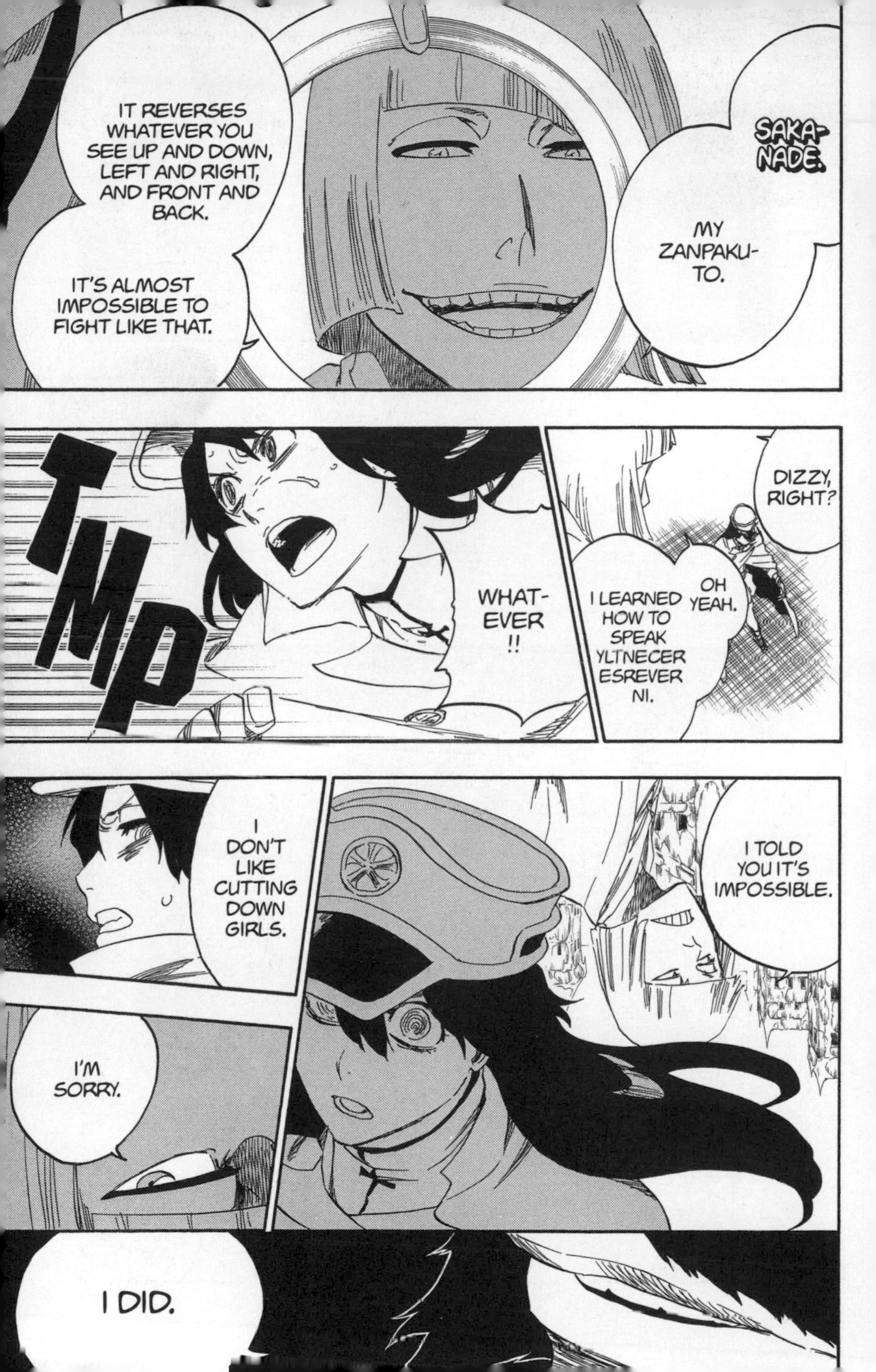
SAKA-NADE.
MY ZANPAKU-TO.
IT REVERSES WHATEVER YOU SEE UP AND DOWN, LEFT AND RIGHT, AND FRONT AND BACK.
IT'S ALMOST IMPOSSIBLE TO FIGHT LIKE THAT.
DIZZY, RIGHT?
OH YEAH.
I LEARNED HOW TO SPEAK YLTNECER ESREVER NI.
WHAT-EVER !!
TMP
I TOLD YOU IT'S IMPOSSIBLE.
I DON'T LIKE CUTTING DOWN GIRLS.
I'M SORRY.
I DID.

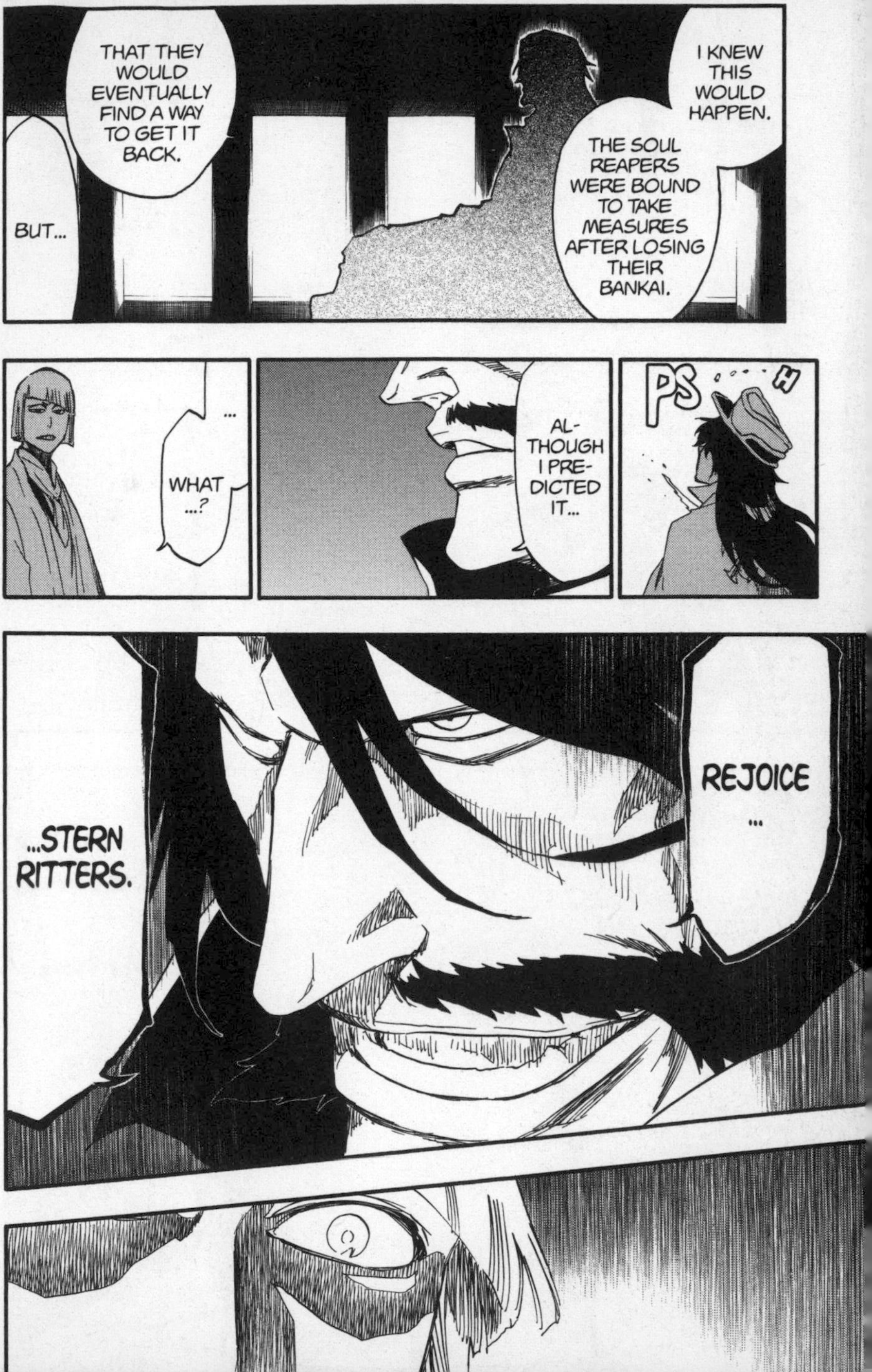
I KNEW THIS WOULD HAPPEN.
THE SOUL REAPERS WERE BOUND TO TAKE MEASURES AFTER LOSING THEIR BANKAI.
THAT THEY WOULD EVENTUALLY FIND A WAY TO GET IT BACK.
BUT...
PSSH
ALTHOUGH I PREDICTED IT...
...
WHAT ...?
REJOICE ...
...STERN RITTERS.

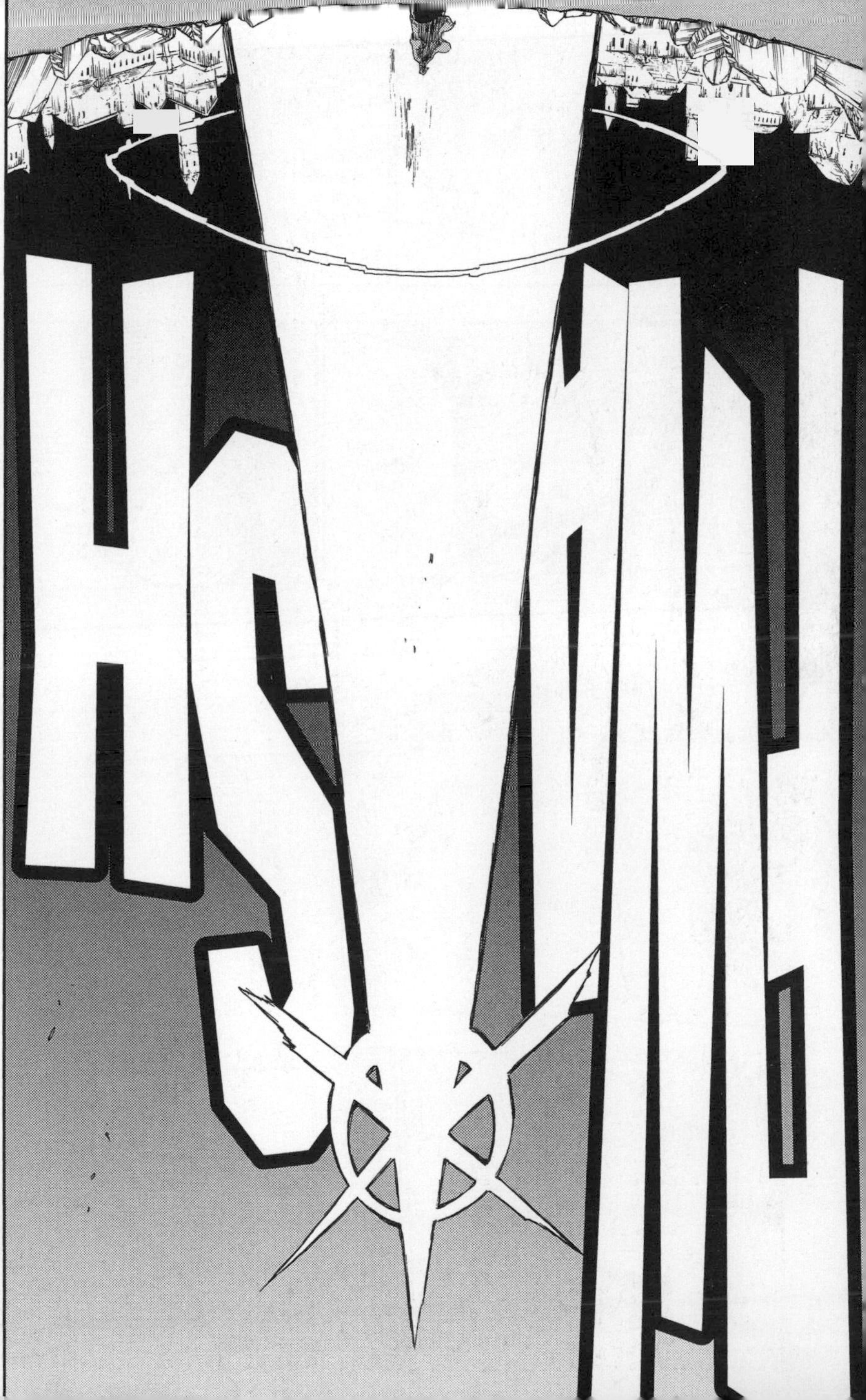

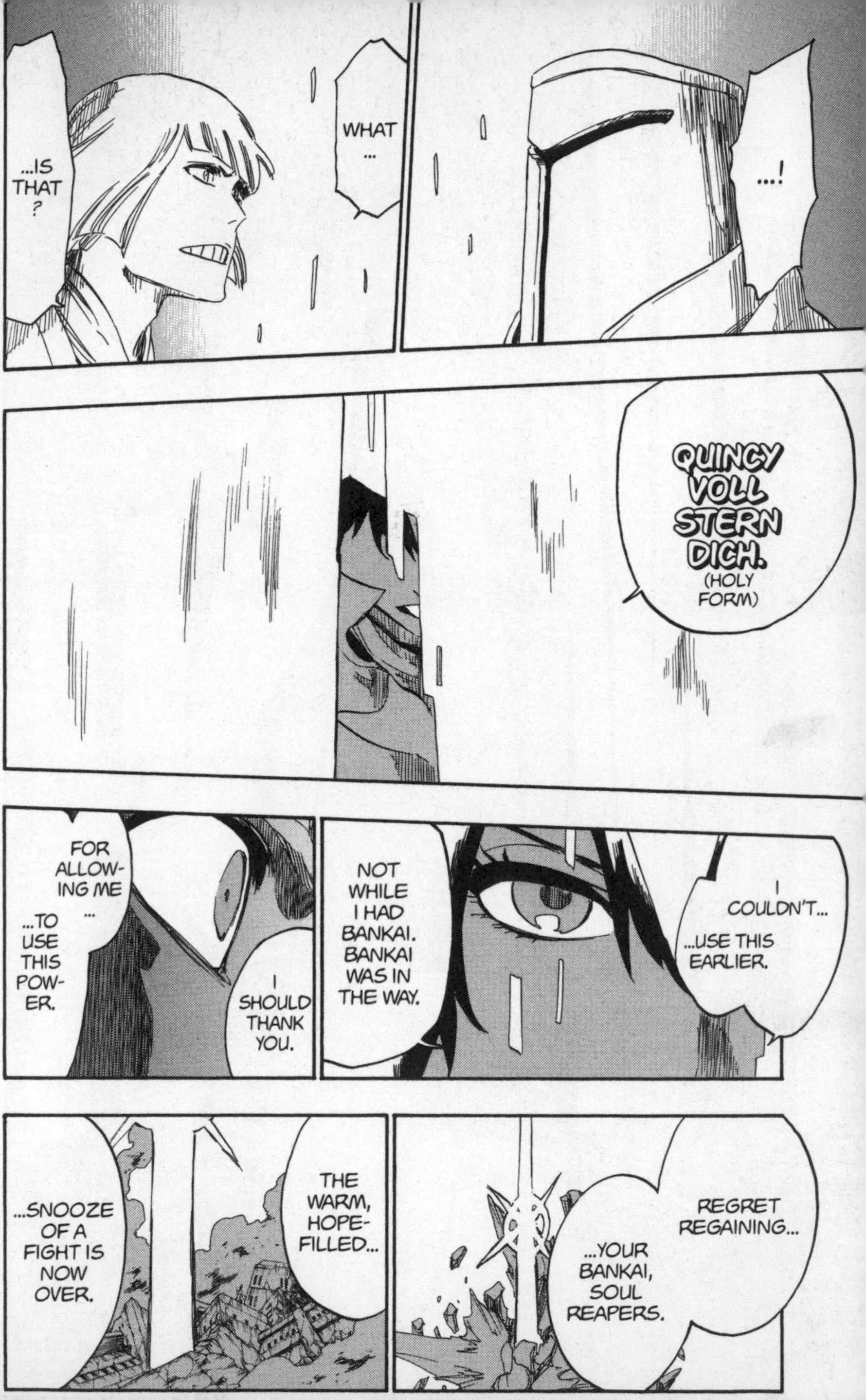
...!
WHAT ...
...IS THAT ?
QUINCY VOLL STERN DICH. (HOLY FORM)
I COULDN'T...
...USE THIS EARLIER.
NOT WHILE I HAD BANKAI. BANKAI WAS IN THE WAY.
I SHOULD THANK YOU.
FOR ALLOWING ME ...
...TO USE THIS POWER.
REGRET REGAINING...
...YOUR BANKAI, SOUL REAPERS.
THE WARM, HOPE-FILLED...
...SNOOZE OF A FIGHT IS NOW OVER.

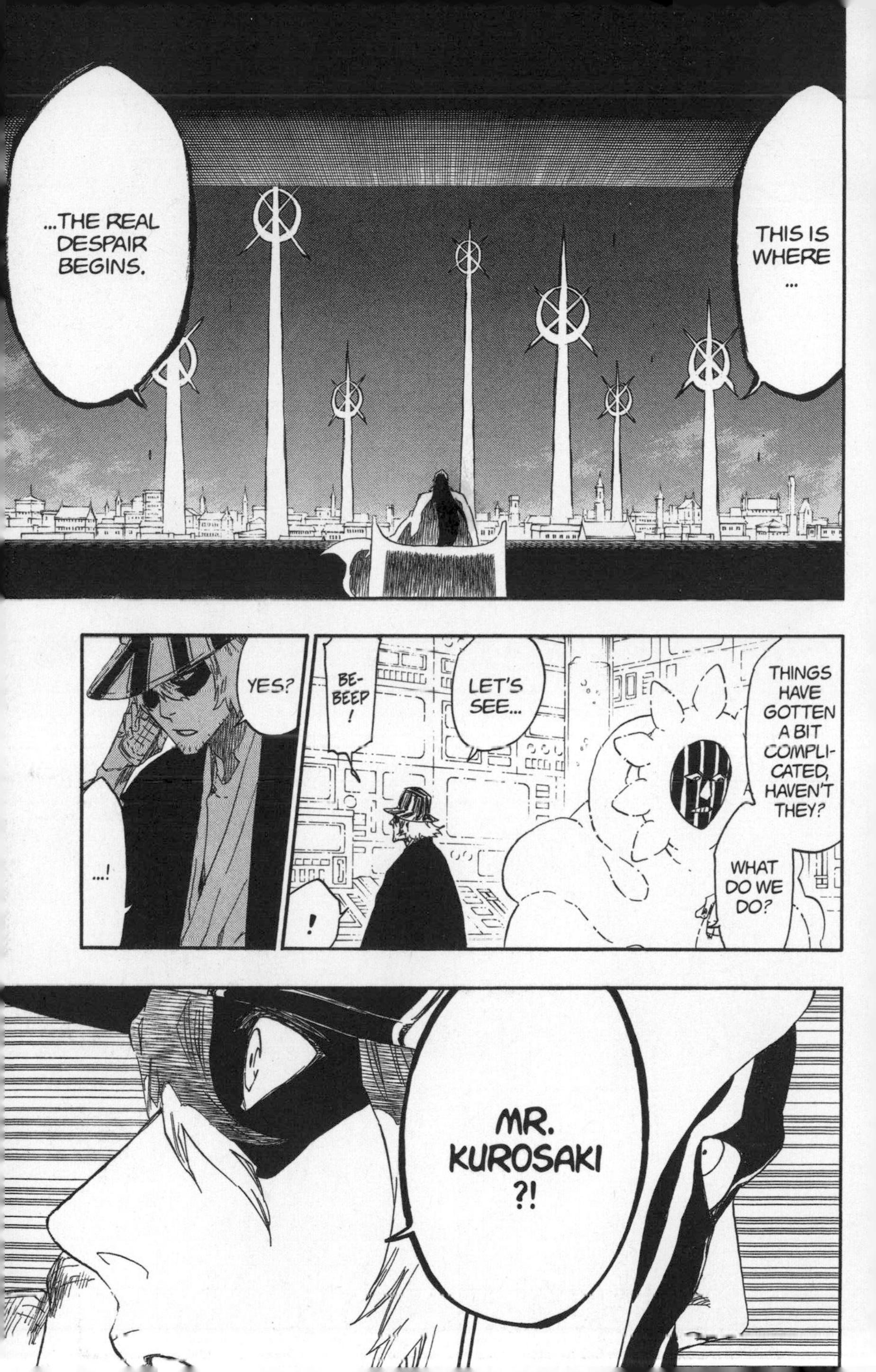
THIS IS WHERE ...
...THE REAL DESPAIR BEGINS.
THINGS HAVE GOTTEN A BIT COMPLI-CATED, HAVEN'T THEY?
WHAT DO WE DO?
LET'S SEE...
BE-BEEP!
!
YES?
...!
MR. KUROSAKI ?!

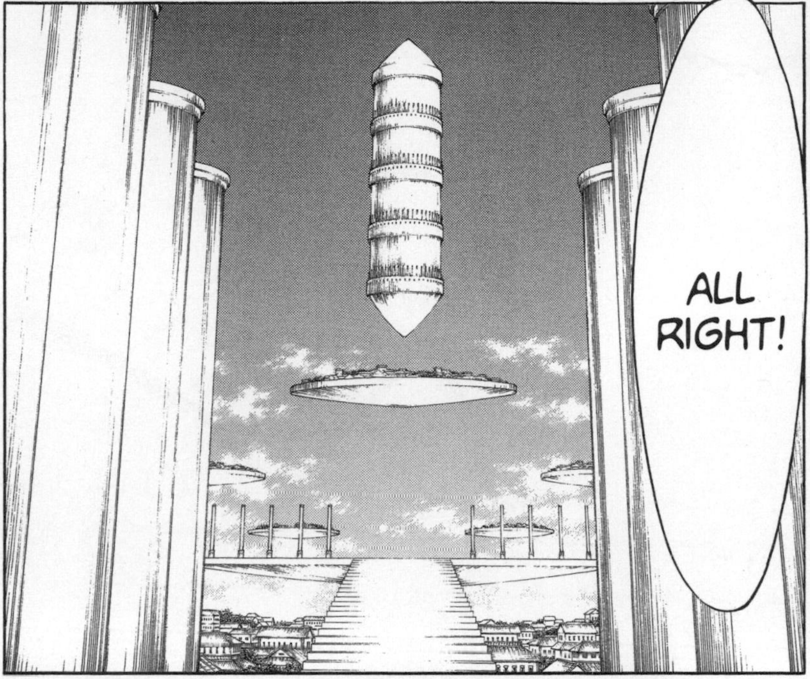
ALL RIGHT!

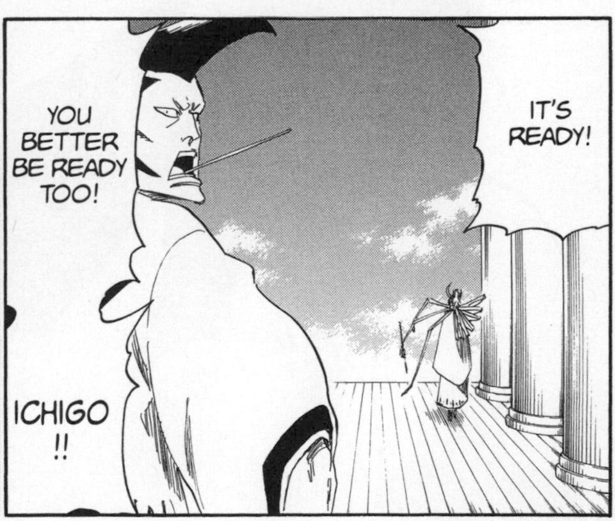
IT'S READY!
YOU BETTER BE READY TOO!
ICHIGO !!

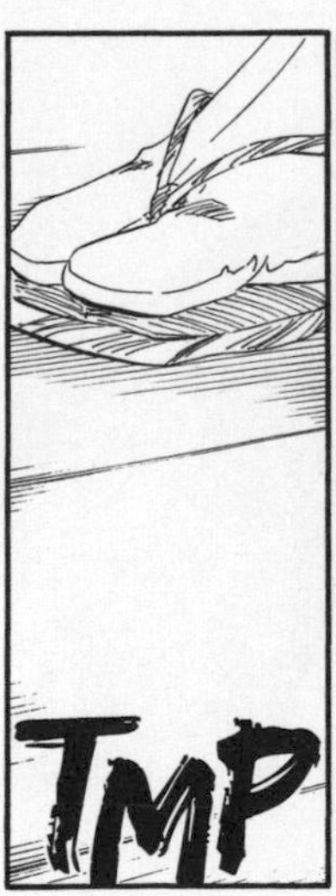
TMP

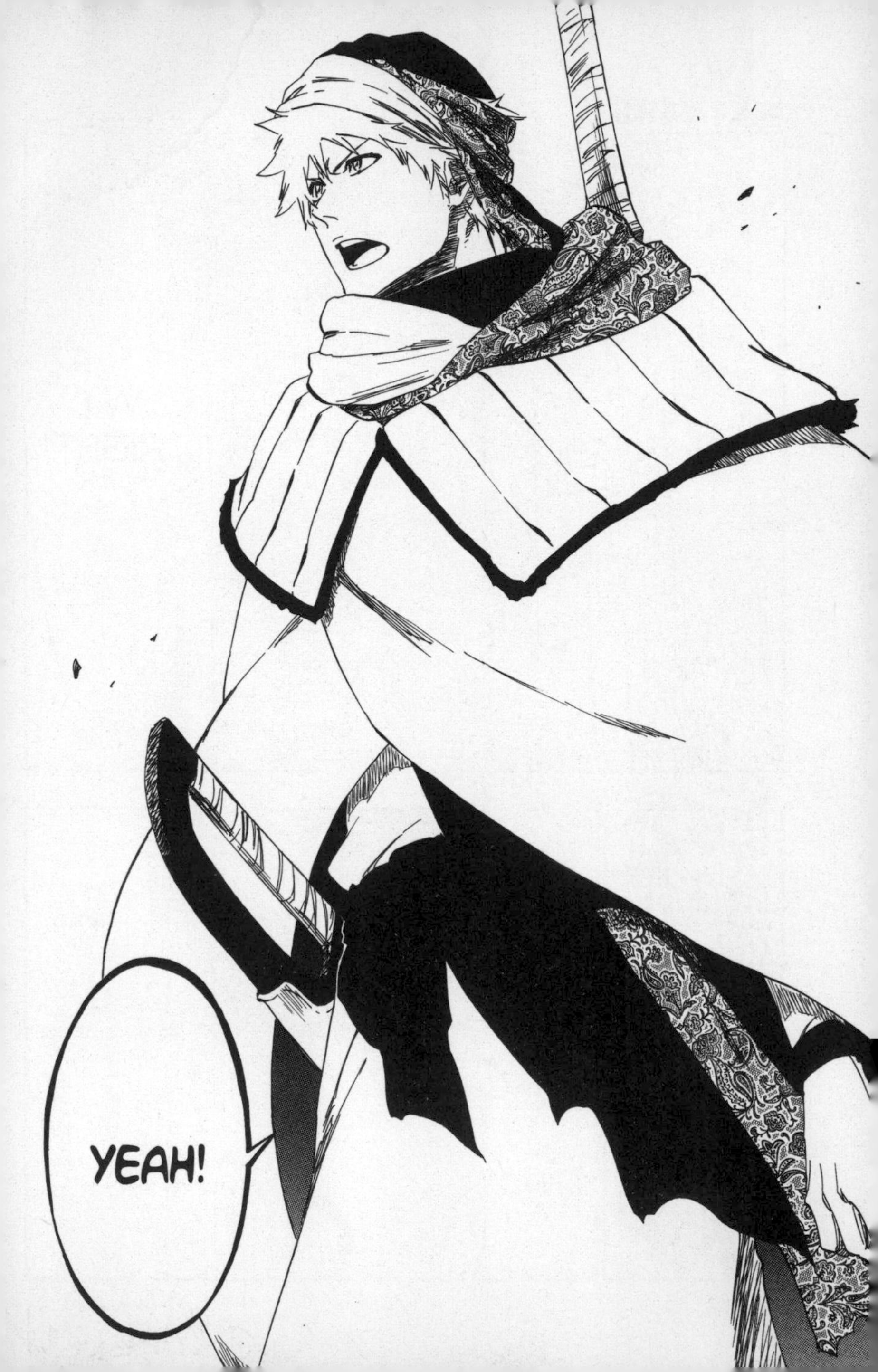
YEAH!

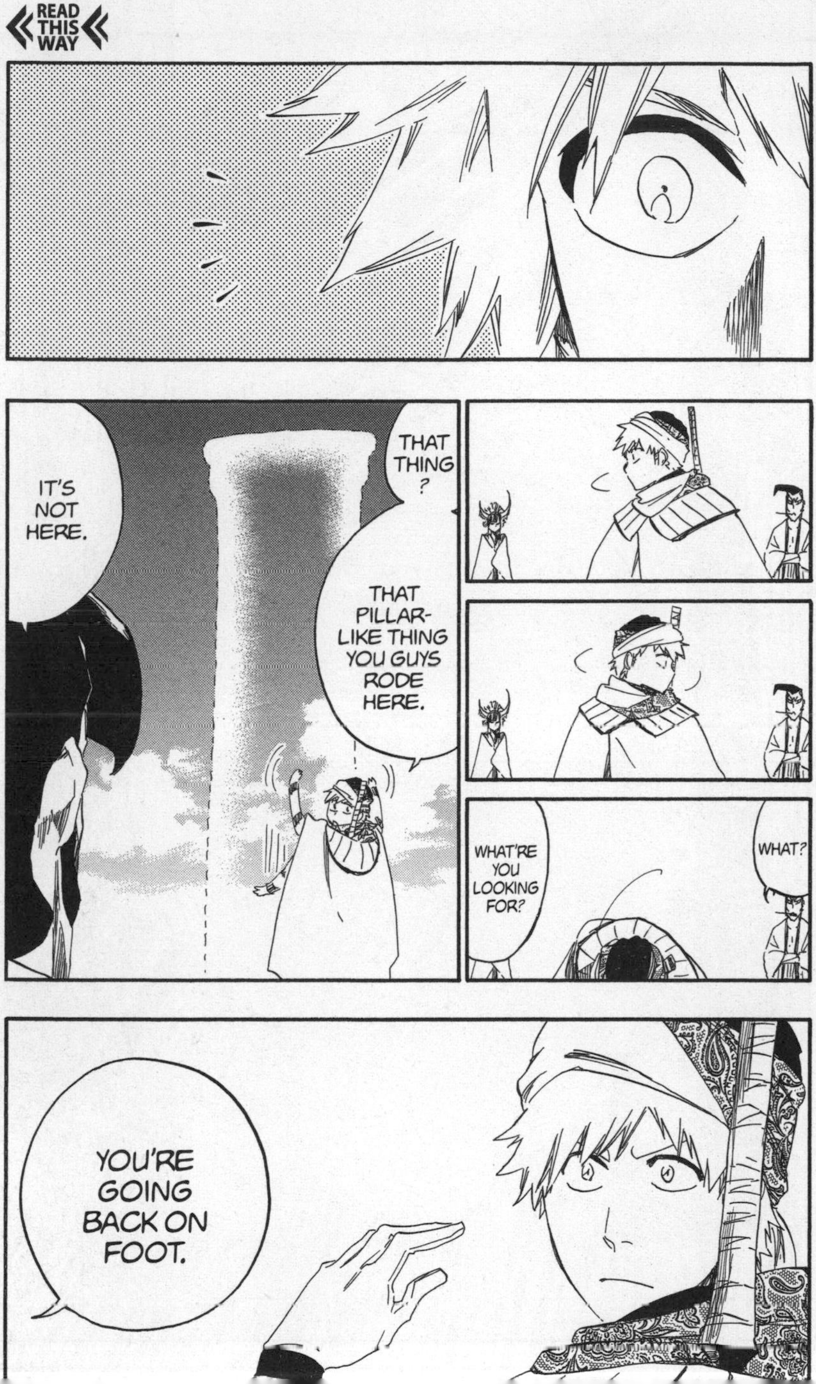
READ THIS WAY
WHAT?
WHAT'RE YOU LOOKING FOR?
THAT THING?
IT'S NOT HERE.
THAT PILLAR-LIKE THING YOU GUYS RODE HERE.
YOU'RE GOING BACK ON FOOT.

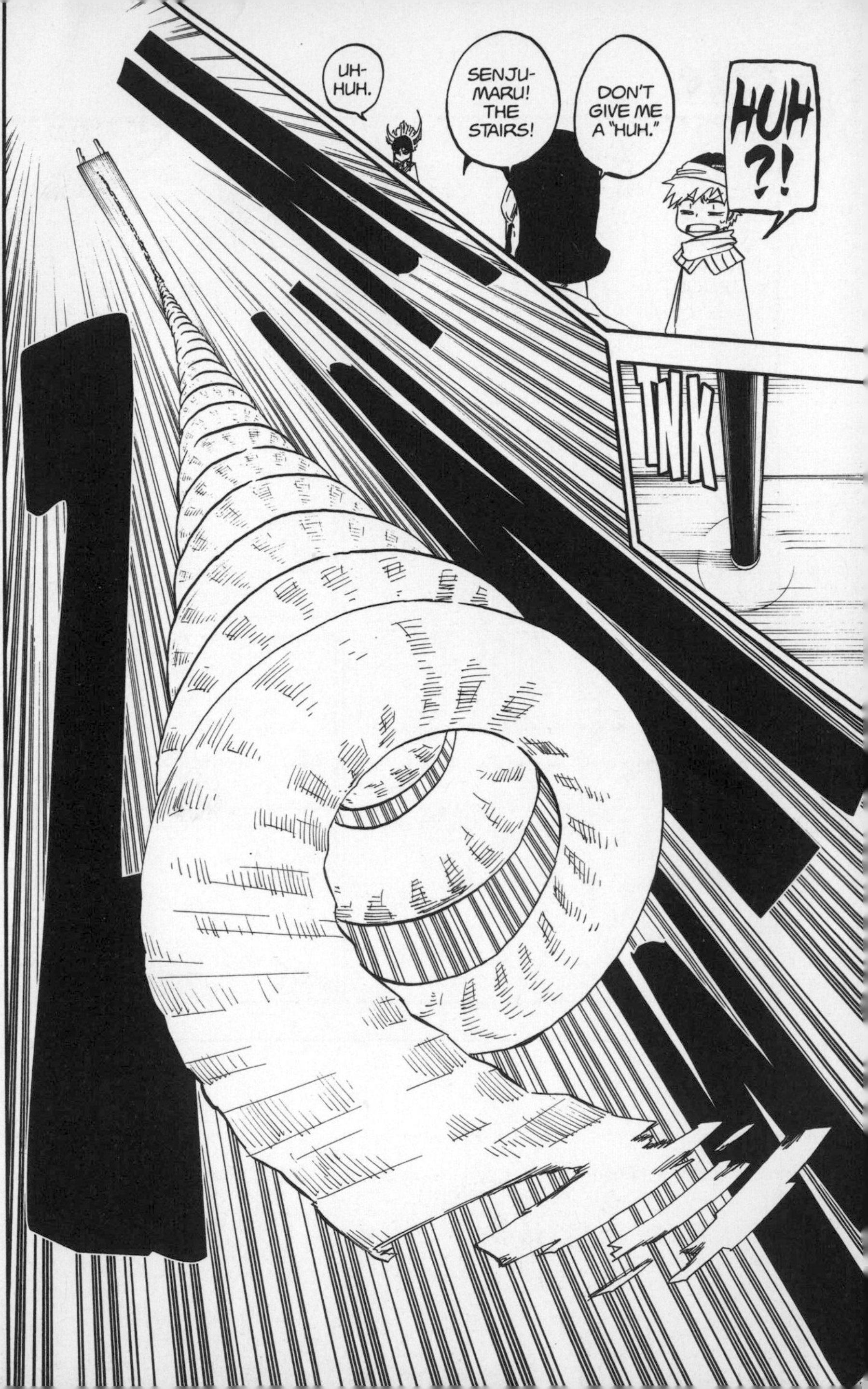
HUH?!
DON'T GIVE ME A "HUH."
SENJU-MARU! THE STAIRS!
UH-HUH.
TNK

READ THIS WAY

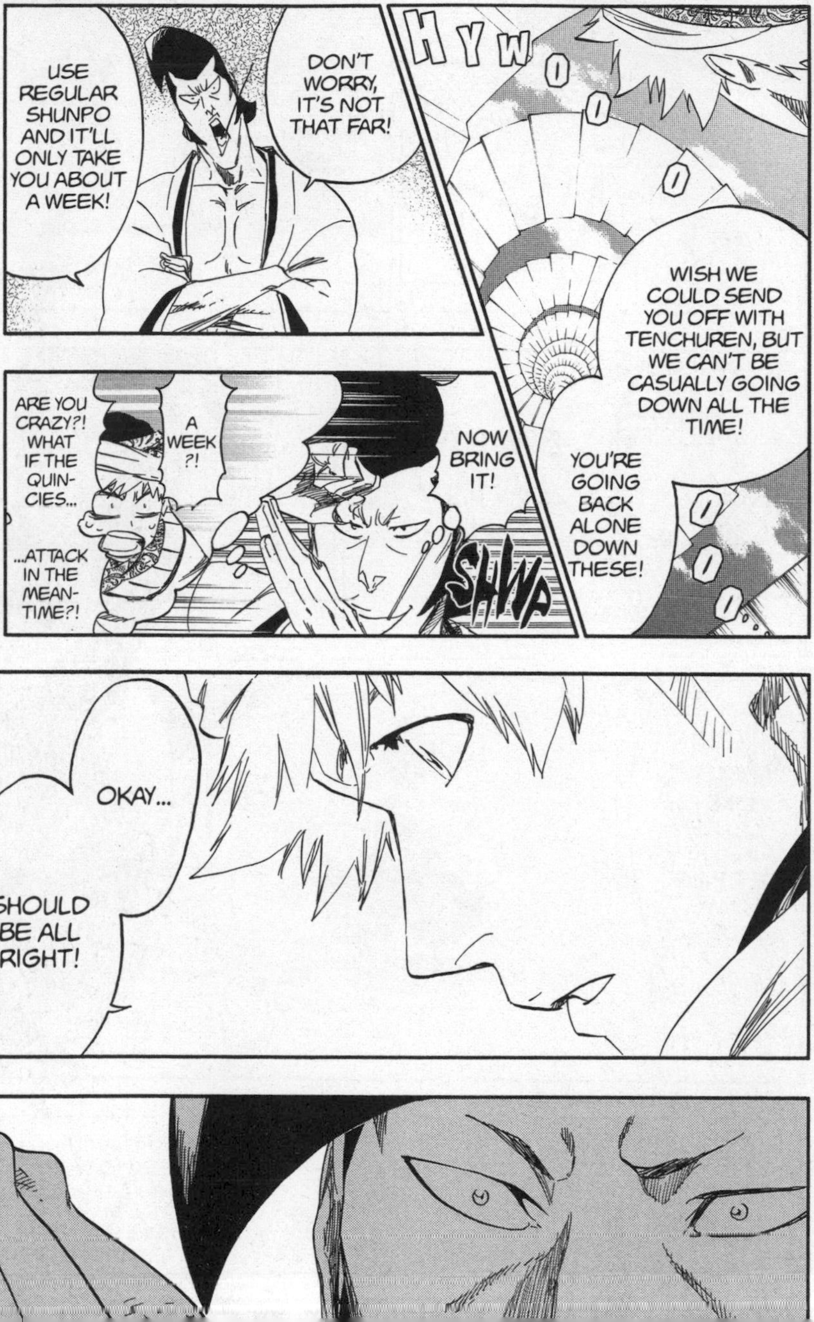
HYWOOOOO
WISH WE COULD SEND YOU OFF WITH TENCHUREN, BUT WE CAN'T BE CASUALLY GOING DOWN ALL THE TIME!
YOU'RE GOING BACK ALONE DOWN THESE!
DON'T WORRY, IT'S NOT THAT FAR!
USE REGULAR SHUNPO AND IT'LL ONLY TAKE YOU ABOUT A WEEK!
SHWP
NOW BRING IT!
A WEEK ?!
ARE YOU CRAZY?! WHAT IF THE QUIN-CIES...
...ATTACK IN THE MEAN-TIME?!
OKAY...
SHOULD BE ALL RIGHT!

HUH?
REALLY ...?
IT'S PRETTY FAR. YOU SURE ...?
WHAT'RE YOU TALKING ABOUT?
YOU SAID YOUR-SELF IT WASN'T THAT FAR.
IF IT TAKES A WEEK USING REGULAR SHUNPO ...
IF I HURRY LIKE HELL, IT'LL ONLY TAKE ME HALF A DAY!
IT'LL BE FINE!
...
BWAHAHA-HAHAHA-HAHAHA !!!
GOOD, GOOD!
LOOKS LIKE YOU'RE FINALLY GETTING SOME BALLS!
AND THERE'S NO NEED TO WORRY ABOUT WHETHER YOU'LL MAKE IT IN TIME FOR THE BATTLE!
THE QUINCIES...

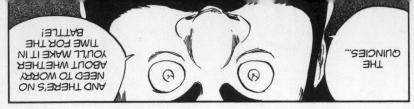

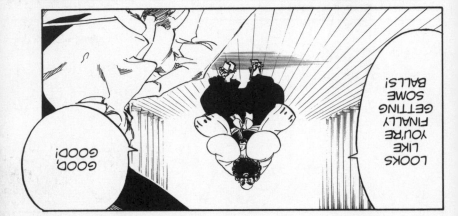

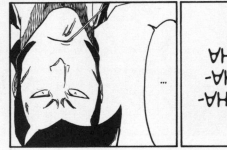

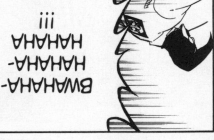

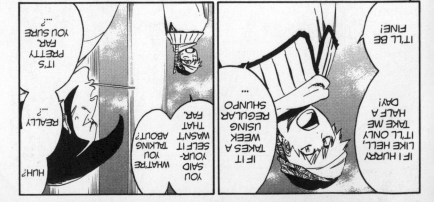

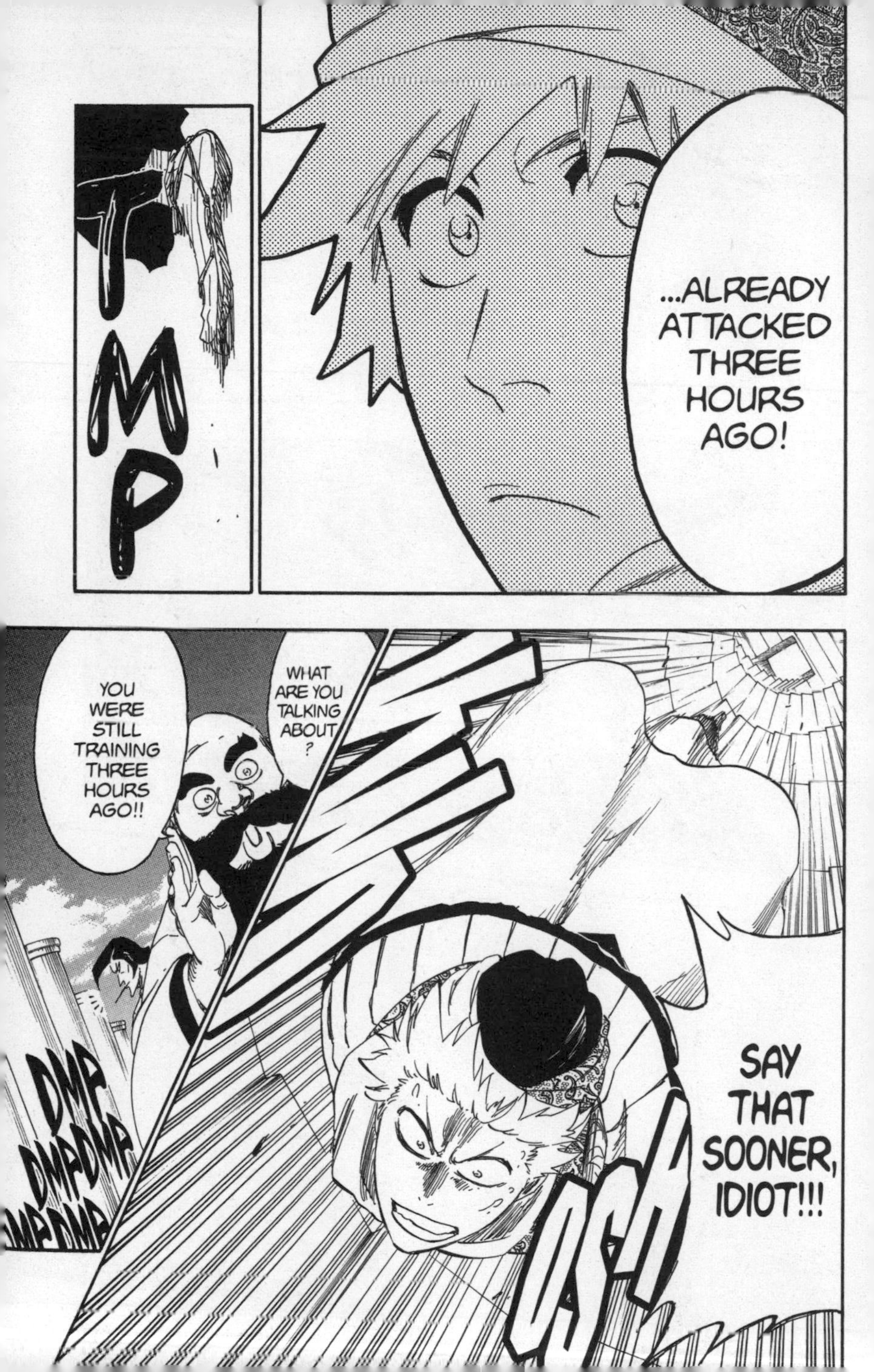
...ALREADY ATTACKED THREE HOURS AGO!
TMP
SAY THAT SOONER, IDIOT!!!
WHAT ARE YOU TALKING ABOUT?
YOU WERE STILL TRAINING THREE HOURS AGO!!
DMP DMPDMP

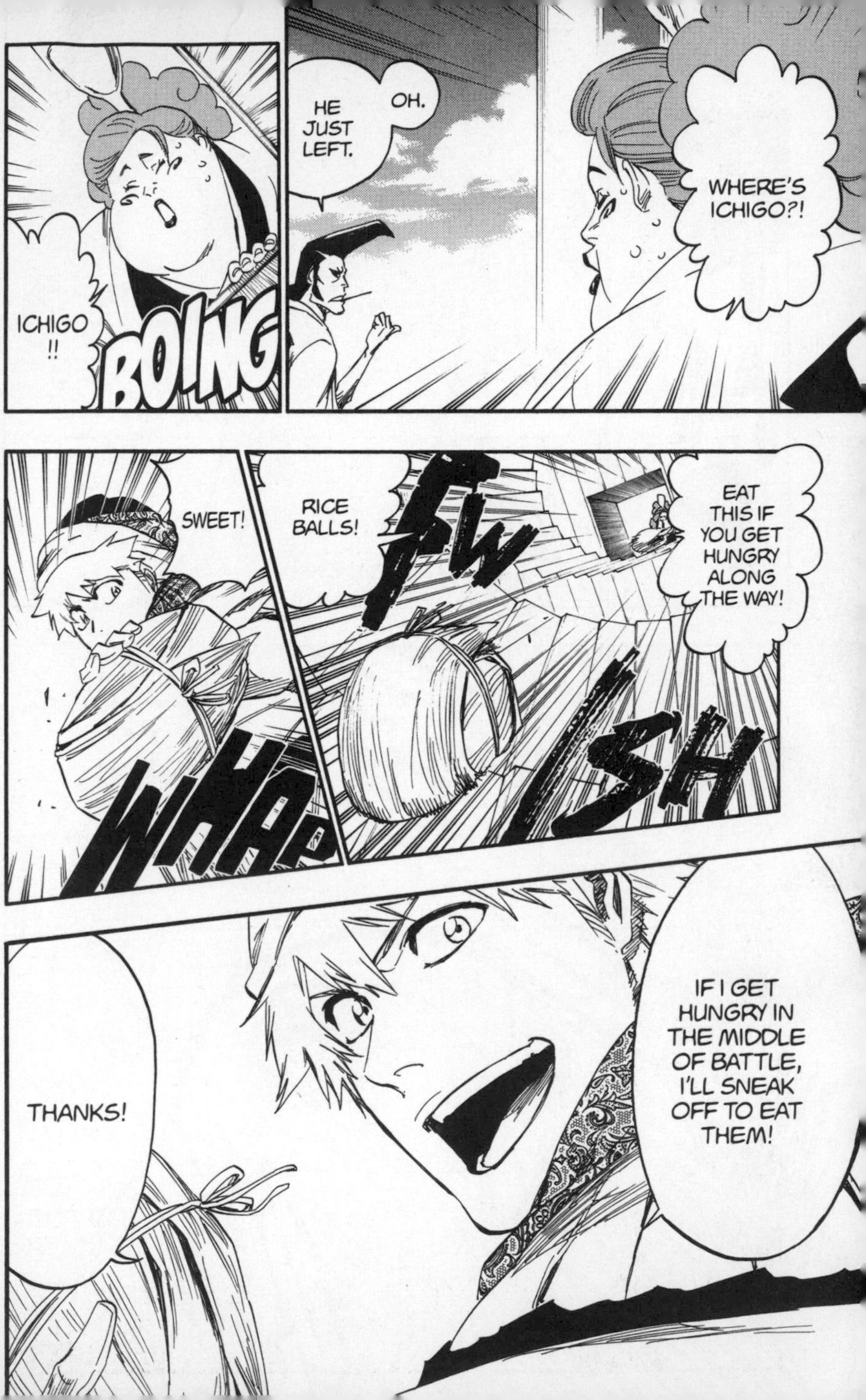
WHERE'S ICHIGO?!
OH.
HE JUST LEFT.
ICHIGO !!
BOING
EAT THIS IF YOU GET HUNGRY ALONG THE WAY!
FWISH
RICE BALLS!
SWEET!
WHAP
IF I GET HUNGRY IN THE MIDDLE OF BATTLE, I'LL SNEAK OFF TO EAT THEM!
THANKS!

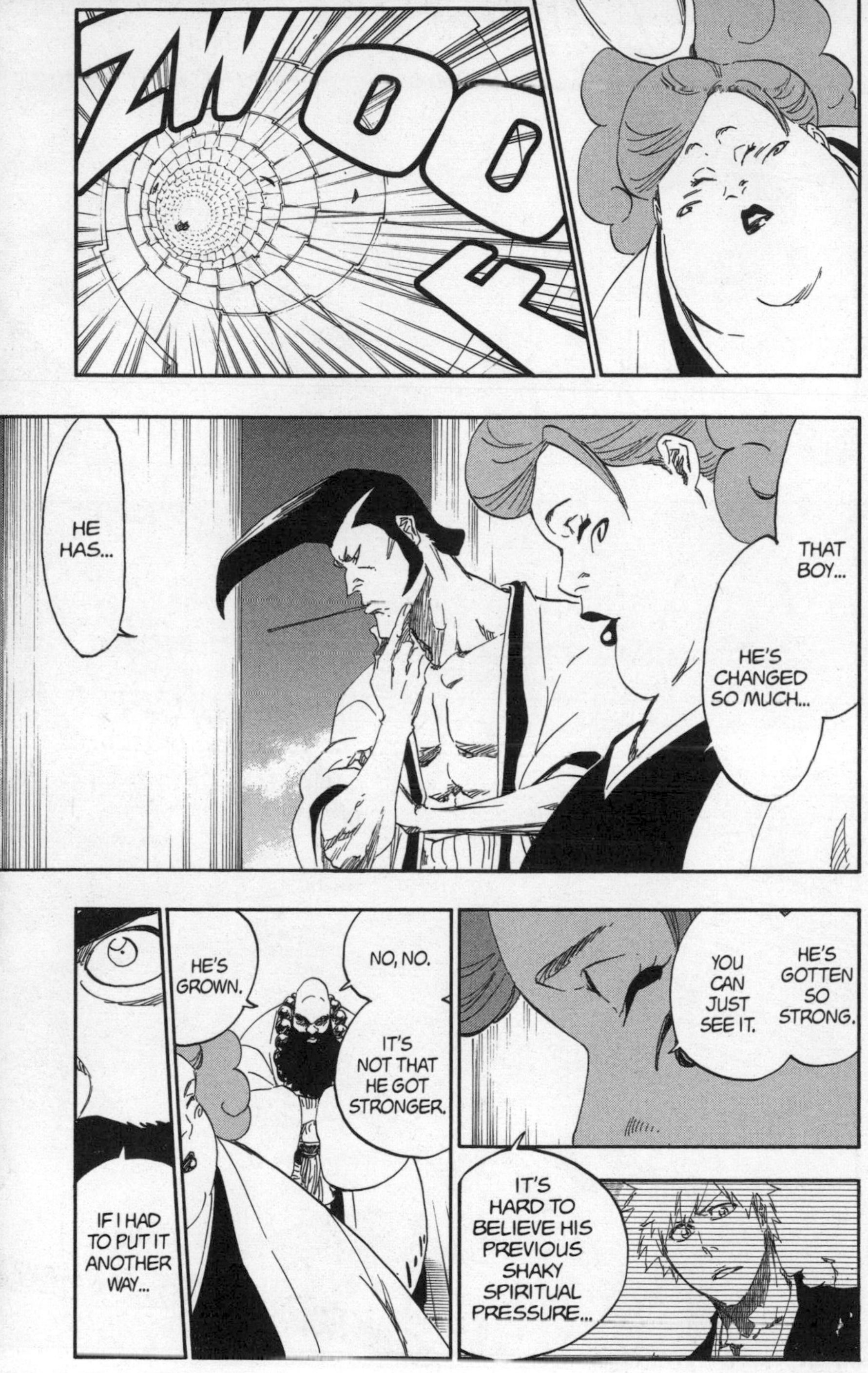
ZWOOF
THAT BOY...
HE'S CHANGED SO MUCH...
HE HAS...
HE'S GOTTEN SO STRONG.
YOU CAN JUST SEE IT.
IT'S HARD TO BELIEVE HIS PREVIOUS SHAKY SPIRITUAL PRESSURE...
NO, NO.
IT'S NOT THAT HE GOT STRONGER.
HE'S GROWN.
IF I HAD TO PUT IT ANOTHER WAY...

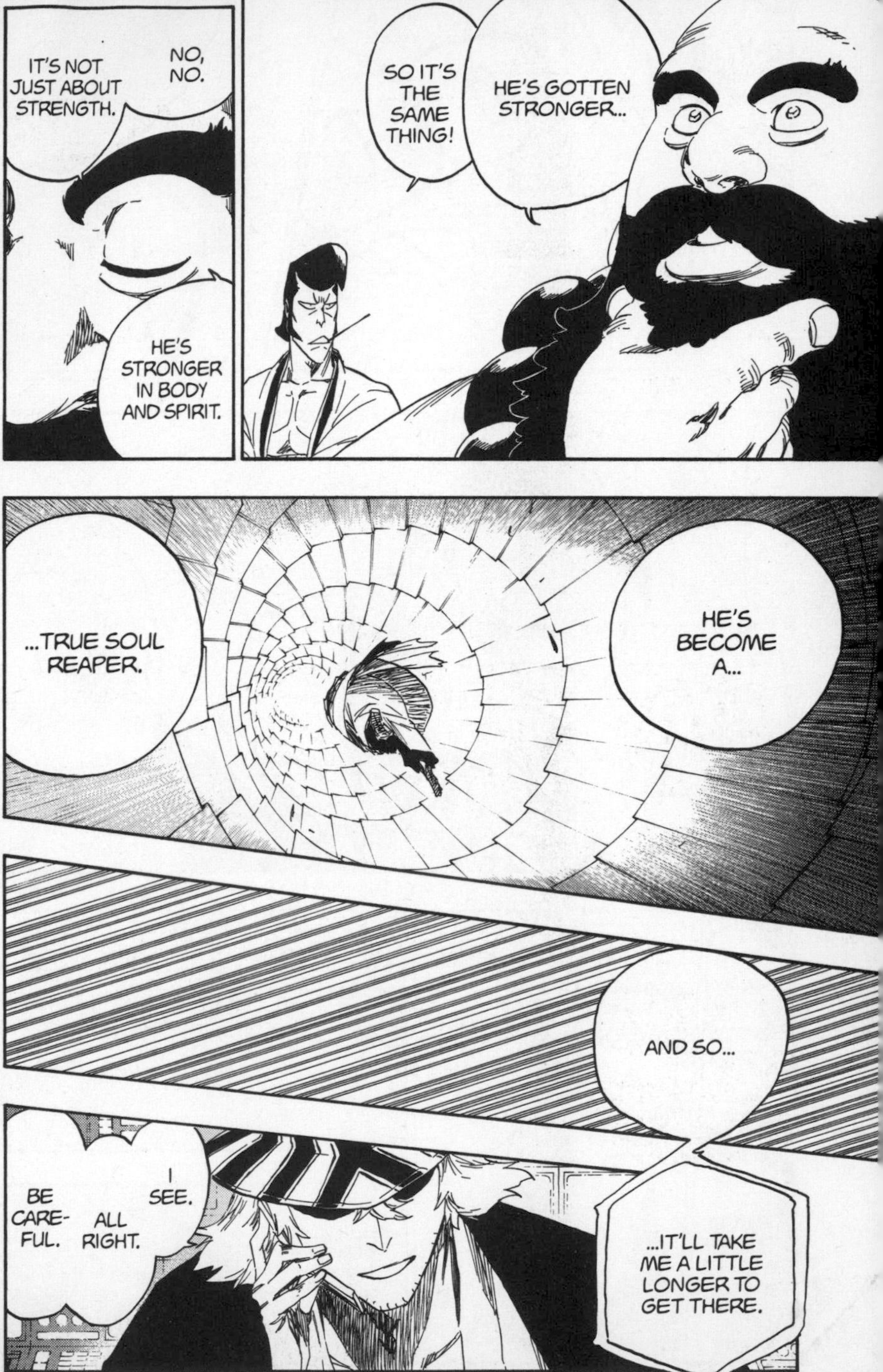
HE'S GOTTEN STRONGER...
SO IT'S THE SAME THING!
NO, NO.
IT'S NOT JUST ABOUT STRENGTH.
HE'S STRONGER IN BODY AND SPIRIT.
HE'S BECOME A...
...TRUE SOUL REAPER.
AND SO...
...IT'LL TAKE ME A LITTLE LONGER TO GET THERE.
I SEE.
ALL RIGHT.
BE CARE-FUL.

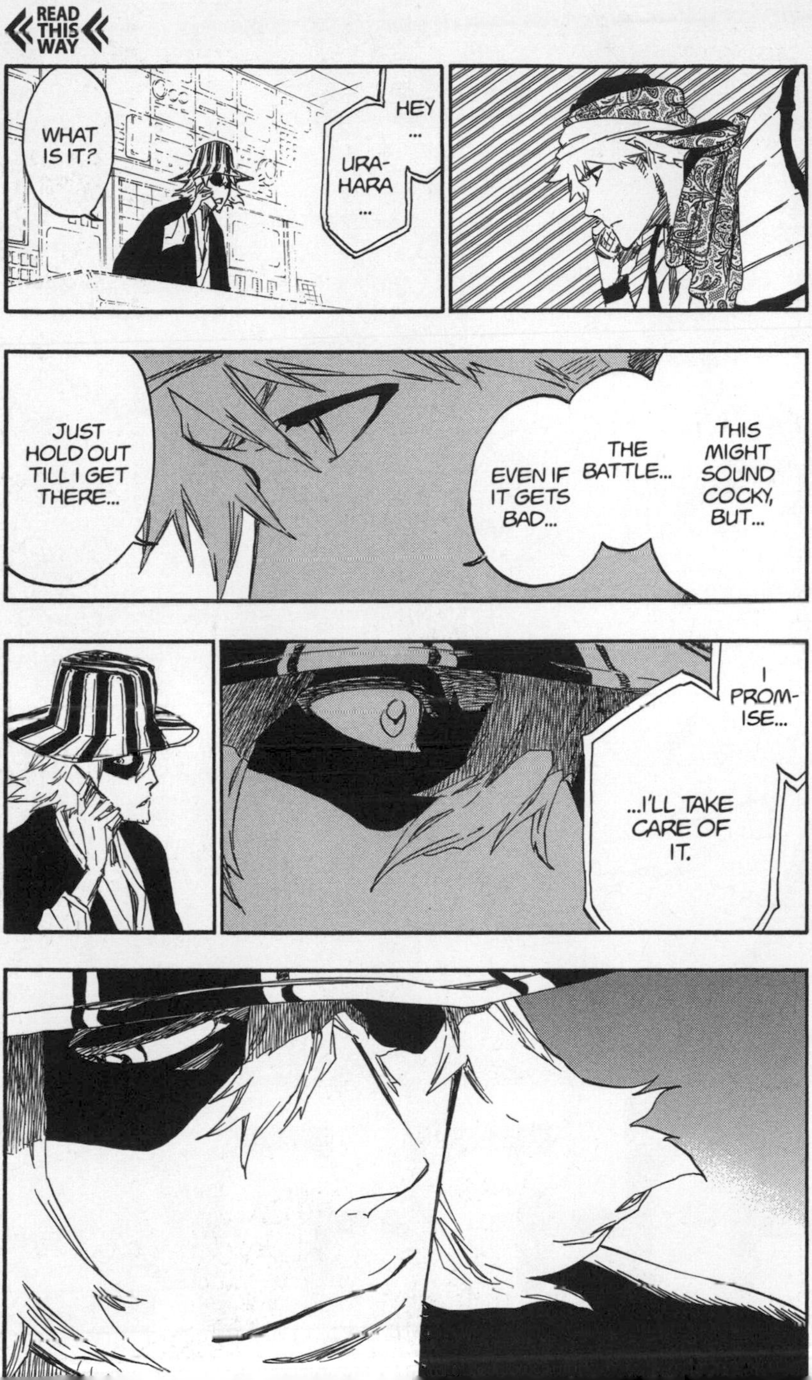
READ THIS WAY
HEY ... URA-HARA ...
WHAT IS IT?
THIS MIGHT SOUND COCKY, BUT...
THE BATTLE...
EVEN IF IT GETS BAD...
JUST HOLD OUT TILL I GET THERE...
I PROM-ISE...
...I'LL TAKE CARE OF IT.

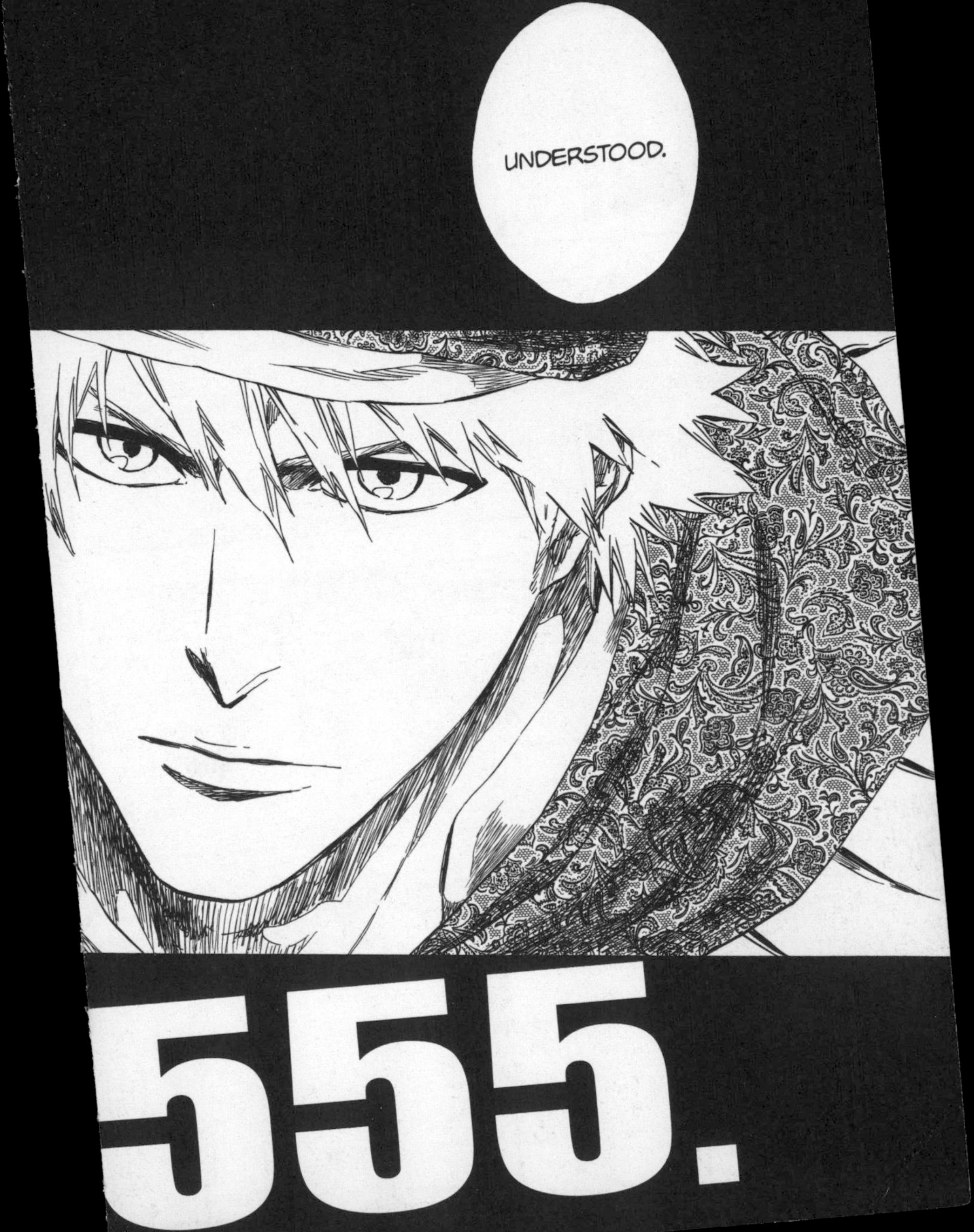
UNDERSTOOD.
555.

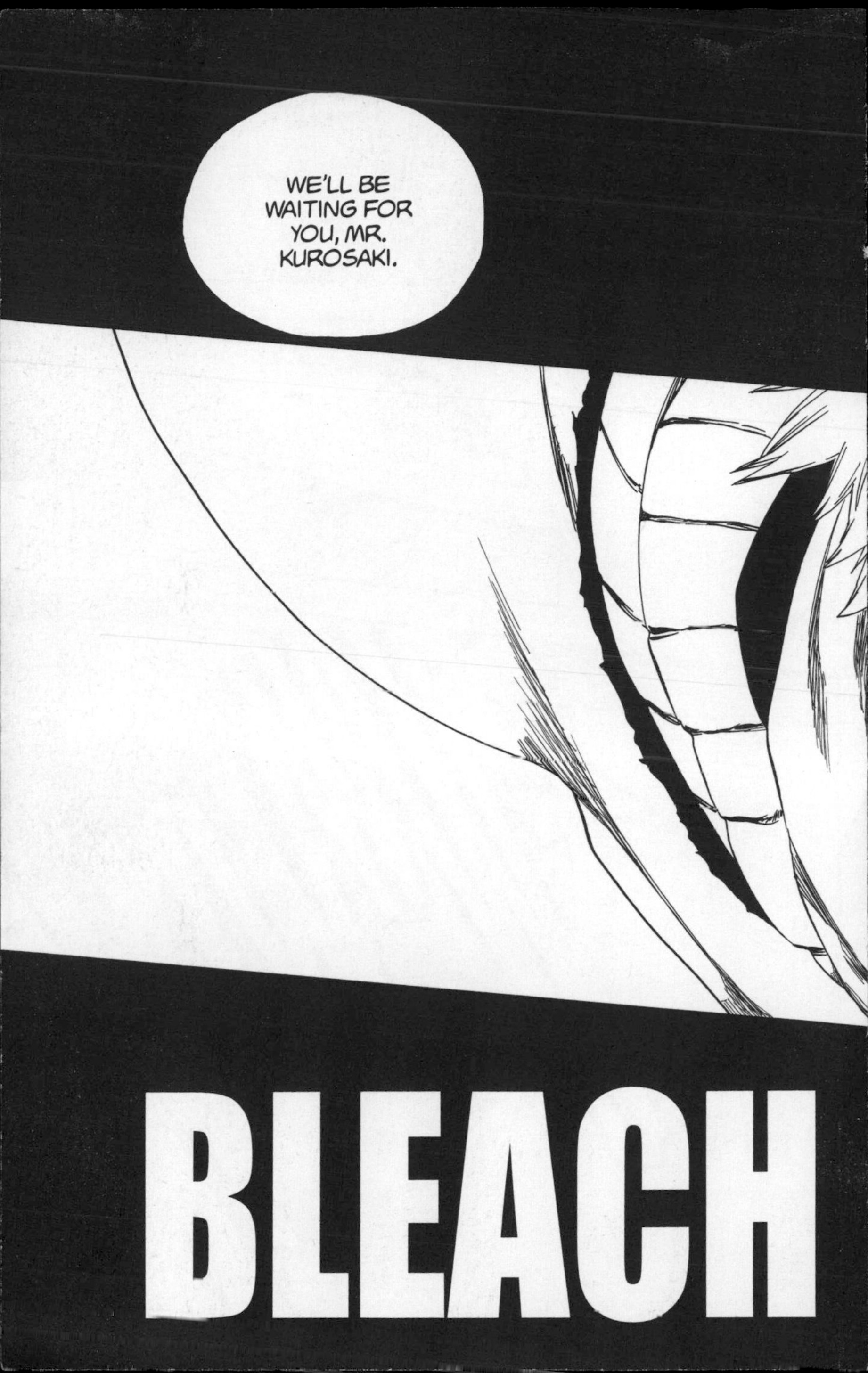
WE'LL BE WAITING FOR YOU, MR. KUROSAKI.
BLEACH

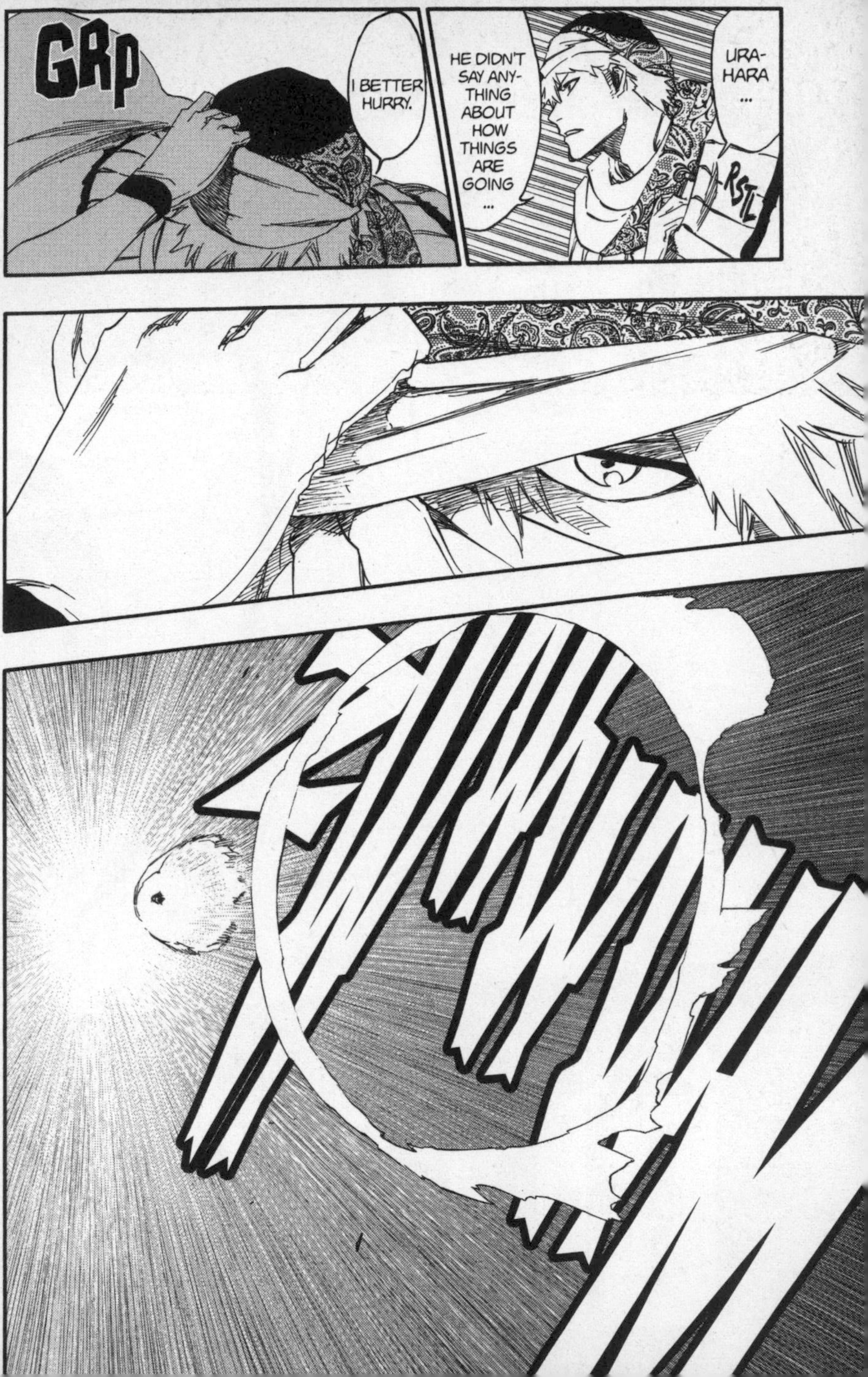
URA-HARA...
RSTL
HE DIDN'T SAY ANYTHING ABOUT HOW THINGS ARE GOING...
I BETTER HURRY.
GRP

THE HERO

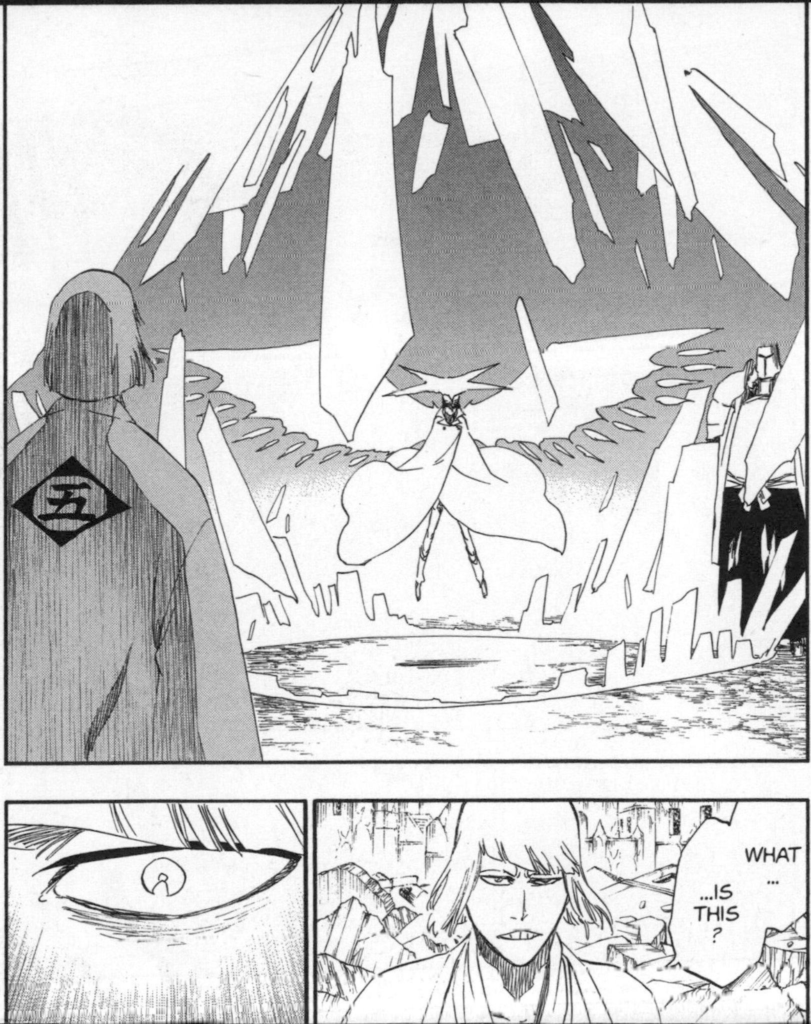
WHAT …
…IS THIS?

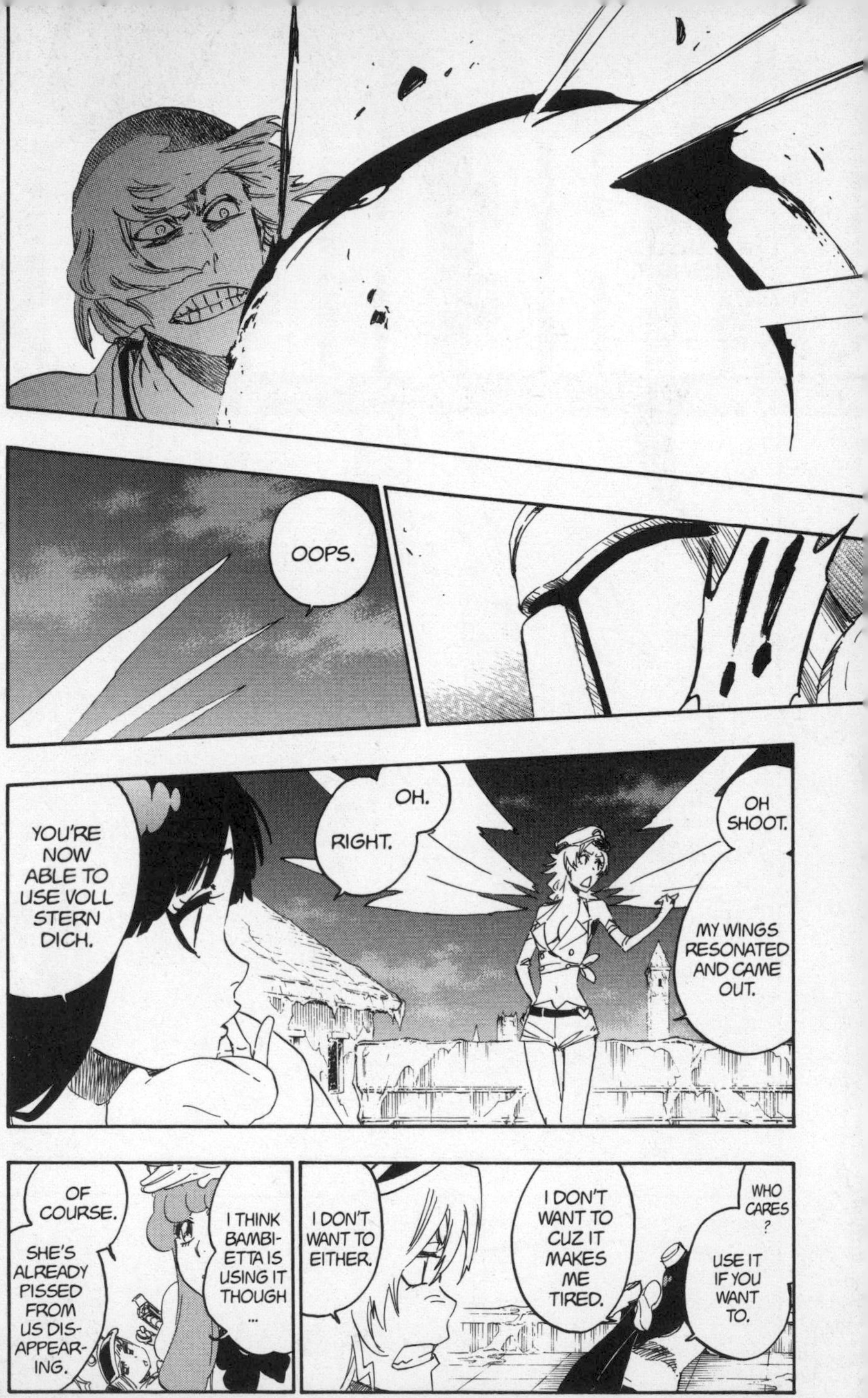
!!
OOPS.
OH SHOOT.
MY WINGS RESONATED AND CAME OUT.
OH.
RIGHT.
YOU'RE NOW ABLE TO USE VOLL STERN DICH.
WHO CARES?
USE IT IF YOU WANT TO.
I DON'T WANT TO CUZ IT MAKES ME TIRED.
I DON'T WANT TO EITHER.
I THINK BAMBI-ETTA IS USING IT THOUGH...
OF COURSE.
SHE'S ALREADY PISSED FROM US DIS-APPEAR-ING.

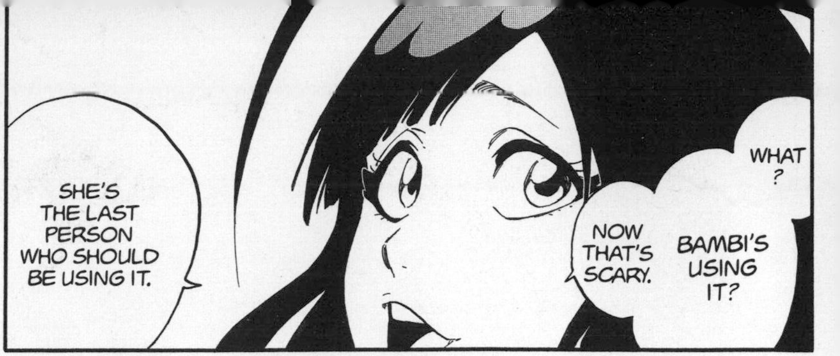
WHAT?
BAMBI'S USING IT?
NOW THAT'S SCARY.
SHE'S THE LAST PERSON WHO SHOULD BE USING IT.

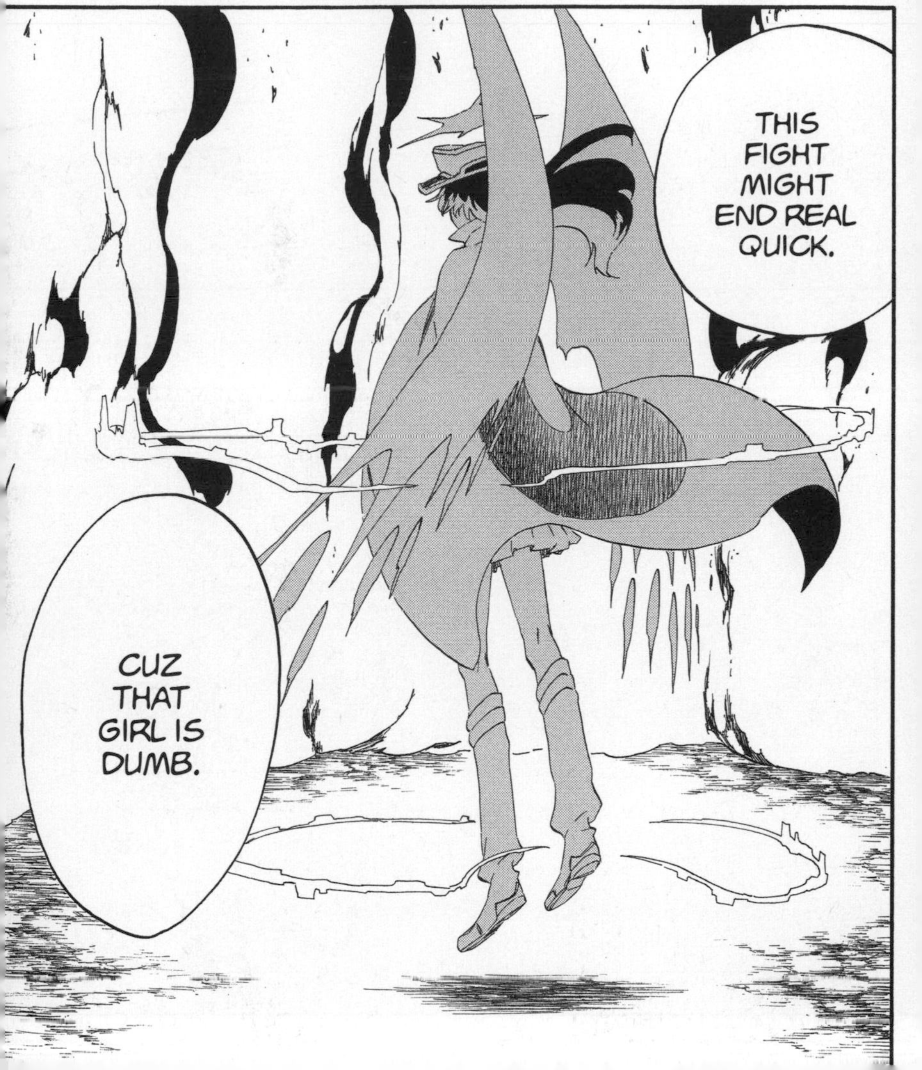
THIS FIGHT MIGHT END REAL QUICK.
CUZ THAT GIRL IS DUMB.

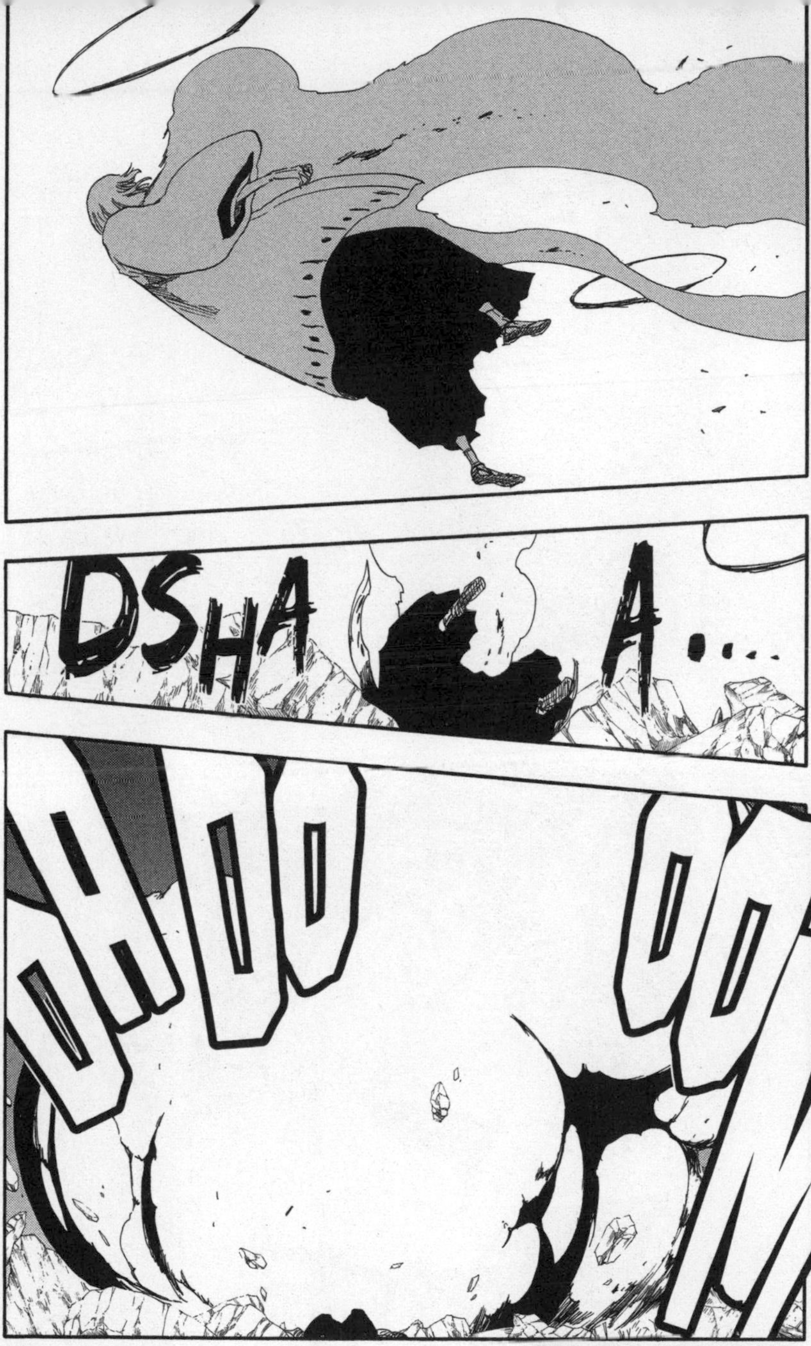
DSHA
A...
GADOOOOM

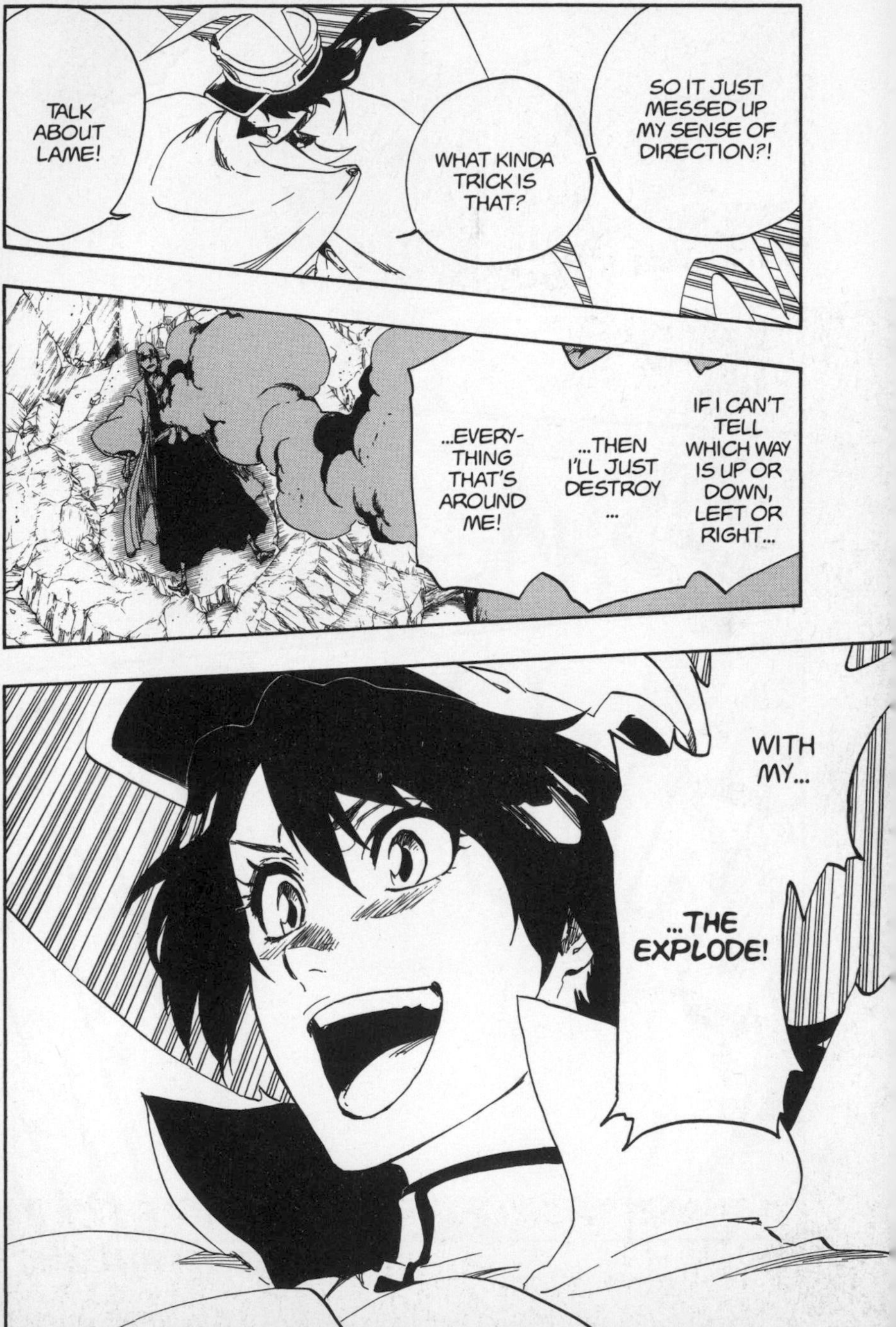
SO IT JUST MESSED UP MY SENSE OF DIRECTION?!
WHAT KINDA TRICK IS THAT?
TALK ABOUT LAME!
IF I CAN'T TELL WHICH WAY IS UP OR DOWN, LEFT OR RIGHT...
...THEN I'LL JUST DESTROY ...
...EVERY-THING THAT'S AROUND ME!
WITH MY...
...THE EXPLODE!

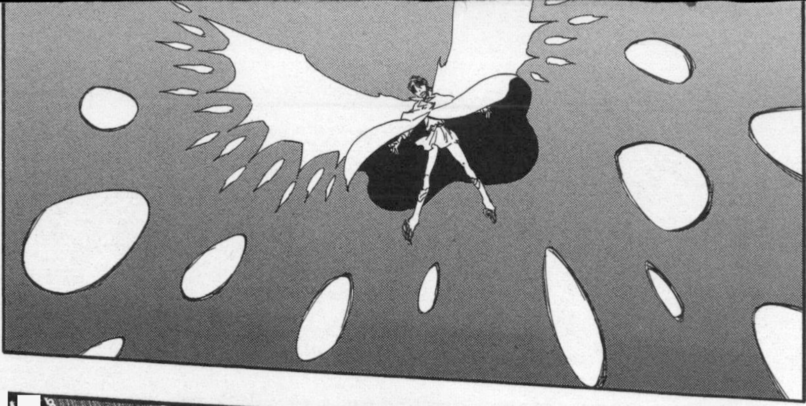

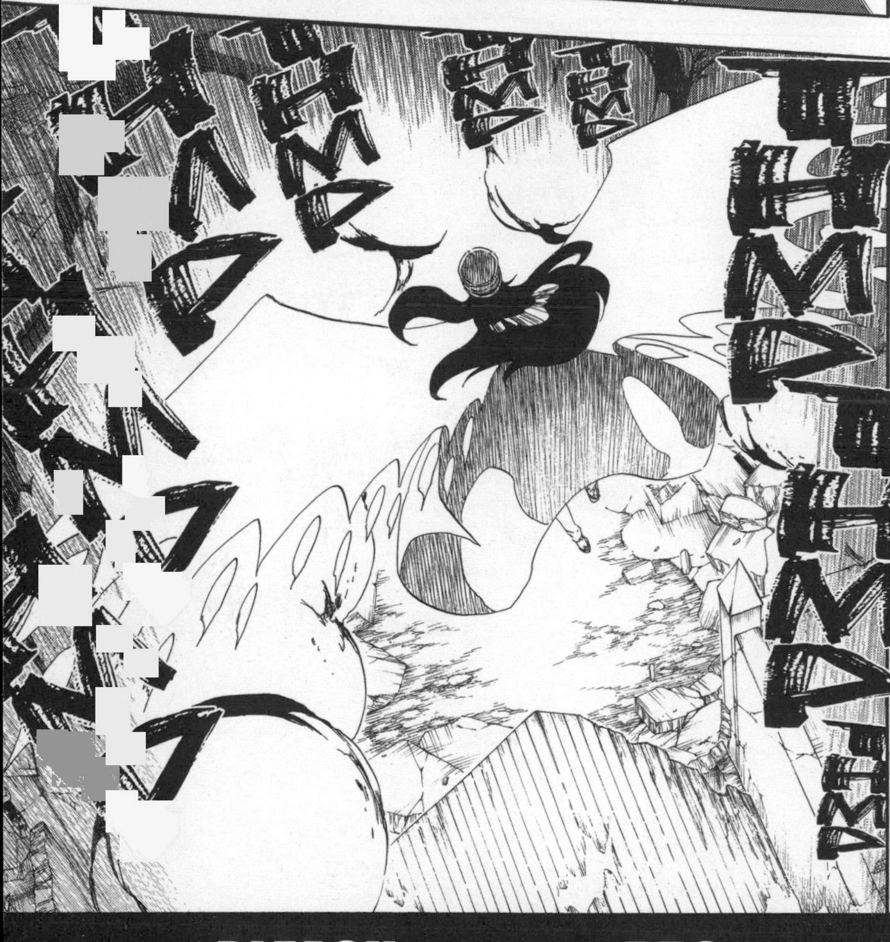

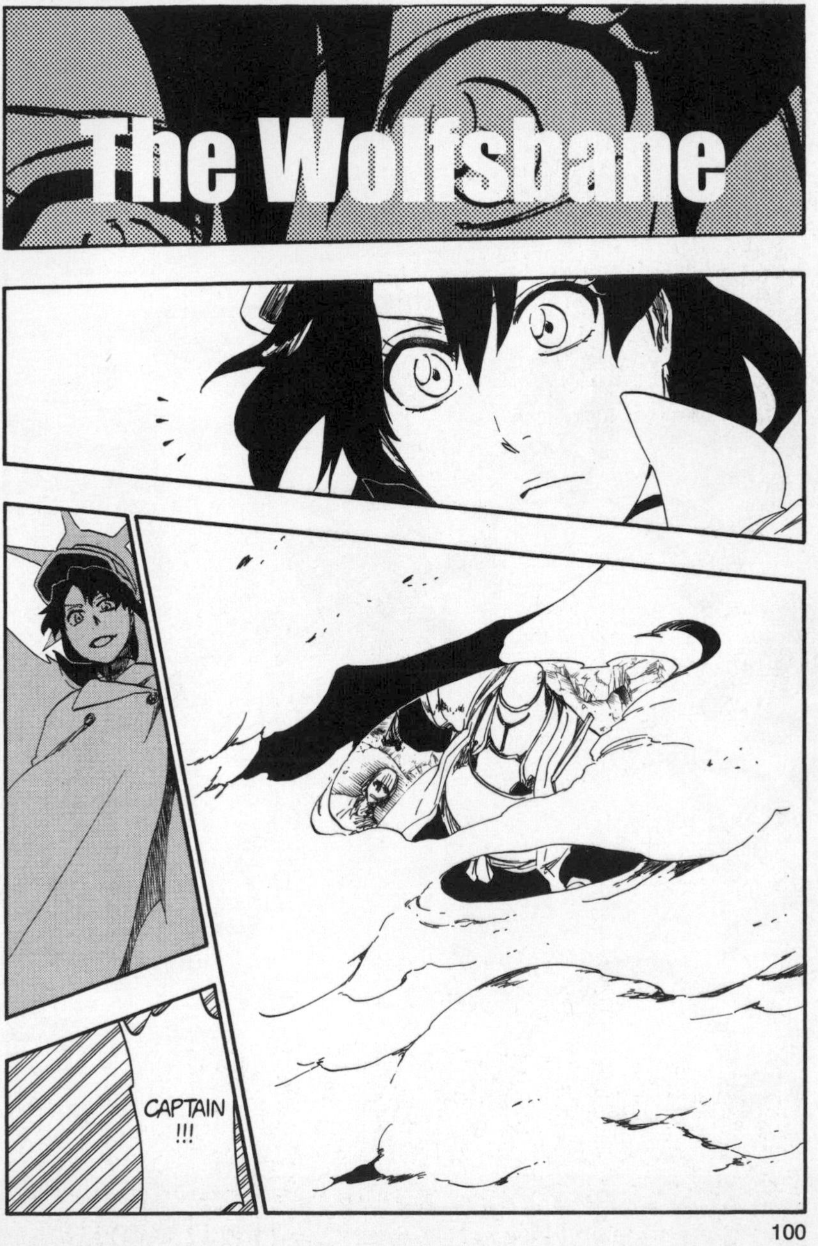
The Wolfsbane
CAPTAIN !!!

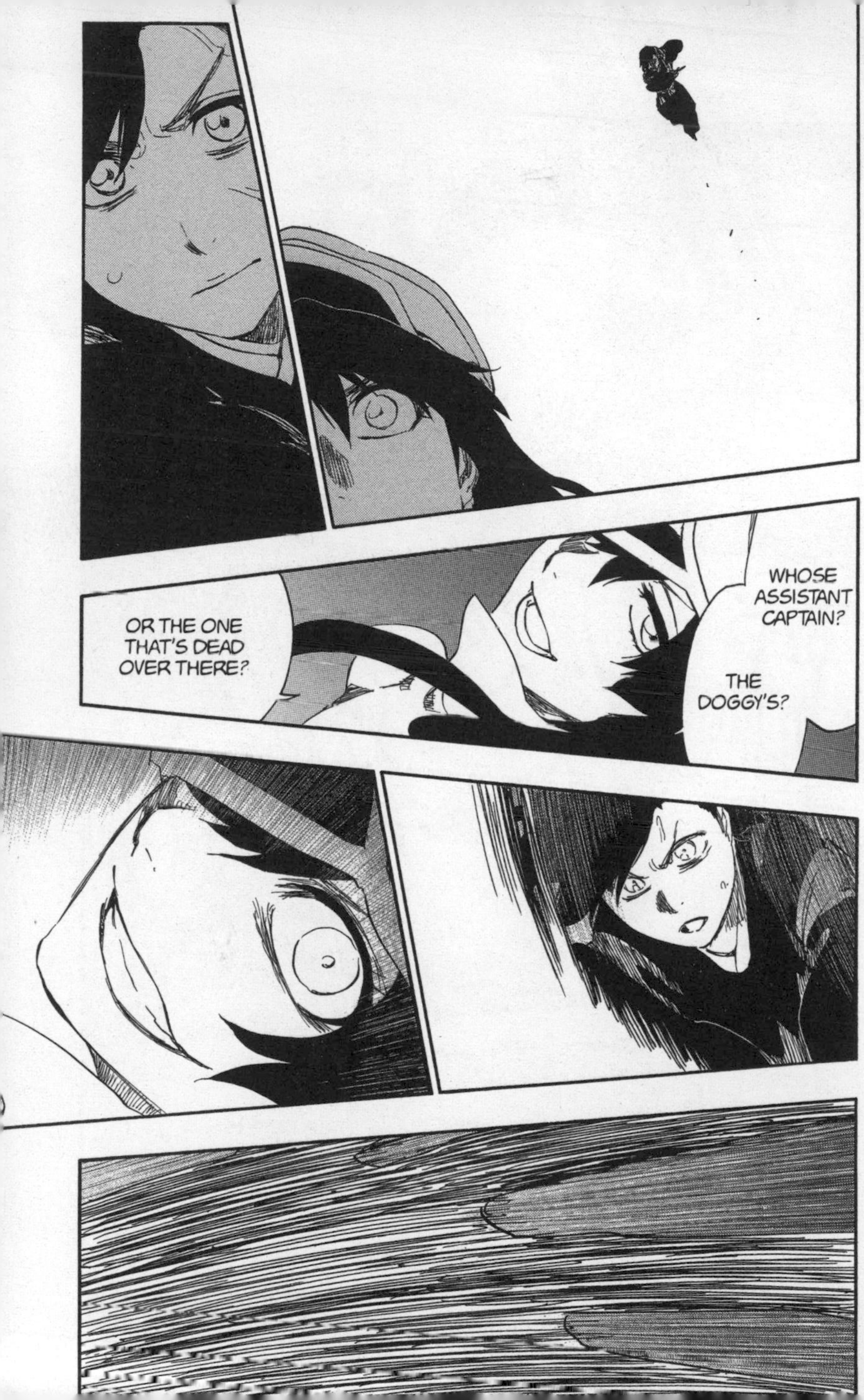
WHOSE ASSISTANT CAPTAIN?
THE DOGGY'S?
OR THE ONE THAT'S DEAD OVER THERE?

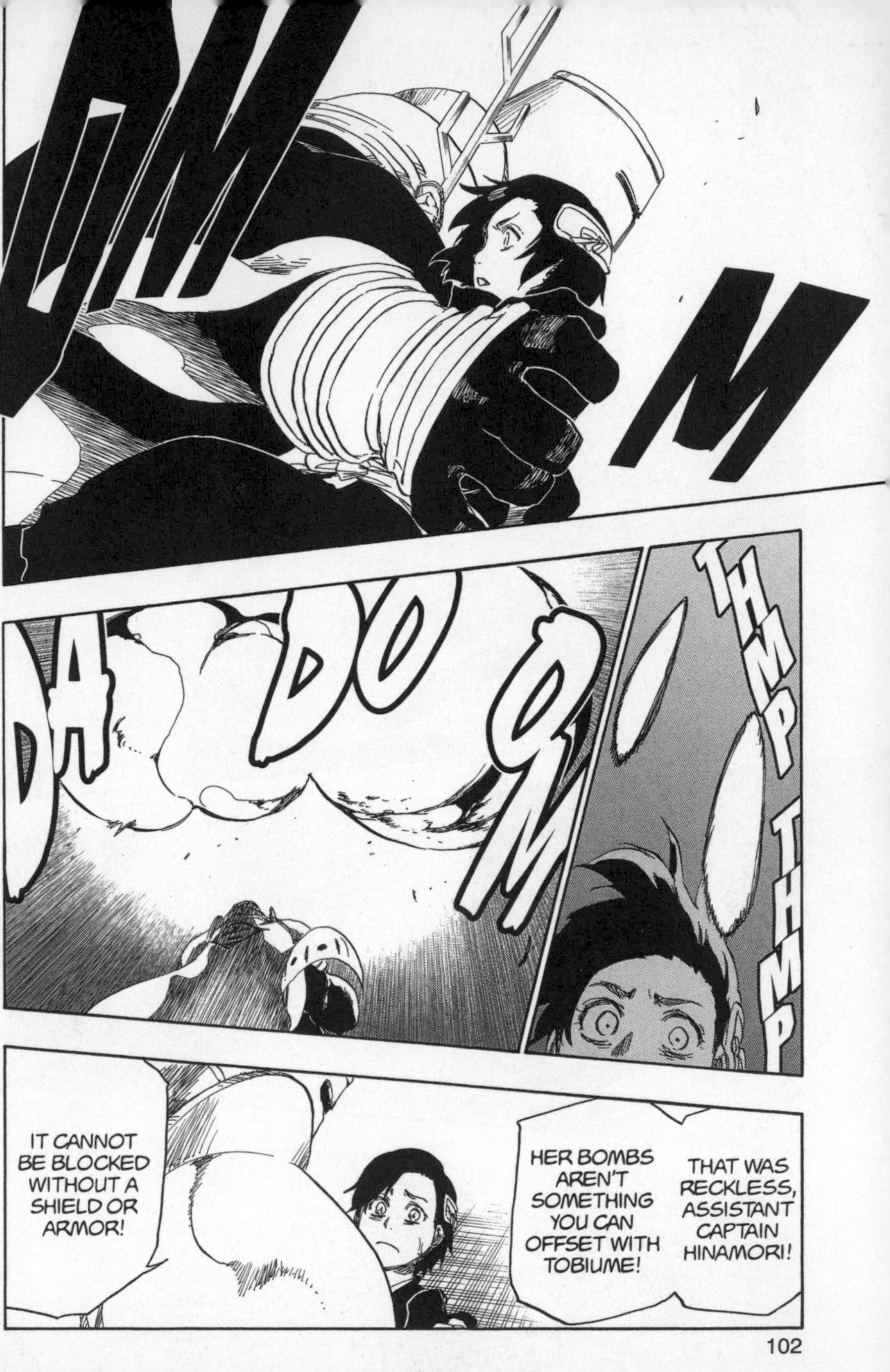
THMP THMP
DADOOM
THAT WAS RECKLESS, ASSISTANT CAPTAIN HINAMORI!
HER BOMBS AREN'T SOMETHING YOU CAN OFFSET WITH TOBIUME!
IT CANNOT BE BLOCKED WITHOUT A SHIELD OR ARMOR!

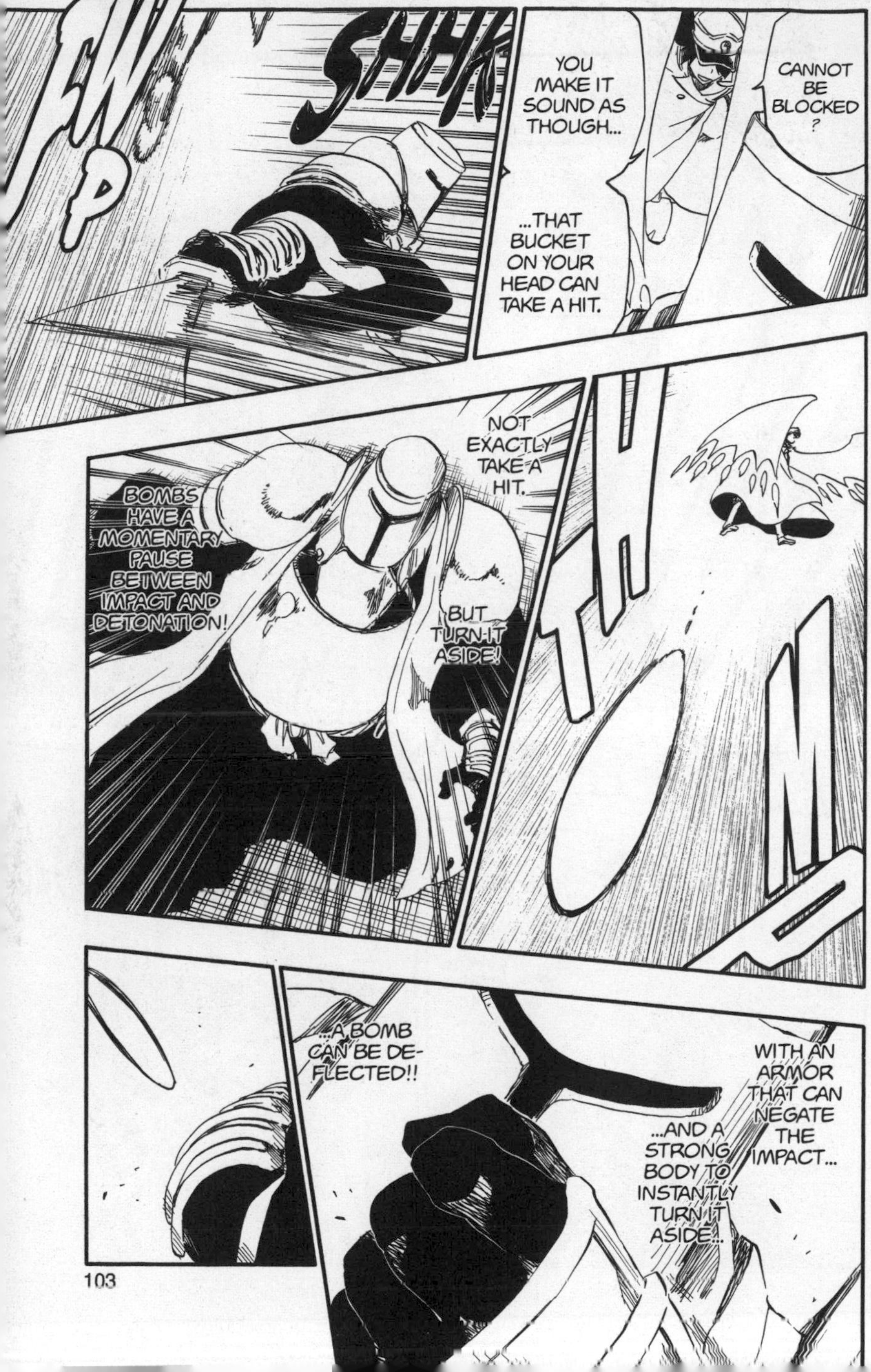
CANNOT BE BLOCKED ?
YOU MAKE IT SOUND AS THOUGH...
...THAT BUCKET ON YOUR HEAD CAN TAKE A HIT.
FWP
SHHK
THOMP
NOT EXACTLY TAKE A HIT.
BUT TURN IT ASIDE!
BOMBS HAVE A MOMENTARY PAUSE BETWEEN IMPACT AND DETONATION!
WITH AN ARMOR THAT CAN NEGATE THE IMPACT...
...AND A STRONG BODY TO INSTANTLY TURN IT ASIDE...
...A BOMB CAN BE DE-FLECTED!!

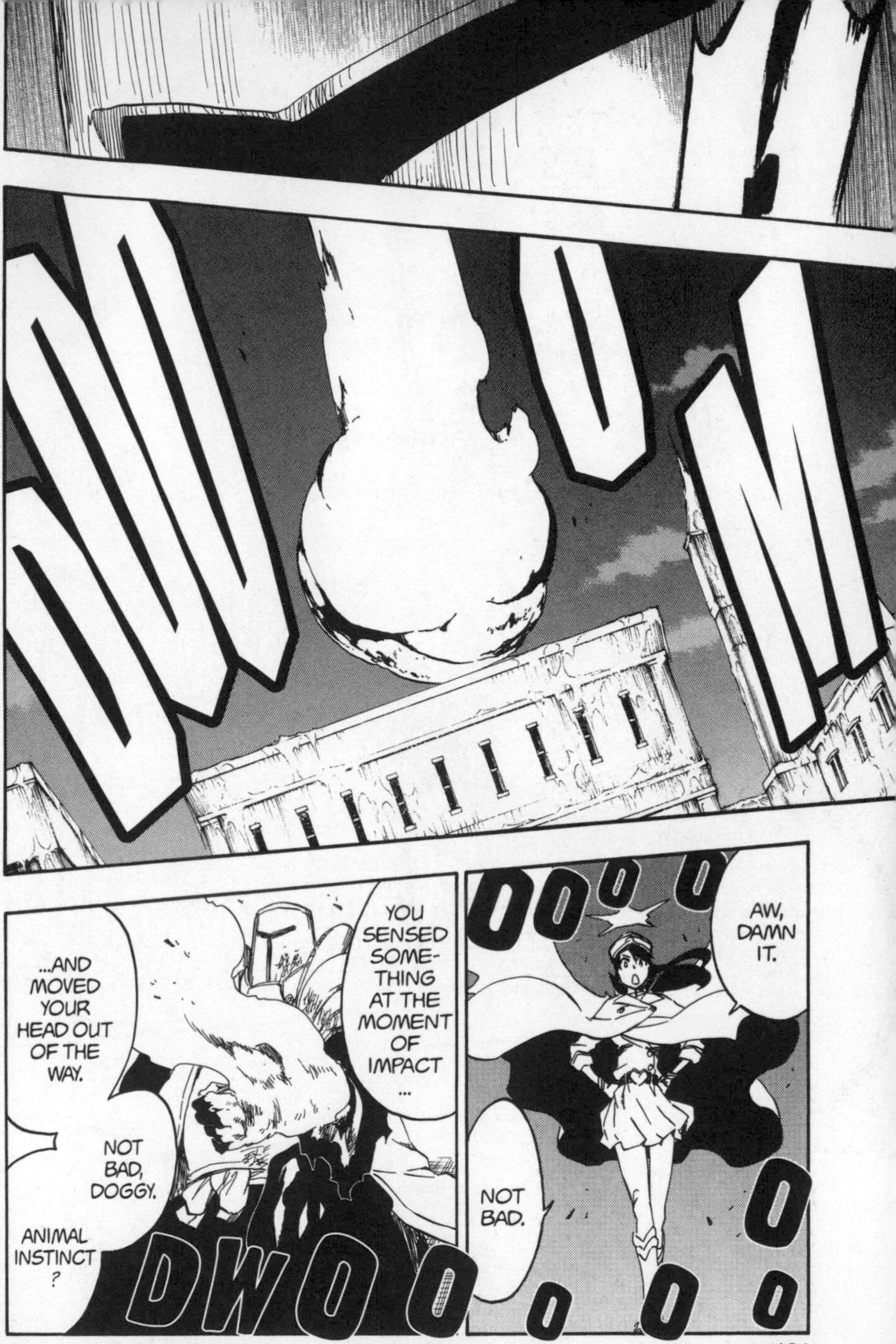
AW, DAMN IT.
DOOOO
NOT BAD.
OOOO
YOU SENSED SOME-THING AT THE MOMENT OF IMPACT ...
...AND MOVED YOUR HEAD OUT OF THE WAY.
NOT BAD, DOGGY.
ANIMAL INSTINCT ?
DWOO

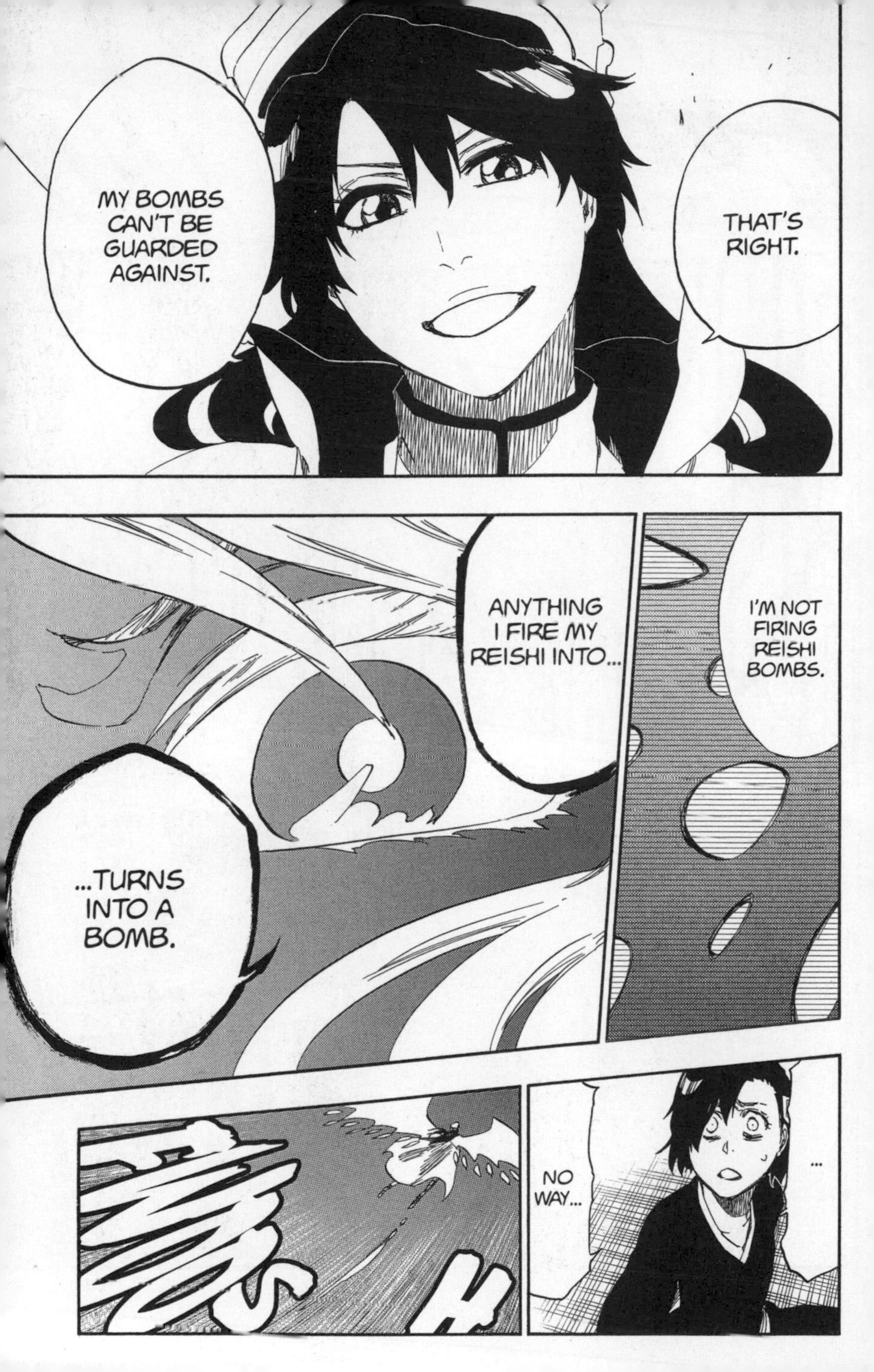
THAT'S RIGHT.
MY BOMBS CAN'T BE GUARDED AGAINST.
I'M NOT FIRING REISHI BOMBS.
ANYTHING I FIRE MY REISHI INTO...
...TURNS INTO A BOMB.
...
NO WAY...

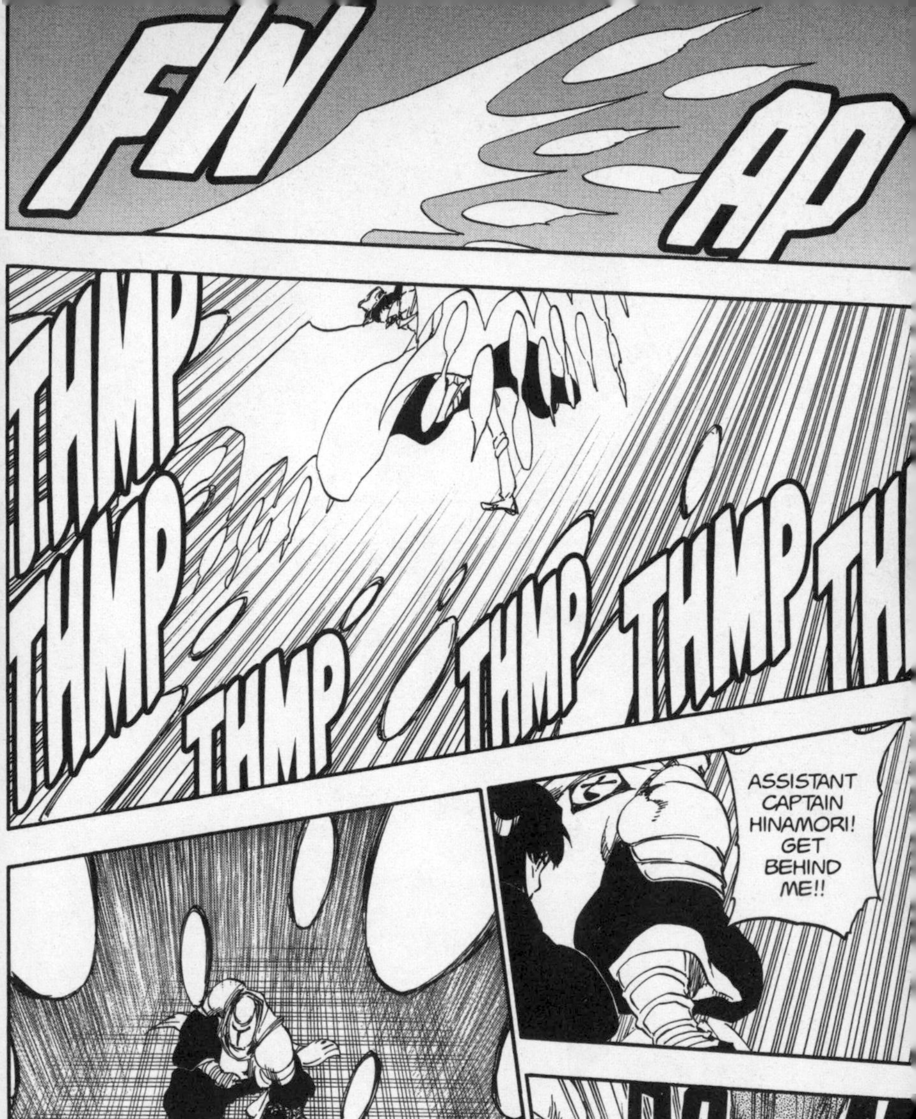
FWAP
THMP
THMP
THMP
THMP
THMP
ASSISTANT CAPTAIN HINAMORI! GET BEHIND ME!!
BAM

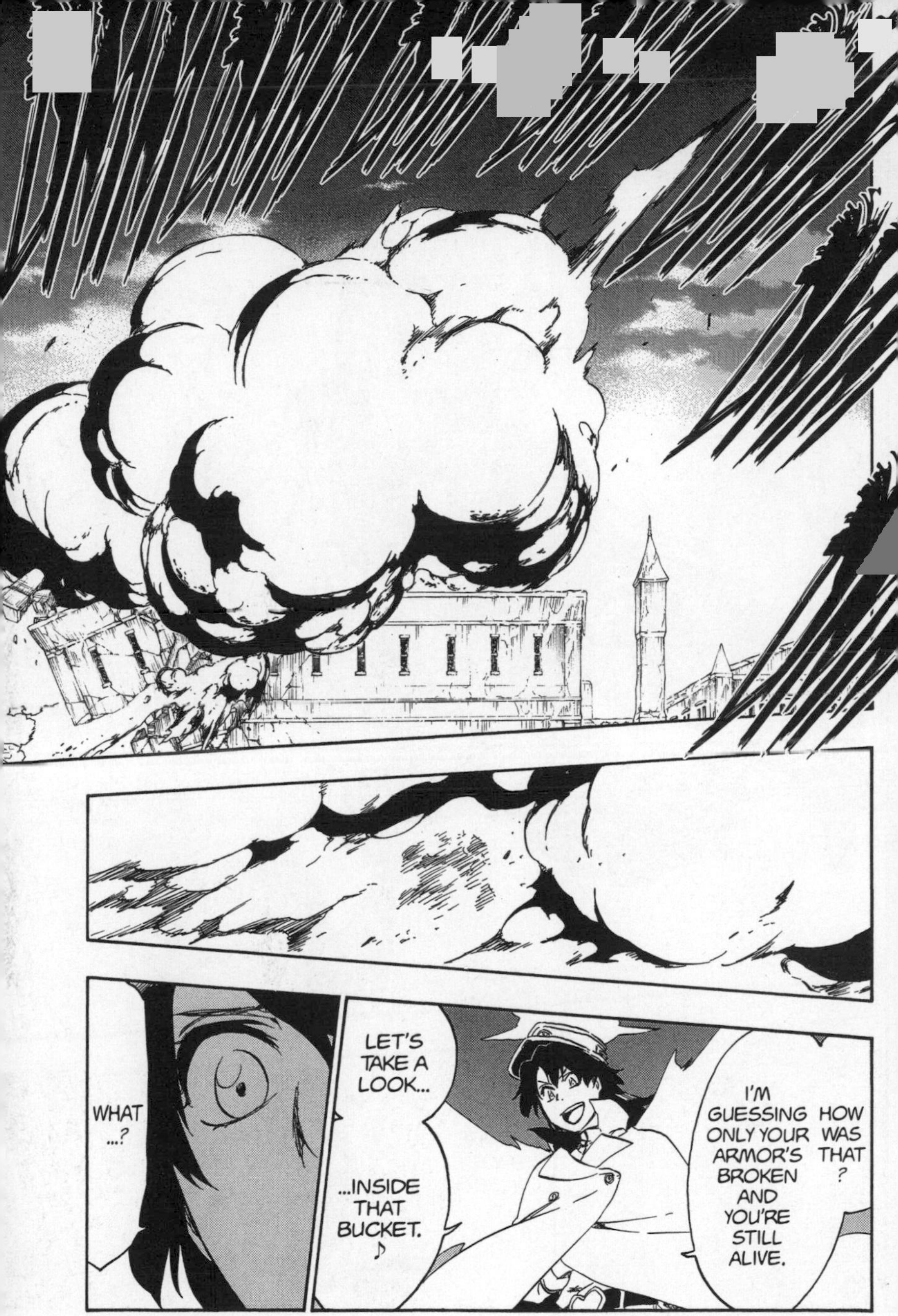
HOW WAS THAT?
I'M GUESSING ONLY YOUR ARMOR'S BROKEN AND YOU'RE STILL ALIVE.
LET'S TAKE A LOOK...
...INSIDE THAT BUCKET. ♪
WHAT...?

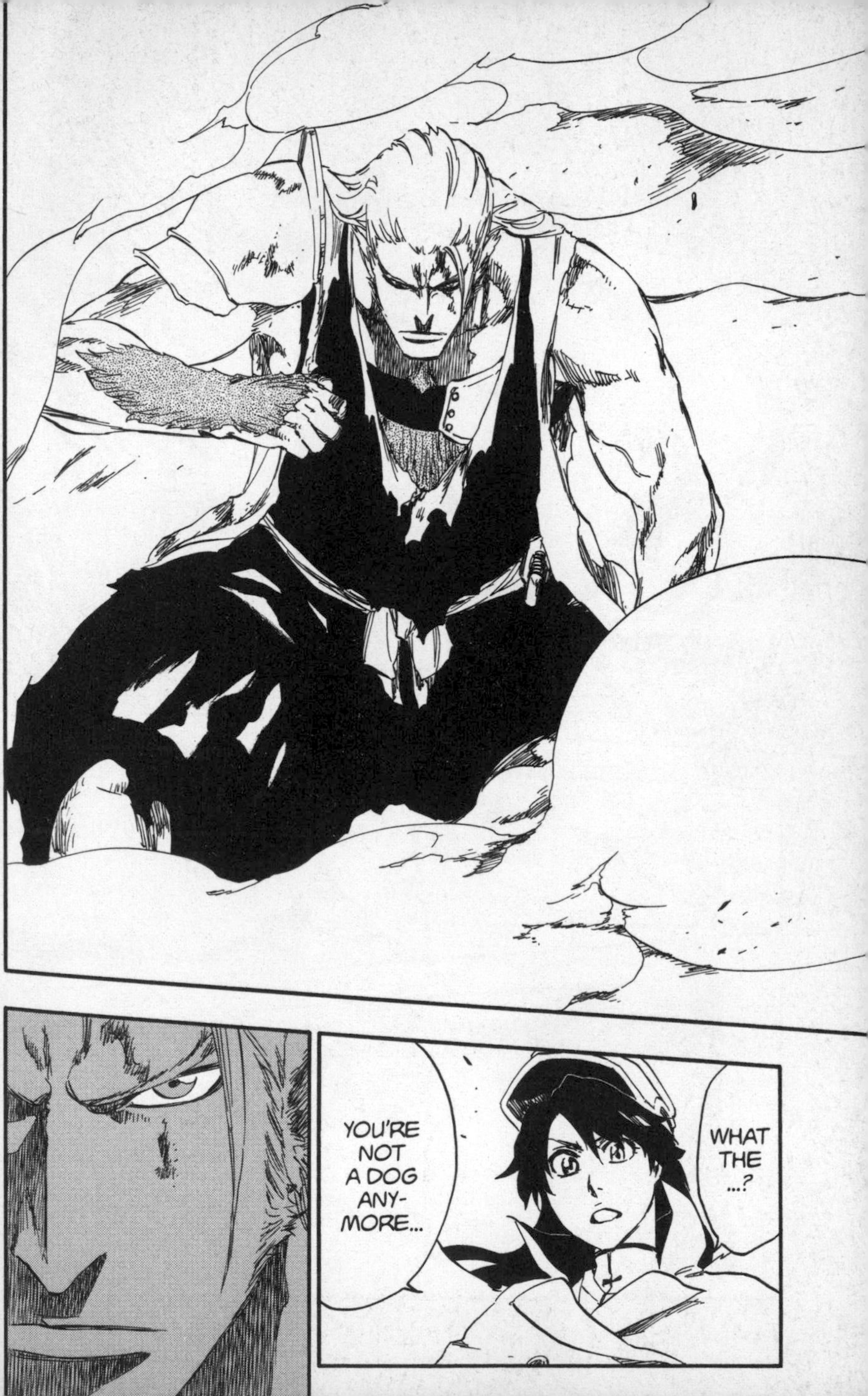
WHAT THE ...?
YOU'RE NOT A DOG ANY-MORE...

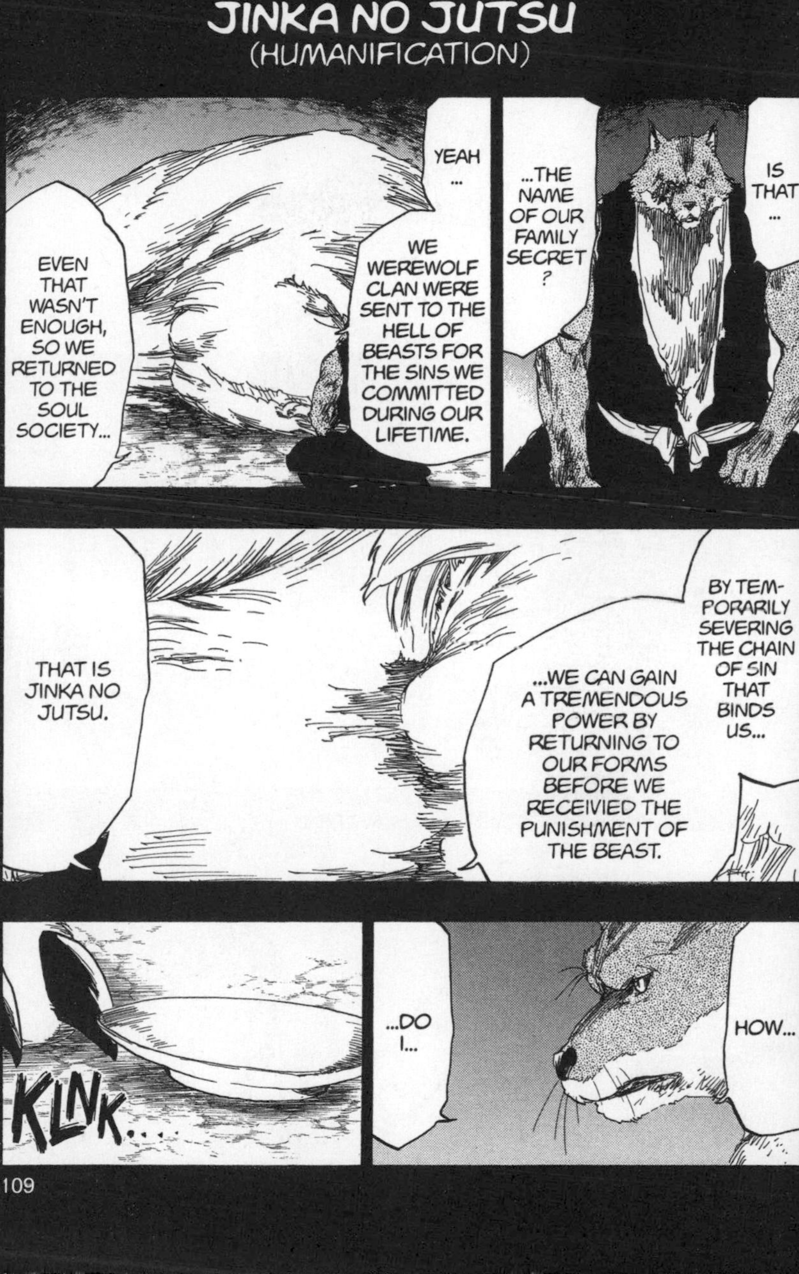
JINKA NO JUTSU
(HUMANIFICATION)
IS THAT ...
...THE NAME OF OUR FAMILY SECRET ?
YEAH ...
WE WEREWOLF CLAN WERE SENT TO THE HELL OF BEASTS FOR THE SINS WE COMMITTED DURING OUR LIFETIME.
EVEN THAT WASN'T ENOUGH, SO WE RETURNED TO THE SOUL SOCIETY...
BY TEM-PORARILY SEVERING THE CHAIN OF SIN THAT BINDS US...
...WE CAN GAIN A TREMENDOUS POWER BY RETURNING TO OUR FORMS BEFORE WE RECEIVIED THE PUNISHMENT OF THE BEAST.
THAT IS JINKA NO JUTSU.
HOW...
...DO I...
KLNK....

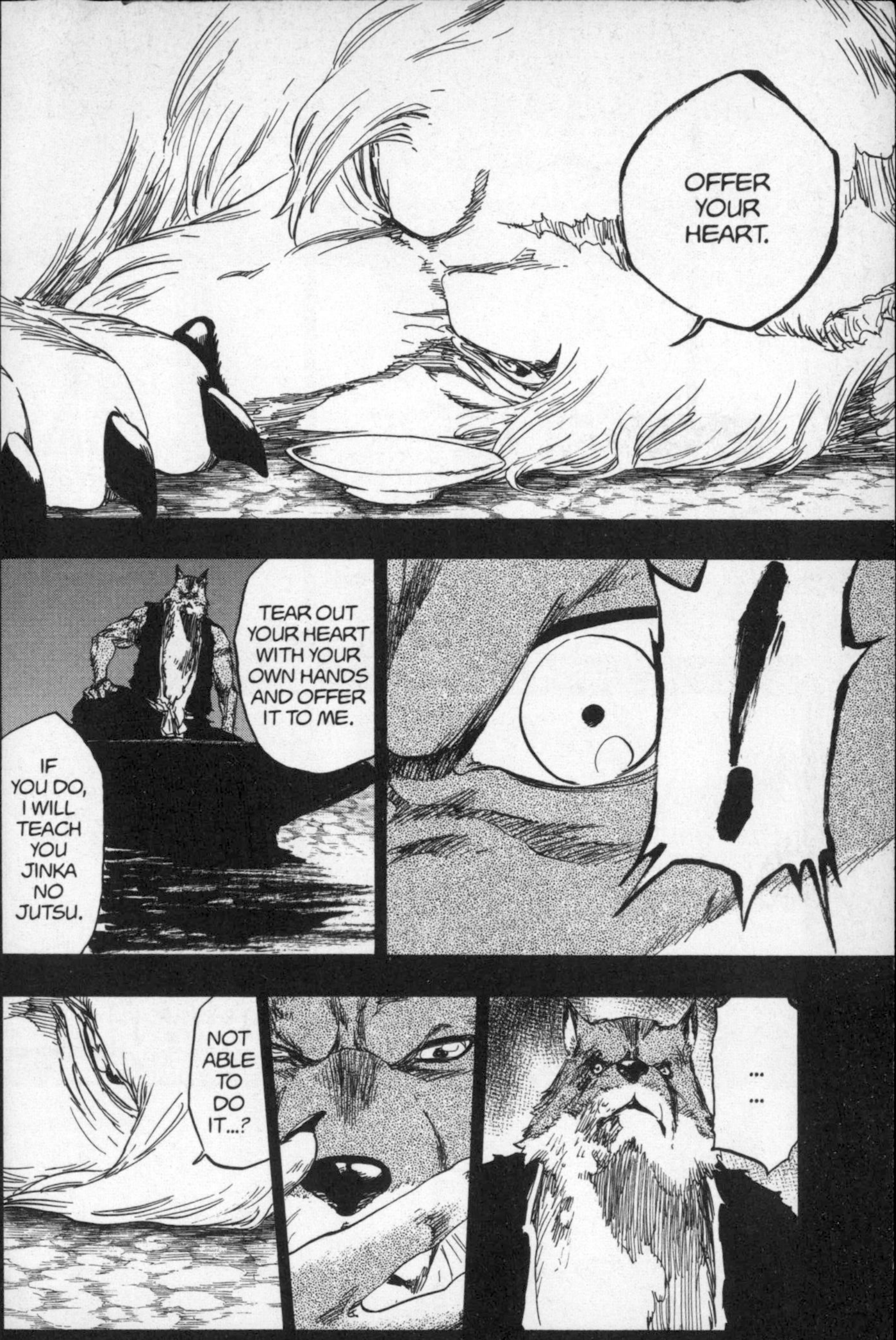
OFFER YOUR HEART.
!
TEAR OUT YOUR HEART WITH YOUR OWN HANDS AND OFFER IT TO ME.
IF YOU DO, I WILL TEACH YOU JINKA NO JUTSU.
...
...
NOT ABLE TO DO IT...?

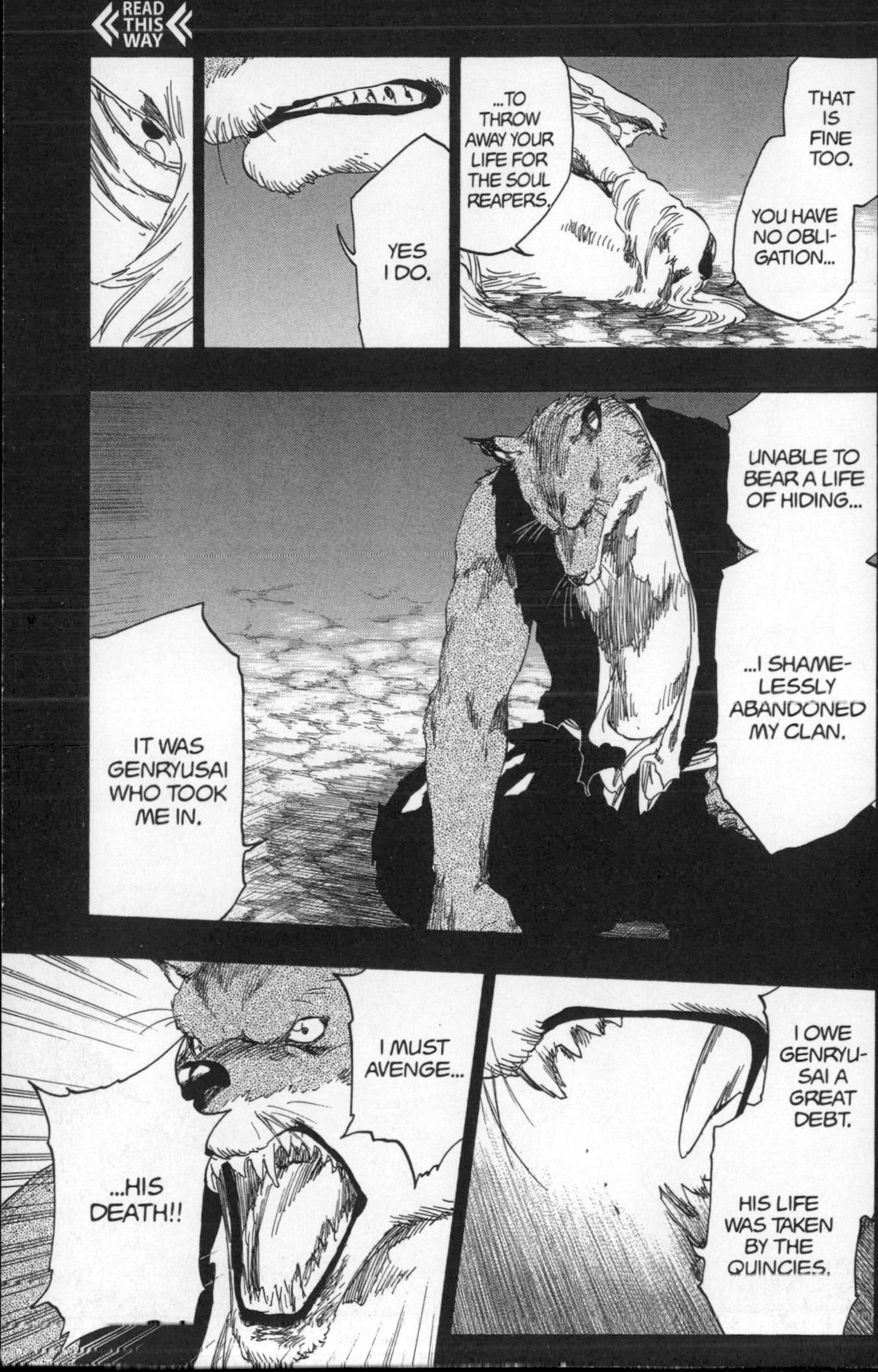
READ THIS WAY
THAT IS FINE TOO.
YOU HAVE NO OBLIGATION...
...TO THROW AWAY YOUR LIFE FOR THE SOUL REAPERS.
YES I DO.
UNABLE TO BEAR A LIFE OF HIDING...
...I SHAMELESSLY ABANDONED MY CLAN.
IT WAS GENRYUSAI WHO TOOK ME IN.
I OWE GENRYUSAI A GREAT DEBT.
HIS LIFE WAS TAKEN BY THE QUINCIES.
I MUST AVENGE...
...HIS DEATH!!

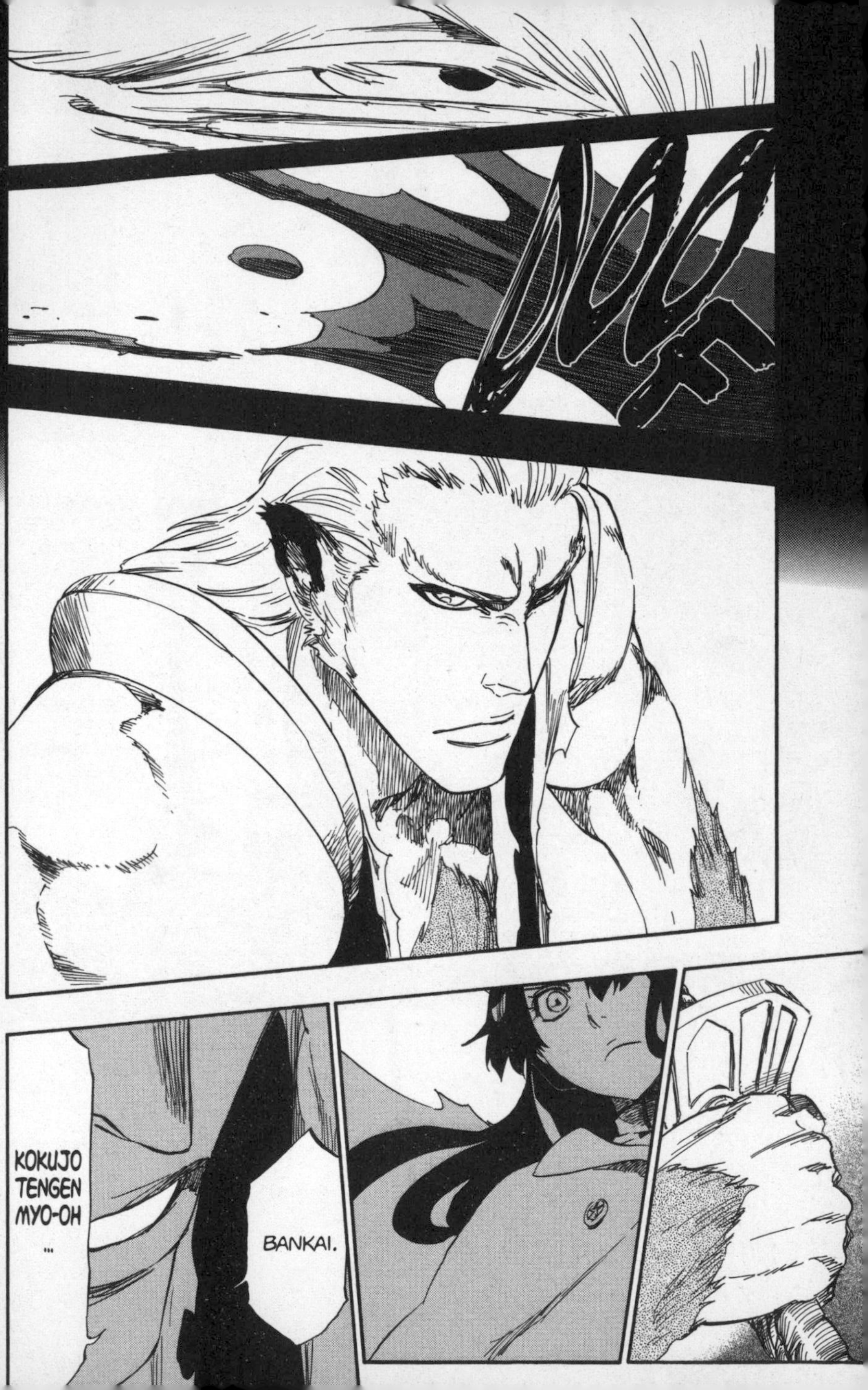
BANKAI.
KOKUJO TENGEN MYO-OH ...

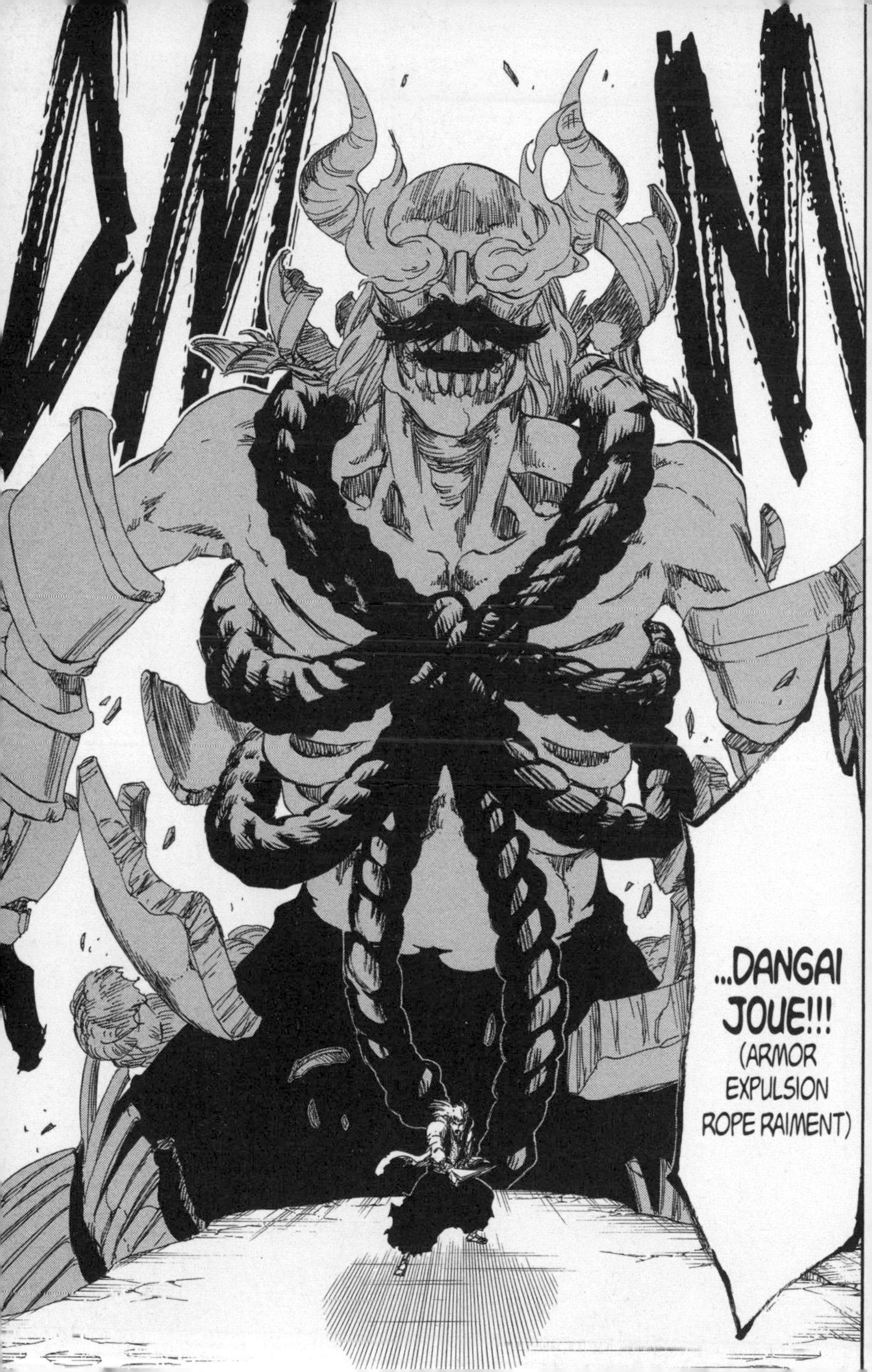
...DANGAI JOUE!!!
(ARMOR EXPULSION ROPE RAIMENT)

The Xplode

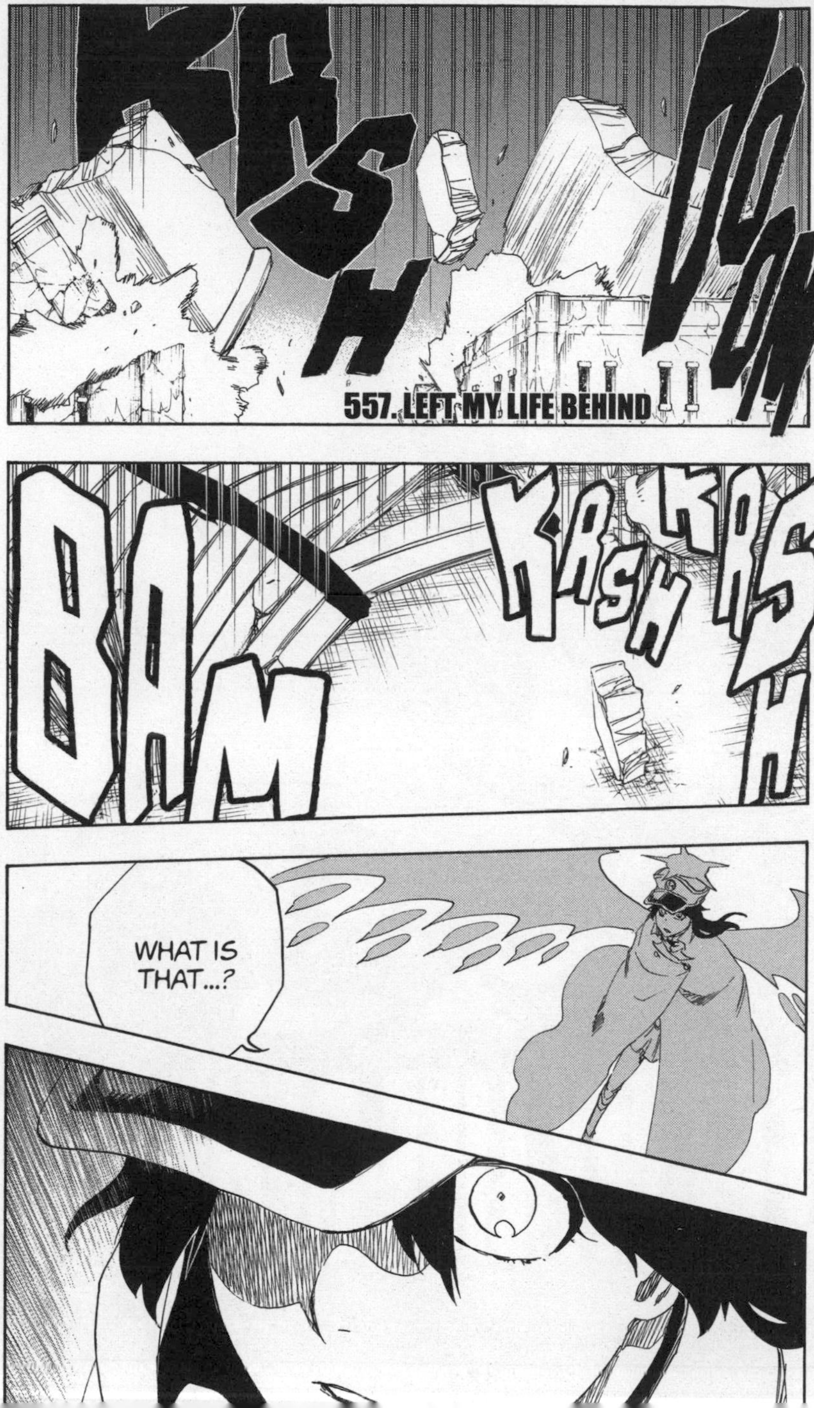
DOOM
KRASH
557. LEFT MY LIFE BEHIND
KRASH
KASH
BAM
WHAT IS THAT...?

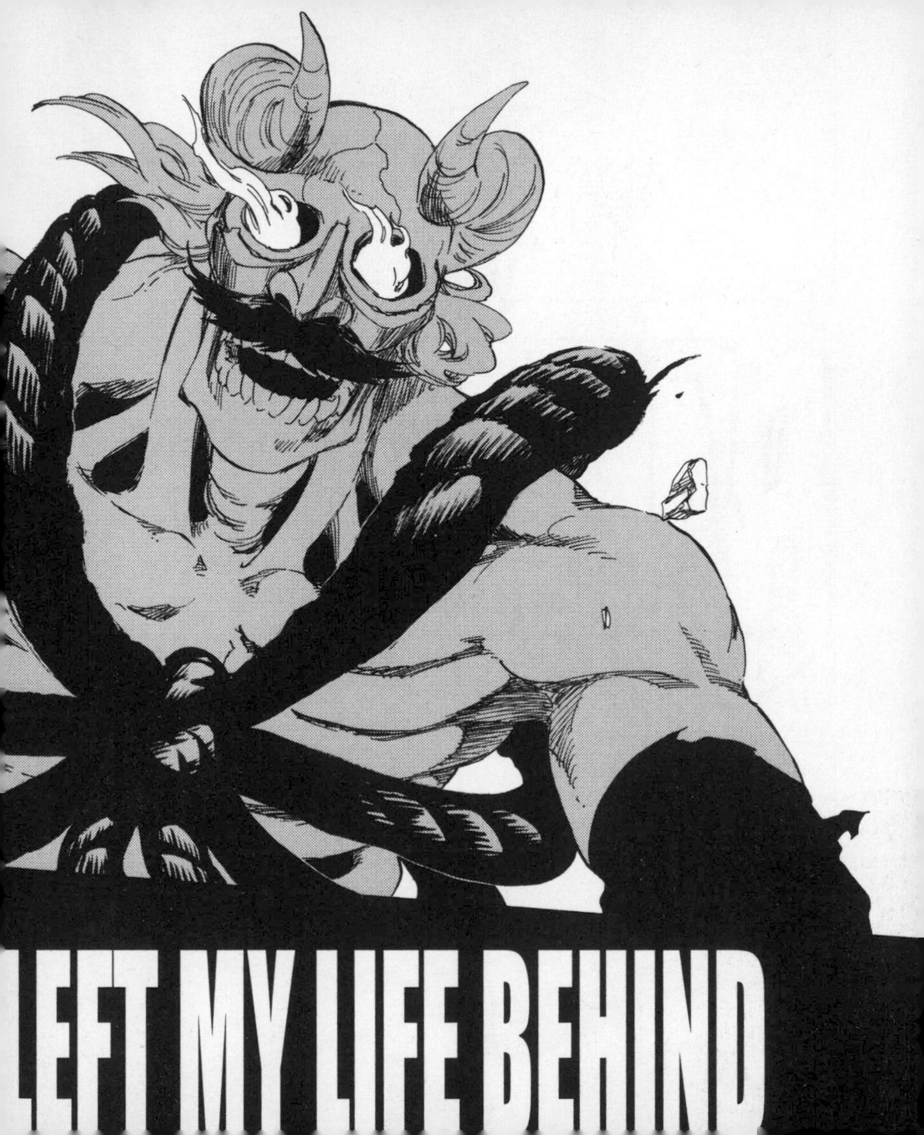
LEFT MY LIFE BEHIND

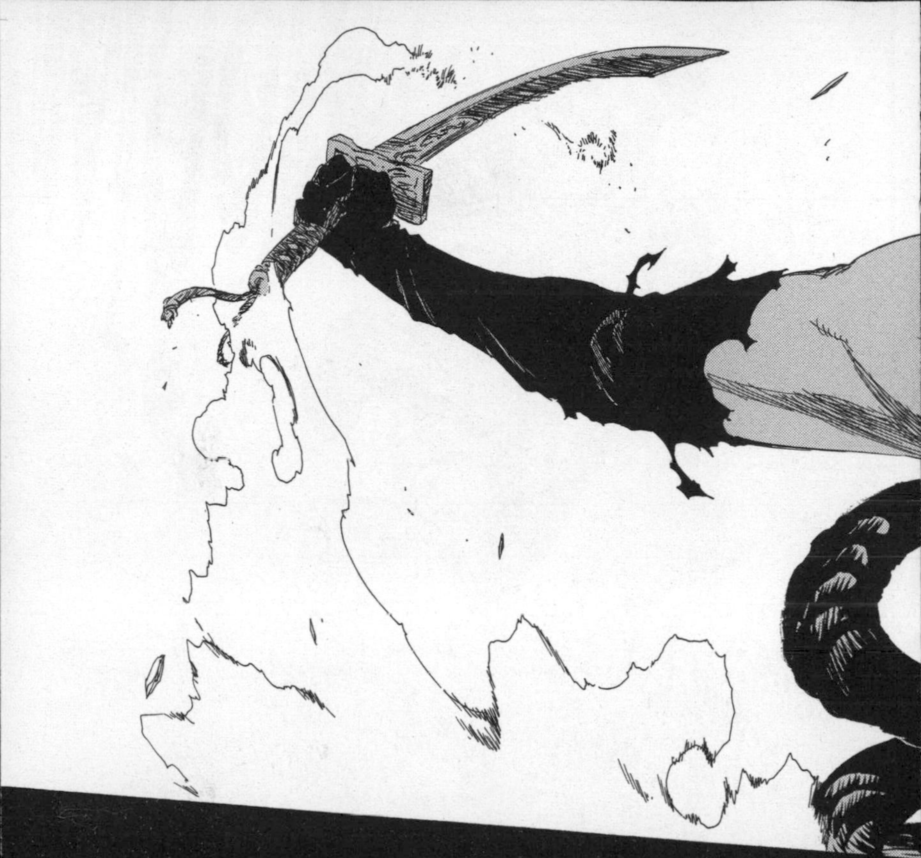

BLEACH 557.

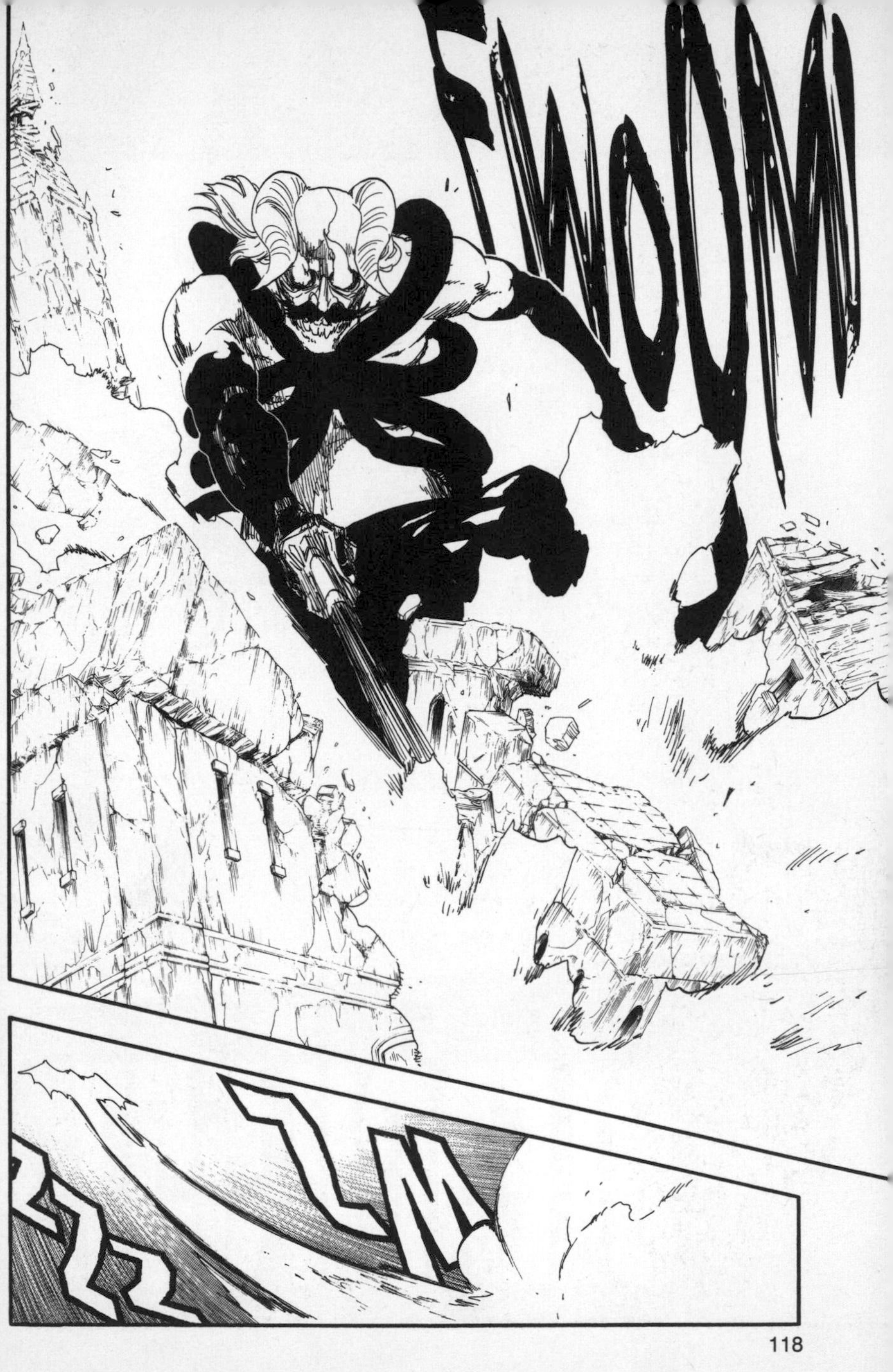
FWOOM

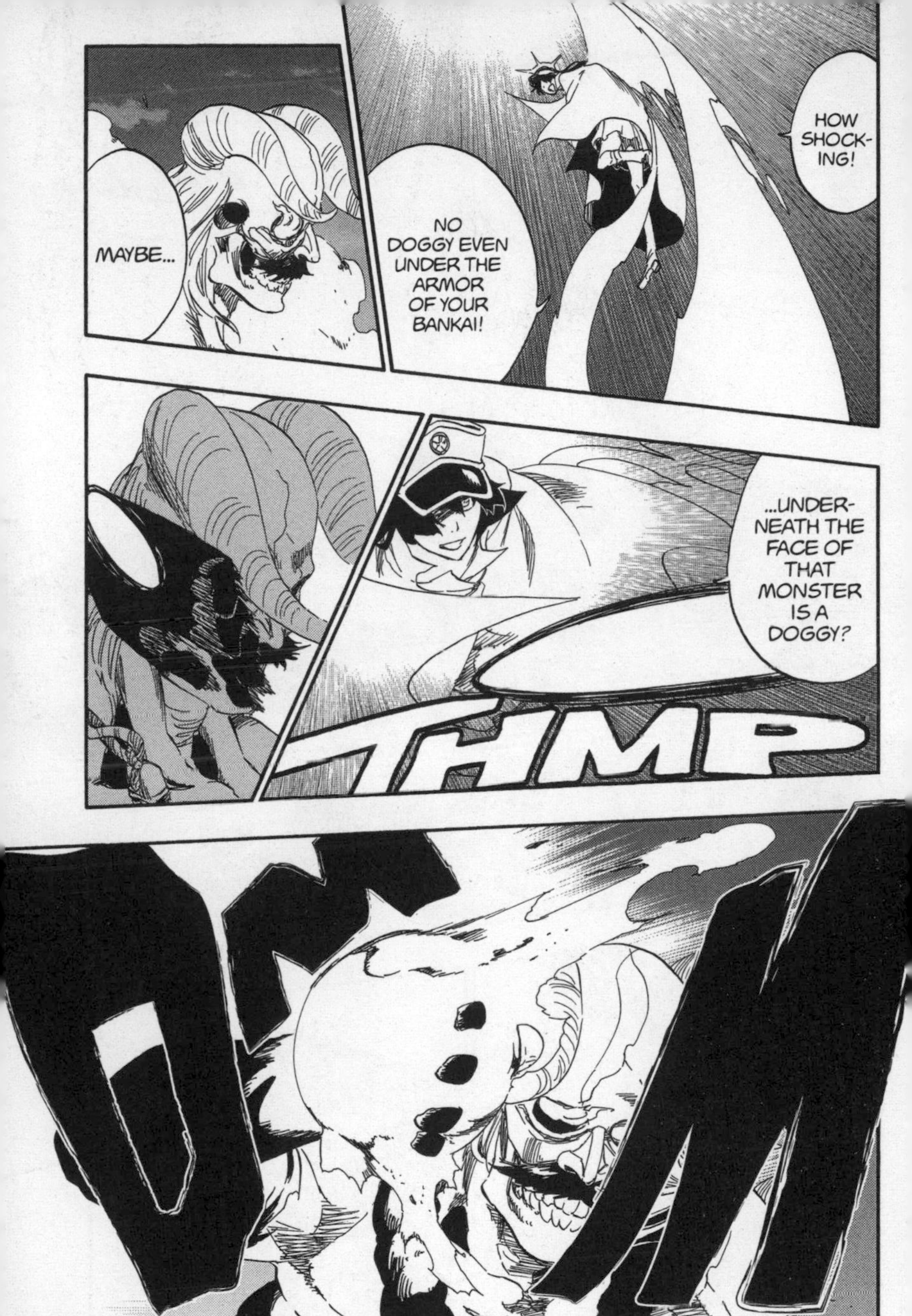
HOW SHOCKING!
NO DOGGY EVEN UNDER THE ARMOR OF YOUR BANKAI!
MAYBE...
...UNDERNEATH THE FACE OF THAT MONSTER IS A DOGGY?
THMP

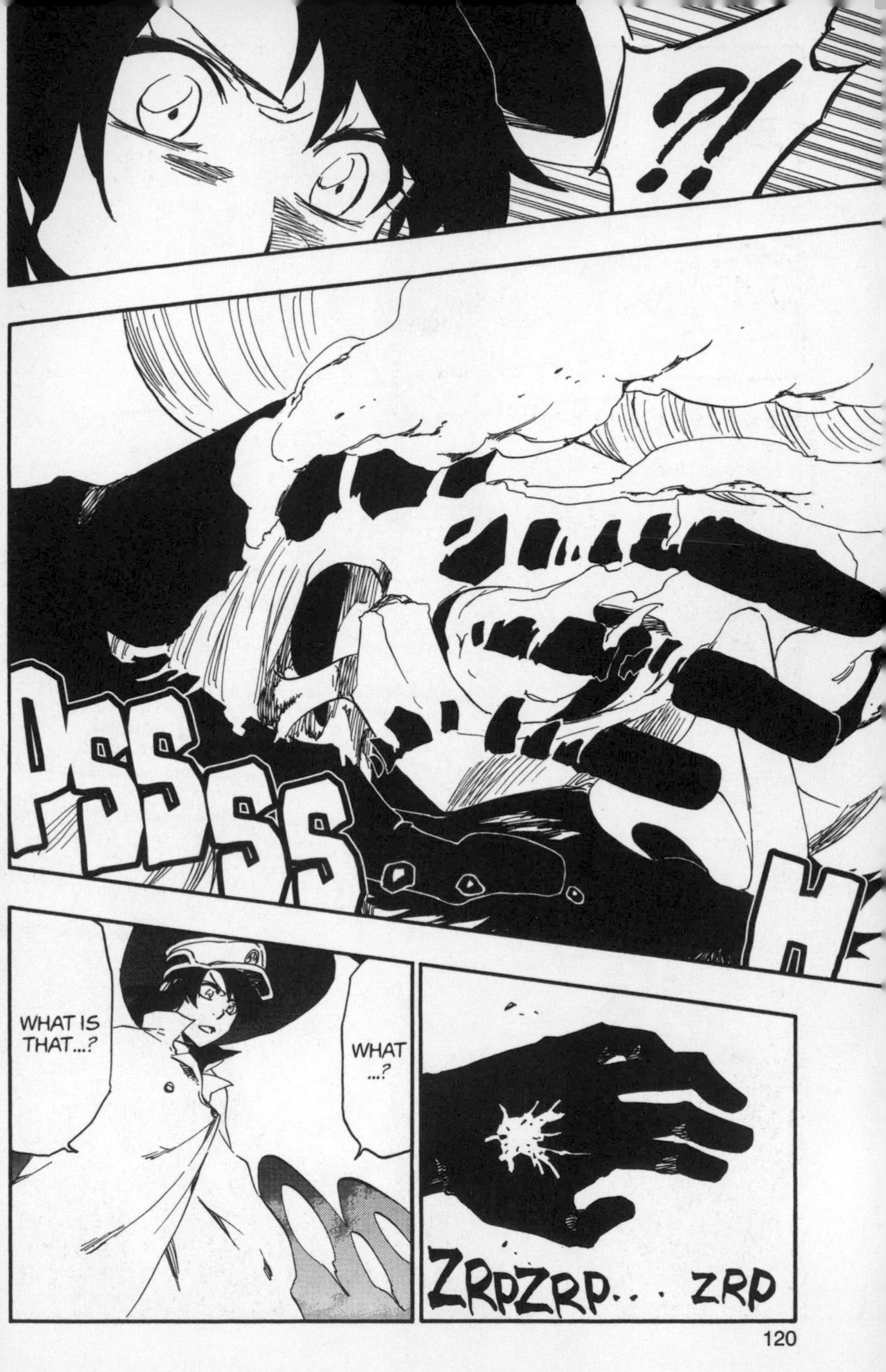
?!
HSSSS
ZRPZRP... ZRP
WHAT ...?
WHAT IS THAT...?

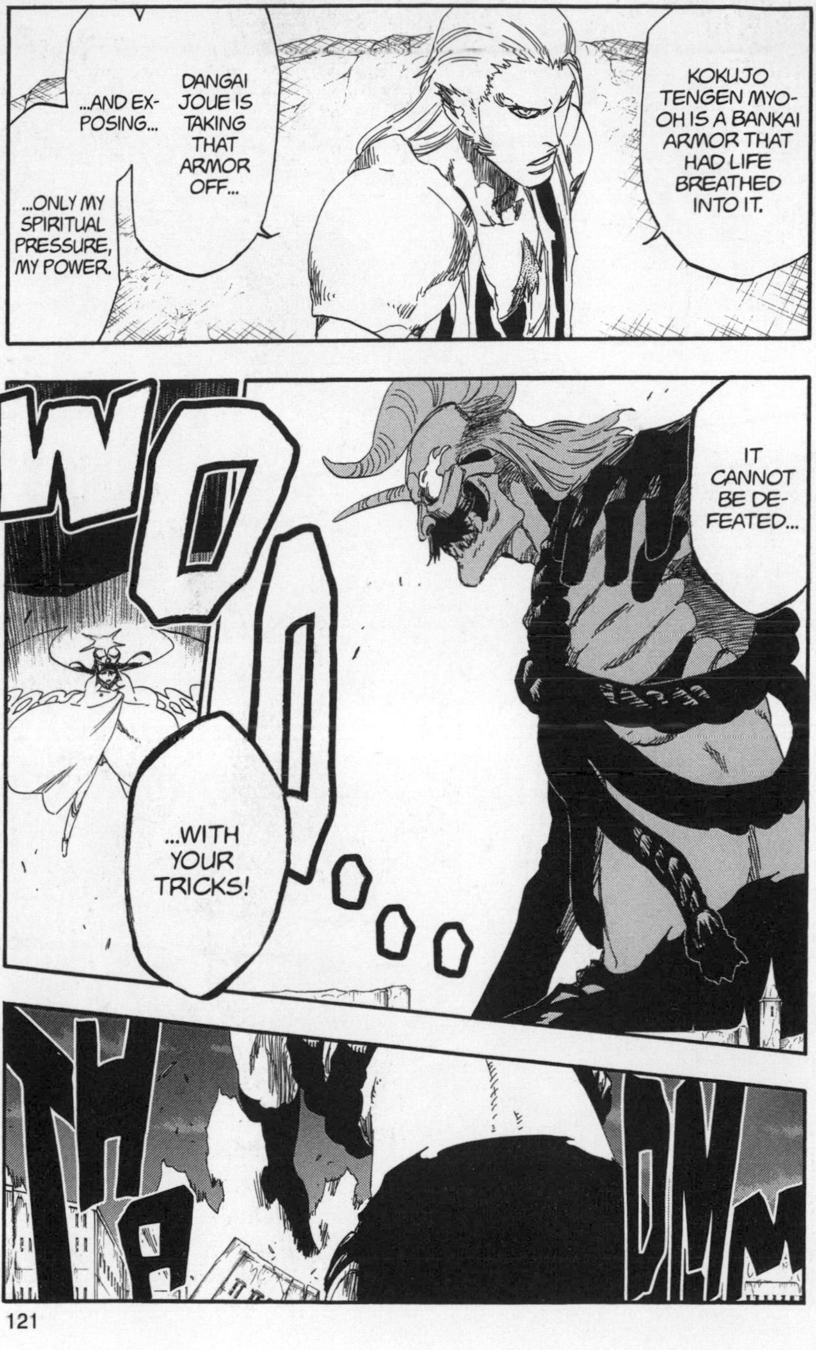
KOKUJO TENGEN MYO-OH IS A BANKAI ARMOR THAT HAD LIFE BREATHED INTO IT.
DANGAI JOUE IS TAKING THAT ARMOR OFF...
...AND EX-POSING...
...ONLY MY SPIRITUAL PRESSURE, MY POWER.
IT CANNOT BE DE-FEATED...
WOOOO...
...WITH YOUR TRICKS!
DMM
THA

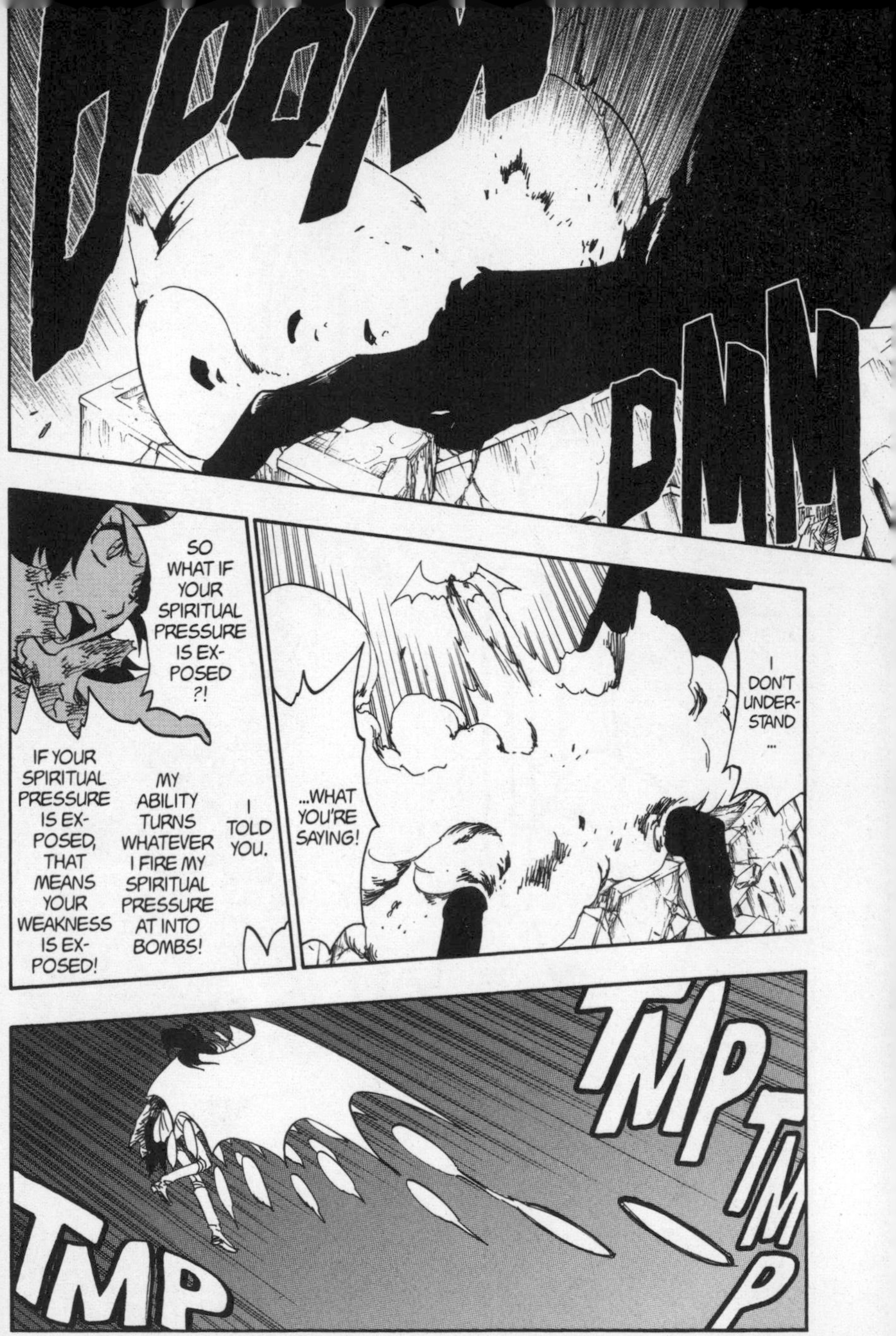
DOOM
DMM
I DON'T UNDERSTAND...
...WHAT YOU'RE SAYING!
SO WHAT IF YOUR SPIRITUAL PRESSURE IS EXPOSED?!
I TOLD YOU.
MY ABILITY TURNS WHATEVER I FIRE MY SPIRITUAL PRESSURE AT INTO BOMBS!
IF YOUR SPIRITUAL PRESSURE IS EXPOSED, THAT MEANS YOUR WEAKNESS IS EXPOSED!
TMP
TMP
TMP

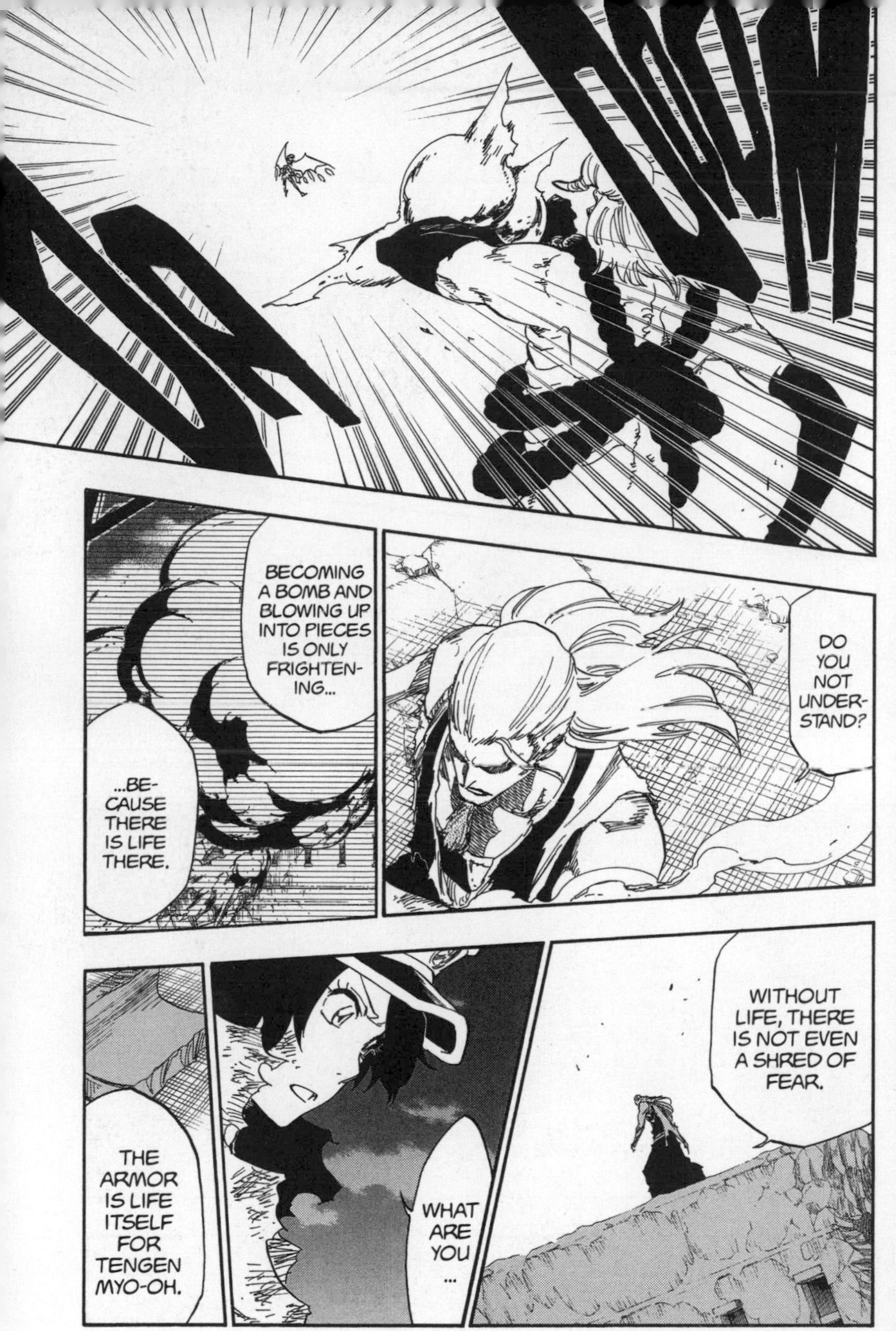
DO YOU NOT UNDER-STAND?
BECOMING A BOMB AND BLOWING UP INTO PIECES IS ONLY FRIGHTEN-ING...
...BE-CAUSE THERE IS LIFE THERE.
WITHOUT LIFE, THERE IS NOT EVEN A SHRED OF FEAR.
WHAT ARE YOU ...
THE ARMOR IS LIFE ITSELF FOR TENGEN MYO-OH.

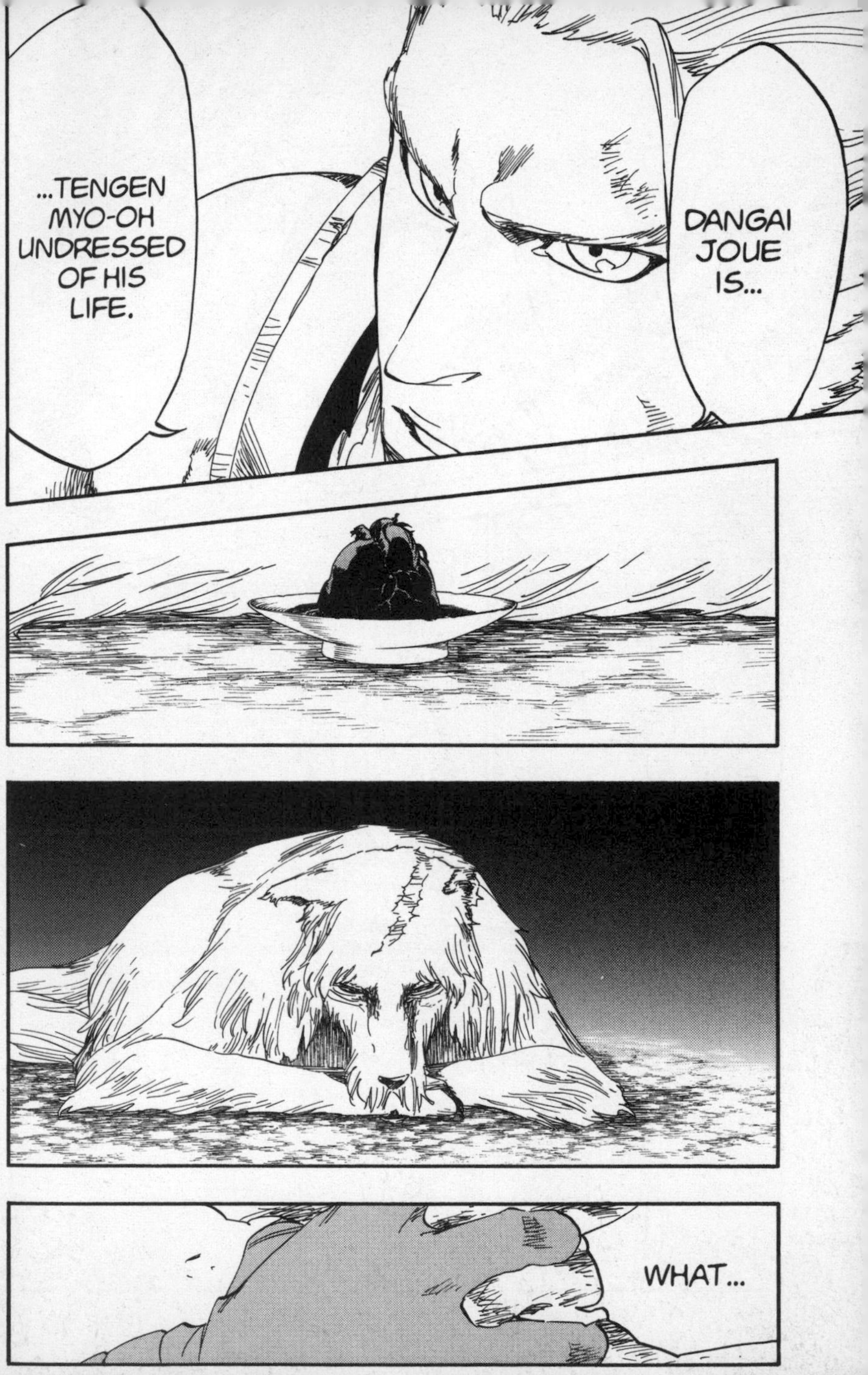
DANGAI JOUE IS...
...TENGEN MYO-OH UNDRESSED OF HIS LIFE.
WHAT...

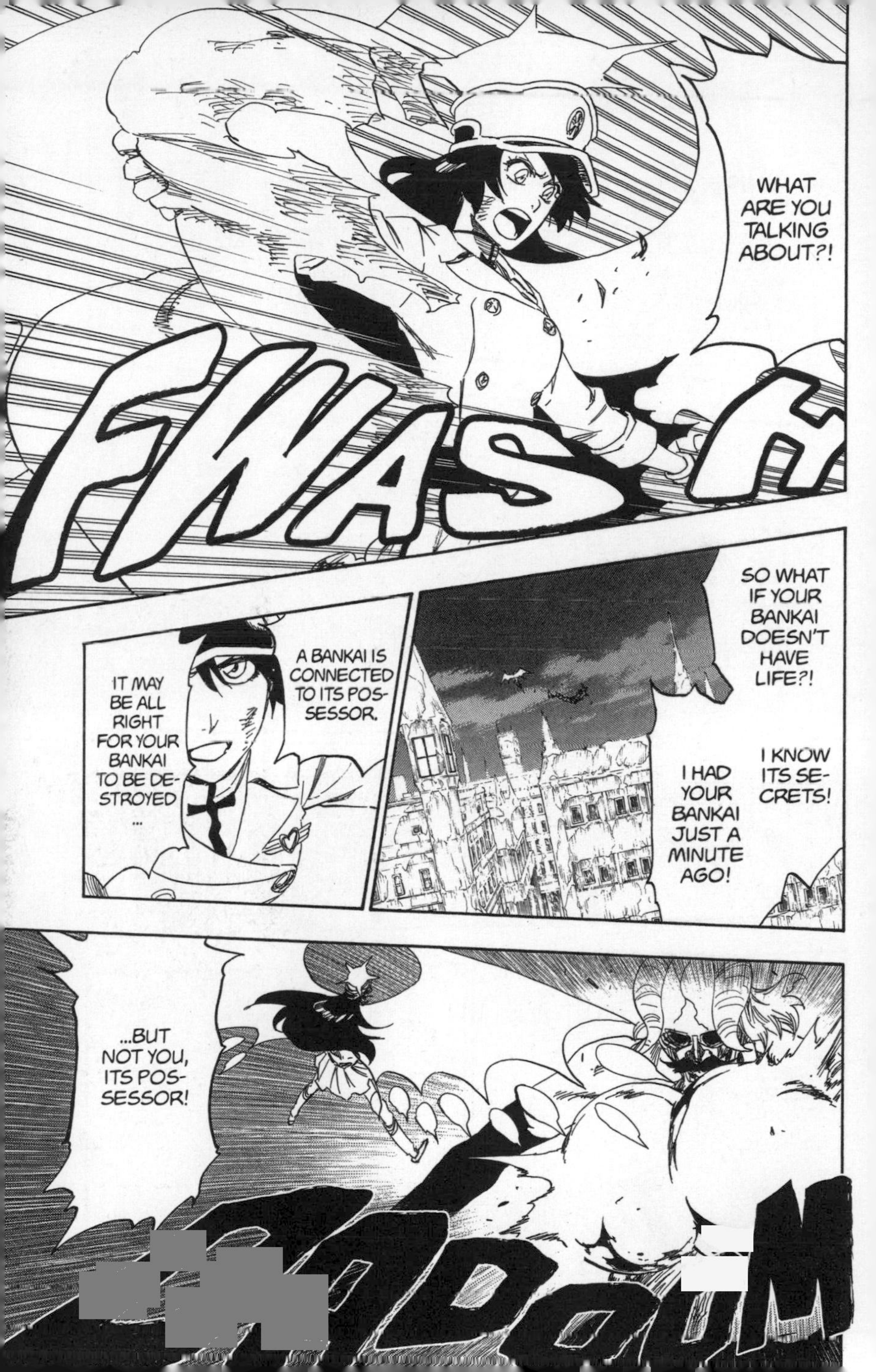
WHAT ARE YOU TALKING ABOUT?!
FWASH
SO WHAT IF YOUR BANKAI DOESN'T HAVE LIFE?!
I KNOW ITS SE-CRETS!
I HAD YOUR BANKAI JUST A MINUTE AGO!
A BANKAI IS CONNECTED TO ITS POS-SESSOR.
IT MAY BE ALL RIGHT FOR YOUR BANKAI TO BE DE-STROYED ...
...BUT NOT YOU, ITS POS-SESSOR!

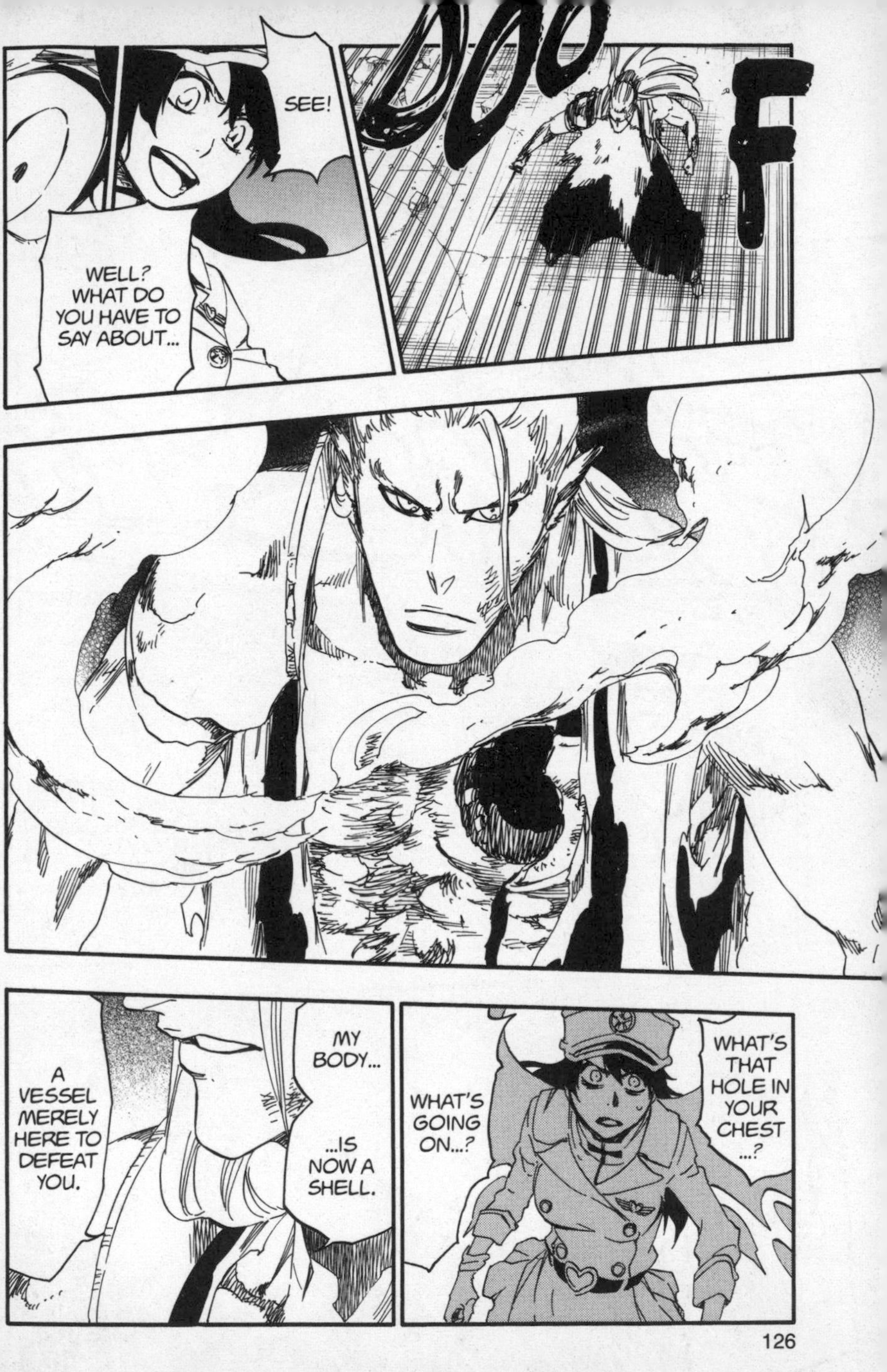
DOOOF
SEE!
WELL? WHAT DO YOU HAVE TO SAY ABOUT...
WHAT'S THAT HOLE IN YOUR CHEST ...?
WHAT'S GOING ON...?
MY BODY...
...IS NOW A SHELL.
A VESSEL MERELY HERE TO DEFEAT YOU.

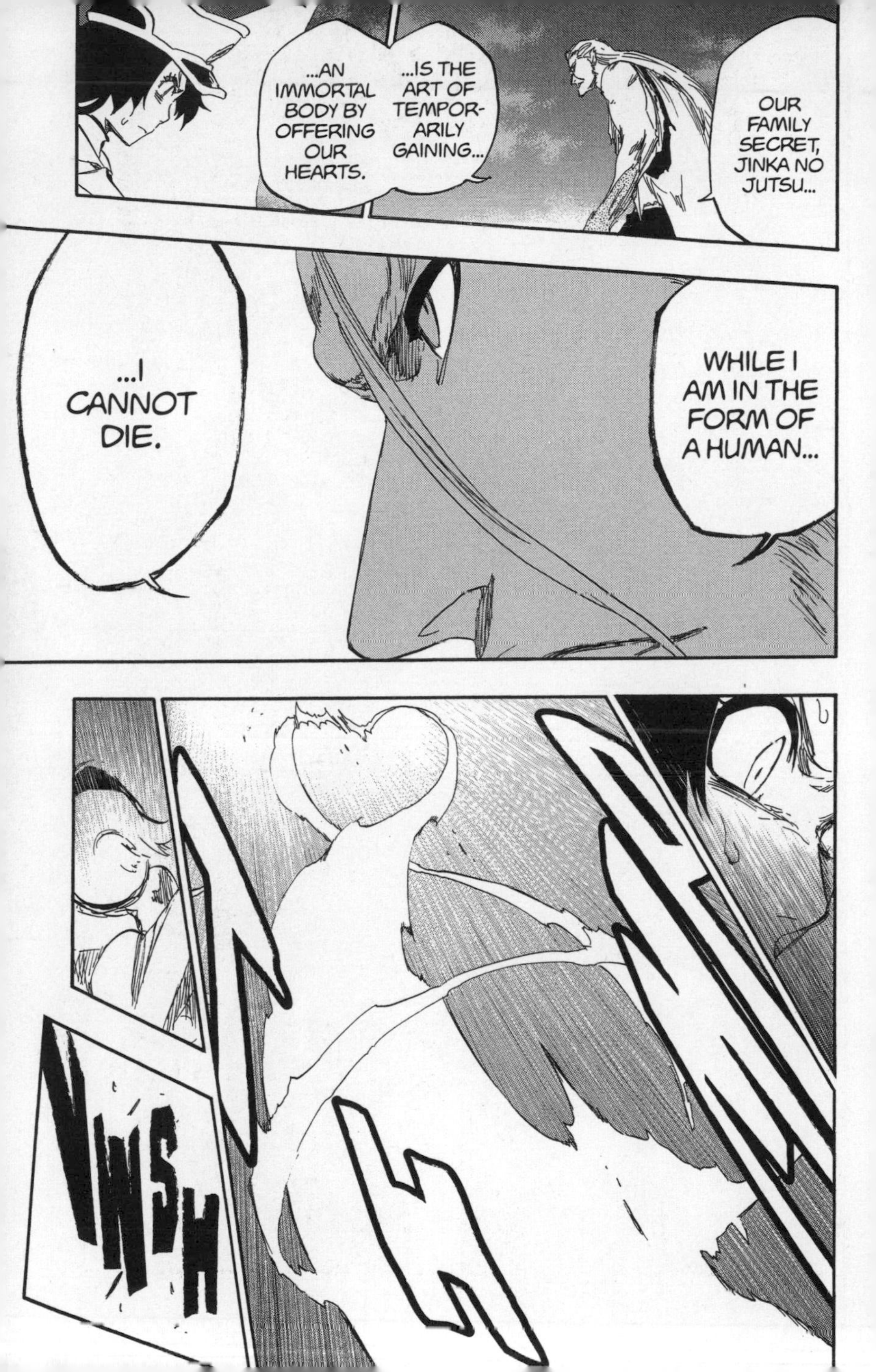
OUR FAMILY SECRET, JINKA NO JUTSU...
...IS THE ART OF TEMPORARILY GAINING...
...AN IMMORTAL BODY BY OFFERING OUR HEARTS.
WHILE I AM IN THE FORM OF A HUMAN...
...I CANNOT DIE.
VWSH

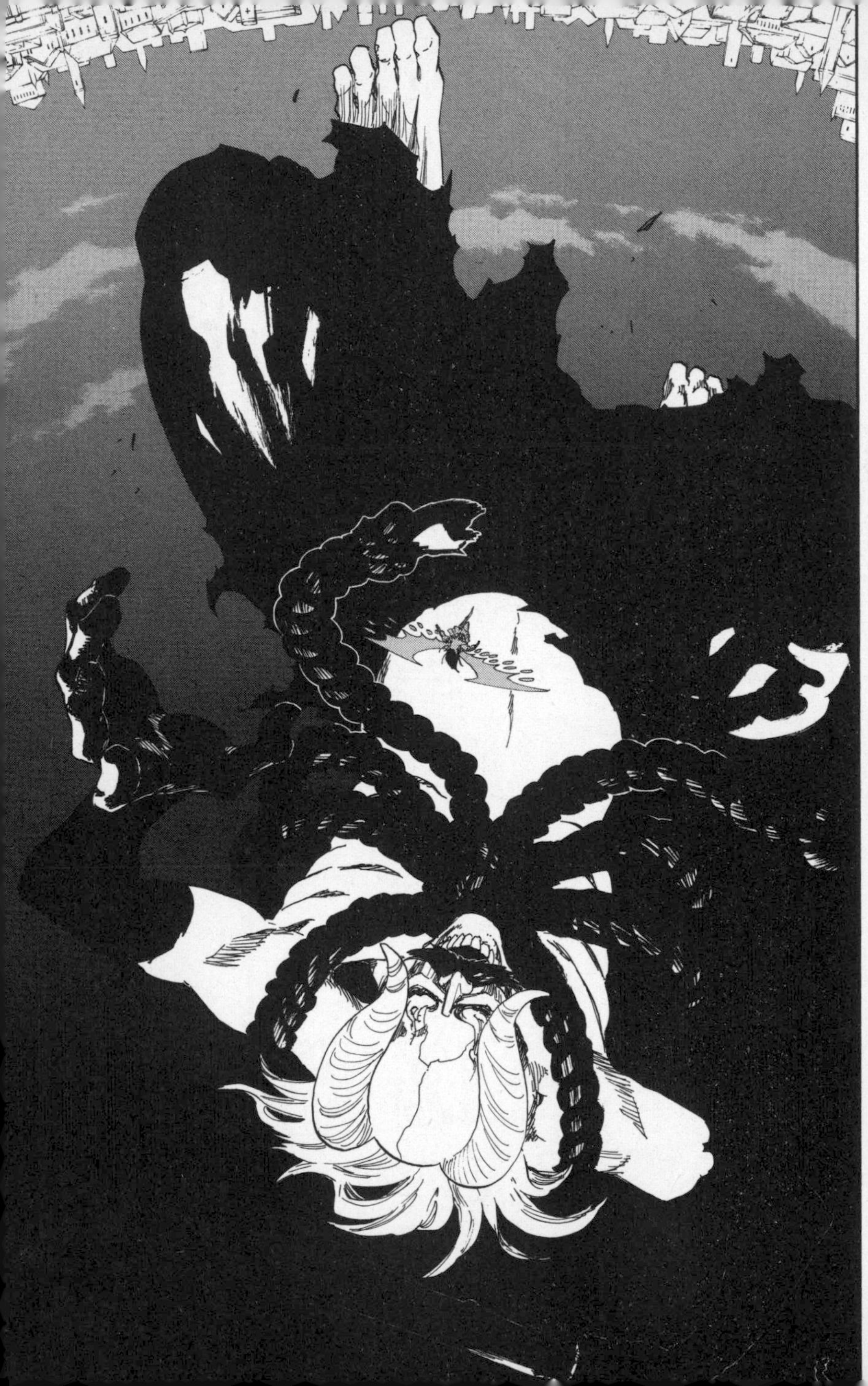

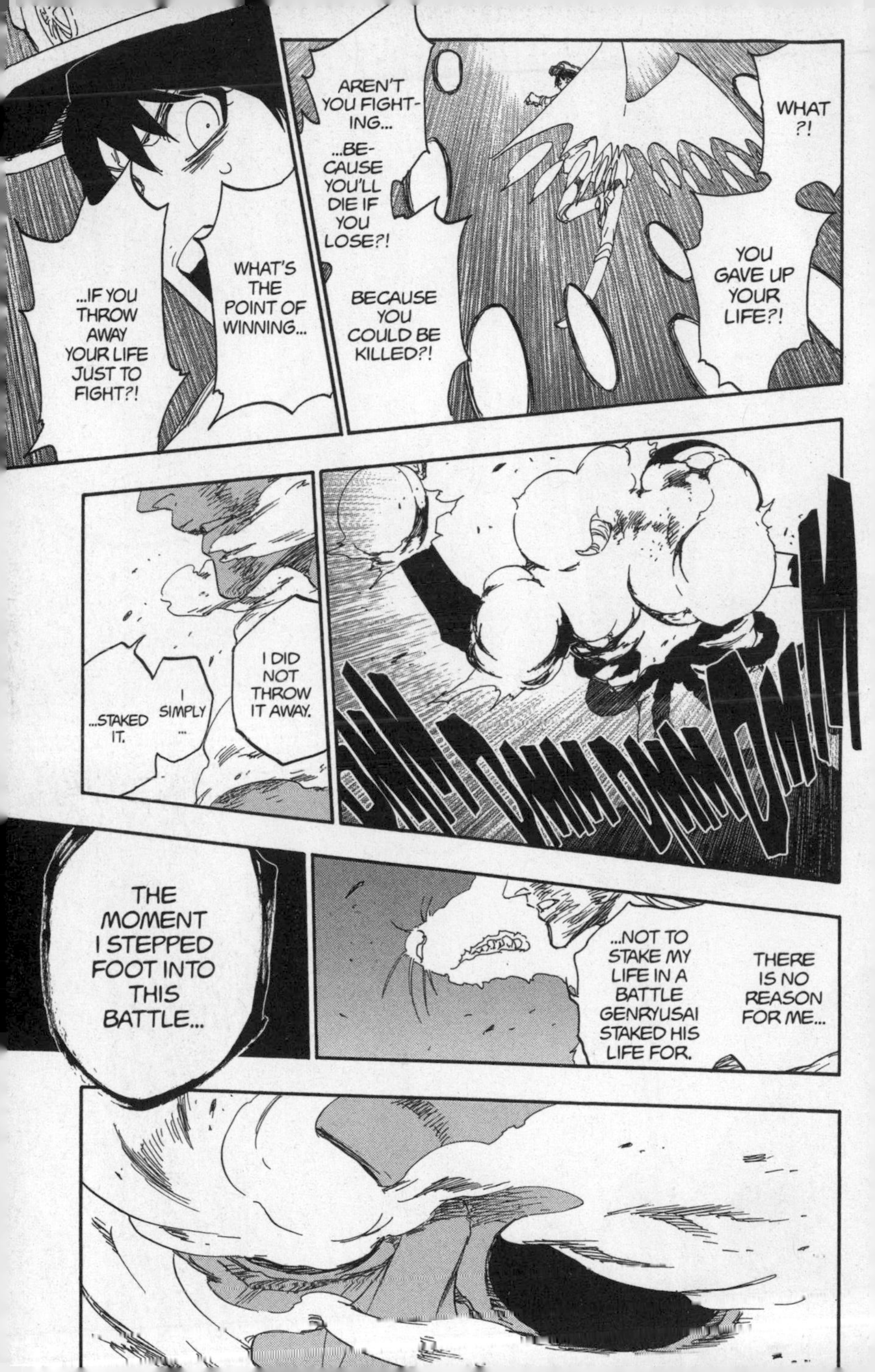
WHAT ?!
YOU GAVE UP YOUR LIFE?!
AREN'T YOU FIGHT-ING...
...BE-CAUSE YOU'LL DIE IF YOU LOSE?!
BECAUSE YOU COULD BE KILLED?!
WHAT'S THE POINT OF WINNING...
...IF YOU THROW AWAY YOUR LIFE JUST TO FIGHT?!
I DID NOT THROW IT AWAY.
I SIMPLY ...
...STAKED IT.
THERE IS NO REASON FOR ME...
...NOT TO STAKE MY LIFE IN A BATTLE GENRYUSAI STAKED HIS LIFE FOR.
THE MOMENT I STEPPED FOOT INTO THIS BATTLE...

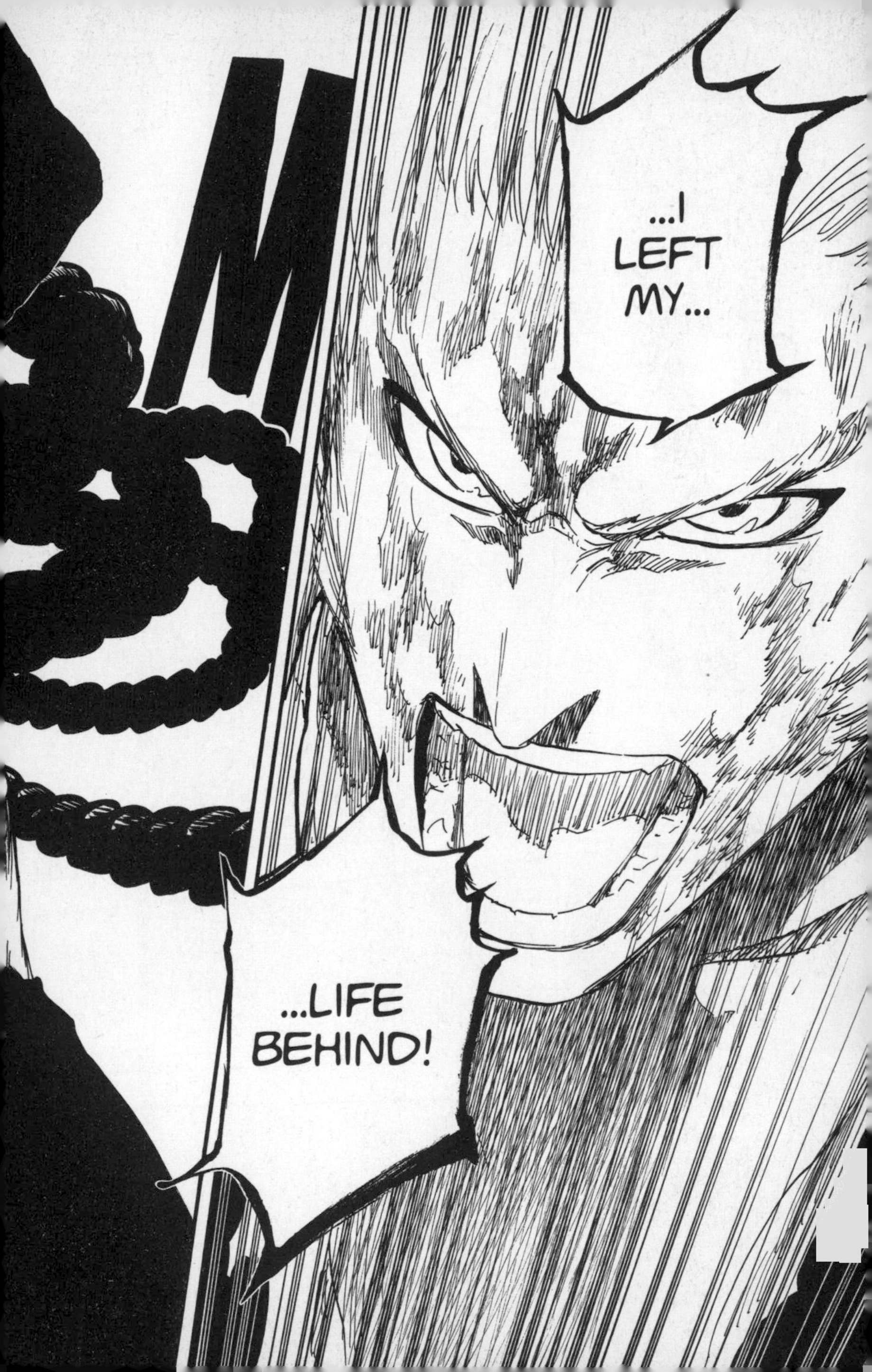
...I LEFT MY...
...LIFE BEHIND!

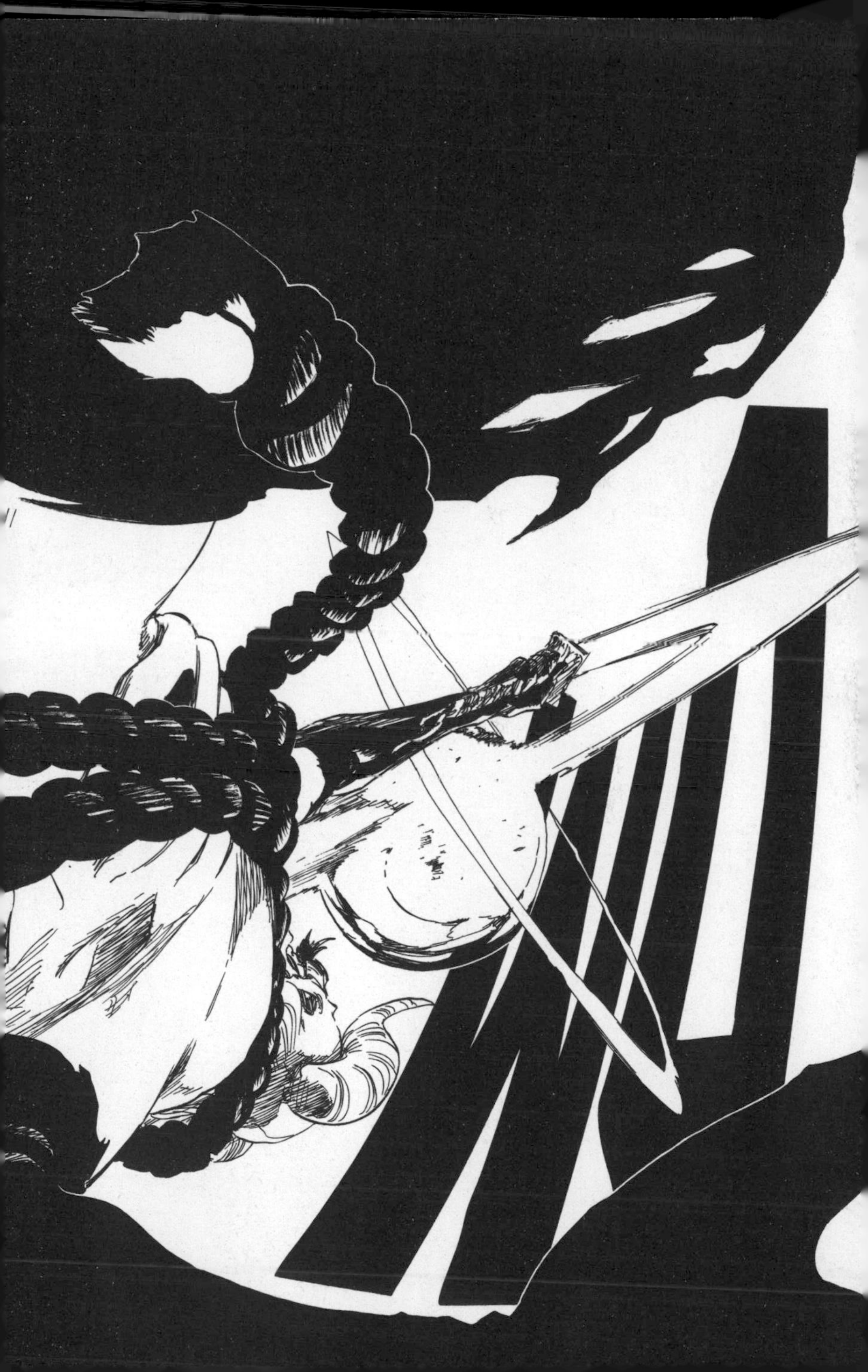

558. HEART OF WOLF

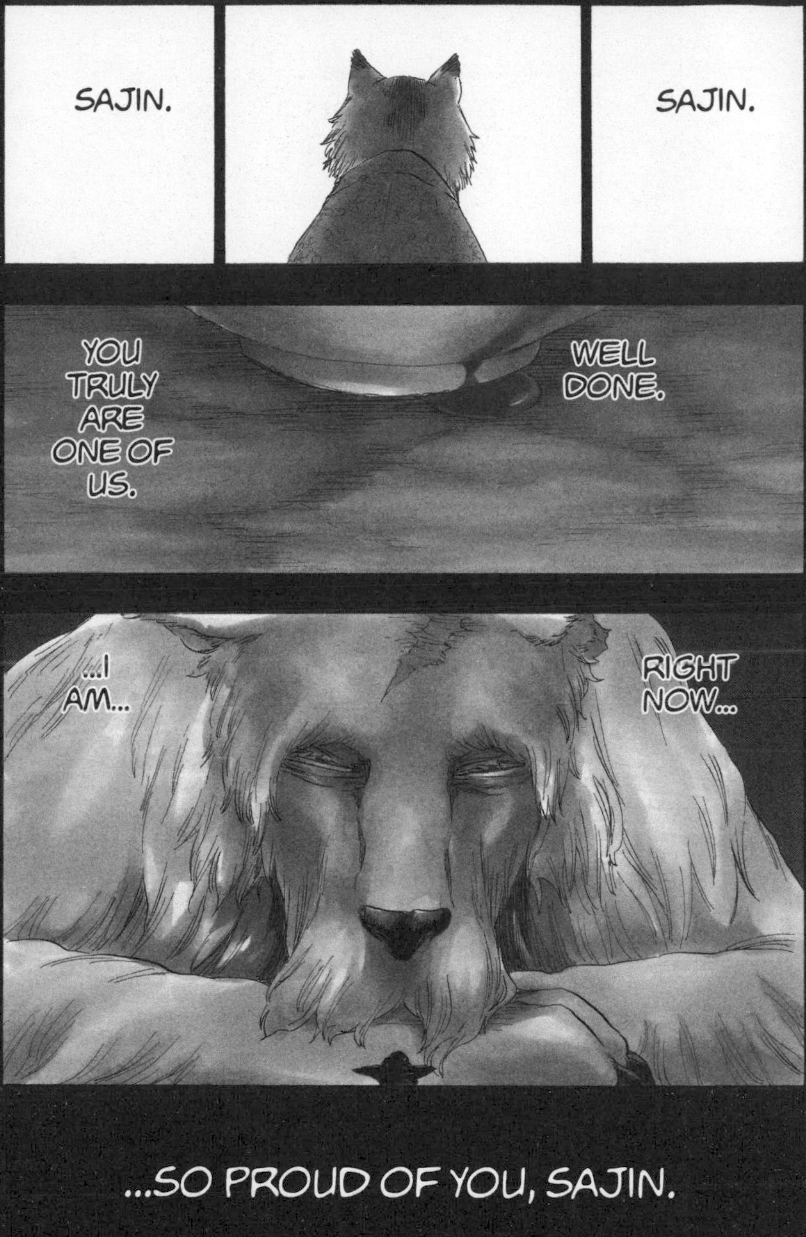
SAJIN.
SAJIN.
WELL DONE.
YOU TRULY ARE ONE OF US.
RIGHT NOW...
...I AM...
...SO PROUD OF YOU, SAJIN.

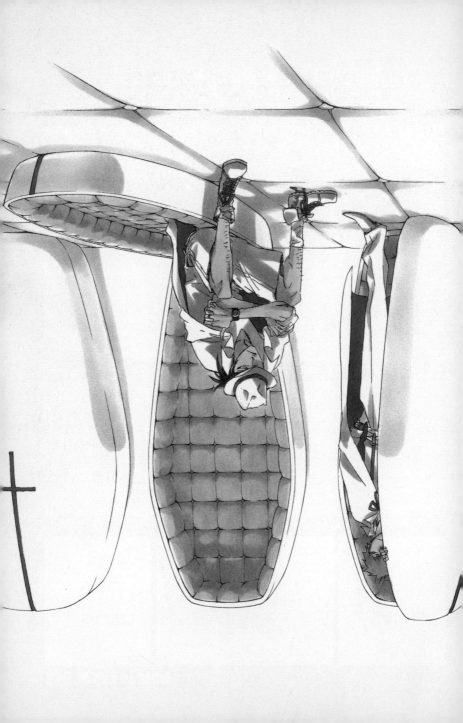

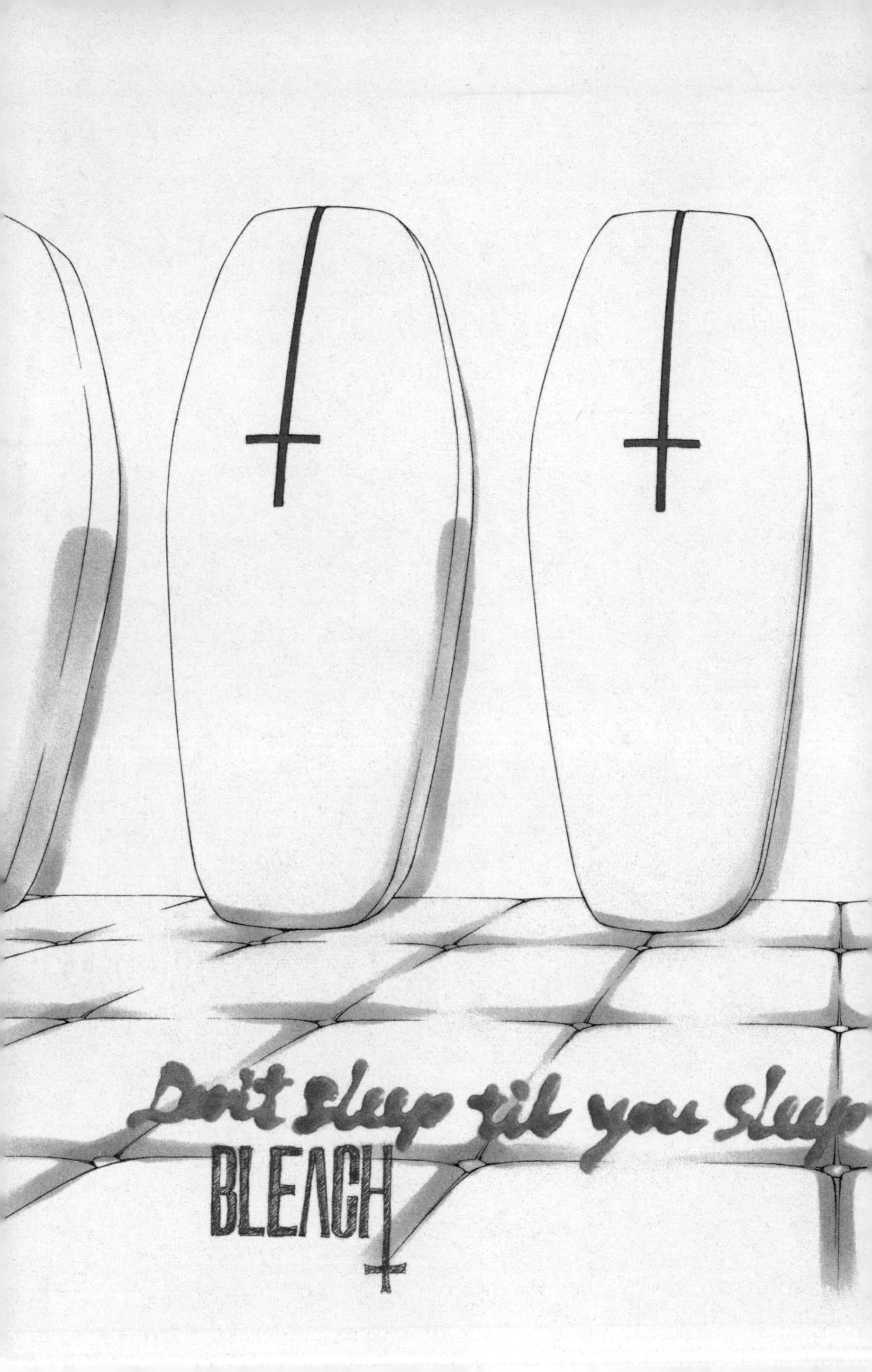
Don't sleep til you sleep
BLEACH

BLEACH
ブリーチ

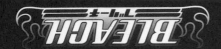

READ THIS WAY

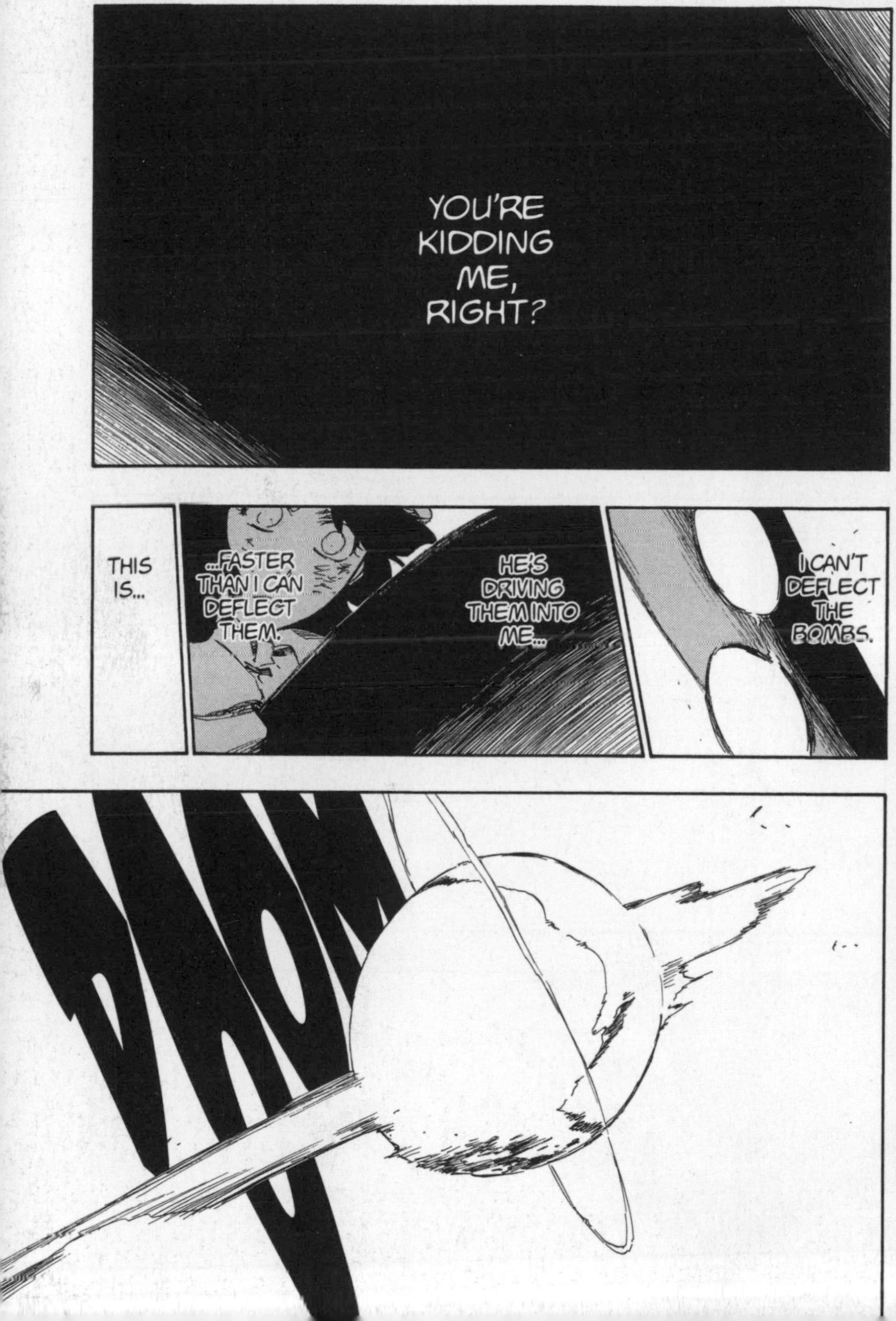
YOU'RE KIDDING ME, RIGHT?
I CAN'T DEFLECT THE BOMBS.
HE'S DRIVING THEM INTO ME...
...FASTER THAN I CAN DEFLECT THEM.
THIS IS...

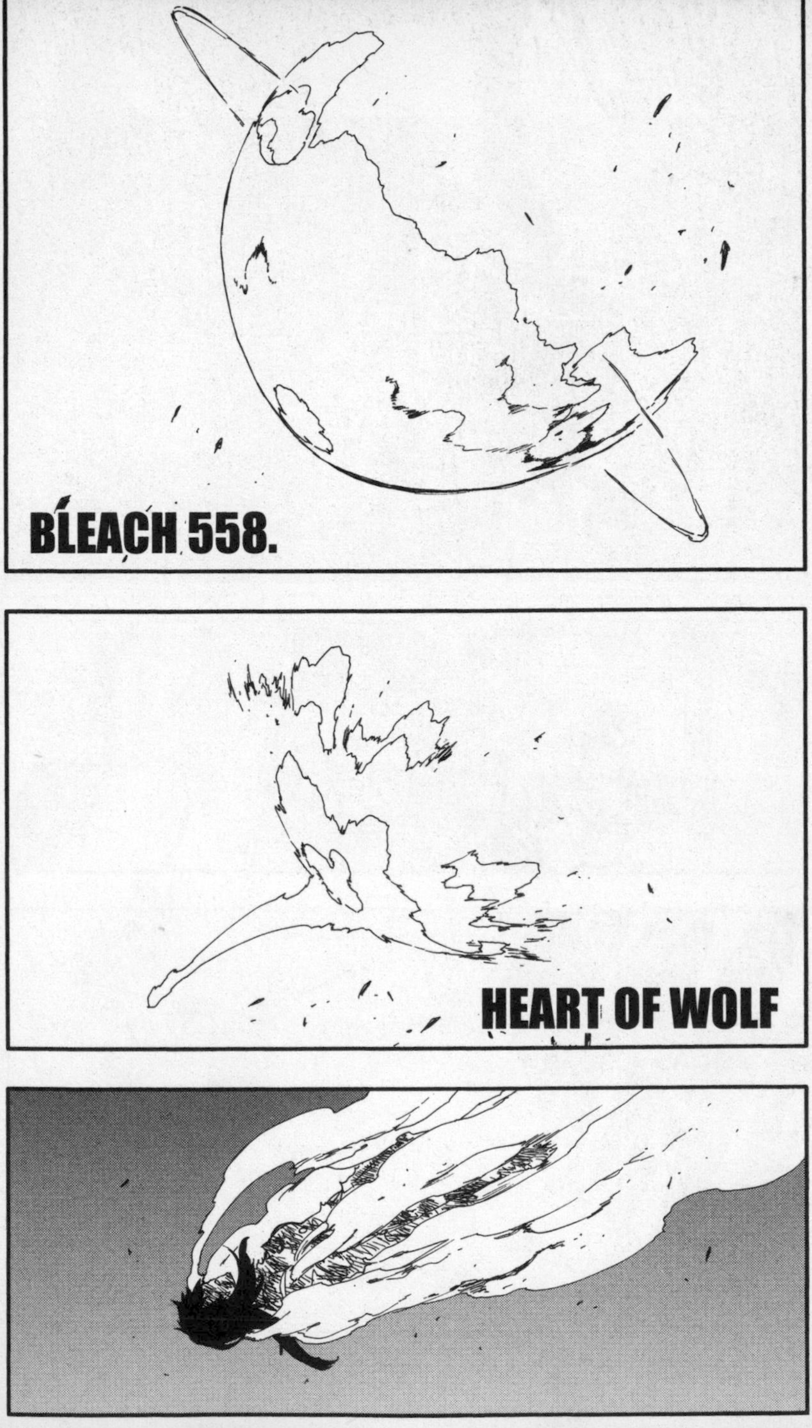
BLEACH 558.
HEART OF WOLF

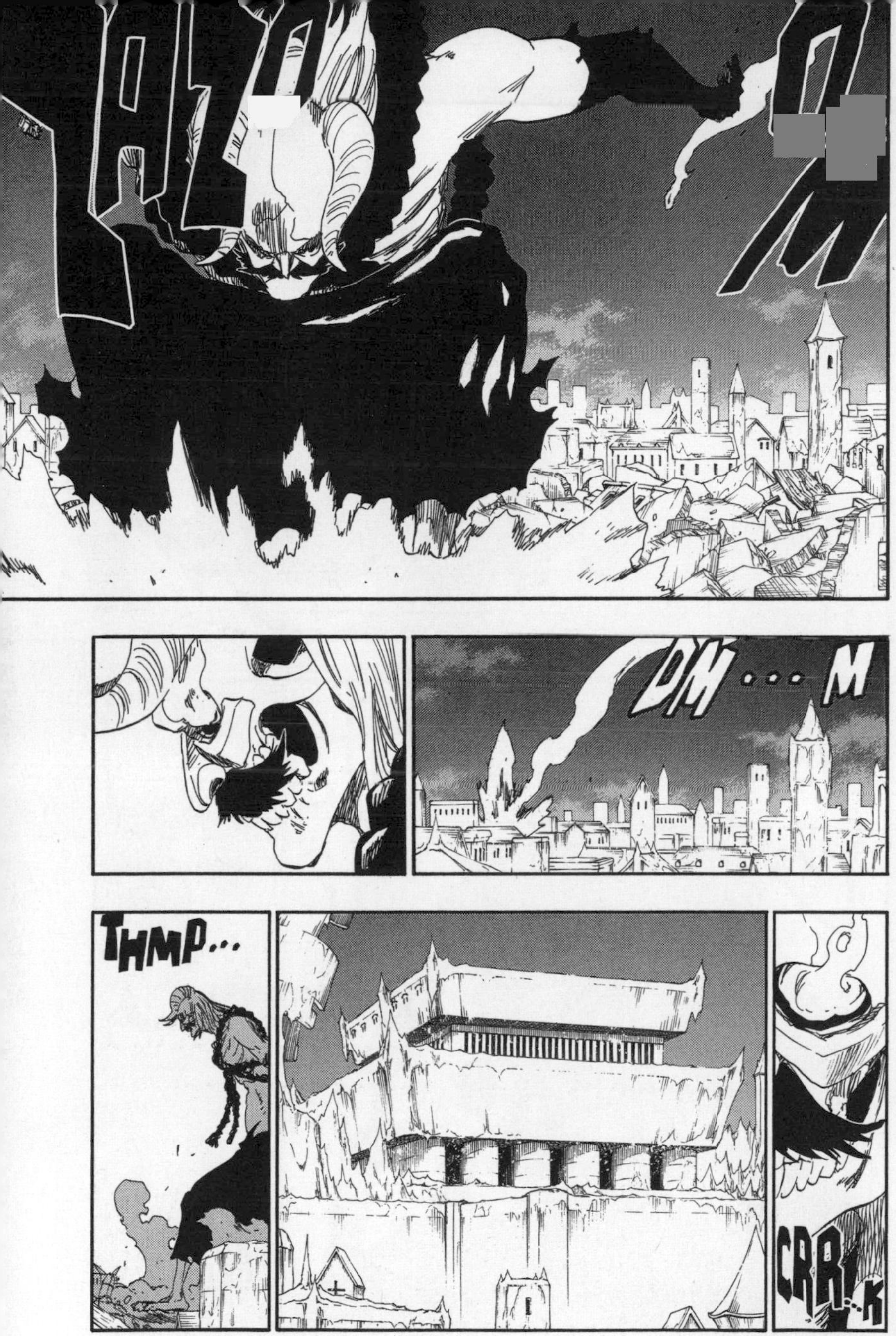
DM . . . M
CRR..K
THMP...

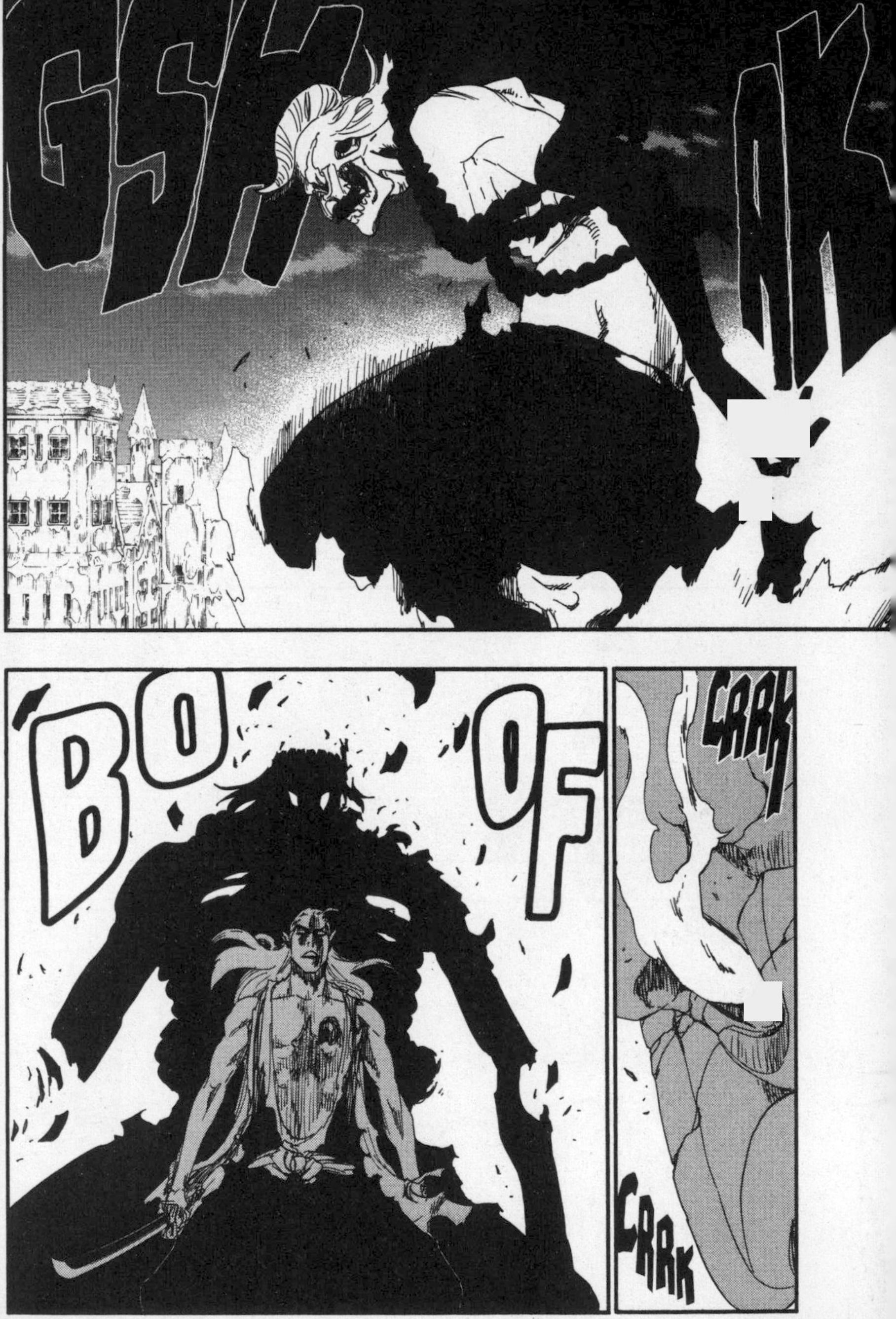
GSHAK
CRRK
CRRK
BOOF

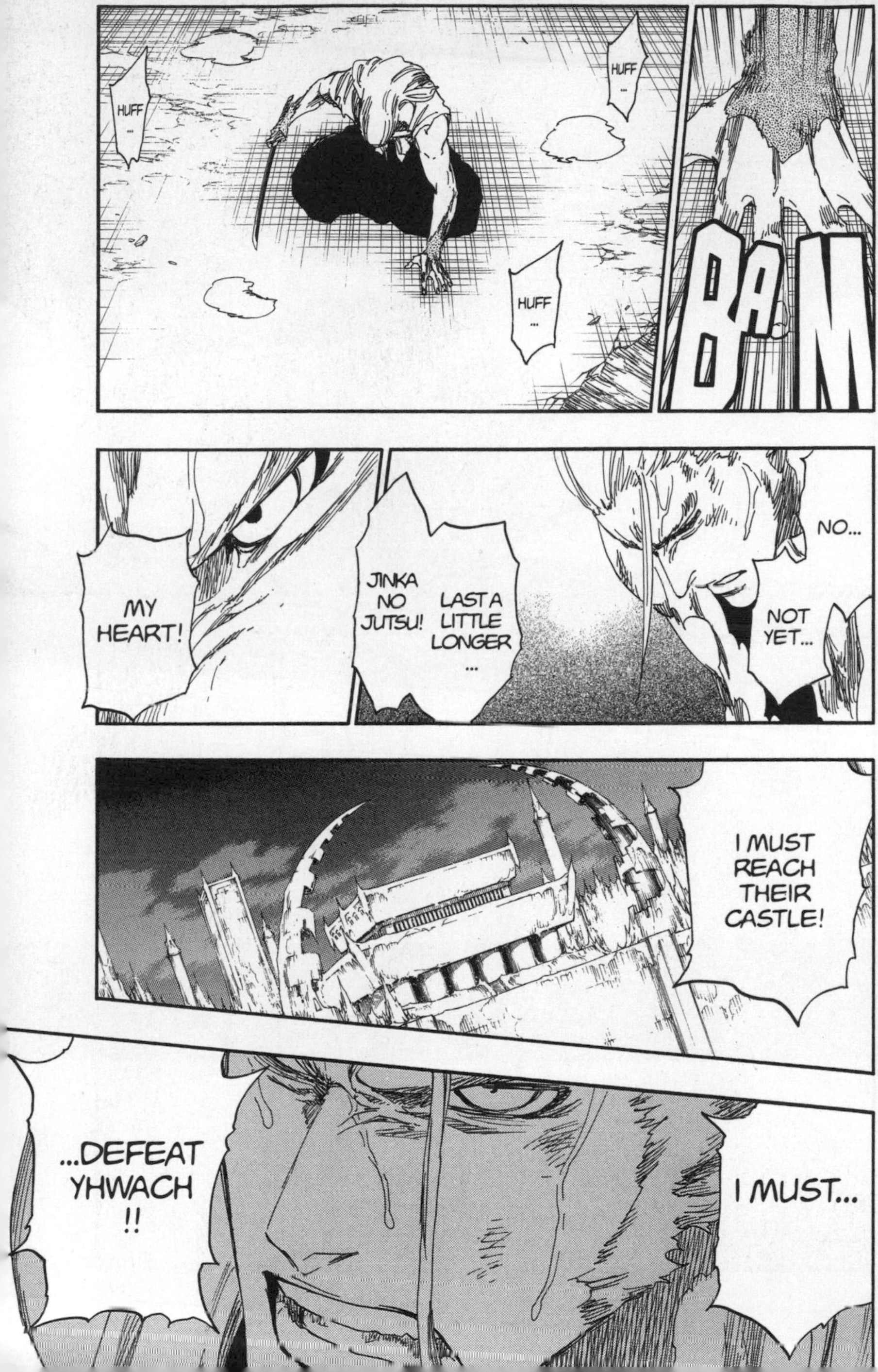
BAM
HUFF ...
HUFF ...
HUFF ...
NO... NOT YET...
JINKA NO JUTSU! LAST A LITTLE LONGER ...
MY HEART!
I MUST REACH THEIR CASTLE!
I MUST...
...DEFEAT YHWACH !!

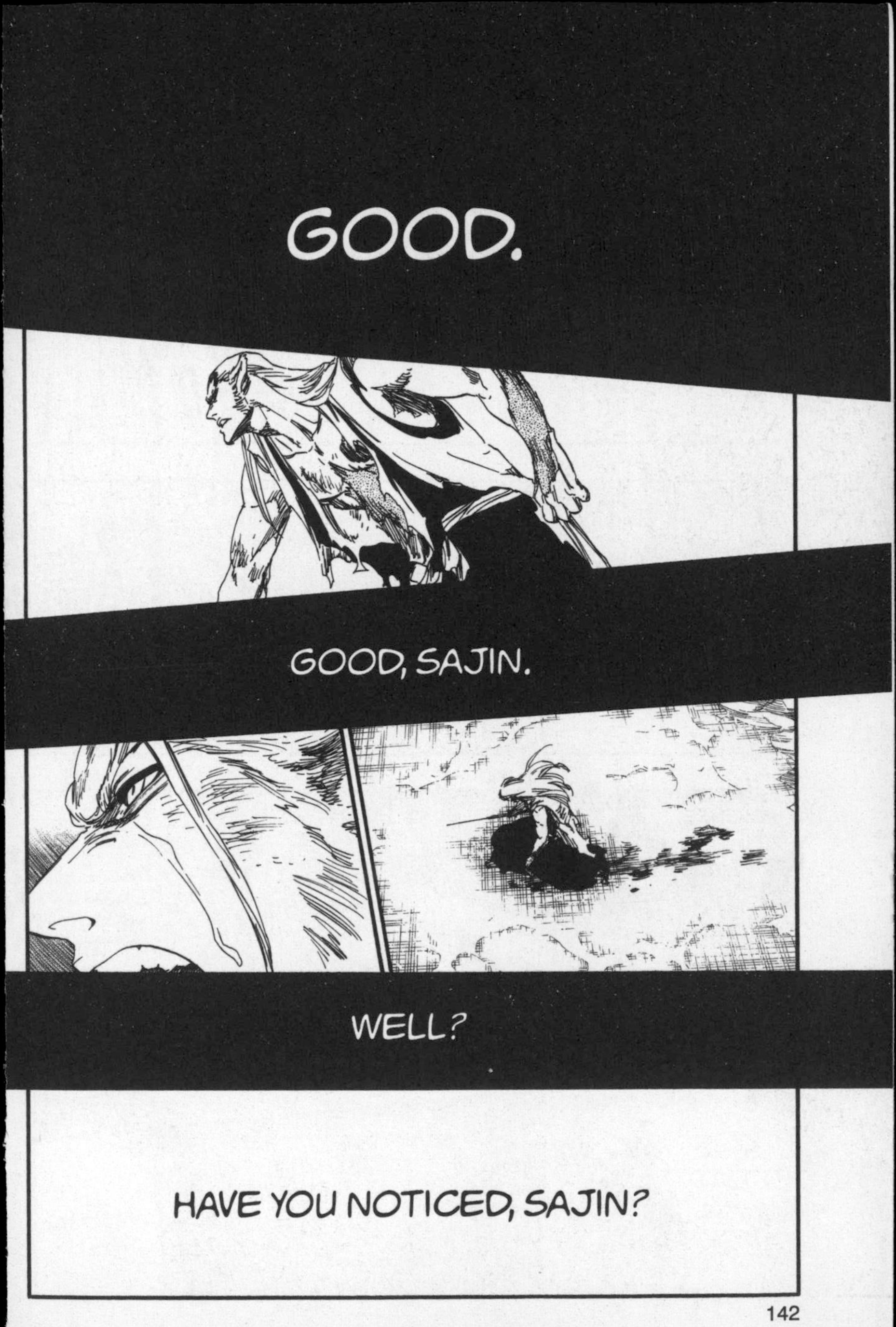
GOOD.
GOOD, SAJIN.
WELL?
HAVE YOU NOTICED, SAJIN?

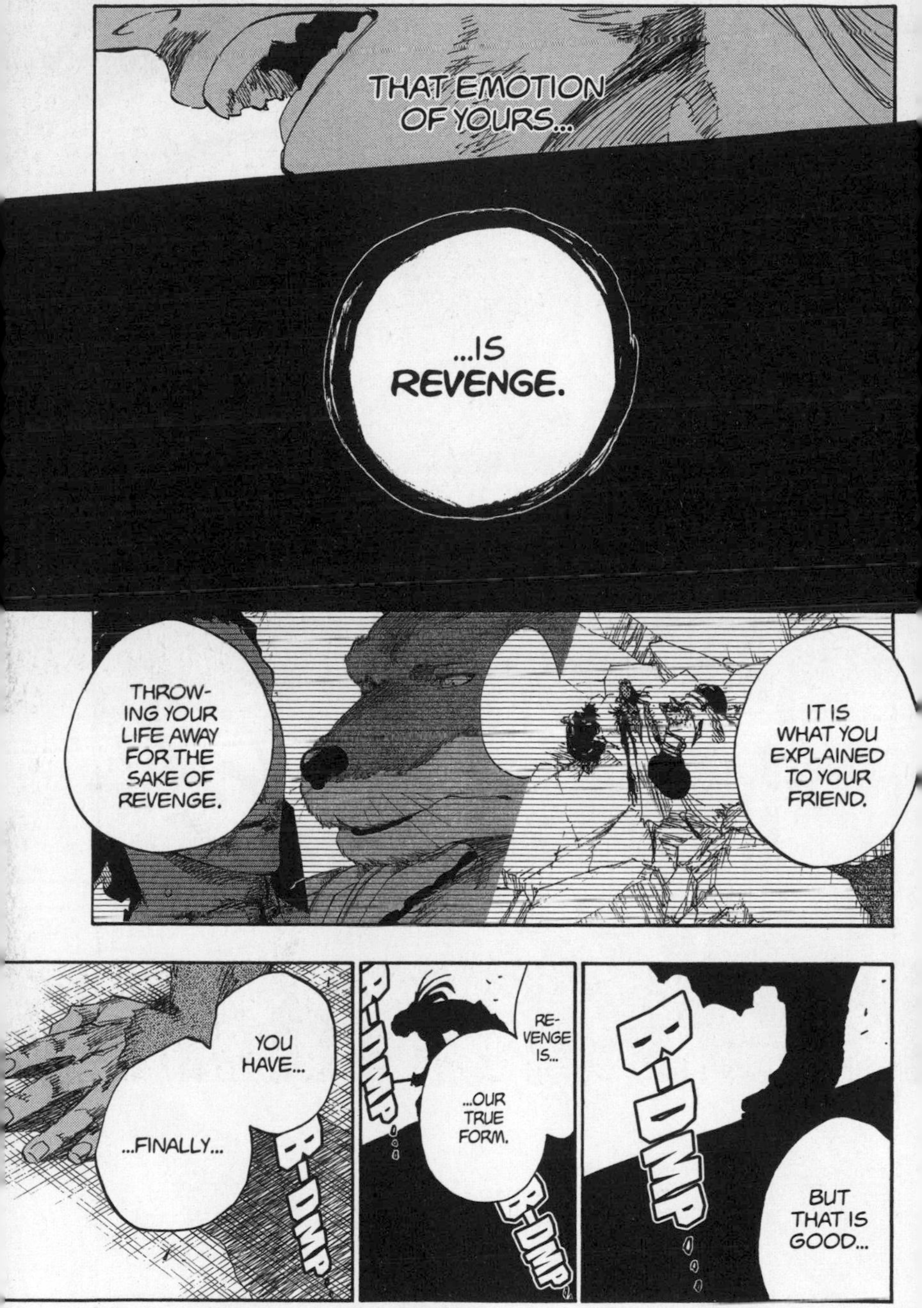
THAT EMOTION OF YOURS...
...IS REVENGE.
IT IS WHAT YOU EXPLAINED TO YOUR FRIEND.
THROWING YOUR LIFE AWAY FOR THE SAKE OF REVENGE.
B-DMP
BUT THAT IS GOOD...
RE-VENGE IS...
...OUR TRUE FORM.
B-DMP
B-DMP
YOU HAVE...
...FINALLY...
B-DMP

...RETURNED TO OUR CLAN.
B-DMP
ZZP
ZWAP

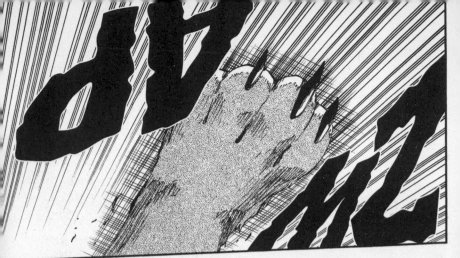

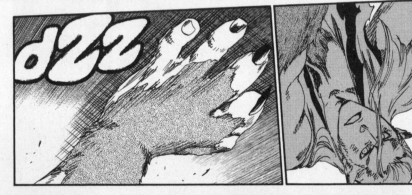

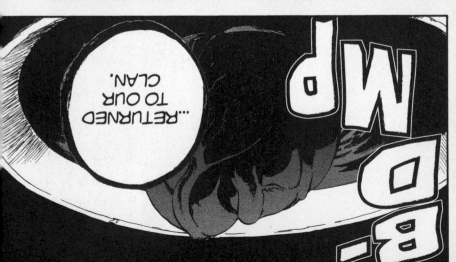

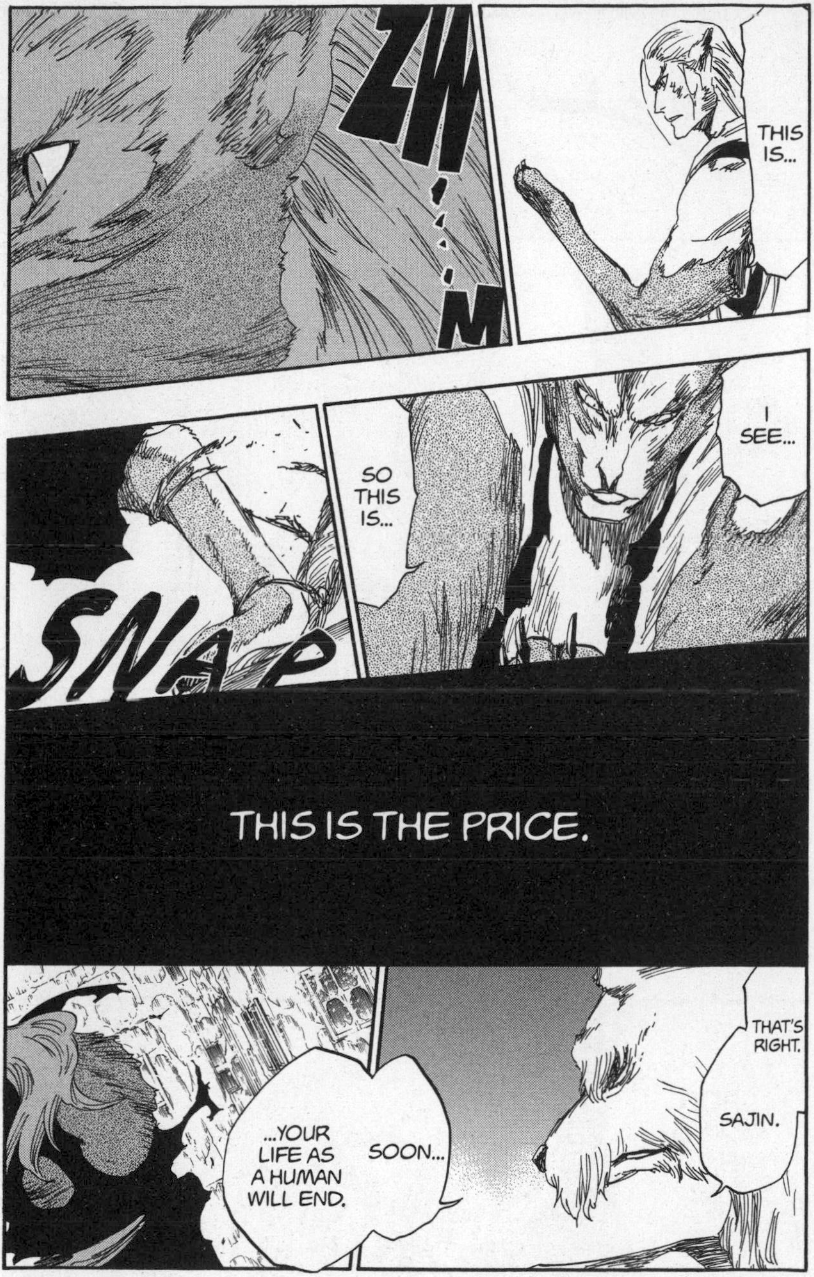
THIS IS...
ZWM...
I SEE...
SO THIS IS...
SNAP
THIS IS THE PRICE.
THAT'S RIGHT.
SAJIN.
SOON...
...YOUR LIFE AS A HUMAN WILL END.

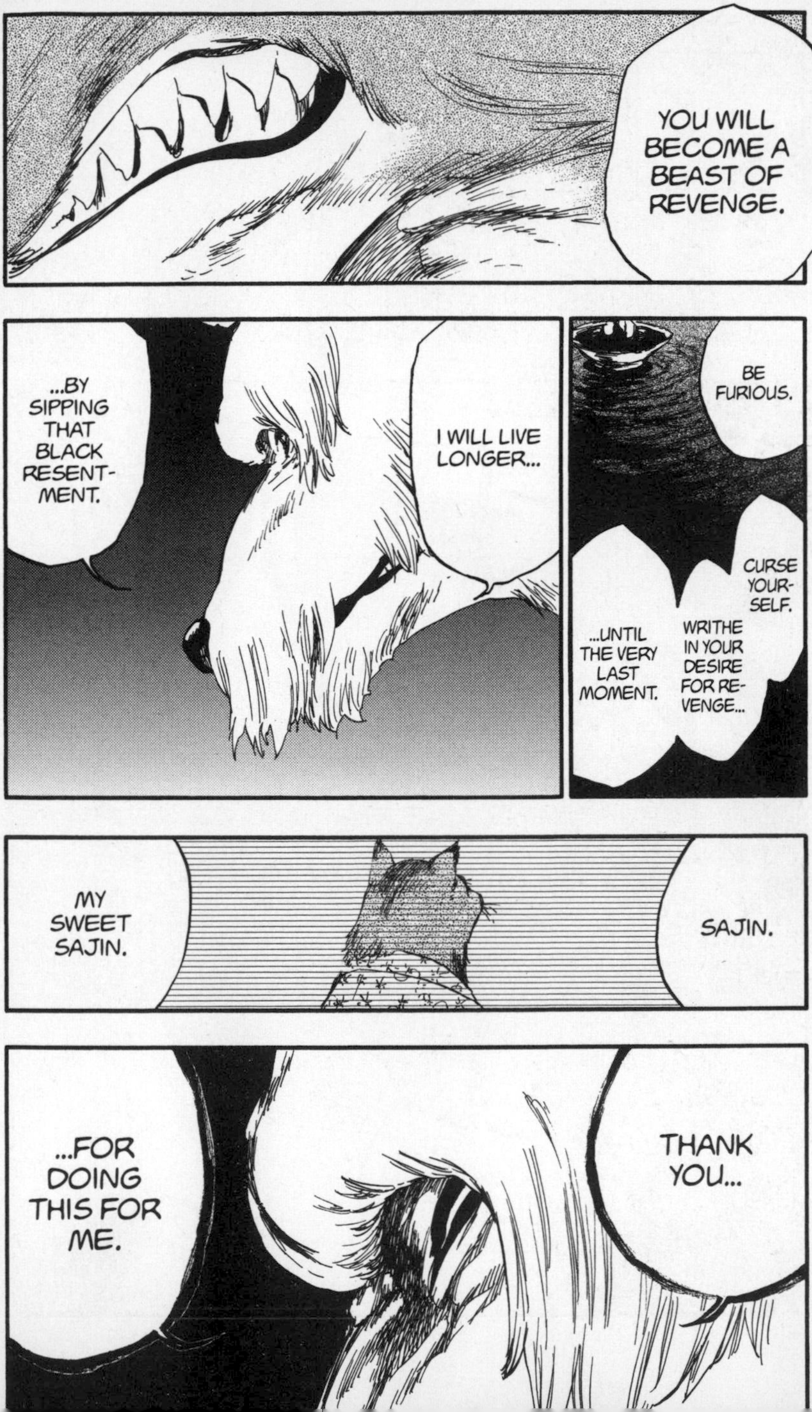
YOU WILL BECOME A BEAST OF REVENGE.
BE FURIOUS.
CURSE YOURSELF.
WRITHE IN YOUR DESIRE FOR REVENGE...
...UNTIL THE VERY LAST MOMENT.
I WILL LIVE LONGER...
...BY SIPPING THAT BLACK RESENTMENT.
SAJIN.
MY SWEET SAJIN.
THANK YOU...
...FOR DOING THIS FOR ME.

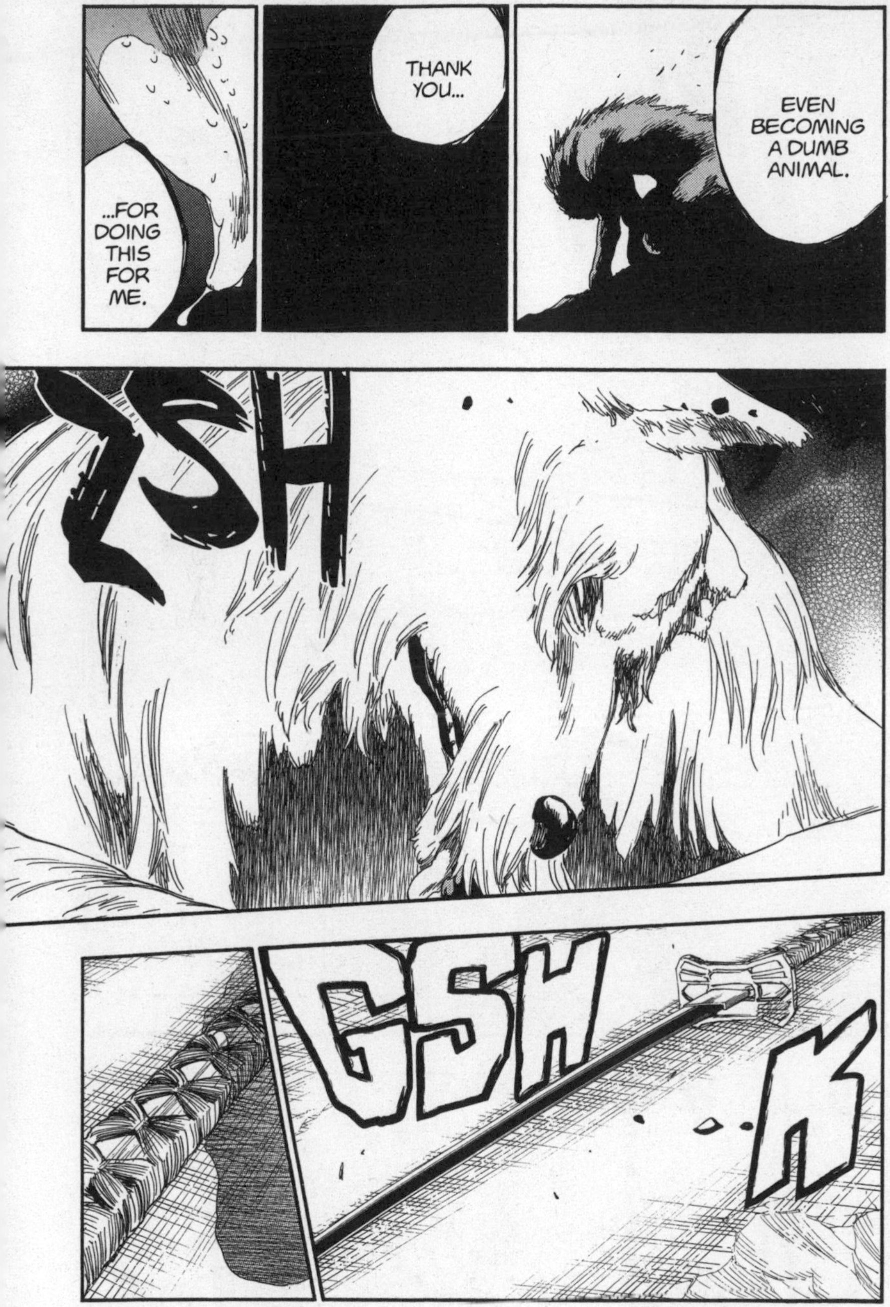
EVEN BECOMING A DUMB ANIMAL.
THANK YOU...
...FOR DOING THIS FOR ME.
SH
GSH
K

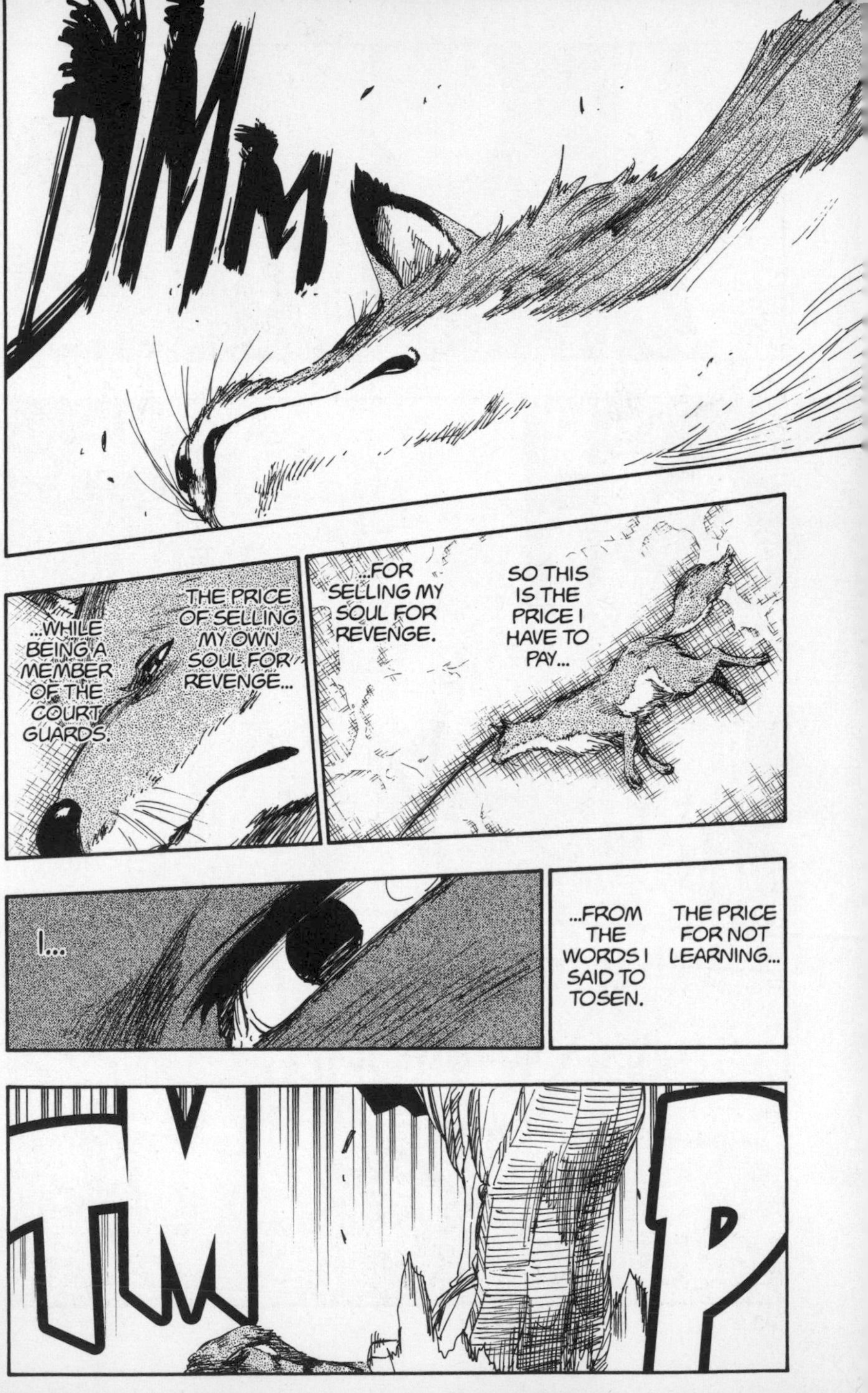
DMM
SO THIS IS THE PRICE I HAVE TO PAY...
...FOR SELLING MY SOUL FOR REVENGE.
THE PRICE OF SELLING MY OWN SOUL FOR REVENGE...
...WHILE BEING A MEMBER OF THE COURT GUARDS.
THE PRICE FOR NOT LEARNING...
...FROM THE WORDS I SAID TO TOSEN.
I...
TMP

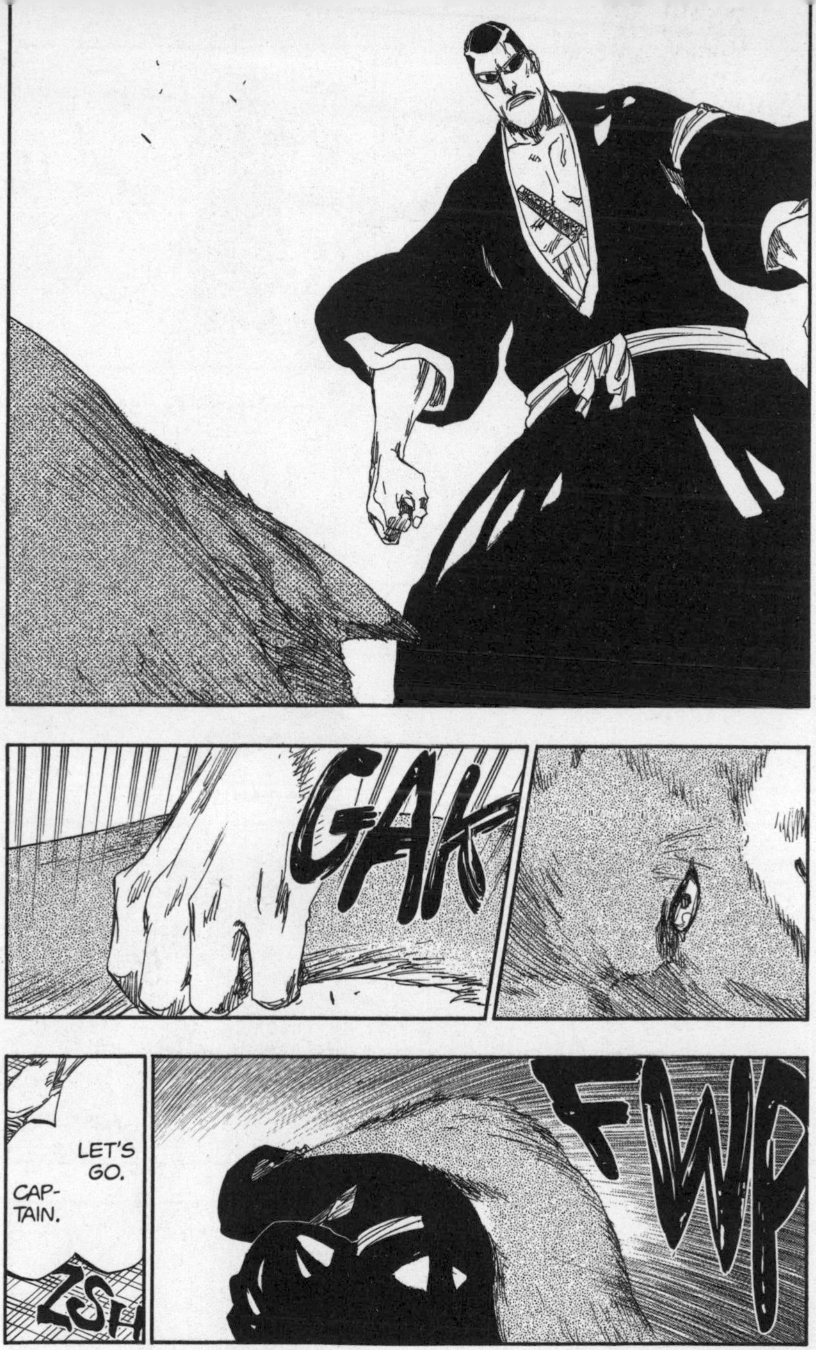
GAK
FWP
LET'S GO.
CAP-TAIN.
ZSH

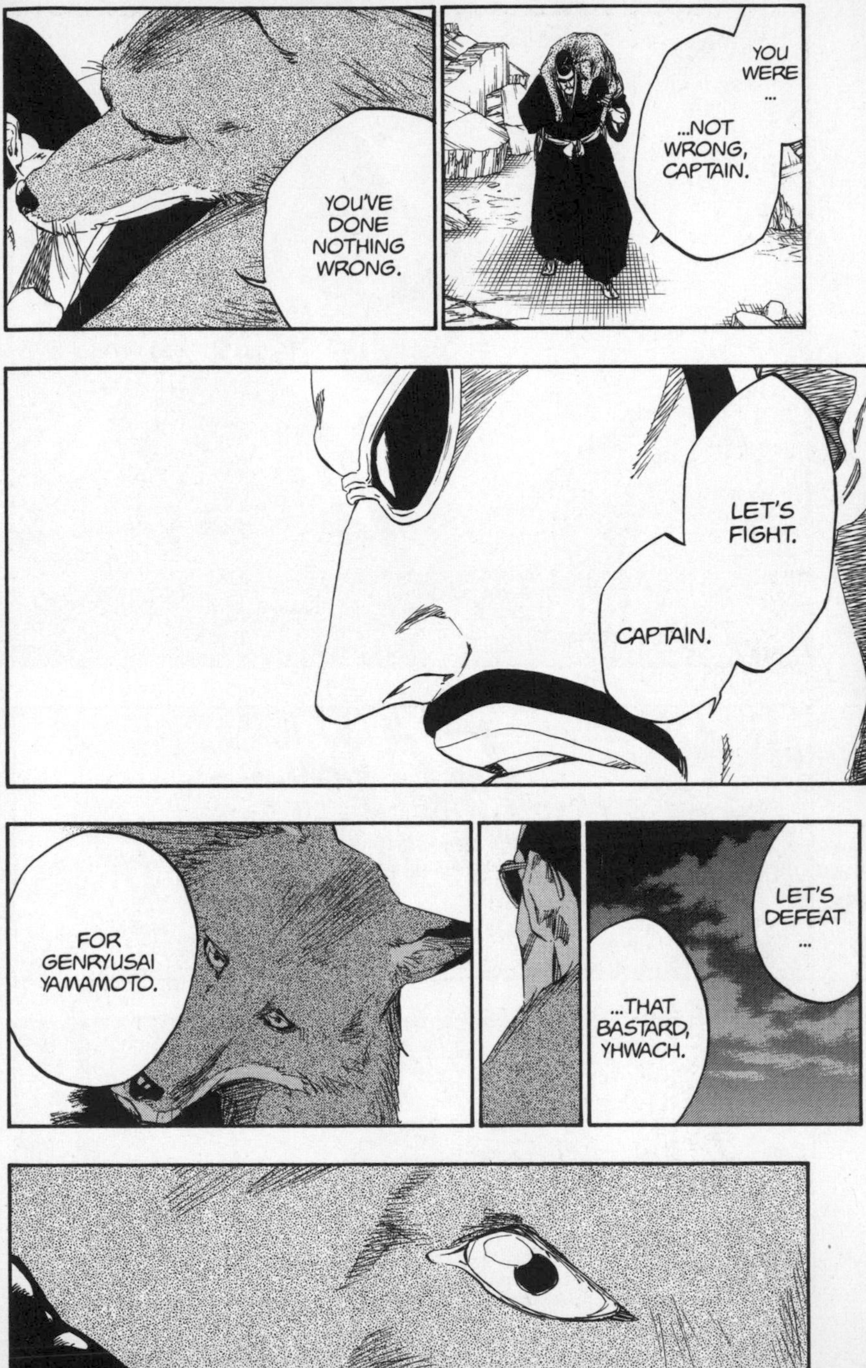
YOU WERE ...
...NOT WRONG, CAPTAIN.
YOU'VE DONE NOTHING WRONG.
LET'S FIGHT.
CAPTAIN.
LET'S DEFEAT ...
...THAT BASTARD, YHWACH.
FOR GENRYUSAI YAMAMOTO.

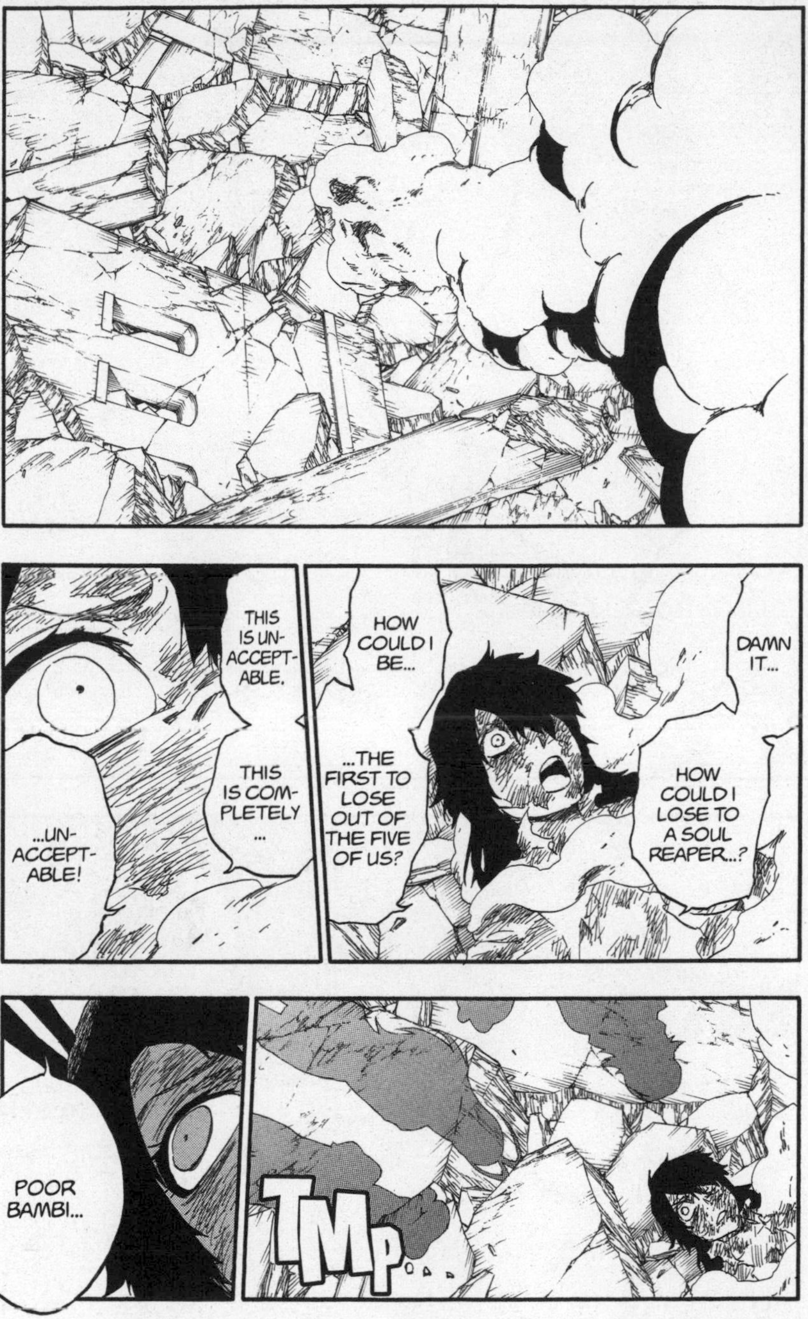
DAMN IT...
HOW COULD I LOSE TO A SOUL REAPER...?
HOW COULD I BE...
...THE FIRST TO LOSE OUT OF THE FIVE OF US?
THIS IS UN-ACCEPT-ABLE.
THIS IS COM-PLETELY ...
...UN-ACCEPT-ABLE!
TMP
POOR BAMBI...

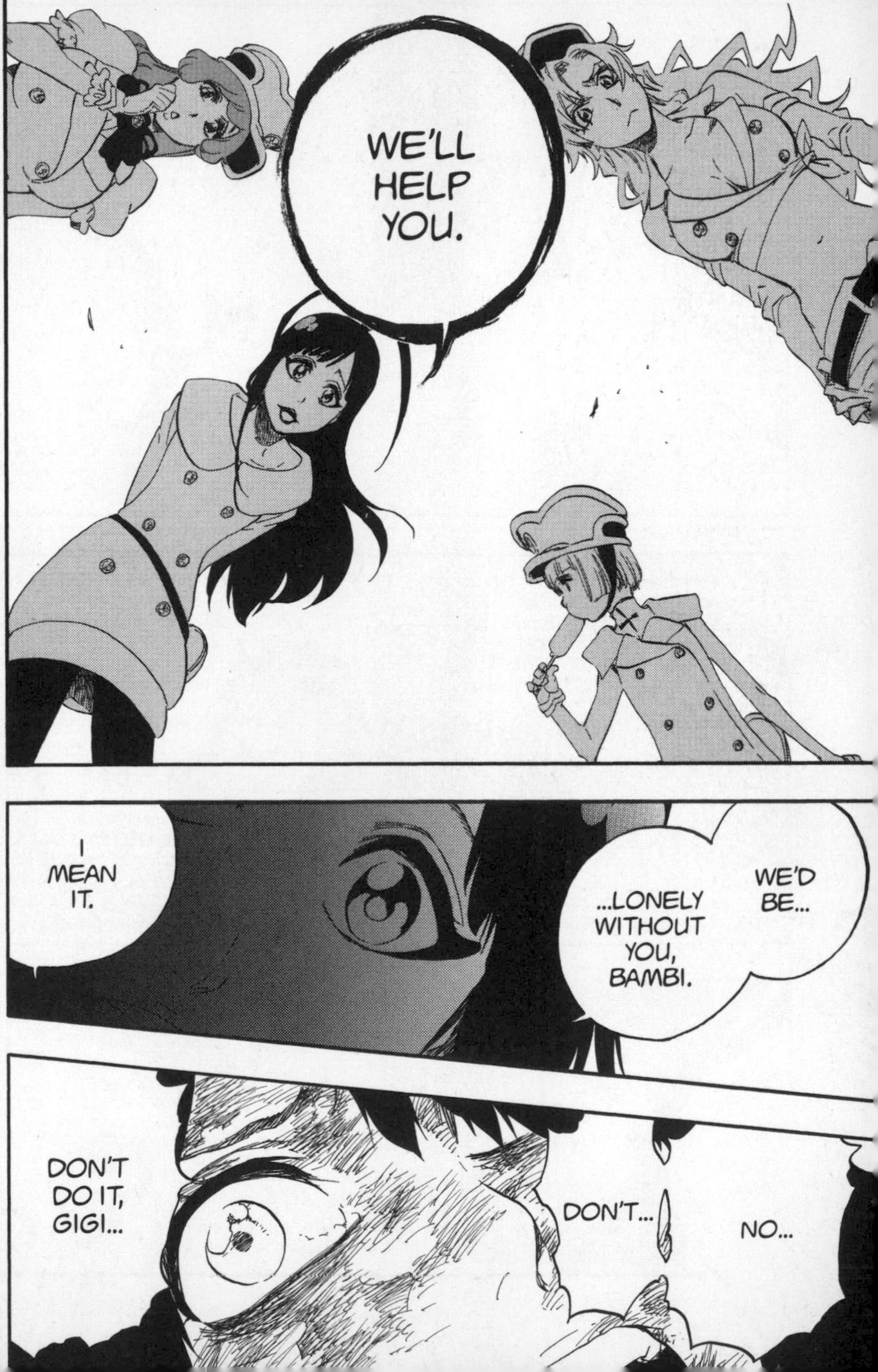
WE'LL HELP YOU.
WE'D BE...
...LONELY WITHOUT YOU, BAMBI.
I MEAN IT.
NO...
DON'T...
DON'T DO IT, GIGI...

READ THIS WAY

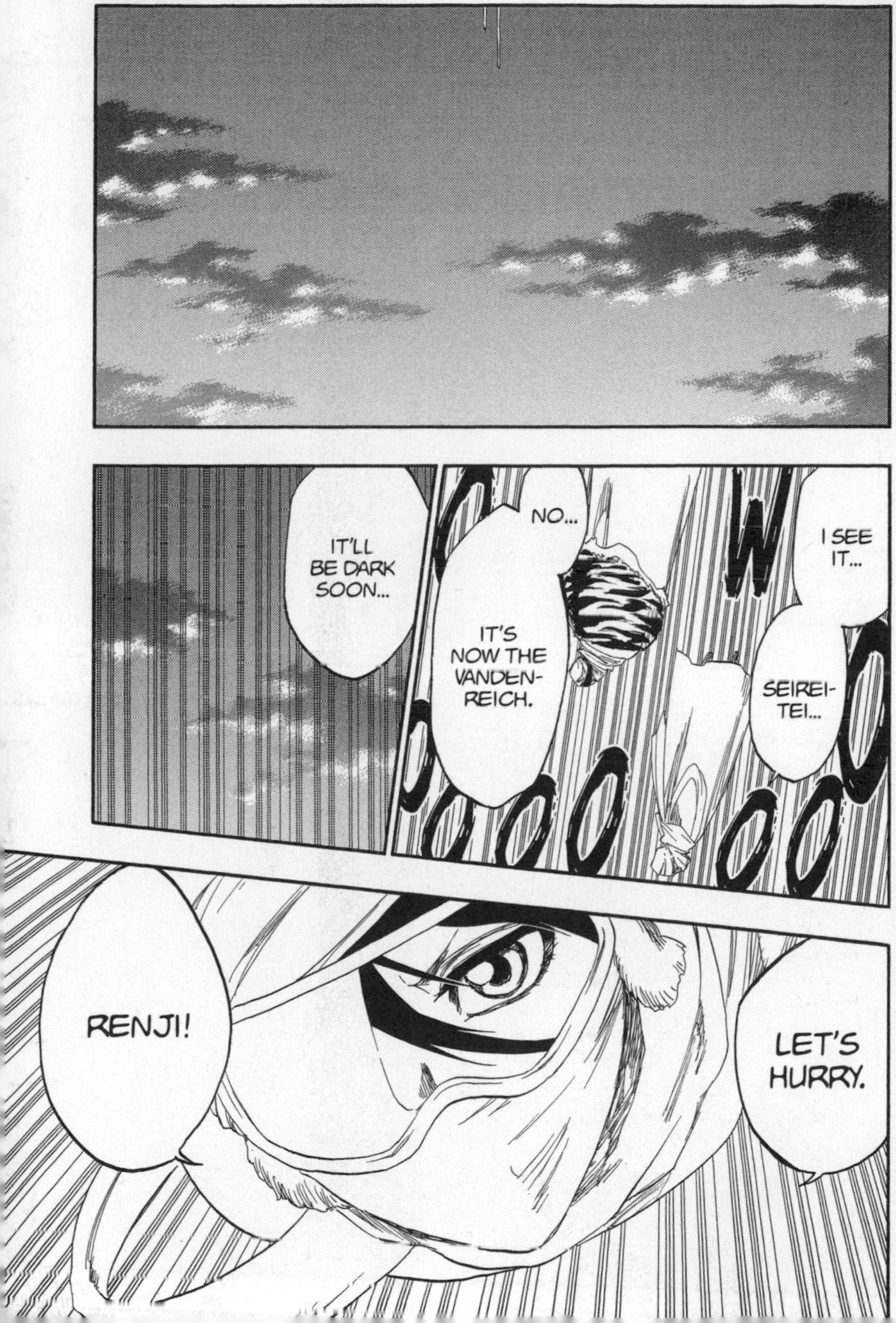
I SEE IT...
SEIREI-TEI...
NO...
IT'S NOW THE VANDEN-REICH.
IT'LL BE DARK SOON...
LET'S HURRY.
RENJI!

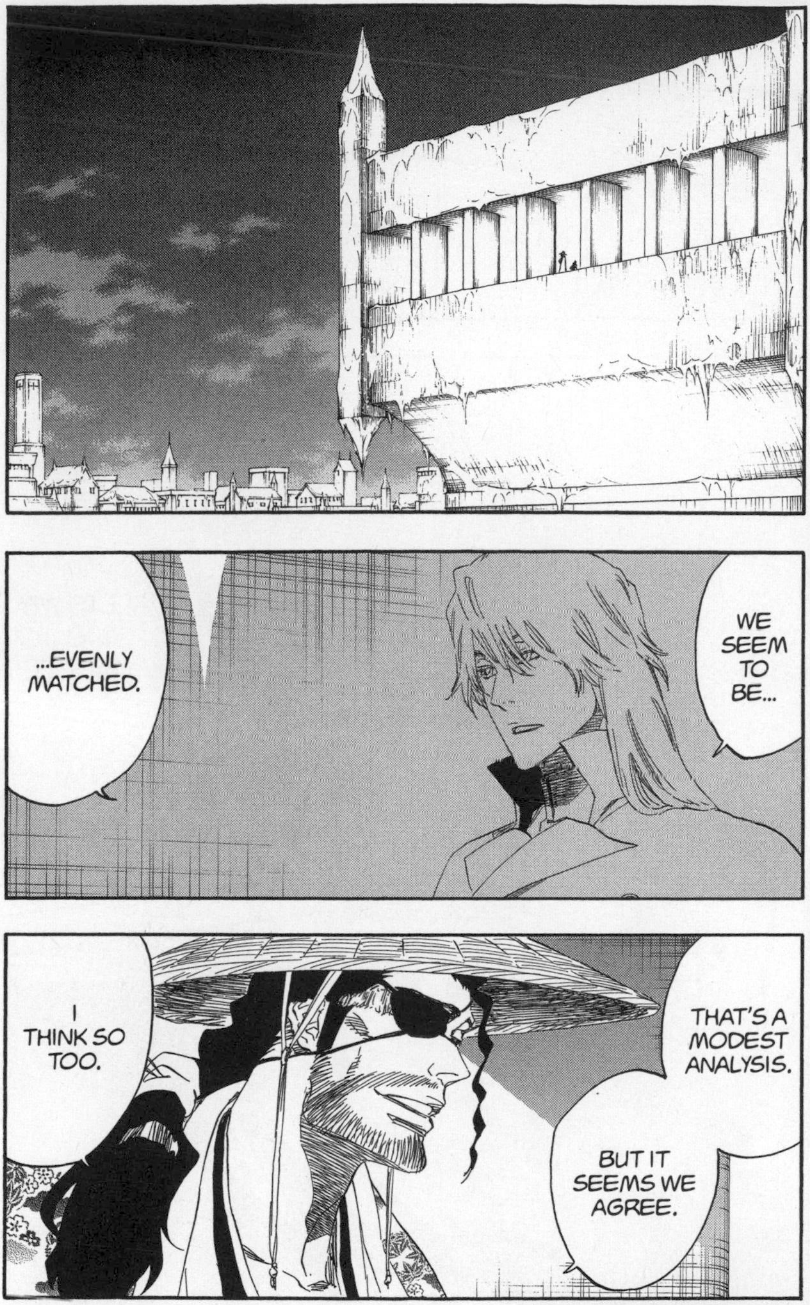
WE SEEM TO BE...
...EVENLY MATCHED.
THAT'S A MODEST ANALYSIS.
BUT IT SEEMS WE AGREE.
I THINK SO TOO.

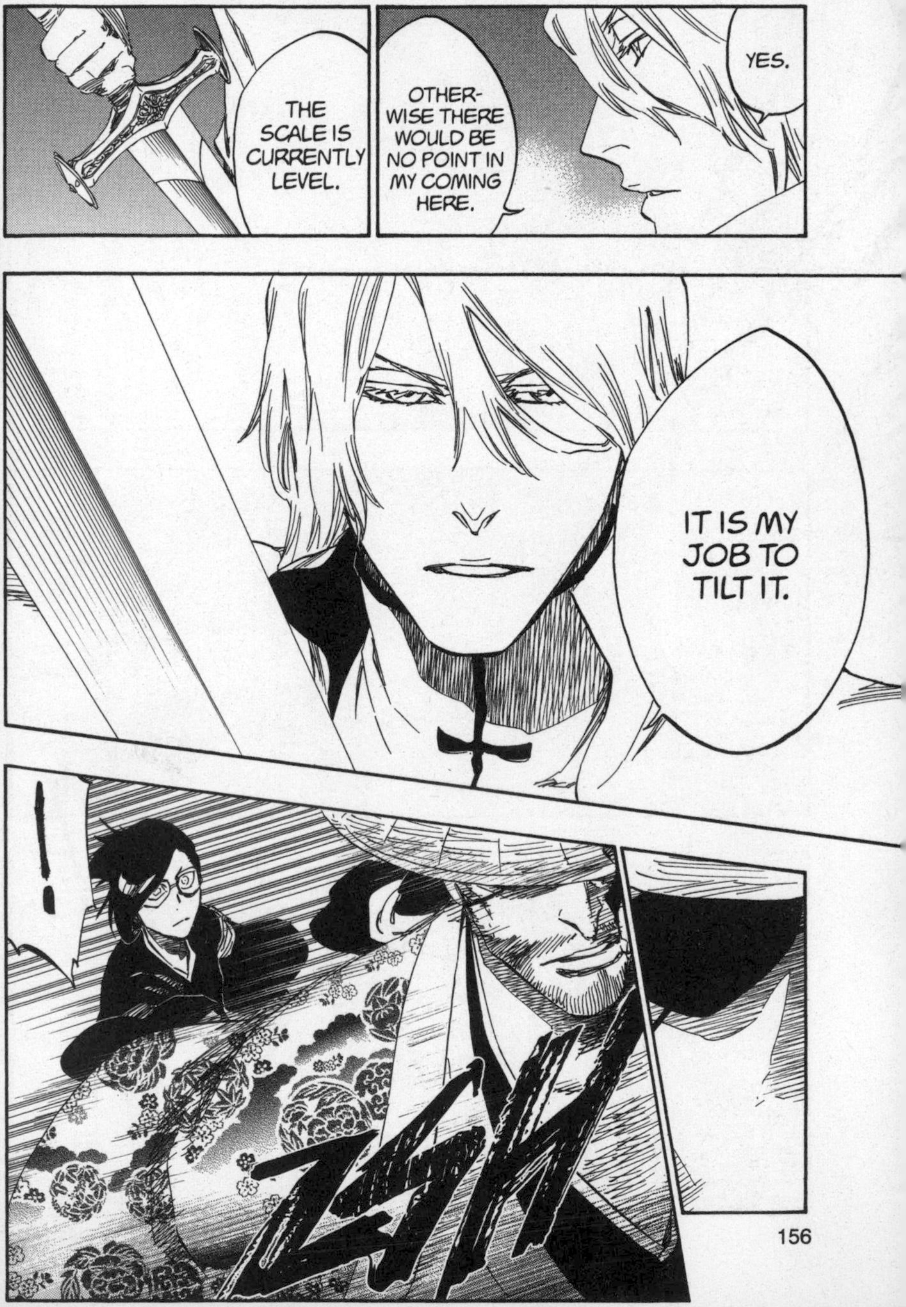
YES.
OTHER-WISE THERE WOULD BE NO POINT IN MY COMING HERE.
THE SCALE IS CURRENTLY LEVEL.
IT IS MY JOB TO TILT IT.
!
ZAK

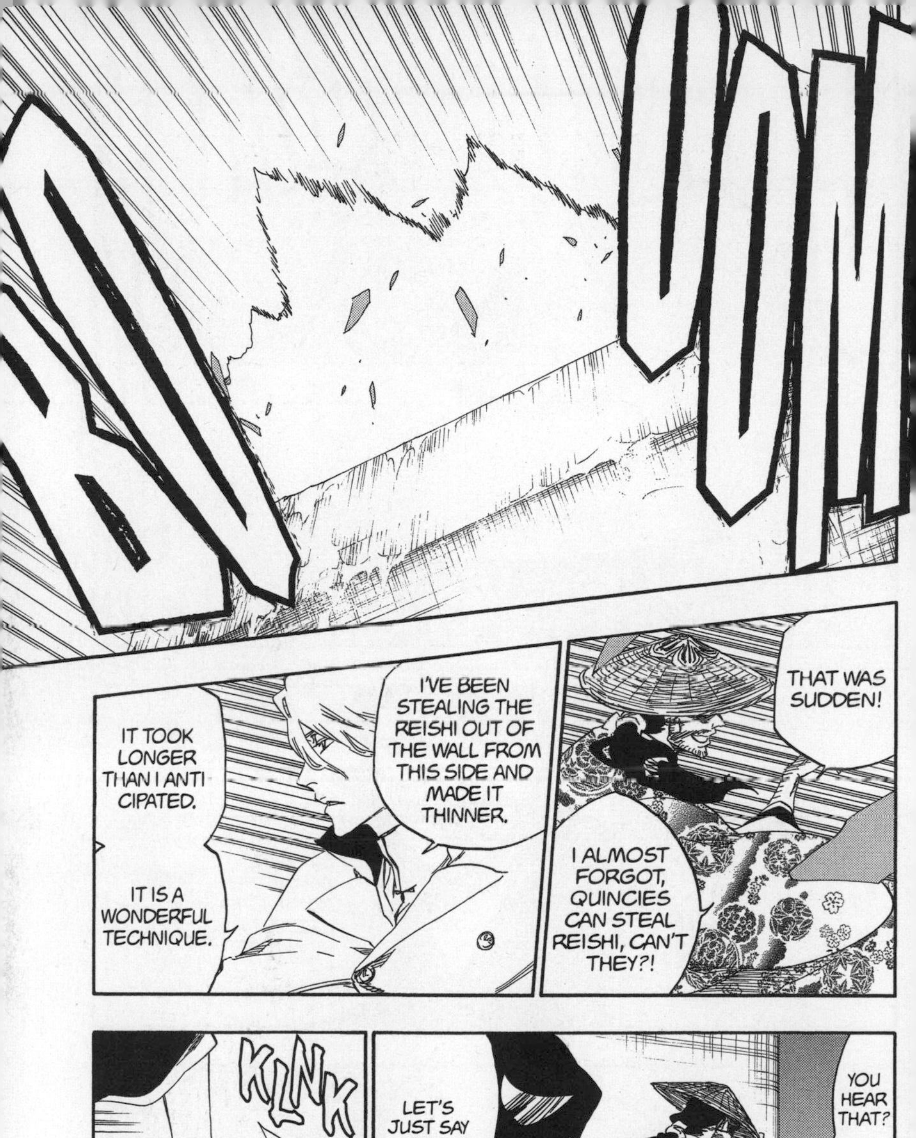
THAT WAS SUDDEN!
I ALMOST FORGOT, QUINCIES CAN STEAL REISHI, CAN'T THEY?!
I'VE BEEN STEALING THE REISHI OUT OF THE WALL FROM THIS SIDE AND MADE IT THINNER.
IT TOOK LONGER THAN I ANTI CIPATED.
IT IS A WONDERFUL TECHNIQUE.
YOU HEAR THAT?
LET'S JUST SAY I FEEL HONORED FOR NOW.
KLNK
BUT...

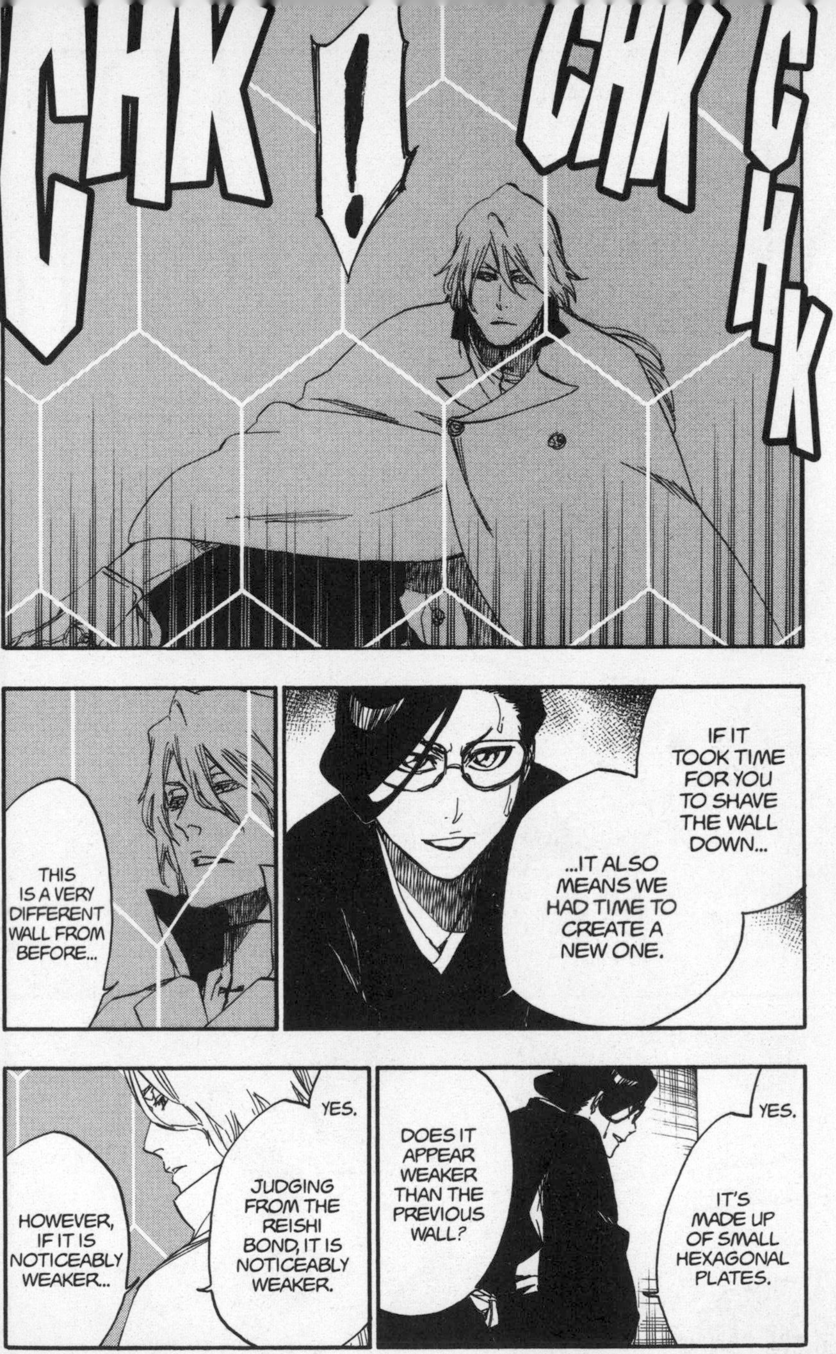
CHK
CHK
!
CHK
IF IT TOOK TIME FOR YOU TO SHAVE THE WALL DOWN...
...IT ALSO MEANS WE HAD TIME TO CREATE A NEW ONE.
THIS IS A VERY DIFFERENT WALL FROM BEFORE...
DOES IT APPEAR WEAKER THAN THE PREVIOUS WALL?
YES.
IT'S MADE UP OF SMALL HEXAGONAL PLATES.
YES.
JUDGING FROM THE REISHI BOND, IT IS NOTICEABLY WEAKER.
HOWEVER, IF IT IS NOTICEABLY WEAKER...

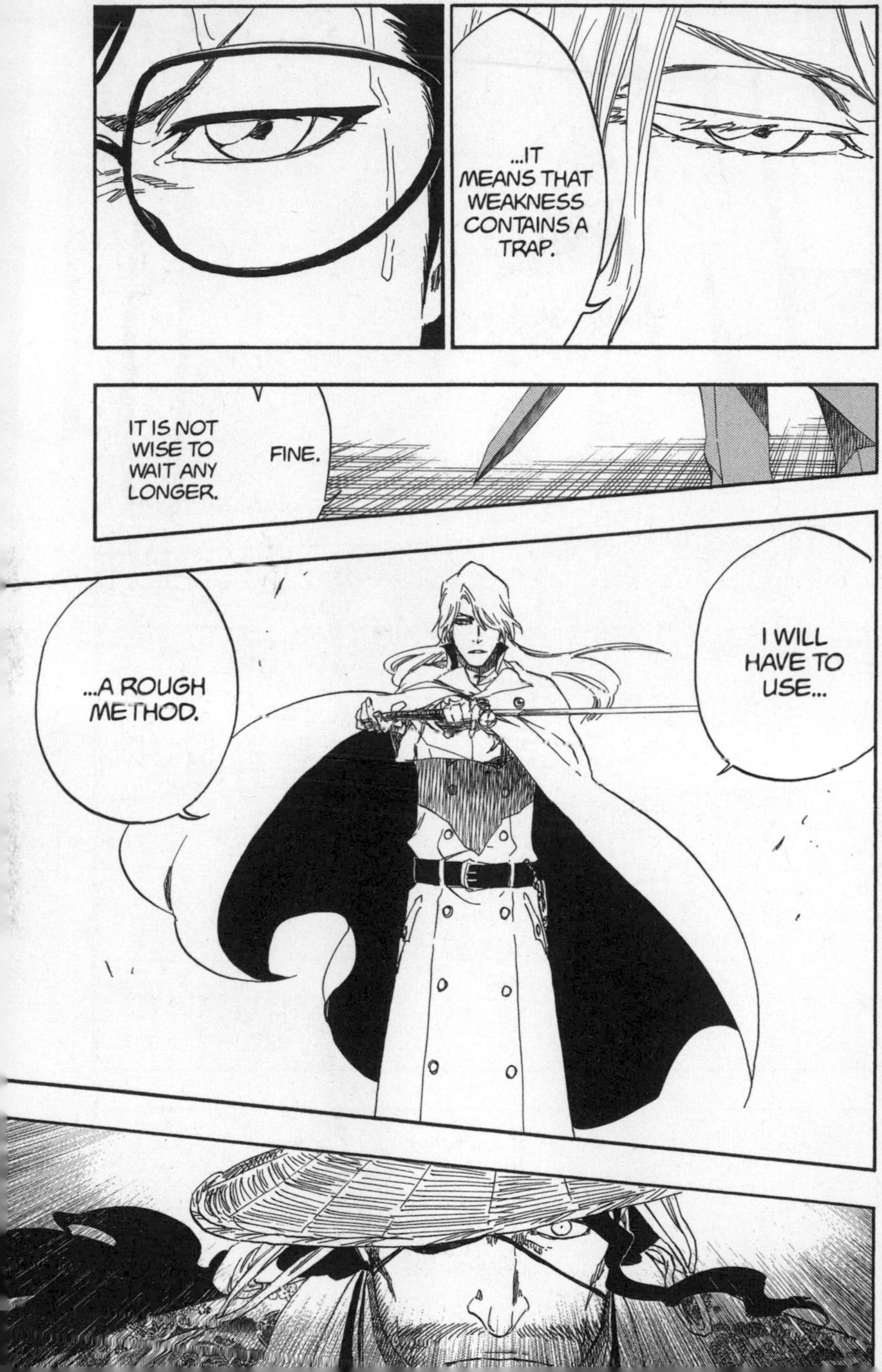
...IT MEANS THAT WEAKNESS CONTAINS A TRAP.
FINE.
IT IS NOT WISE TO WAIT ANY LONGER.
I WILL HAVE TO USE...
...A ROUGH METHOD.

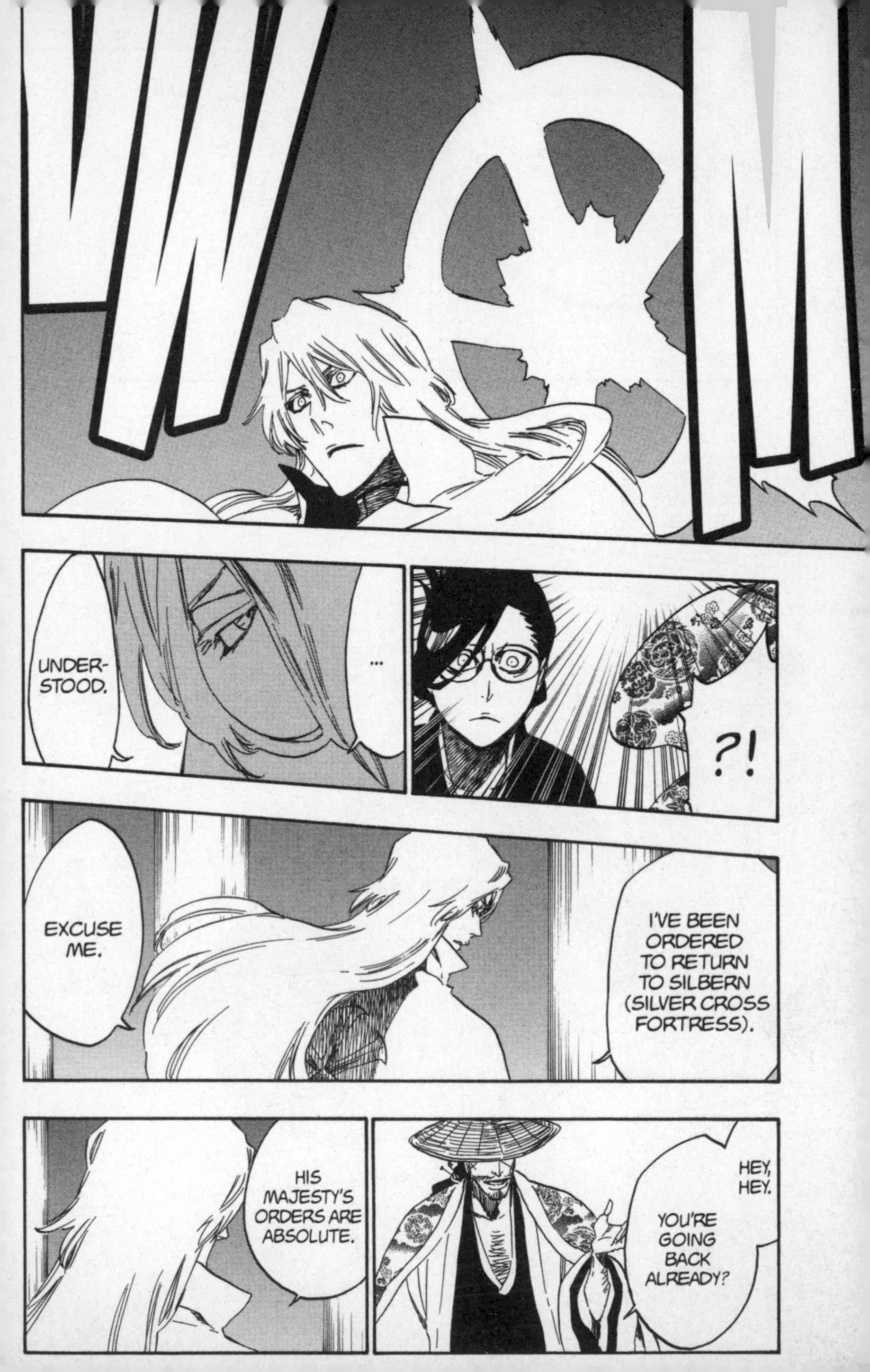
?!
...
UNDER-STOOD.
I'VE BEEN ORDERED TO RETURN TO SILBERN (SILVER CROSS FORTRESS).
EXCUSE ME.
HEY, HEY.
YOU'RE GOING BACK ALREADY?
HIS MAJESTY'S ORDERS ARE ABSOLUTE.

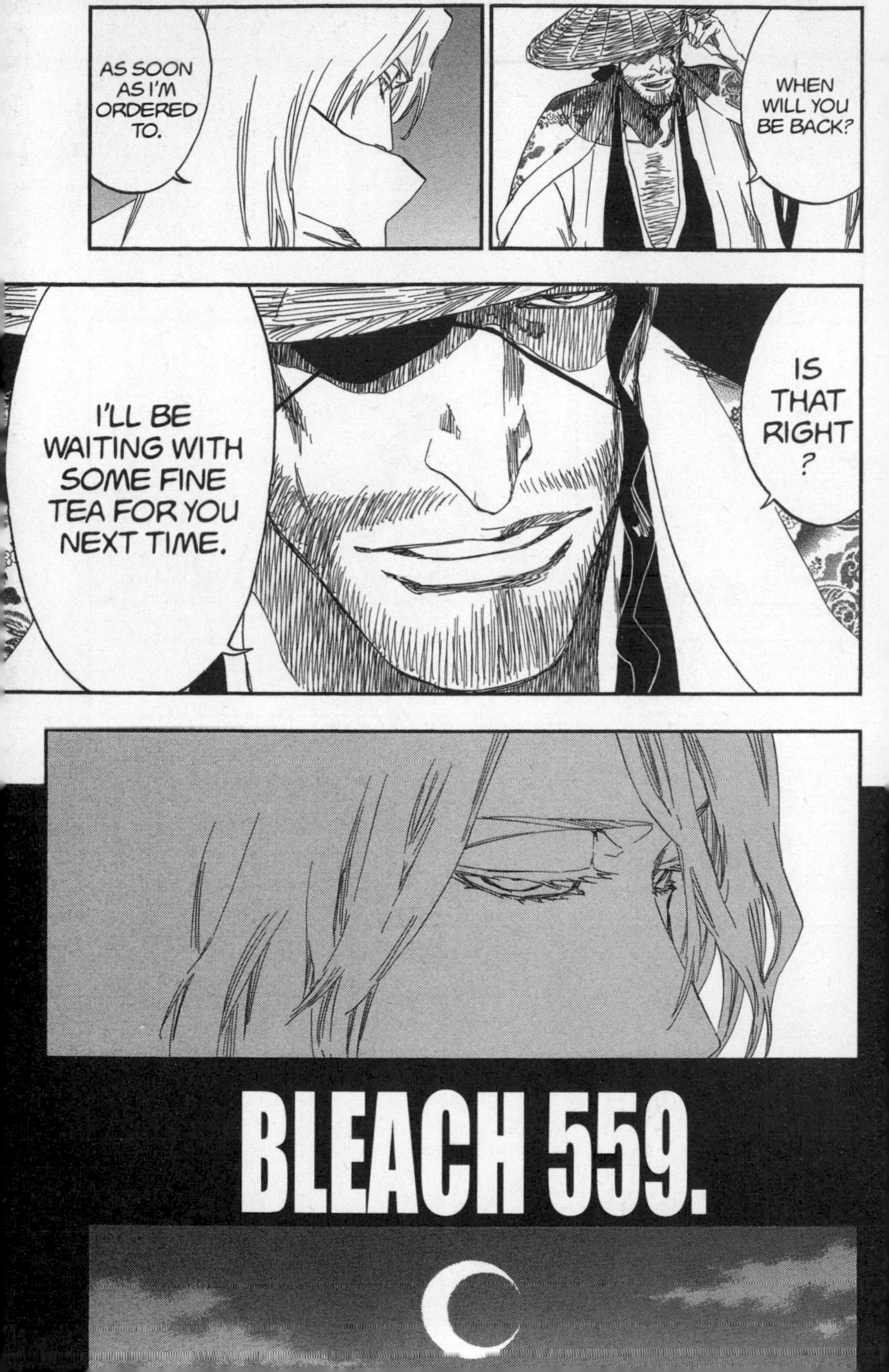
WHEN WILL YOU BE BACK?
AS SOON AS I'M ORDERED TO.
IS THAT RIGHT?
I'LL BE WAITING WITH SOME FINE TEA FOR YOU NEXT TIME.
BLEACH 559.

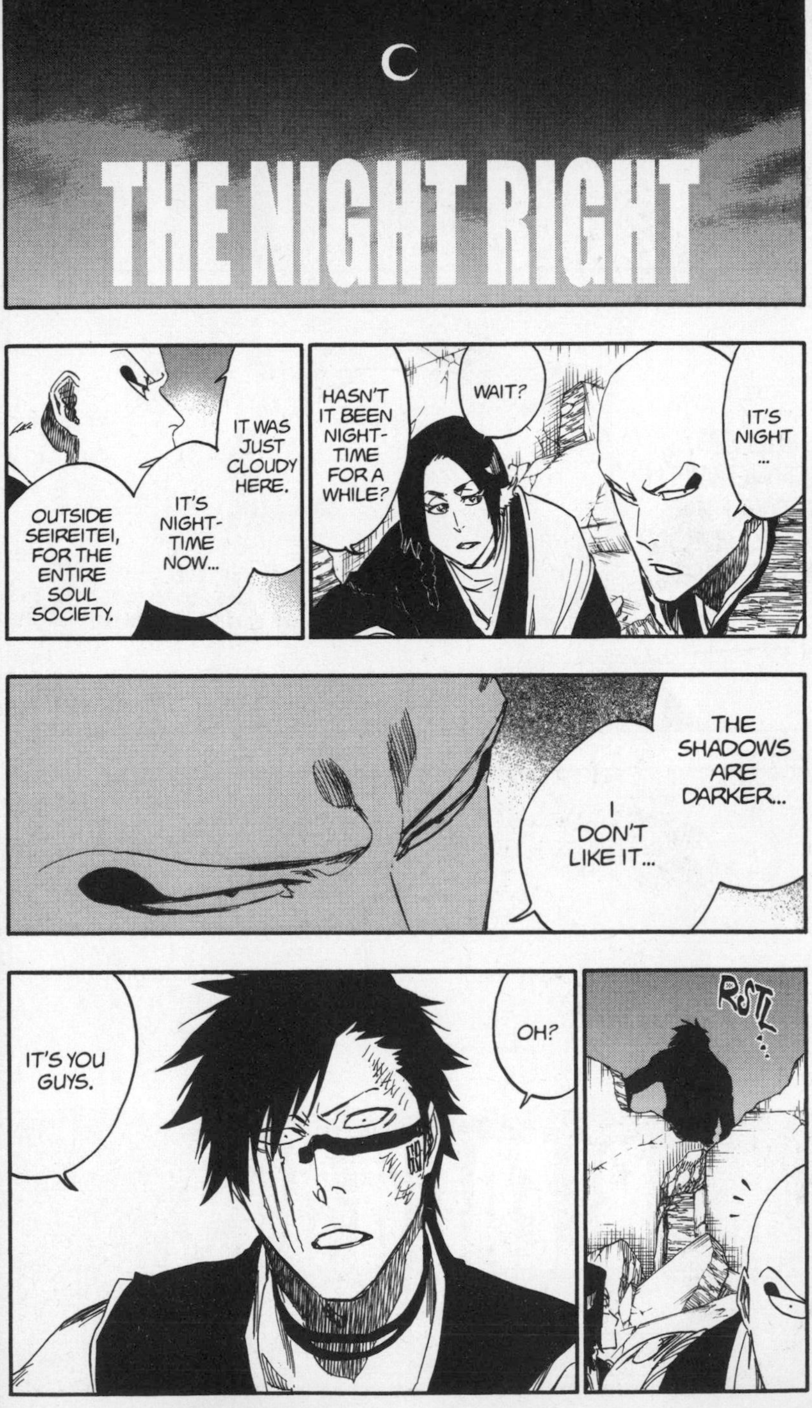
THE NIGHT RIGHT
IT'S NIGHT ...
WAIT?
HASN'T IT BEEN NIGHT-TIME FOR A WHILE?
IT WAS JUST CLOUDY HERE.
IT'S NIGHT-TIME NOW...
OUTSIDE SEIREITEI, FOR THE ENTIRE SOUL SOCIETY.
THE SHADOWS ARE DARKER...
I DON'T LIKE IT...
RSTL
OH?
IT'S YOU GUYS.

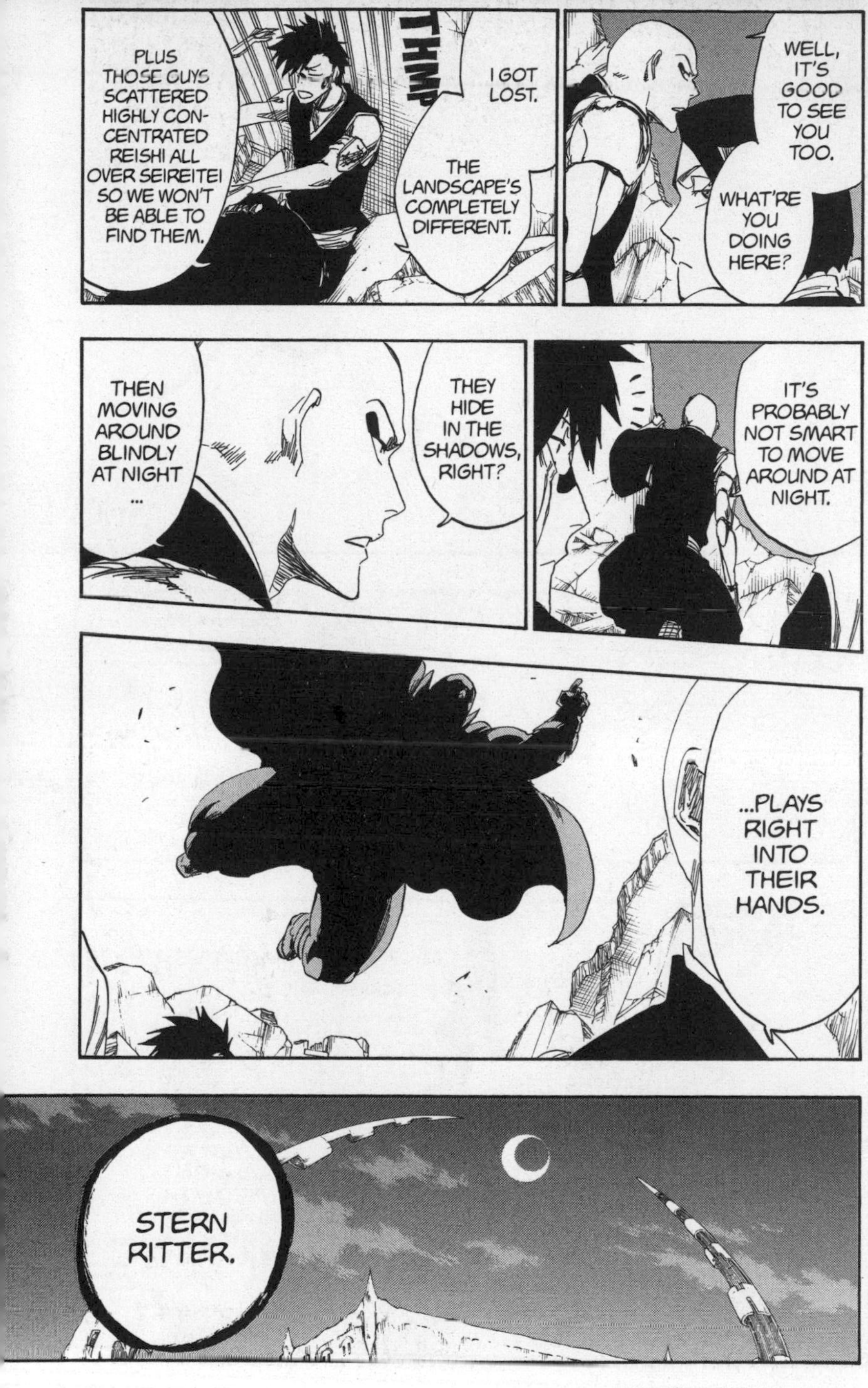
WELL, IT'S GOOD TO SEE YOU TOO.
WHAT'RE YOU DOING HERE?
I GOT LOST.
THMP
THE LANDSCAPE'S COMPLETELY DIFFERENT.
PLUS THOSE GUYS SCATTERED HIGHLY CON-CENTRATED REISHI ALL OVER SEIREITEI SO WE WON'T BE ABLE TO FIND THEM.
IT'S PROBABLY NOT SMART TO MOVE AROUND AT NIGHT.
THEY HIDE IN THE SHADOWS, RIGHT?
THEN MOVING AROUND BLINDLY AT NIGHT ...
...PLAYS RIGHT INTO THEIR HANDS.
STERN RITTER.

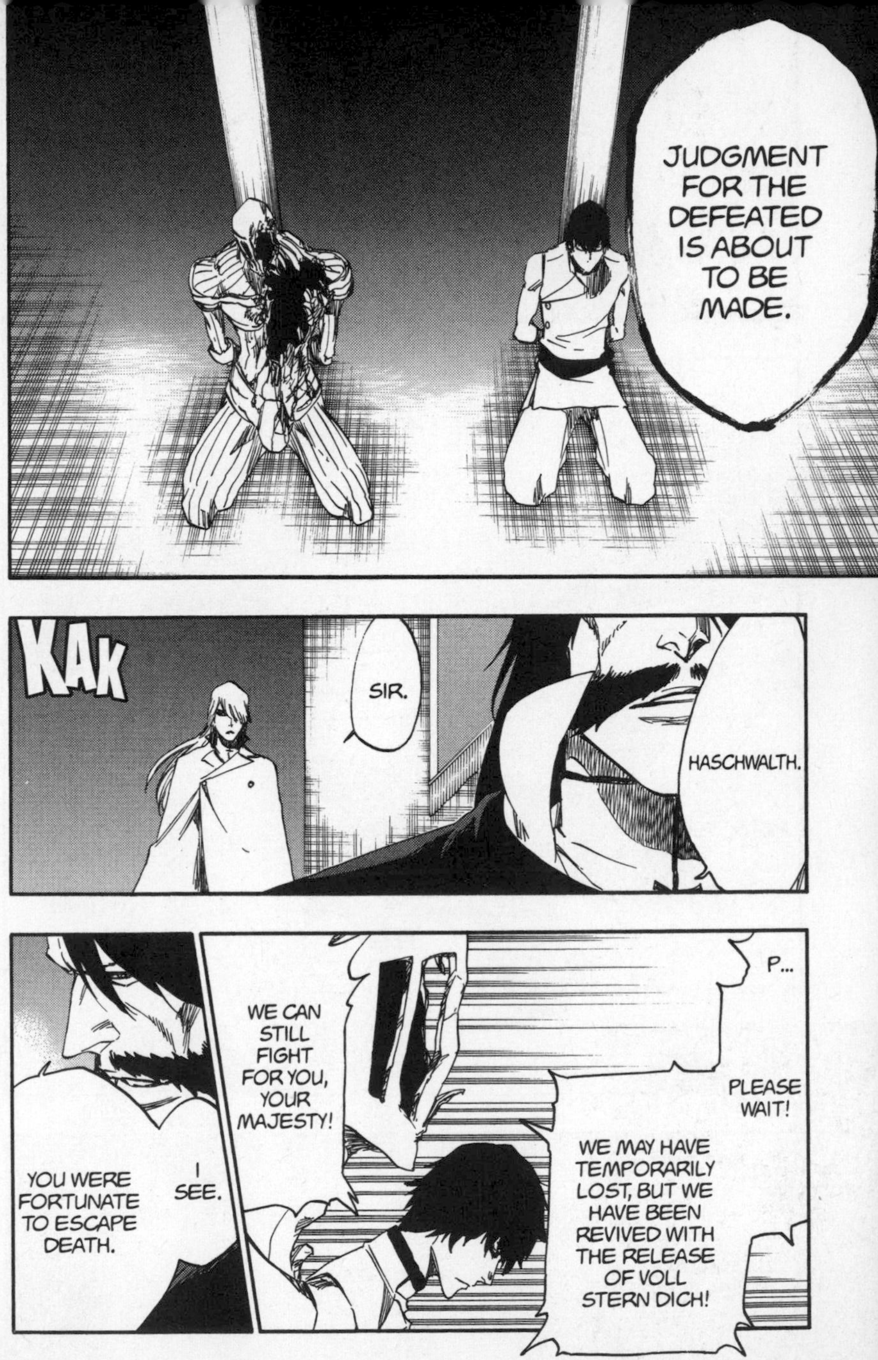
JUDGMENT FOR THE DEFEATED IS ABOUT TO BE MADE.
HASCHWALTH.
SIR.
KAK
P...
PLEASE WAIT!
WE MAY HAVE TEMPORARILY LOST, BUT WE HAVE BEEN REVIVED WITH THE RELEASE OF VOLL STERN DICH!
WE CAN STILL FIGHT FOR YOU, YOUR MAJESTY!
I SEE.
YOU WERE FORTUNATE TO ESCAPE DEATH.

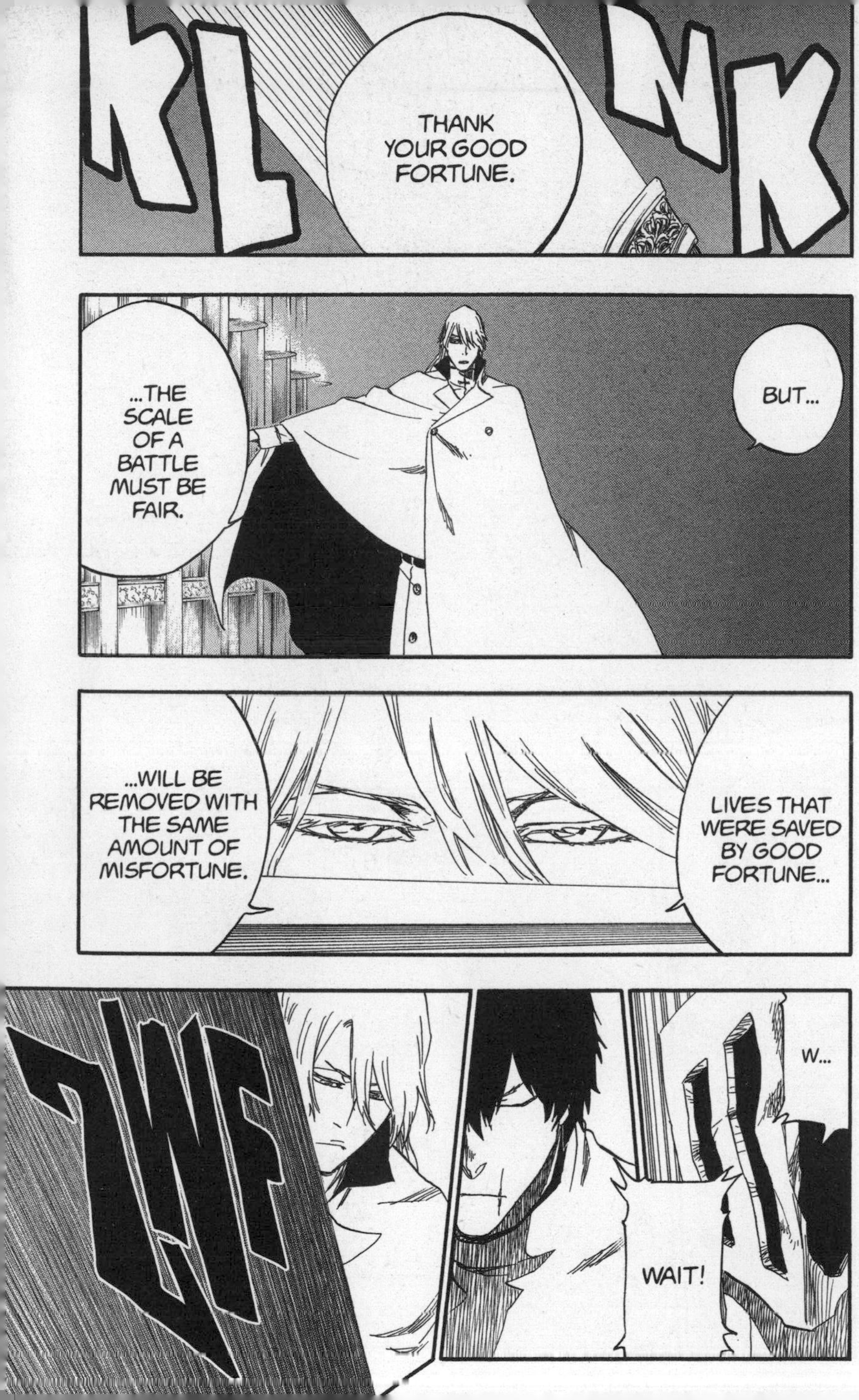
KL
NK
THANK YOUR GOOD FORTUNE.
BUT...
...THE SCALE OF A BATTLE MUST BE FAIR.
LIVES THAT WERE SAVED BY GOOD FORTUNE...
...WILL BE REMOVED WITH THE SAME AMOUNT OF MISFORTUNE.
W...
WAIT!

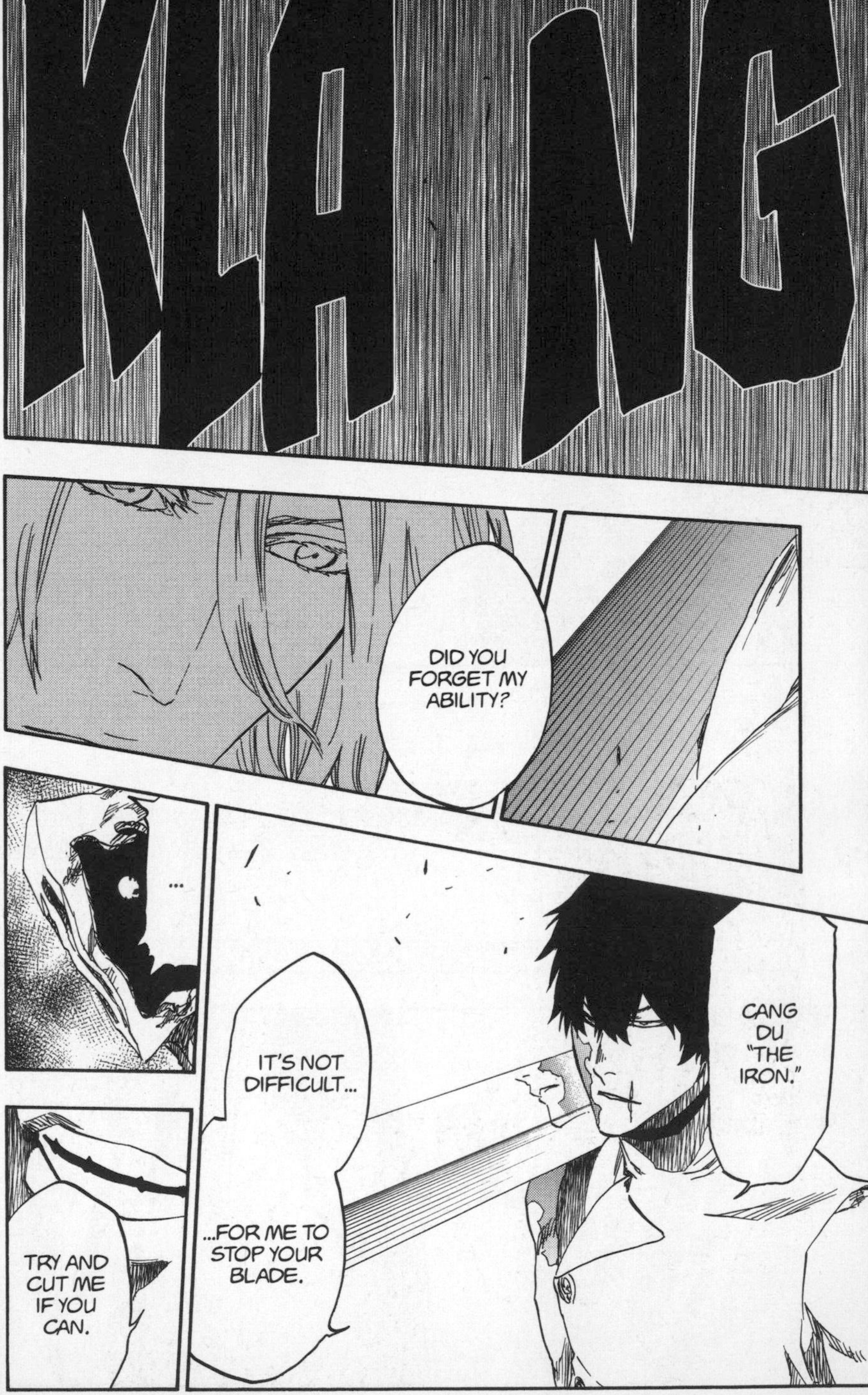
KLANG
DID YOU FORGET MY ABILITY?
CANG DU "THE IRON."
IT'S NOT DIFFICULT...
...FOR ME TO STOP YOUR BLADE.
...
TRY AND CUT ME IF YOU CAN.

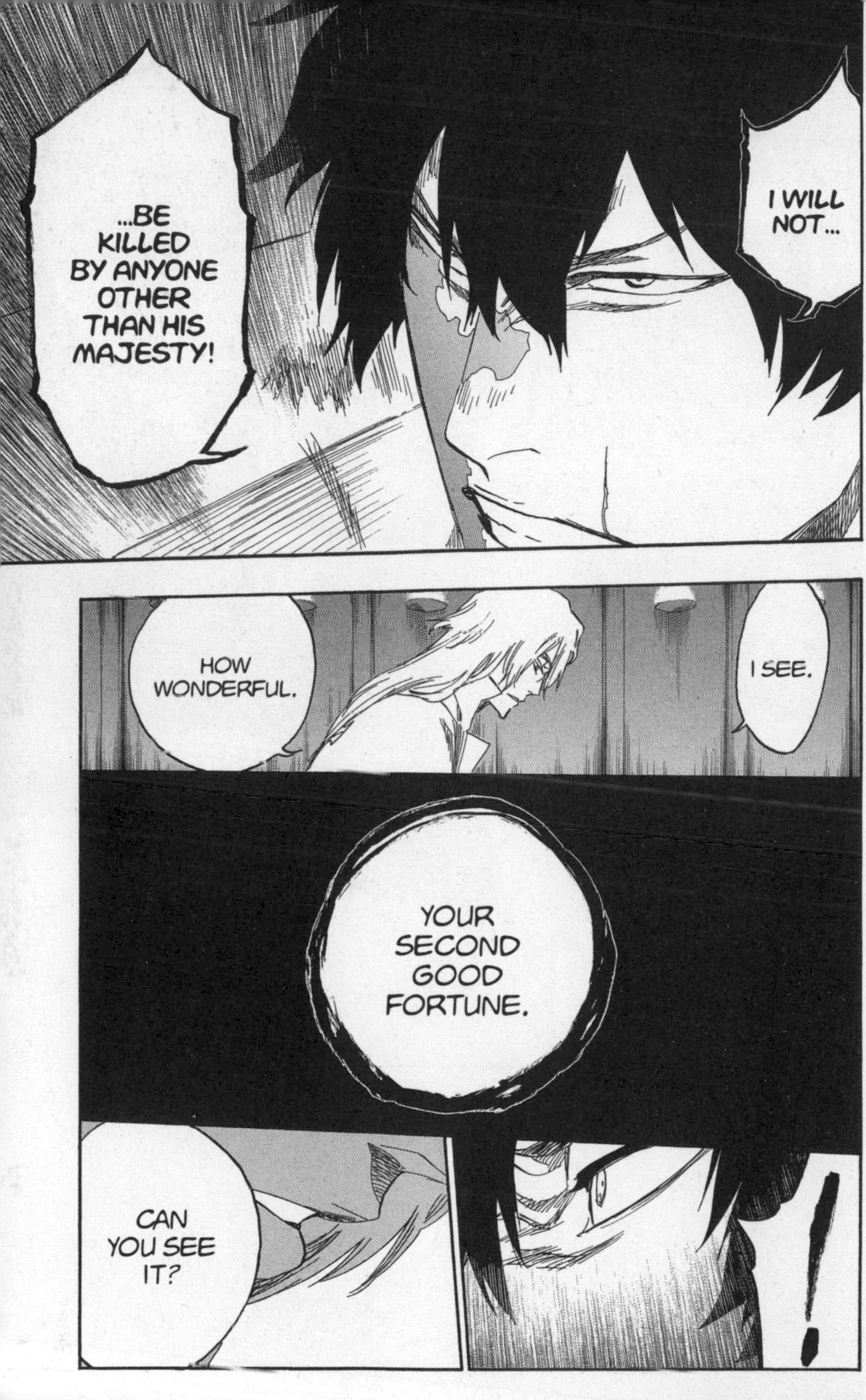
I WILL NOT...
...BE KILLED BY ANYONE OTHER THAN HIS MAJESTY!
I SEE.
HOW WONDERFUL.
YOUR SECOND GOOD FORTUNE.
!
CAN YOU SEE IT?

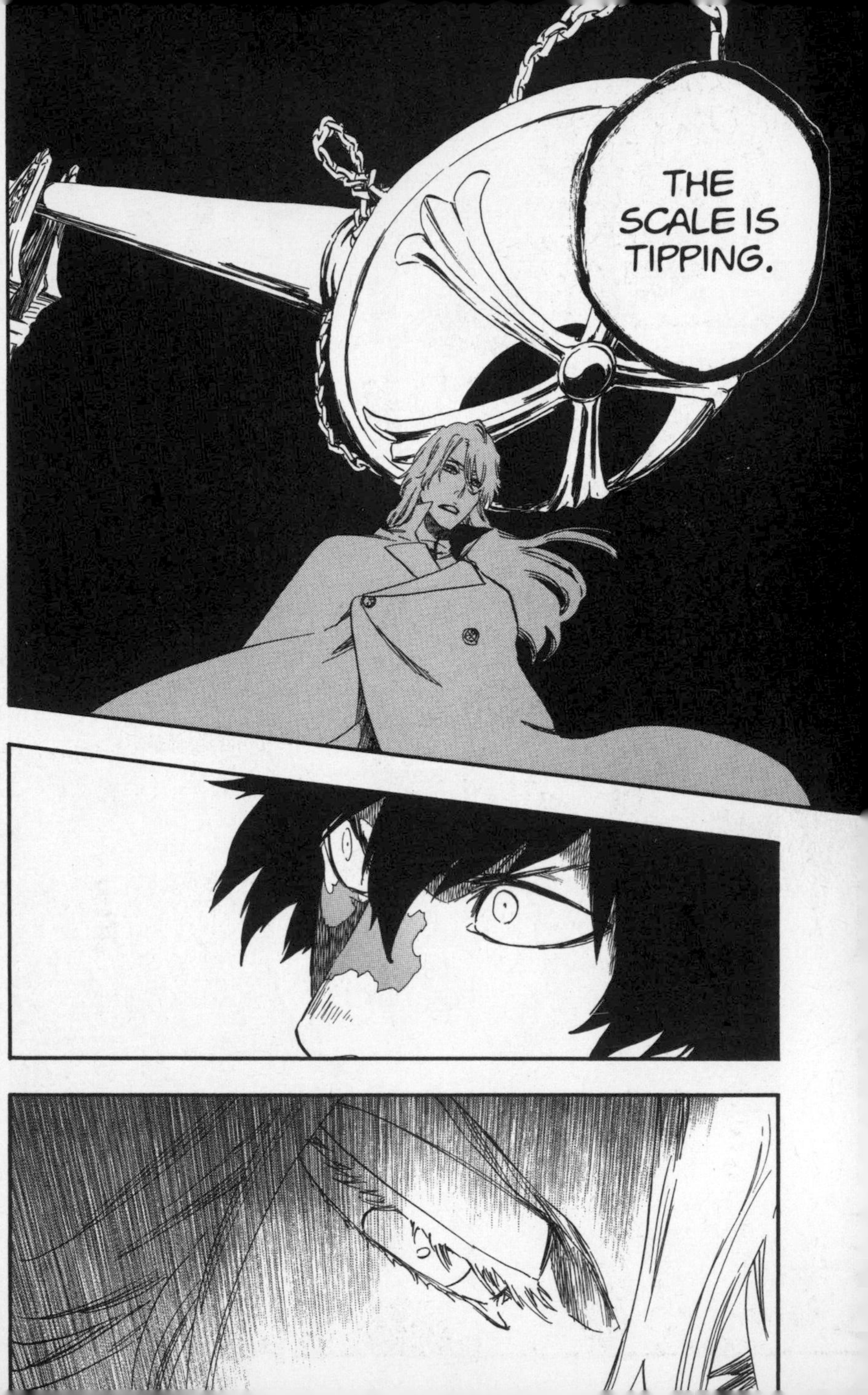
THE SCALE IS TIPPING.

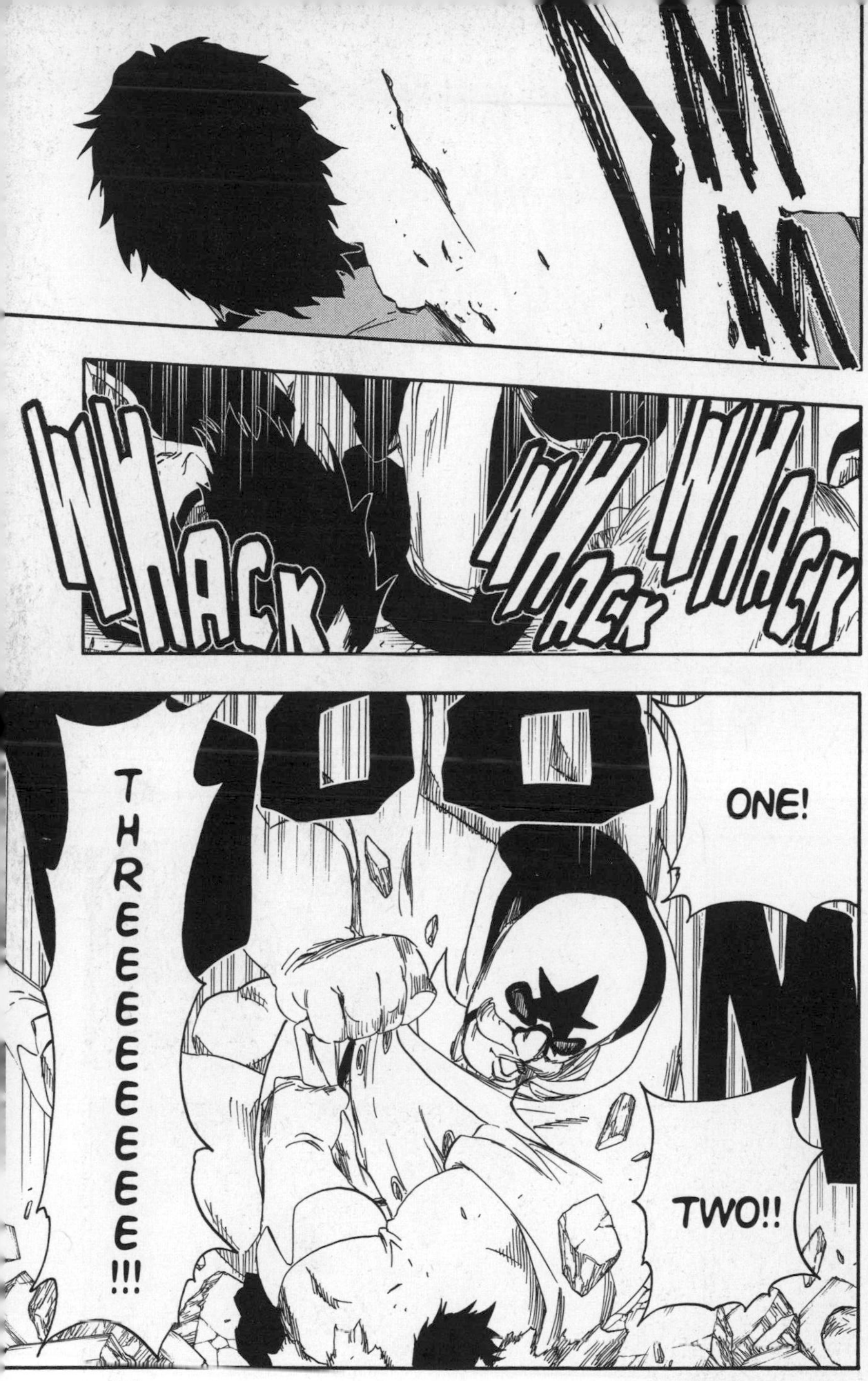
WHACK
WHACK
WHACK
ONE!
TWO!!
THREEEEEEEEEEE!!!

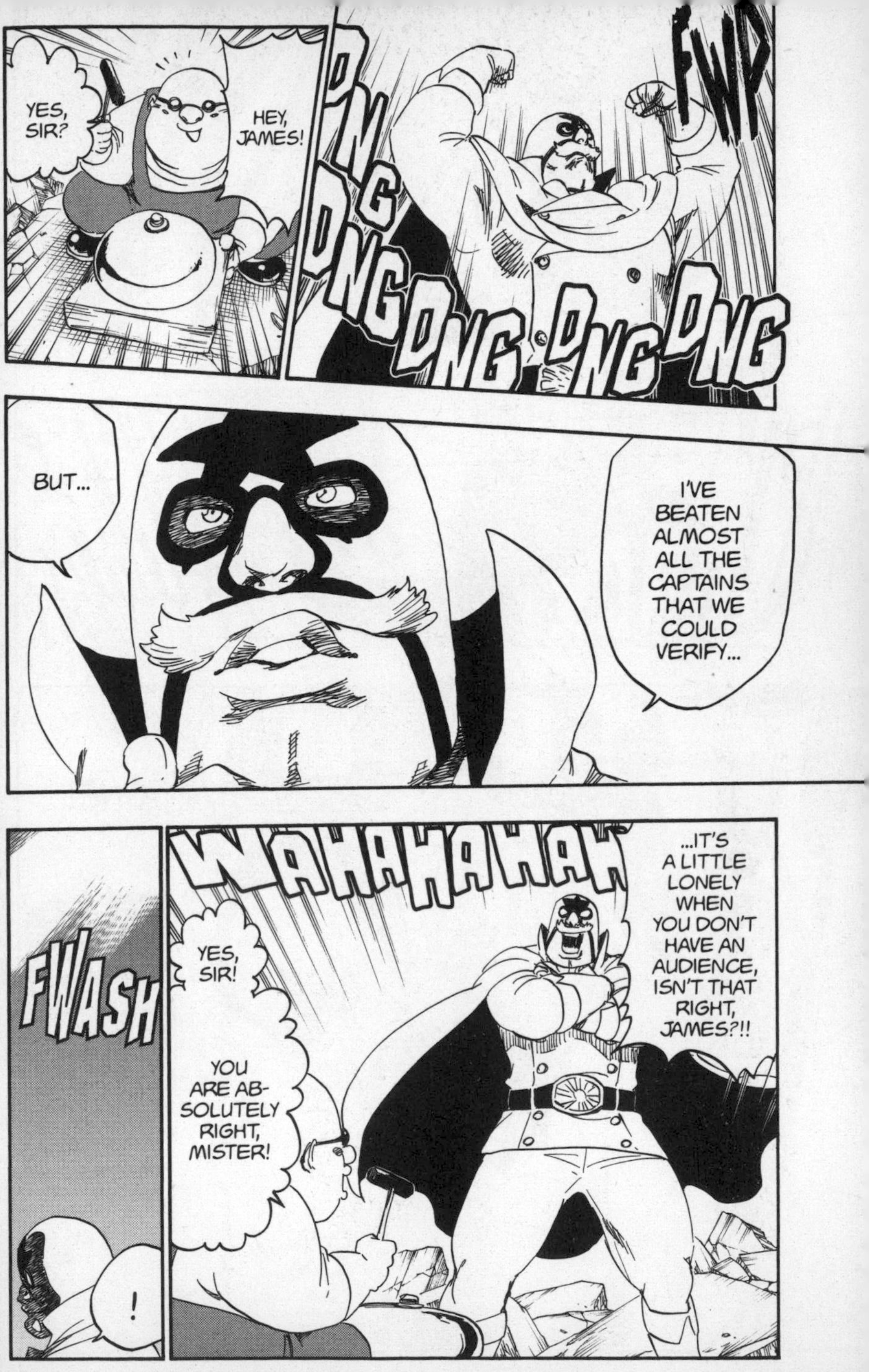
FWP
DNG DNG DNG DNG DNG DNG
HEY, JAMES!
YES, SIR?
I'VE BEATEN ALMOST ALL THE CAPTAINS THAT WE COULD VERIFY...
BUT...
WAHAHAHAHAH
...IT'S A LITTLE LONELY WHEN YOU DON'T HAVE AN AUDIENCE, ISN'T THAT RIGHT, JAMES?!!
YES, SIR!
YOU ARE AB-SOLUTELY RIGHT, MISTER!
FWASH
!

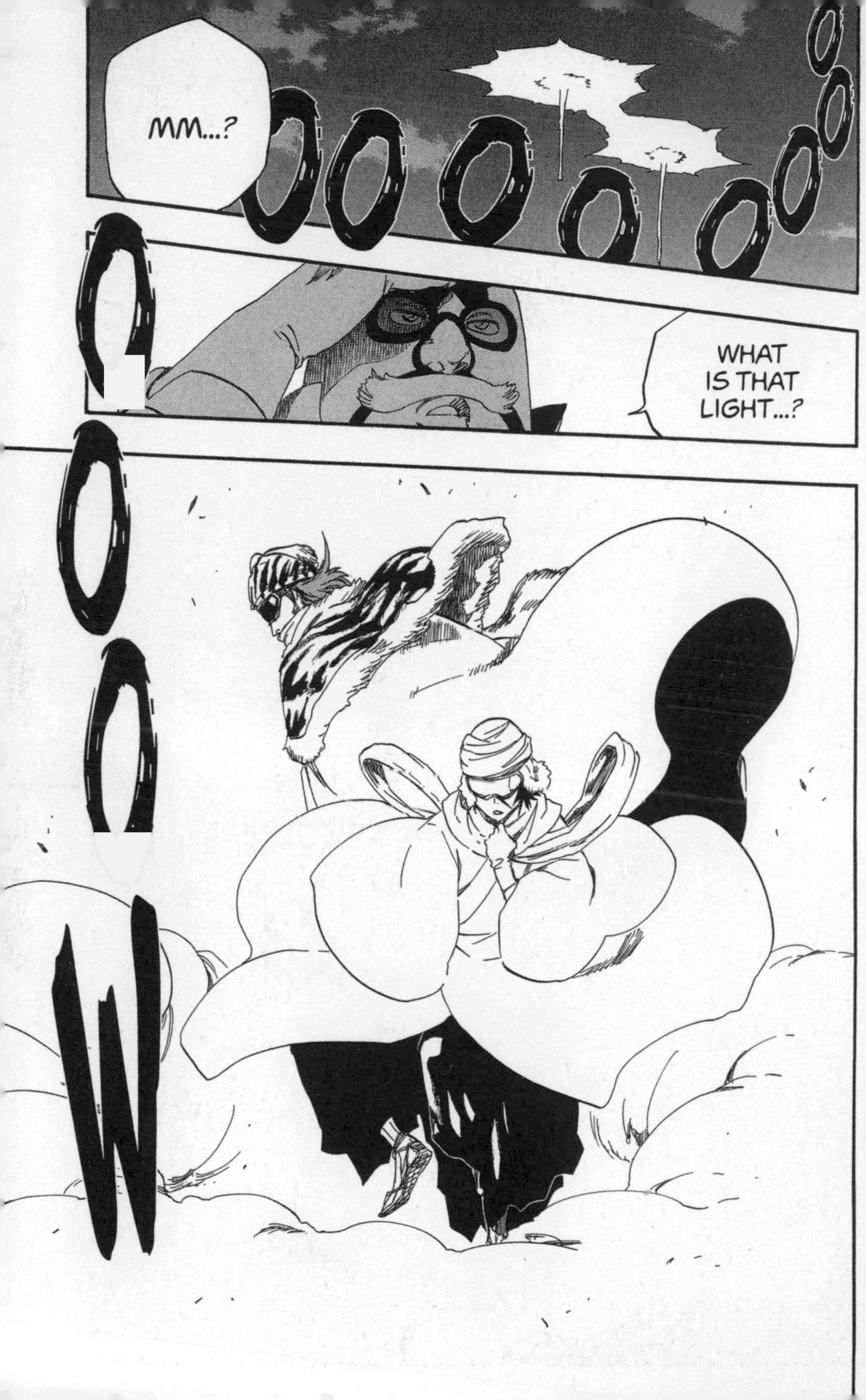
MM...?
WHAT IS THAT LIGHT...?

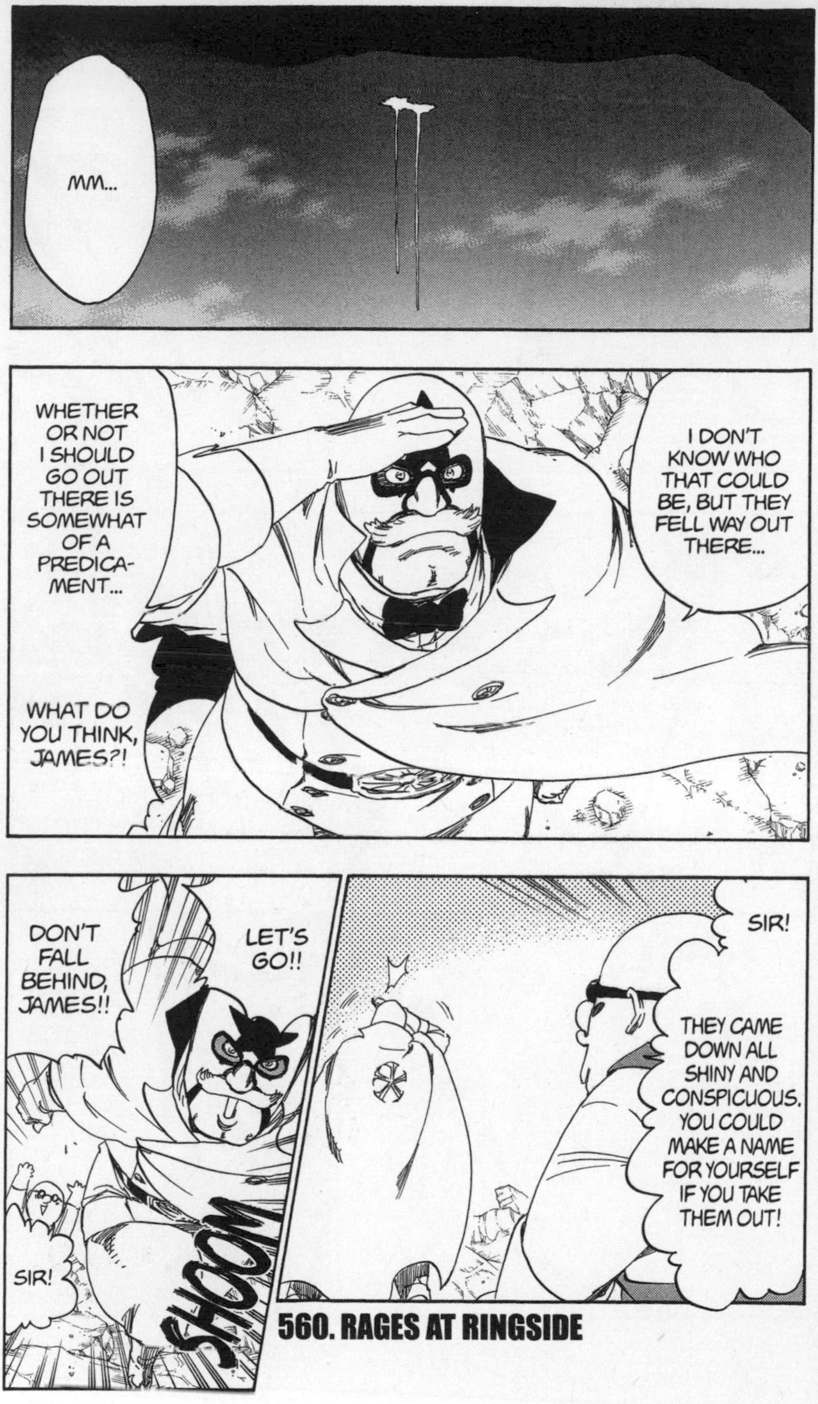
MM...
I DON'T KNOW WHO THAT COULD BE, BUT THEY FELL WAY OUT THERE...
WHETHER OR NOT I SHOULD GO OUT THERE IS SOMEWHAT OF A PREDICA-MENT...
WHAT DO YOU THINK, JAMES?!
SIR!
THEY CAME DOWN ALL SHINY AND CONSPICUOUS. YOU COULD MAKE A NAME FOR YOURSELF IF YOU TAKE THEM OUT!
LET'S GO!!
DON'T FALL BEHIND, JAMES!!
SHOOM
SIR!

560. RAGES AT RINGSIDE

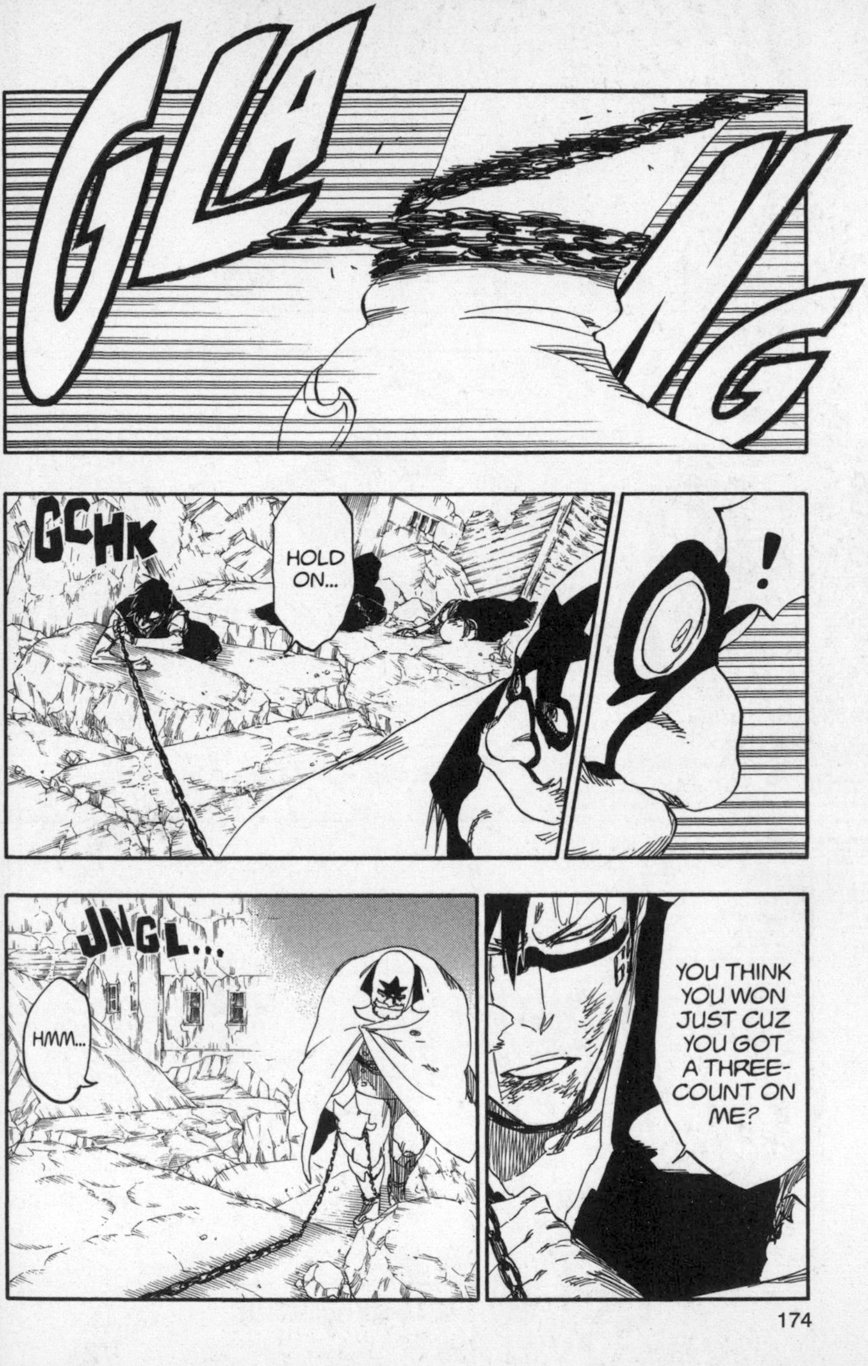
GLANG
!
GCHK
HOLD ON...
YOU THINK YOU WON JUST CUZ YOU GOT A THREE-COUNT ON ME?
JNGL...
HMM...

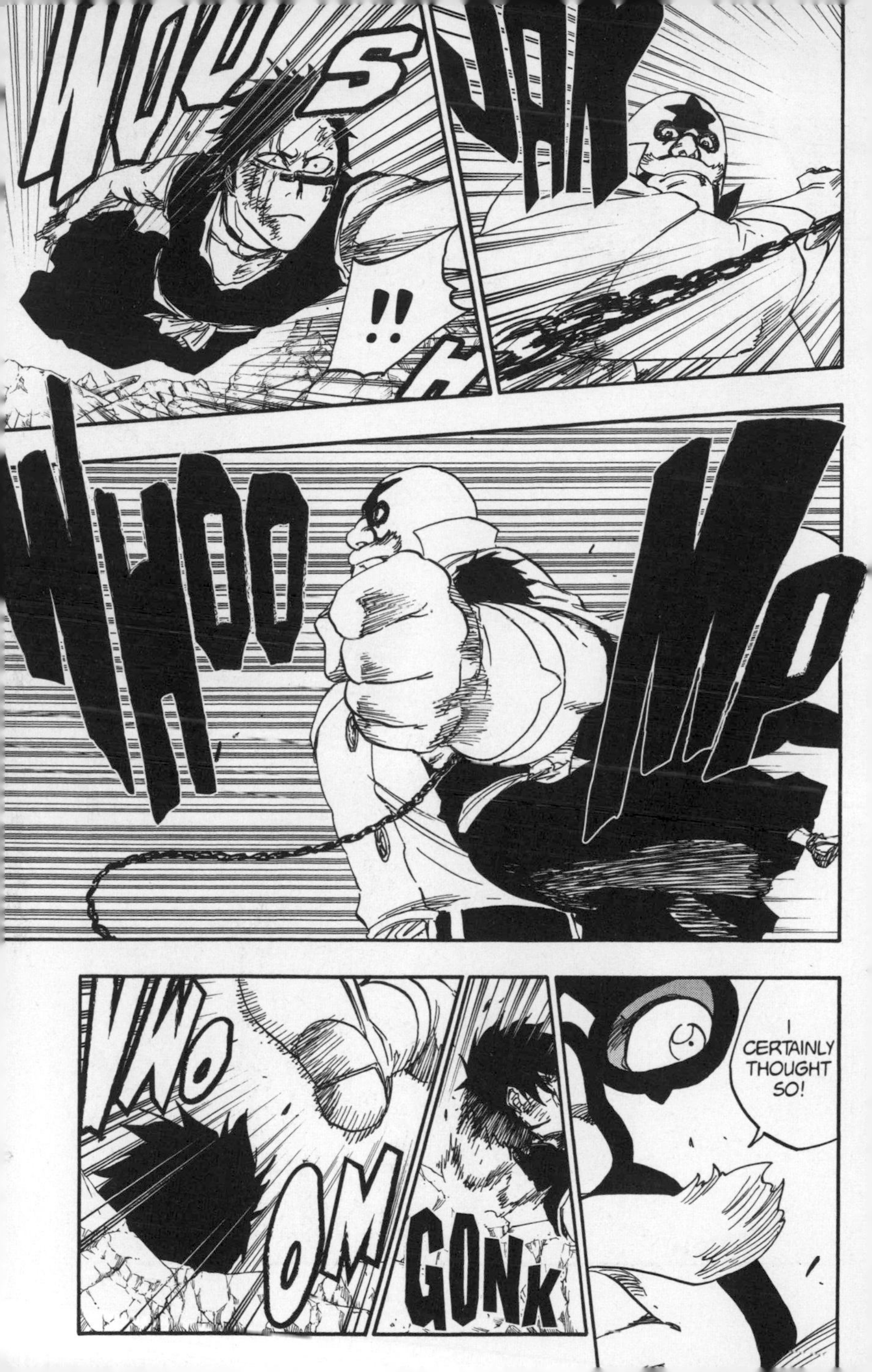
JAK
!!
WHOOMP
I CERTAINLY THOUGHT SO!
GONK
WHOOM

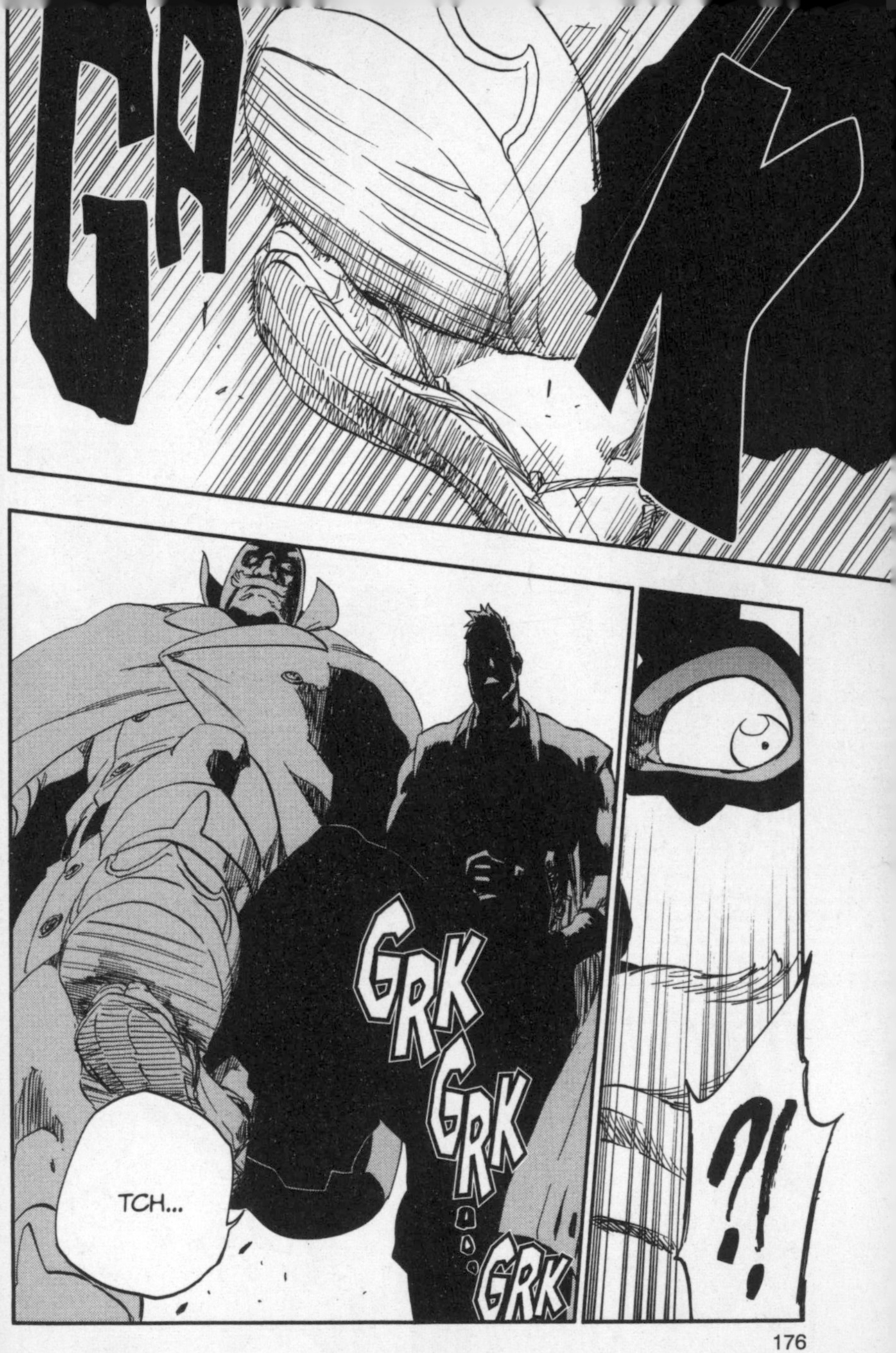
GA
?!
GRK GRK
GRK
TCH...

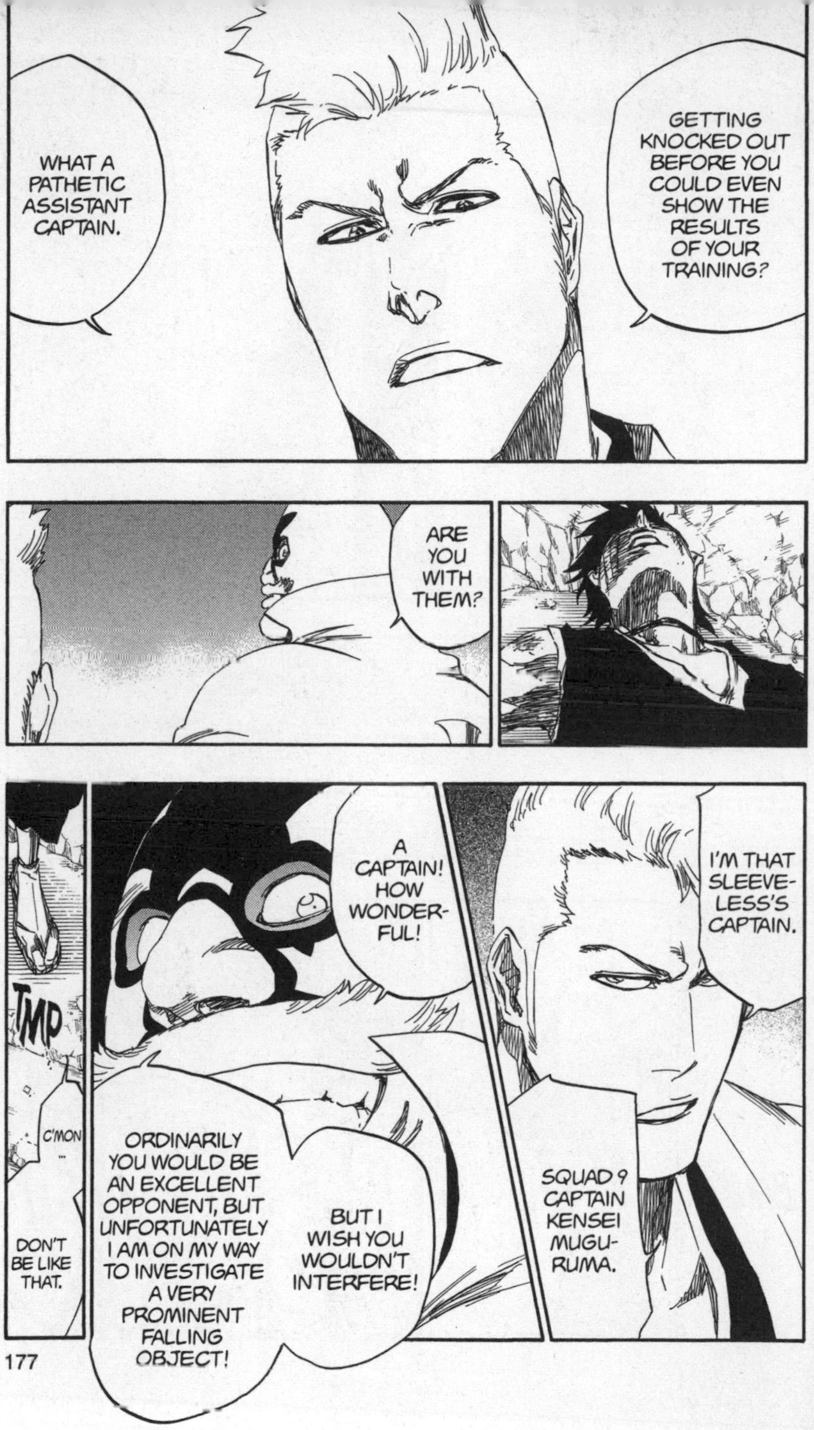
GETTING KNOCKED OUT BEFORE YOU COULD EVEN SHOW THE RESULTS OF YOUR TRAINING?
WHAT A PATHETIC ASSISTANT CAPTAIN.
ARE YOU WITH THEM?
I'M THAT SLEEVE-LESS'S CAPTAIN.
SQUAD 9 CAPTAIN KENSEI MUGU-RUMA.
A CAPTAIN! HOW WONDER-FUL!
BUT I WISH YOU WOULDN'T INTERFERE!
ORDINARILY YOU WOULD BE AN EXCELLENT OPPONENT, BUT UNFORTUNATELY I AM ON MY WAY TO INVESTIGATE A VERY PROMINENT FALLING OBJECT!
TMP
C'MON ...
DON'T BE LIKE THAT.

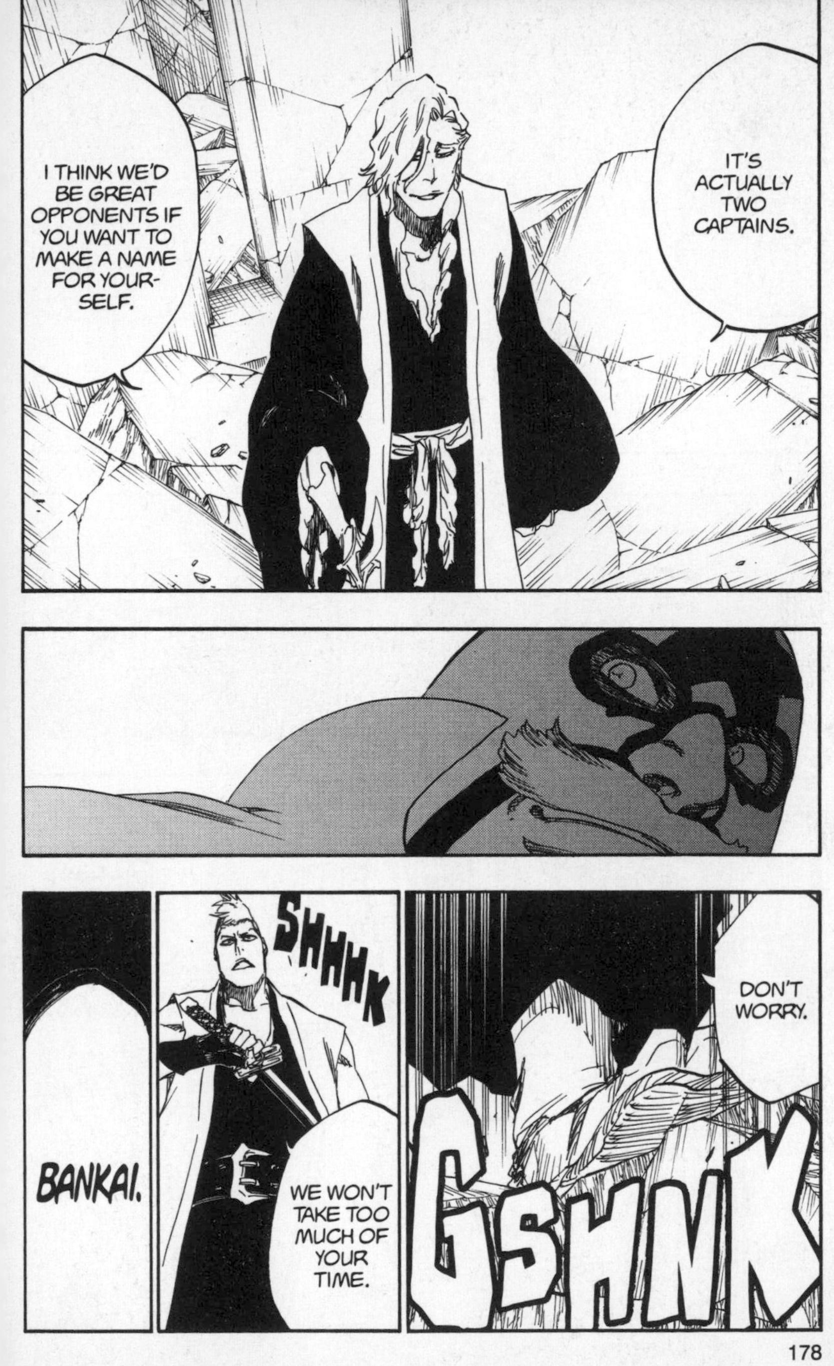
IT'S ACTUALLY TWO CAPTAINS.
I THINK WE'D BE GREAT OPPONENTS IF YOU WANT TO MAKE A NAME FOR YOURSELF.
DON'T WORRY.
GSHNK
SHHHK
WE WON'T TAKE TOO MUCH OF YOUR TIME.
BANKAI.

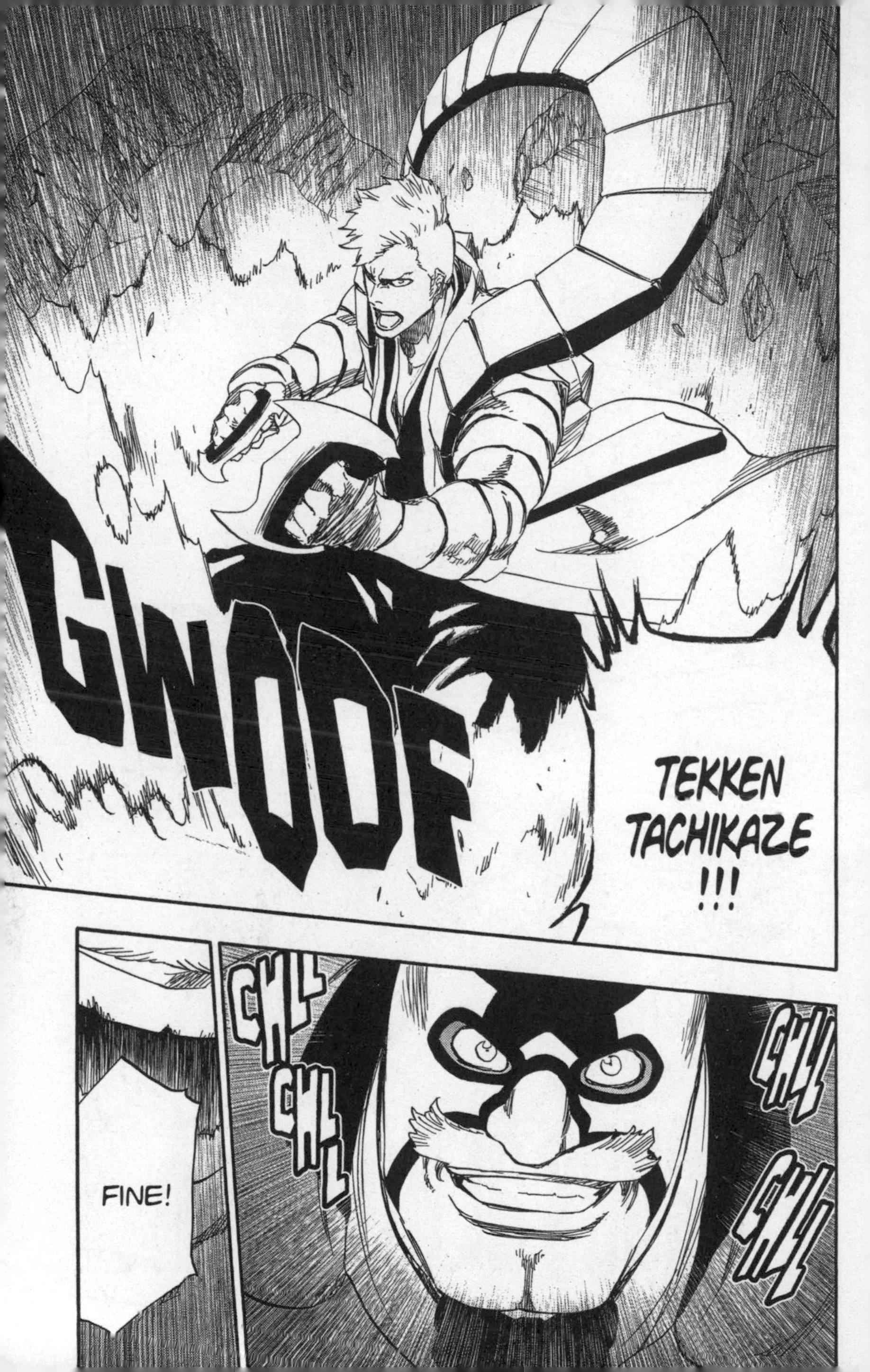
TEKKEN TACHIKAZE !!!
GWOOF
CHL CHL
CHL CHL CHL
FINE!

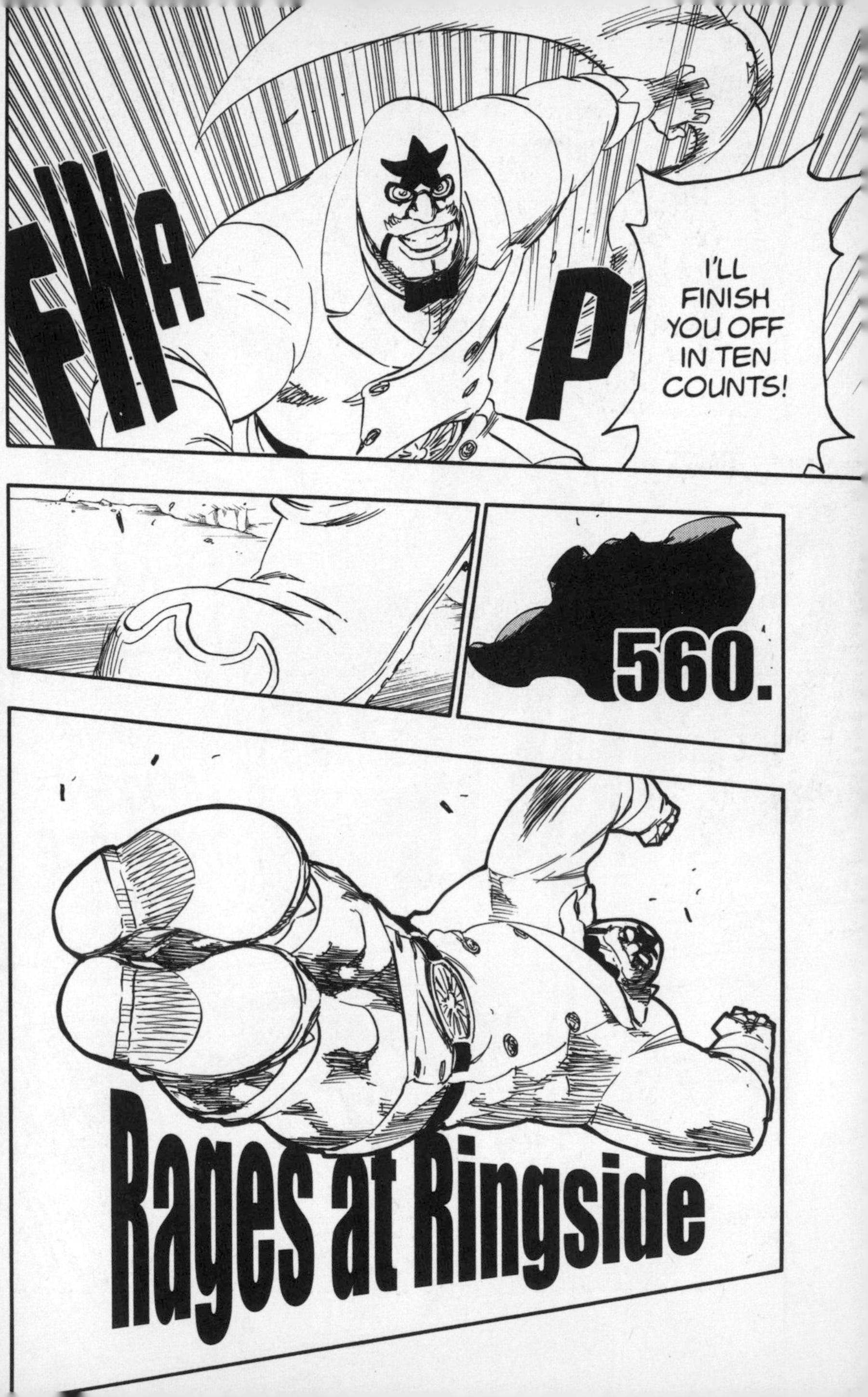
I'LL FINISH YOU OFF IN TEN COUNTS!
FWAP
560.
Rages at Ringside

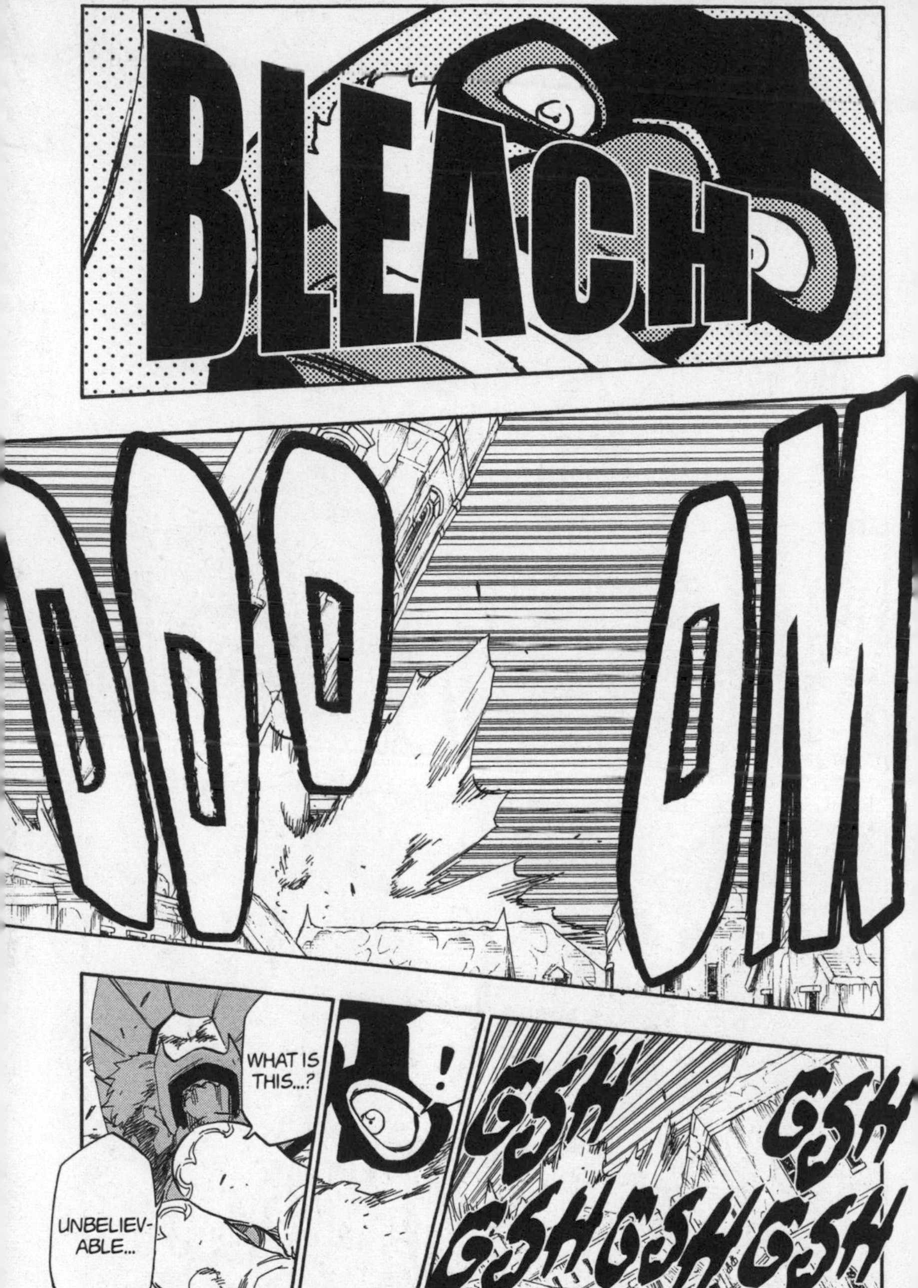
BLEACH
DOOOM
GSH GSH
GSHGSHGSH
!
WHAT IS THIS...?
UNBELIEV-ABLE...

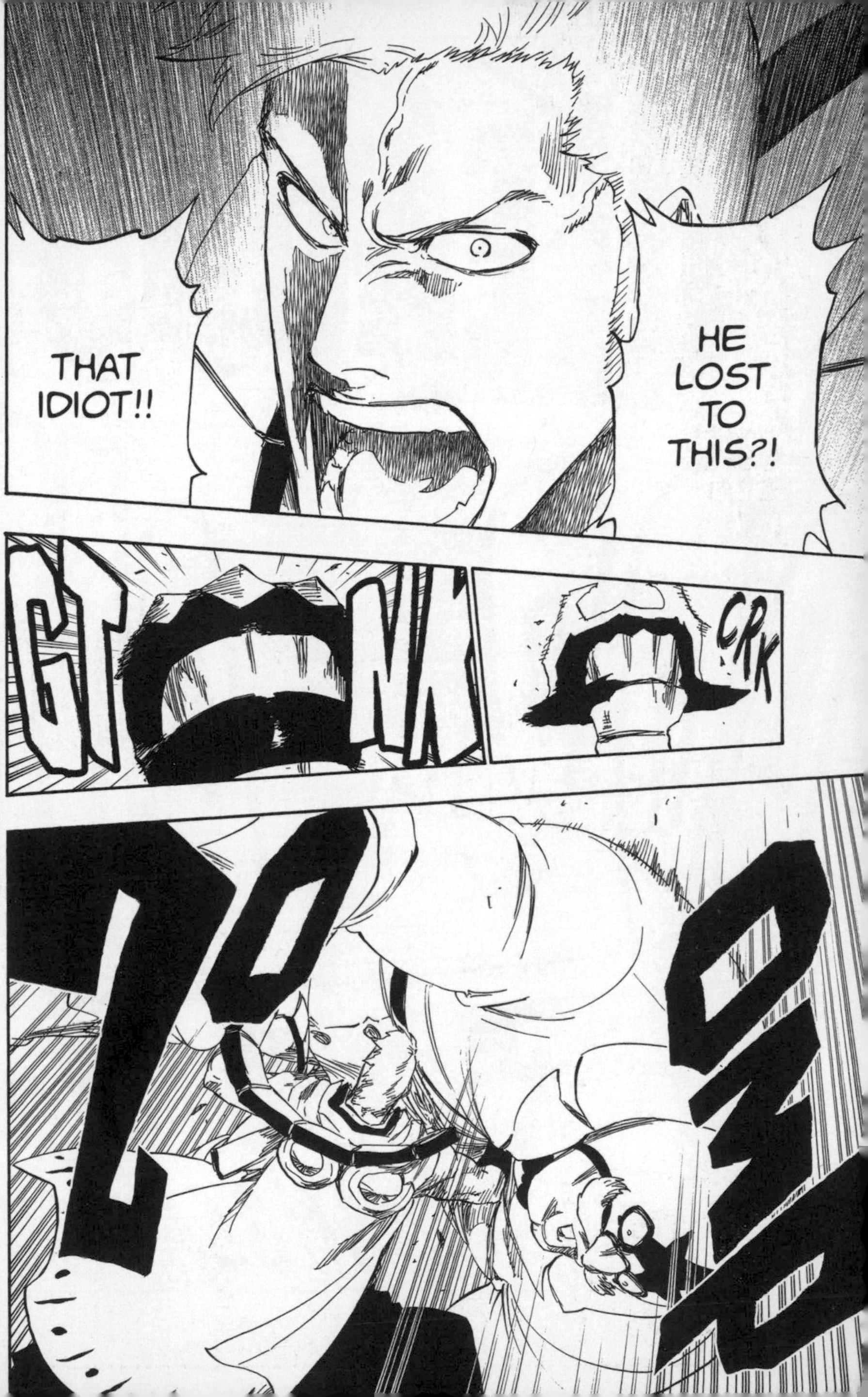
HE LOST TO THIS?!
THAT IDIOT!!
CRK

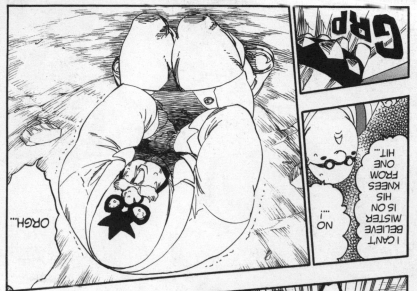

ORGH....

I CAN'T BELIEVE MISTER IS ON HIS KNEES FROM ONE HIT...

NO...!

ORGH...?!

WOMM

HURTS, DON'T IT?
GRRK
K
MY TACHIKAZE IS A ZANPAKU-TO WITH AN EXPLOSIVE SWING.
TEKKEN TACHIKAZE IS A BANKAI THAT PACKS THE POWER OF THAT EXPLOSION INTO THE FIST.
THE POWER OF THE EXPLOSION...
...CONTINUES TO BE POUNDED IN INFINITELY WHILE THE FIST IS IN CONTACT.
DOOF

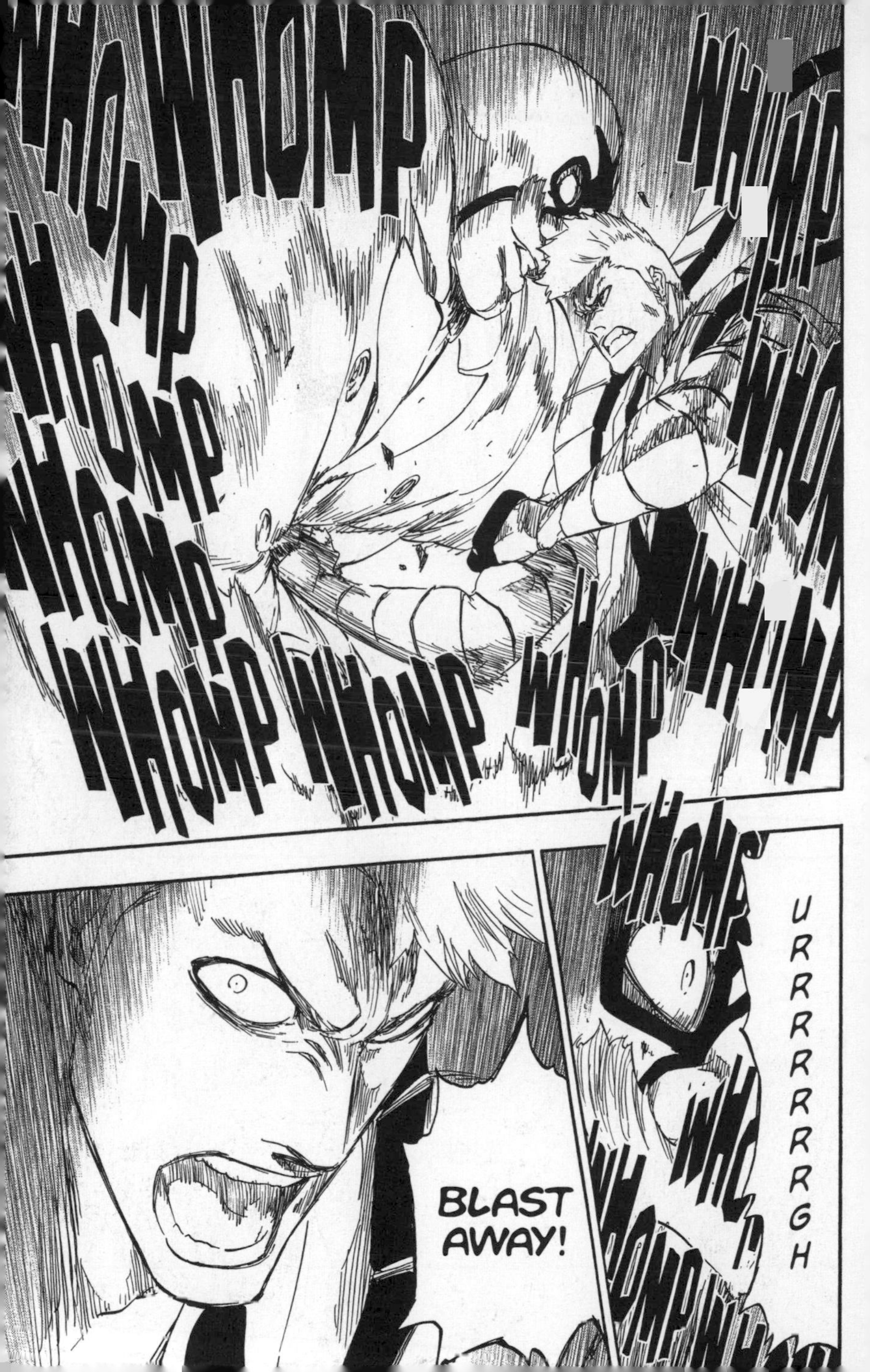
WHUMP WHUMP WHUMP
WHOMP WHOMP
WHOMP WHOMP WHOMP
WHOMP WHOMP WHOMP
URRRRRRRRGH
WHOMP
WHOMP WHOMP
BLAST
AWAY!

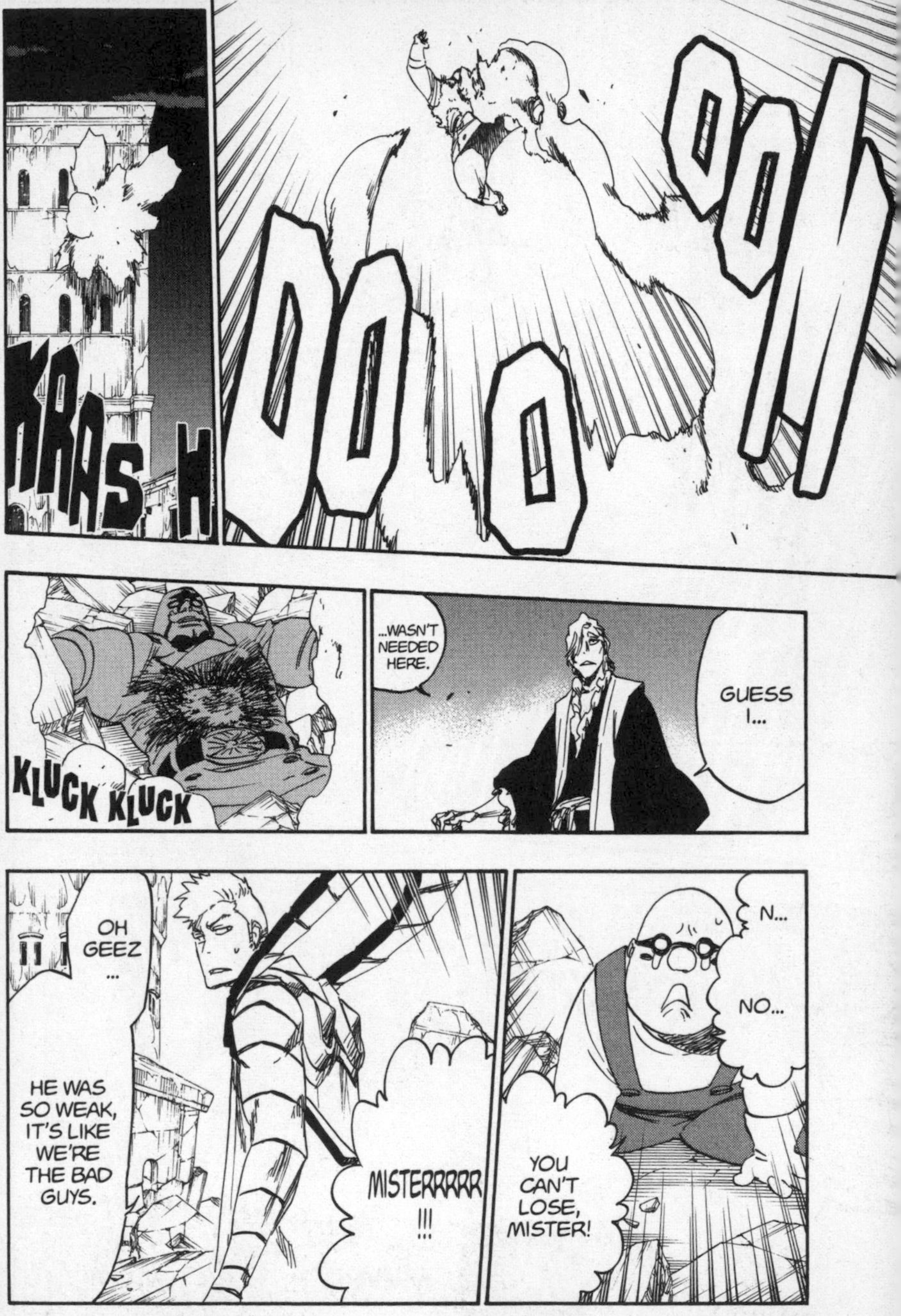
DOOOOOM!!
KRASH
GUESS I...
...WASN'T NEEDED HERE.
KLUCK KLUCK
N...
NO...
YOU CAN'T LOSE, MISTER!
MISTERRRRR !!!
OH GEEZ ...
HE WAS SO WEAK, IT'S LIKE WE'RE THE BAD GUYS.

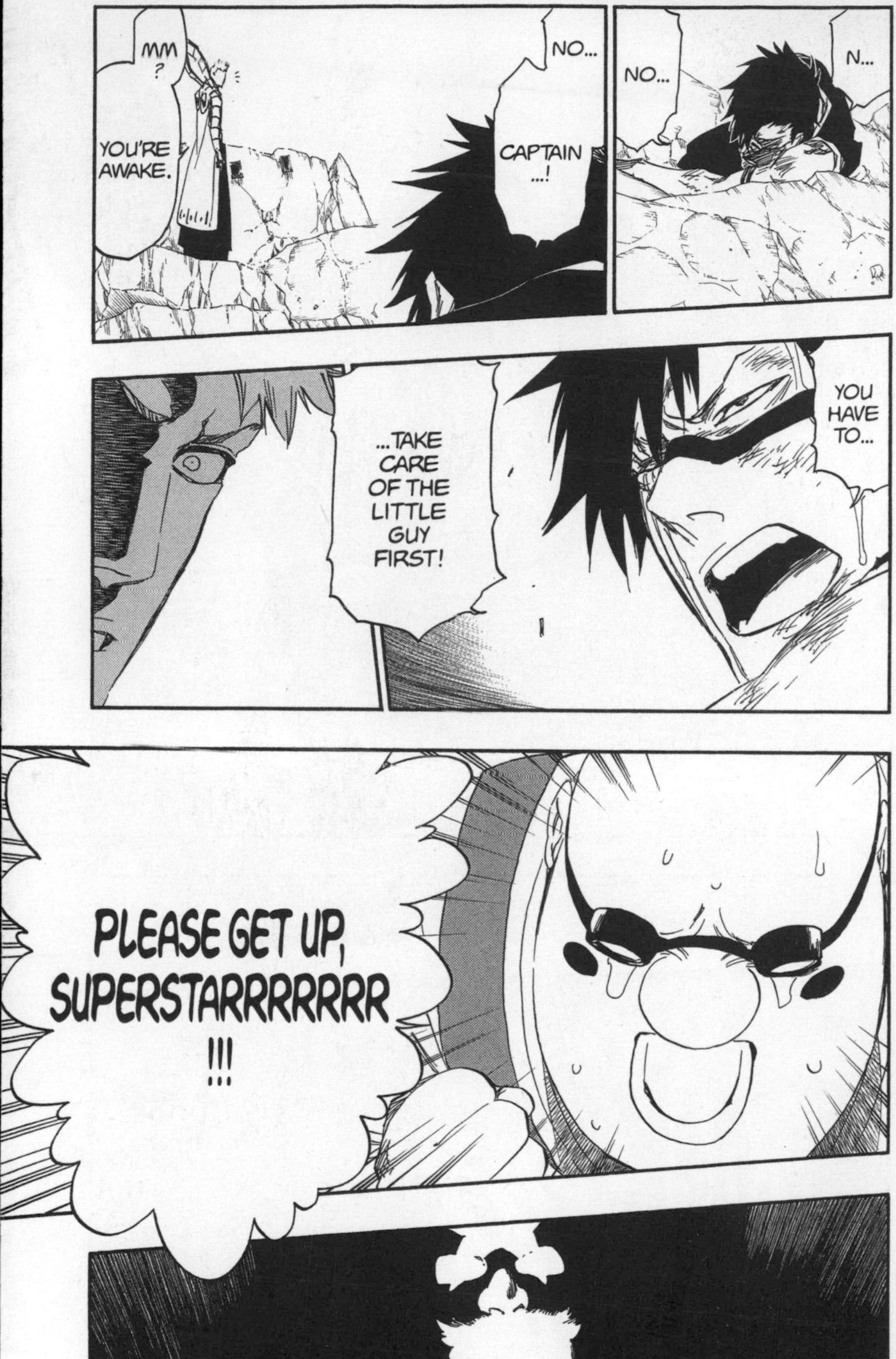
N...
NO...
NO...
CAPTAIN ...!
MM ?
YOU'RE AWAKE.
YOU HAVE TO...
...TAKE CARE OF THE LITTLE GUY FIRST!
PLEASE GET UP, SUPERSTARRRRRRR !!!

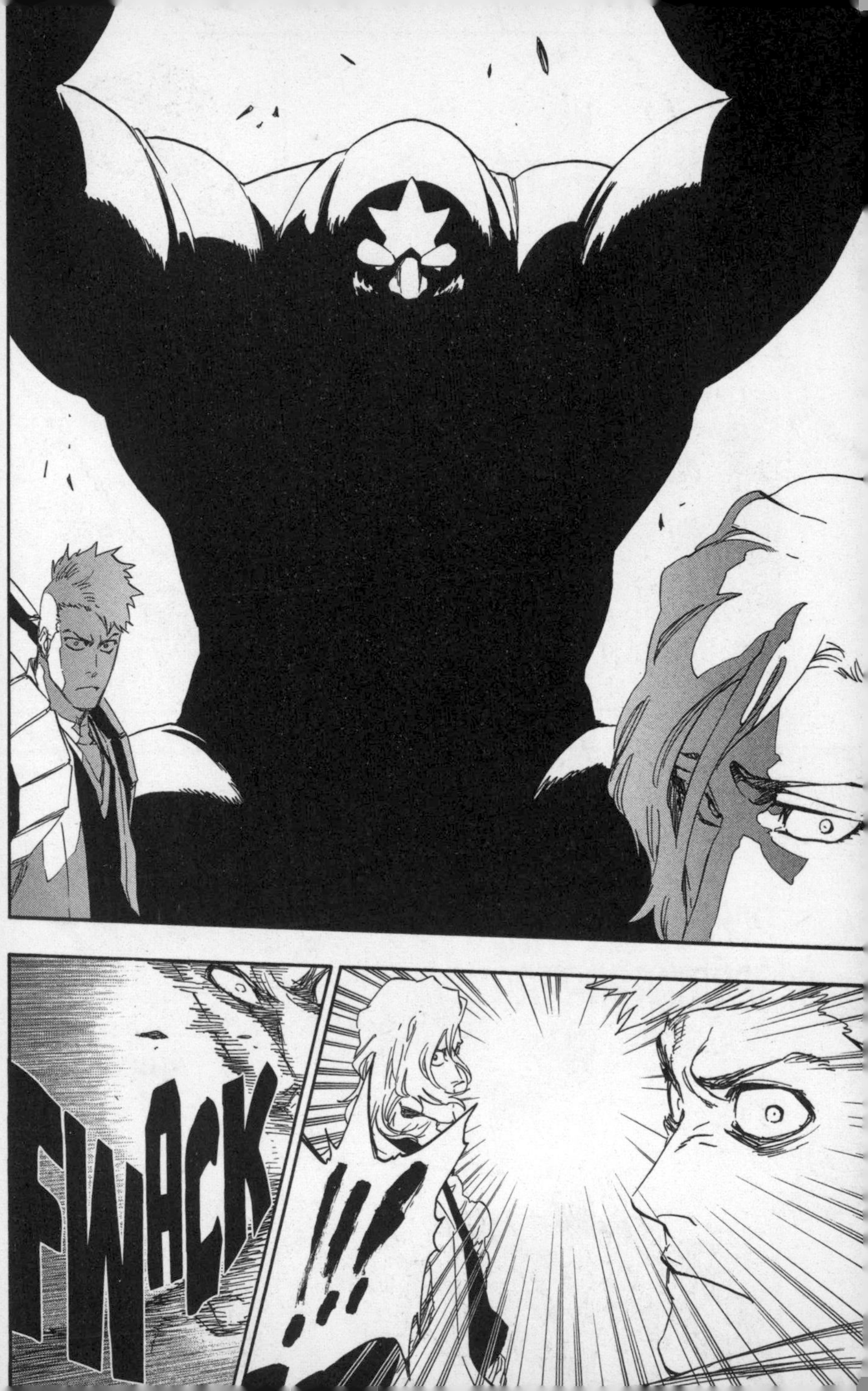
!!!
FWACK

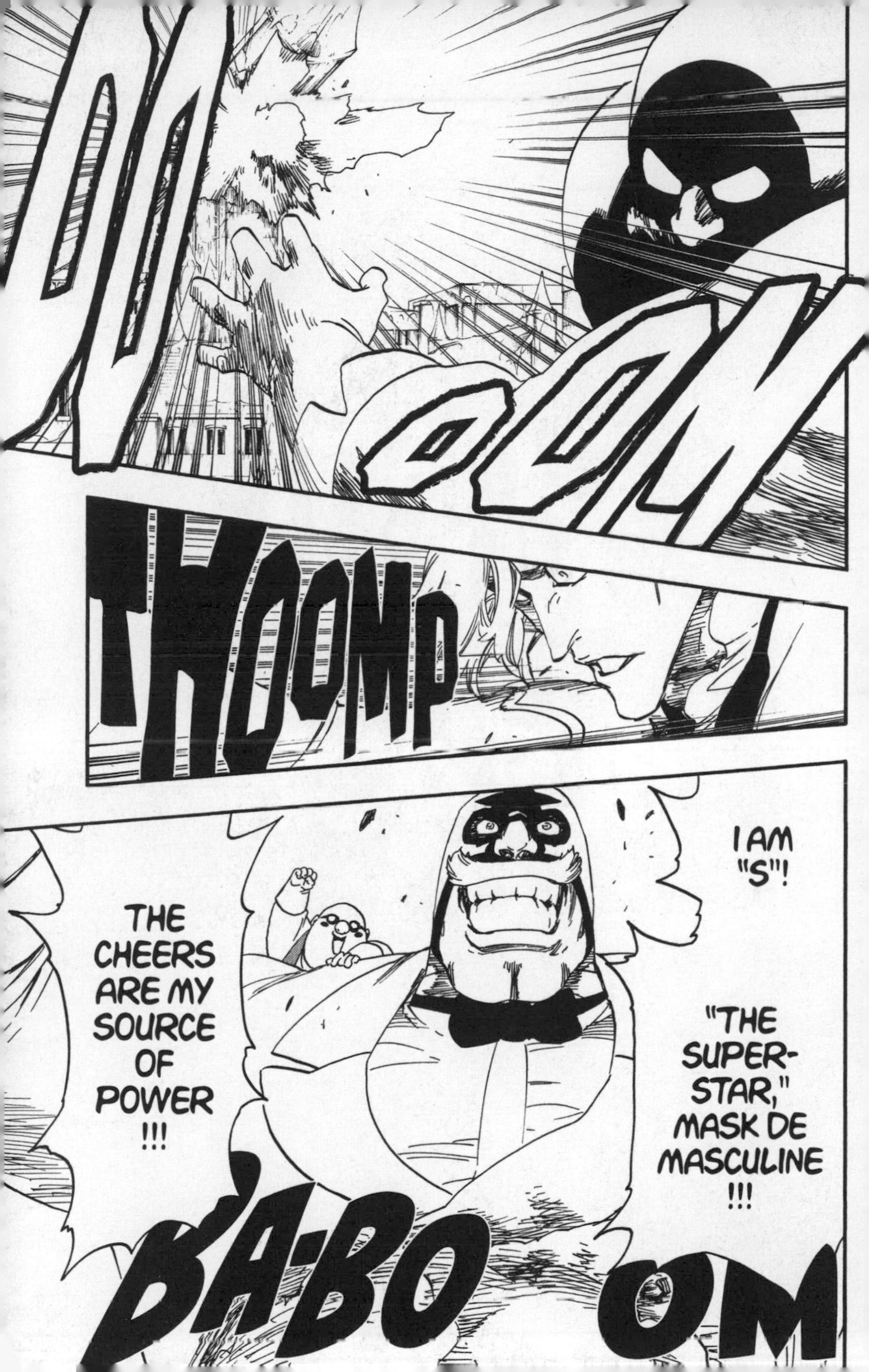
THOOMP
I AM "S"!
"THE SUPER-STAR," MASK DE MASCULINE !!!
THE CHEERS ARE MY SOURCE OF POWER !!!
KA-BOOM

CONTINUED IN BLEACH 63

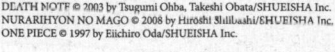

You're Reading in the Wrong Direction!!

Whoops! Guess what? You're starting at the wrong end of the comic!

…It's true! In keeping with the original Japanese format, **Bleach** is meant to be read from right to left, starting in the upper-right corner.

Unlike English, which is read from left to right, Japanese is read from right to left, meaning that action, sound effects and word-balloon order are completely reversed… something which can make readers unfamiliar with Japanese feel pretty backwards themselves. For this reason, manga or Japanese comics published in the U.S. in English have sometimes been published "flopped"—that is, printed in exact reverse order, as though seen from the other side of a mirror.

By flopping pages, U.S. publishers can avoid confusing readers, but the compromise is not without its downside. For one thing, a character in a flopped manga series who once wore in the original Japanese version a T-shirt emblazoned with "M A Y" (as in "the merry month of") now wears one which reads "Y A M"! Additionally, many manga creators in Japan are themselves unhappy with the process, as some feel the mirror-imaging of their art skews their original intentions.

We are proud to bring you Tite Kubo's **Bleach** in the original unflopped format. For now, though, turn to the other side of the book and let the adventure begin…!

—Editor

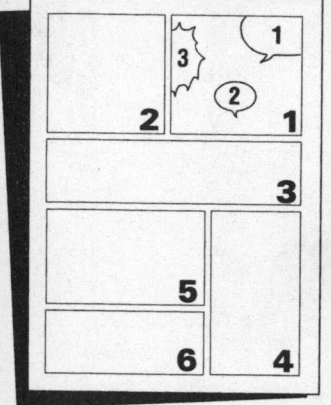

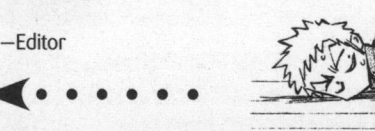